Chesapeake Prehistory
Old Traditions, New Directions

INTERDISCIPLINARY CONTRIBUTIONS TO ARCHAEOLOGY

Series Editor: Michael Jochim, *University of California, Santa Barbara*
Founding Editor: Roy S. Dickens, Jr., *Late of University of North Carolina, Chapel Hill*

Current Volumes in This Series:

A Continuation Order Plan is available for this series. A continuation order will bring delivery of each new volume immediately upon publication. Volumes are billed only upon actual shipment. For further information please contact the publisher.

Chesapeake Prehistory

Old Traditions, New Directions

RICHARD J. DENT, JR.

The American University
Washington, D.C.

PLENUM PRESS • NEW YORK AND LONDON

Library of Congress Cataloging-in-Publication Data

Dent, Richard J.
    Chesapeake prehistory : old traditions, new directions / Richard
J. Dent, Jr.
        p.   cm. -- (Interdisciplinary contributions to archaeology)
    Includes bibliographical references and index.
    ISBN 0-306-45028-3
    1. Indians of North America--Chesapeake Bay Region (Md. and Va.)-
-Antiquities.   2. Chesapeake Bay Region (Md. and Va.)--Antiquities.
3. Archaeology--Chesapeake Bay Region (Md. and Va.).   I. Title.
II. Series.
E78.M3D45   1995
975.5'1801--dc20   95-11340
                                                                    CIP

ISBN 0-306-45028-3

© 1995 Plenum Press, New York
A Division of Plenum Publishing Corporation
233 Spring Street, New York, N. Y. 10013

10 9 8 7 6 5 4 3 2 1

Printed in the United States of America

To the memory of
Phyllis Webster Dent

Preface

This is not the first book to address Chesapeake archaeology. Just over a century ago, in 1894, William Henry Holmes completed a manuscript on the archaeology of the greater Chesapeake region. Between the covers of the *Fifteenth Annual Report, Bureau of Ethnology, 1893-1894*, which was issued several years later in 1897, he would describe and interpret regional archaeology as it was then known. While Holmes had a number of agendas in the production of that volume, his book stands as the first comprehensive presentation of Chesapeake prehistory. Today the publication is rightfully acknowledged as a landmark in early American archaeology. Nevertheless, this text has now collected the dust of almost a century. Even Holmes would be astounded at what has since been unearthed across the region, and at the changes in archaeology today.

The present book is an effort to bring Chesapeake prehistory up into the world of contemporary archaeology, from the standpoints of both data presentation and interpretation. As a result of the emergence in recent years of new avenues for archaeological excavation, the pace of archaeological research has quickened in the region. Significant numbers of scholars have joined faculties at various local educational institutions. Archaeologists have expanded the ranks of many regional governmental agencies and museums, and cultural resources managers are working to mitigate the tremendous impact of development around the bay. An active corps of amateur archaeologists also continues to work in the area. As a result of all this activity, a large corpus of data on over 11,000 years of Chesapeake prehistory has now accumulated. This book presents a comprehensive and current synthesis of these data. As part of this process I also make an effort to situate the archaeological record of the study area into the broader context of eastern North America. The prehistoric Chesapeake area was a cross-roads between the greater Southeast and Northeast regions and, ultimately, late in prehistory, it was the meeting place of the Old and New Worlds.

Ideas about the nature of the past have changed significantly over the course of scholarly interest in Chesapeake prehistory. This book traces the history of those changes, and it attempts to critically evaluate the legacy of these various ideas in contemporary archaeological interpretation. At the same time, I also offer my own interpretations of the patterns and processes evident in the whole of Chesapeake prehistory. Some of these interpretations draw on existing ideas and others go in new directions. Throughout the book I have made my best effort to produce interpretation that is accessible to the many audiences that have an interest in Chesapeake prehistory.

Books such as this depend on the charity of many. A number of friends and colleagues have been supportive of my work over the years. A partial list of these folks includes Mike Agar, Erve Chambers, Paul Cissna, June and Warren Evans, Diane Gelburd, Russ Handsman, Mike Johnson, Louana Lackey, Mark Leone, Sydne Marshall, the late Mac McDaniel, Barbara McMillan, Charlie McNett, Stephen Potter, Rich Sacchi, Harry Schuckel, Bill Stuart, Henry Wright, and Anne Yentsch. I owe a special debt of gratitude to the College of Arts and Sciences at American University and to the entire faculty of the Department of Anthropology. My students at that university, both undergraduate and graduate, have likewise contributed to my thinking. And with the effort to produce this book now a protracted affair, I have no doubt forgotten a few people that should be listed above. Their support, however, is no less appreciated.

A number of institutions, in the Chesapeake region and elsewhere, shared freely of their information on regional prehistory. The British Museum, Museum of Mankind in London, and the Ashmolean Museum in Oxford let me rummage through their collections of eastern North American artifacts. The John Wesley Powell Anthropology Library and National Anthropological Archives at the Smithsonian Institution allowed me access to their treasures. The Maryland Historical Trust, Office of Archaeology, was another invaluable ally. I especially want to acknowledge the help of Dennis Curry, Tyler Bastian, Maureen Kavanagh, and Richard Hughes. In the same sense, the Virginia Department of Historic Resources hosted me on a number of occasions. Special thanks go to Mary Ellen Hodges (now at VDOT), Keith Egloff, and Beth Acuff. Joe McAvoy of the Nottoway River Survey shared some important early radiocarbon dates with me. Governor's Land Associates and the James River Institute for Archaeology let me reproduce unpublished drawings of some important house patterns from the lower Chesapeake. I recently left the Virginia Commonwealth University, Center for Archaeological Research, filled with many new ideas and an armful of scarce, but important, reports. Dan Mouer, Doug McLearen, and Chris Egghart have my special thanks. In fact, everywhere I turned, people went out of their way to lend a hand. If called upon, I would be hard pressed to return the hospitality of these folks and their institutions.

The original proposal for this book to Plenum Press received the careful attention of several reviewers, including Ken Sassaman, William Gardner, and another anonymous reviewer. All offered good suggestions for its development. In particular I have learned much over the years from the writings and preaching of William Gardner. Howard MacCord, Dave Meltzer, and Jay Custer offered detailed and helpful comments on an earlier draft of this manuscript. My special thanks for their efforts to turn my writing into a book go to Eliot Werner, executive editor, and the staff at

Plenum Press as well as to the series editor, Mike Jochim at the University of California, Santa Barbara. All listed above are absolved of any responsibility for my statements, but certainly deserve credit for what is good about this book.

Last, but certainly not least, I want to thank my family, both immediate and extended, for their long support of my interest in archaeology. This includes Richard Dent, Sr., Carolyn, Mike, and Michael, as well as Grace, Phil, Stan, Doris, Tracey, and Allan. Finally, there are no words to express my gratitude, both personally and intellectually, to my wife and good friend, Christine Jirikowic. This book has benefited in so many ways, as have I, from her support.

Thank you all, again.

Richard J. Dent

Washington, D.C.

Contents

Chapter *1*

Archaeology and the Chesapeake

INTRODUCTION

The Chesapeake Bay has evoked a steady stream of interest and written comment from its observers. Spanish mariners made note of a great bay in the middle reaches of the North American continent's Atlantic coast by the first quarter of the sixteenth century. In the early seventeenth century, Captain John Smith, promoting English settlement through virtual biblical metaphor, described it as a place where "heaven and earth never agreed better to frame a place for man's habitation." Almost three centuries later, H. L. Mencken, the noted Baltimore journalist, more succinctly portrayed the Chesapeake Bay as "one giant protein factory." The Bay, as it is colloquially known, continues to inspire contemporary writers from James Michener to William Warner to John Barth. Those who write about it are no doubt influenced by the Chesapeake Bay's phenomenal ecological richness as well as by its distinctive folk, sense of place, and seemingly timeless quality. It is evident to many that this is a special place that has somehow uniquely shaped and defined its inhabitants.

Nevertheless, much of what we commonly associate with the Chesapeake Bay region is set in only a small fraction of more recent time. A prehistoric past, reflected in the archaeological remains of countless North American Indian groups, stands beyond the more well known historic era. This prehistory of the land that borders the Chesapeake Bay spans at least another 11 millennia.

Paleoindians, occupying the very basement of known archaeological time, left a rich record of their lifeways in the region. One of the earliest recognized and most substantial of all such sites, the Williamson site, was discovered in the lower Chesapeake province. A number of other similarly early sites have since been reported. After this initial settlement, a long record of adjustment to the land and its resources is fossilized at regional archaeological sites. This adjustment, consuming much of the Archaic period, occurred against a dramatic backdrop of ecological change that transformed the surrounding landscape.

Within the last 4200 years of prehistory, during the latter portions of the Archaic and through the Woodland period, social experiment began an equally radical

transformation of aboriginal lifeways culminating in complex and sedentary agriculturally based societies. It was into this world, late in time, that the first European
explorers and settlers stepped. While ultimately ushering the native world they
encountered into collapse, these outsiders themselves left behind a graphic written
record of their interactions. All in all, the prehistory of the Chesapeake region
presents a microcosm of the patterns and processes that, in many other areas of the
world, have piqued scholarly interest.

Archaeology, itself, has a long but sporadic history in the Chesapeake region. In
fact, the last comprehensive archaeological treatment of the Chesapeake Bay tidewater area was offered by the prominent early archaeologist William Henry Holmes,
based on research undertaken between the years of 1889 and 1894. This research was
published a few years later, in 1897, in the *Fifteenth Annual Report* of the United States
Bureau of American Ethnology at the Smithsonian Institution. Almost a century has
now elapsed since this early landmark study of the region was published. As time has
passed, remarkable amounts of new data and thought have accumulated on various
aspects of the area's prehistoric past. It seems appropriate to once again take stock of
our knowledge as it relates to the archaeological record of the Chesapeake region.

Specific goals of the present study are straightforward. First, the discipline
deserves a comprehensive and current synthesis of the prehistoric culture history of
the Chesapeake province; none now exists. A great deal of excavation has obviously
been completed since Holmes's report. In recent years the pace of archaeological
research in the region has accelerated. Many scholars have now turned to the region,
and cultural resources management is moving to keep pace with land development
and concomitant archaeological site destruction. Much of this more recent research,
however, has been specific to particular sites or limited areas. Political subdivision of
the region into three states (parts of Virginia, Maryland, and Delaware) and one
federal district (District of Columbia) has done little to encourage regional synthesis. I
think it is therefore important that both existing old data as well as new data be drawn
together. The production of a regional culture history is perhaps one of the more
fundamental and lasting contributions a study such as this can hope to achieve given
the changes in interpretative frameworks that have occurred and will continue to
occur within the discipline of archaeology.

As a second goal, if the Chesapeake region does represent a sort of natural
analytical unit within eastern North American prehistoric archaeology (see Holmes
1897:19–20 for an early argument that it does), some attempt at an integrated
explanation of its past is necessary. Countless archaeologists, in the past and today,
have speculated on the common threads that bind together the many individual sites
of the region. In order to advance archaeology in the Chesapeake region, an explanation of the overall patterns and processes reflected in the area's archaeological record
is very much needed. This statement should be mindful of what has been said before
but it should also look toward the production of a more theoretically current
explanation of the data now available to us. In a broader sense, the discipline of
archaeology as a whole will perhaps reap some benefit from such an understanding of
prehistory in this region.

Third, another goal of this book is to further stimulate interest, scholarly questioning, and debate on Chesapeake prehistory. I am under no illusion that the culture history and interpretation advanced through this volume will, in every instance, concur with the thoughts and explanations of all others. There are a number of ways to know the past. Regardless of this, if the present study stimulates further reflection, or even debate and reaction, it will have served a very useful purpose. I strongly believe that the critical tension between different interpretations of the past is healthy; it is what moves archaeology toward the production of another, hopefully better, view of the past. In this light, my interpretations of Chesapeake prehistory through this volume are, in part, an invitation to others to do the same.

This first chapter serves to introduce the reader to the geographic and organizational boundaries of this study. In regards to the former, I will describe and define the spatial limits of the study area. In terms of the latter domain, I will discuss how I intend to go about making sense of the archaeological record of the Chesapeake region. This is done from the standpoints of both data organization as well as interpretational protocol. Each concern will be addressed in turn below. The chapter will conclude with a brief prospectus on the remaining sections of the book.

CHESAPEAKE BAY STUDY AREA

This volume focuses on the prehistoric archaeological record of what is known as the Chesapeake tidewater area (Figure 1.1). This study area is situated within the Middle Atlantic Bight on the Atlantic coast of the North American continent. The region, of course, takes its principal definition from the great estuary known as the Chesapeake Bay. In its present configuration, the northern portion of the Chesapeake Bay meets the Susquehanna River at Havre de Grace, Maryland (39°35′ north latitude, 76°05′ west longitude), and its southernmost reaches join the Atlantic Ocean at Cape Henry, Virginia (36°55′ north latitude, 76°00′ west longitude). The state of Maryland borders the northern portion of the estuary and the state of Virginia, below the mouth of the Potomac River, flanks the southern Chesapeake Bay. Portions of the state of Delaware, drained by streams that are tributaries of the Chesapeake Bay, and the District of Columbia also fall within this region.

Of the thousands of estuaries and bays within the United States, the Chesapeake Bay is today the largest and most varied. The Chesapeake Bay itself is approximately 320 km long and varies in width from 6.5 to 48 km. It is bordered by over 7400 km of sinuous shoreline and has a surface area of approximately 11,200 km². These figures are greatly increased when the lower embayed portions of its lateral tributaries, themselves small estuaries, are considered. The tributaries, of which there are over 150, drain a vast 167,000-km² region of eastern North America.

The freshwater contribution from these tributaries mixes with the salt water of the Atlantic Ocean in the Chesapeake Bay at about a one to ten ratio, respectively. This mix is what defines the body of water as an estuary. More than 2000 aquatic and terrestrial species thrive in the Chesapeake Bay and on the land that surrounds the

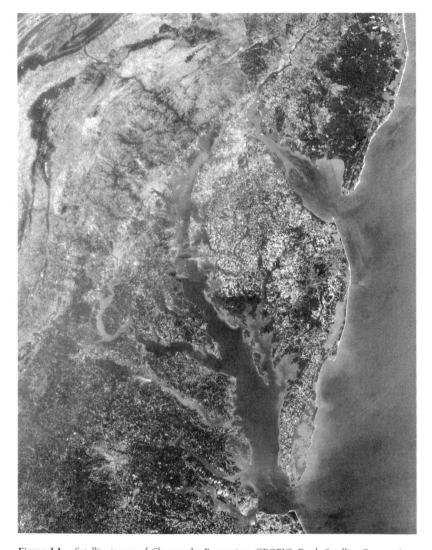

Figure 1.1.   Satellite image of Chesapeake Bay region. GEOPIC, Earth Satellite Corporation.

estuary. Some of these species are present in phenomenal numbers. Today these resources combine to make the Chesapeake Bay region one of the richest and most productive natural ecosystems on this planet.

A substantial, relatively low-lying area of land, colloquially called the tidewater area and technically known as the Coastal Plain physiographic province, surrounds the estuary. This Coastal Plain today extends (east to west) from the Atlantic coast of what is locally referred to as the Eastern Shore of the Chesapeake Bay to the western fall line of the estuary's tributaries on the opposite shore. The fall line (Figure 1.2), generally arcing from present-day Baltimore, Maryland, to Washington, D.C., to Richmond, Virginia, marks the edge of the Piedmont physiographic province. The area of land between the Atlantic coast to the east and the Piedmont physiographic province to the west, as it runs the length of the Chesapeake Bay, is the focus of this study. But the precise description of the study area landscape is more complicated than this.

What I have written above briefly describes the Chesapeake Bay study area today. The temporal length of the archaeological record in this region, however, forces us also to talk about the area before the formation of this estuary. It is well established that the Chesapeake Bay is a relatively recent post-Pleistocene phenomenon. The present estuary only began to form circa 10,000 years ago. It was not complete until approximately 3000 years ago. Before this time, an earlier Pleistocene estuary had been drained by the marine regression associated with that epoch's last glacial advance. During that period, instead of the Chesapeake Bay, an extension of the Susquehanna River, herein referred to as the ancestral Susquehanna River, coursed down through the region and flowed further out onto the exposed continental shelf where it emptied into the somewhat reduced Atlantic Ocean. With this, the actual land mass of the Coastal Plain of that earlier era was greatly expanded (by up to one-third). Areas of land now under the estuary and now submerged by the Atlantic Ocean were exposed.

Given all this, the study area for this research was a dynamic location during the course of prehistory. It actively changed its configuration in an evolution from an ancestral riverine-dominated landscape into one covered by an estuary. This transformation required almost 7000 years. Land mass available for prehistoric occupation during this period varied accordingly. While I can define the absolute geographic boundaries of the study area, the reader must remain aware that the landscape and ecology of this same area changed dramatically through time. More will be said about this in subsequent chapters.

CONSTRUCTING THE PAST

Archaeology has three interrelated spheres of activity: data recovery, taxonomy and description, and interpretation or explanation (follows Clarke 1978:12). The first two realms represent the "sensory organs" of the discipline and the latter concern is that which seeks to place archaeology within the boundaries of the anthropological science. At the same time, there is no more truer statement than Lewis Binford's often repeated remark (e.g., Binford 1983:19) that the archaeological record is a contemporary phenomenon and any observations made about its nature are contemporary observations. While the primary concern of archaeology is most often with the past, our perceptions are necessarily rooted in the present. Archaeologists therefore con-

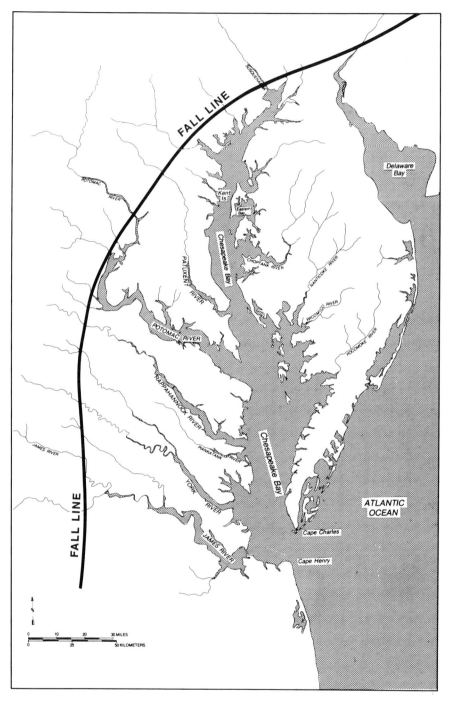

Figure 1.2. Map of Chesapeake Bay region with fall line indicated.

struct the past, they do not discover it. This section of the introductory chapter is designed to offer a statement on how I have chosen to construct Chesapeake prehistory.

Data Recovery

No new program of excavation specifically oriented toward the production of this volume was initiated. The reason is simple. I am convinced that there is no real shortage of data on Chesapeake prehistory. Archaeological excavations and collections have been undertaken over the years by many different individuals, myself included. Active archaeological field research continues in the region today. The detritus of much of this research resides in a rather substantial but scattered corpus of literature, both published and unpublished, that has been accumulating over many years. In addition, some of our knowledge of regional prehistory is only accessible in the form of what can be politely labeled oral tradition. Large and often deteriorating artifact collections reside in various repositories within and outside the region. While the prudent collection of new data must continue, a time should come when archaeology as a discipline stops and begins to account for already existing data. I hope my efforts through this volume will be viewed as one such point in time.

As consolation to those disappointed by this situation, I offer the following admission and encouragement. There is certainly no denial on my part that the currently known archaeological record of the Chesapeake province is incomplete as well as, at a few points, questionable or even contradictory. Archaeological records are this way by nature and the Chesapeake region's record certainly shares this trait with those of many other areas of the world. Nevertheless, in completing the research for this volume, I was often struck by how much we have discovered about the prehistoric Chesapeake. Paralysis, induced by the wait for yet more data, is not an answer. Instead, in what is hopefully a positive step forward, it is time to take stock of what we do know. We should let such exercises stimulate us all to fill in the gaps that are inevitably exposed in our present knowledge.

Taxonomy/Description

It is axiomatic to state that archaeological data must be placed in defined contexts of time and space. The practice of archaeology revolves around analytical decisions that descriptively and analytically group sets of data. Archaeologists are then obliged to assign meaning to and defend artifact taxons or types as well as to make important decisions about how such groupings relate to one another along temporal and spatial axes. The received wisdom (e.g., Clarke 1978; Griffin 1967; McKern 1939; Stoltman 1978; Willey 1966; Willey and Phillips 1958; and many others) indicates the path to taxonomic nirvana is a difficult one.

An undertaking such as this labors under somewhat of a burden as far as taxonomy is concerned. Prehistoric data from the Chesapeake study area have been collected over the years by a number of investigators for a wide variety of purposes. Often they have been collected for no purpose other than to collect them. Taxonomy is not theoretically neutral: the purpose for which the data were collected has a significant impact on the way that they are described and eventually explained. As Ian Hodder (1991:16) comments, fact and theory confront each other, but each changes in relation to the other. In the purest sense, we rightfully argue that taxonomies should strive solely for maximum "scientific objectivity."

In this instance, I would argue that while objectivity is an important factor, it is not the only factor relevant to what essentially in another dimension becomes a tool of communication. Taxonomy or typology produces types. Types are formulated to include particular classes of related data. As Marshall Sahlins (1972:75) comments, the "ideal type is a logical construct founded at once on pretended knowledge *and* on pretended ignorance of the real diversity in the world—with the mysterious power of rendering intelligible any particular case." William Adams and Ernest Adams (1991:4) make the argument that, in any discussion of typology, objectivity should also be tempered by matters of purpose and practicality.

A book such as this inhabits a very real and practical world. In many ways it is a world with limitations. This volume seeks to synthesize and interpret about 11,000 years of prehistory over a rather broad area. In addition, the accumulated data on which it depends have often not been collected specifically for this purpose. Some measure of practicality is therefore necessary. This suggests the need for a broad system intelligible to all. The situation ultimately argues for a flexible, back-to-basics approach. The organizational categories discussed below follow this dictum.

Chesapeake prehistory is divided into gross temporal units labeled periods. The nature, number, and chronological boundaries of such periods are always somewhat arbitrary. As will be demonstrated in the chapter that follows, for a long period of time prehistory in this region was thought to have little chronological depth. As late as 1939, for example, the widely employed Midwestern Taxonomic Method (McKern 1939) accommodated only a rather shallow past. Shortly thereafter, however, temporal horizons began to expand (e.g., Ford and Willey 1941; Martin, Quimby, and Collier 1947). The term *Woodland* eventually came to be employed for the latter portions of prehistory, and attempts were made to define the exact nature of this period (Woodland Conference 1943). William Ritchie (1932a,b) added *Archaic* to our terminology, and Joseph Caldwell (1958) did much to substantiate the uniqueness of such a period. With the discovery of sites attributable to the terminal Pleistocene and the advent of chronometric dating, the temporal vista was further extended into what might be labeled deep time. By the time of James Griffin's edited landmark volume, the *Archaeology of Eastern United States* (1952), the now standard periods of Paleoindian, Archaic, and Woodland were in active use. For many years these units have been employed by Chesapeake prehistorians to temporally define regional prehistory.

The basis of these three major periods has always been the presence or absence of certain diagnostic artifacts. Throughout the usage of this tripartite system, concerns (as early as 1948 by Sears) have been raised about utility and definition of this scheme. In this vein, a different sequence of periods has recently been proposed and adopted by some in the literature of the broader Middle Atlantic region (e.g., Custer 1984, 1989; Gardner 1982). These new units—Paleoindian, Archaic, Woodland I, Woodland II, and Contact—are defined as a culturally evolutionary sequence of adaptation to a changing environment through time. While some find this new sequence totally unnerving, justification for such a system is not difficult given current interests in cultural adaptation.

Two factors mitigated against the adoption of the alternative system in this research. First, while it is evident that adaptation is an important part of the story in terms of prehistoric culture change it is only part of the story. A shift to a taxonomic system based exclusively on adaptation creates problems of its own. Second, in my opinion, the alternative system seems to mystify an old, familiar archaeological record, read from the certainly flawed, but commonly employed, tripartite scheme. For this reason, in a bow to tradition and practicality, I decided to work within the Paleoindian, Archaic, and Woodland periods as they have been traditionally defined. It is a local sequence that has stood the test of time and debate. As Gordon Willey and Philip Phillips (1958:24–25) have commented, local sequences are the "very stuff of archaeology," and however obtained, "the local sequence has this important feature: it is local." Table 1.1 outlines the temporal periods and subperiods utilized in this research.

On the next level of abstraction, these broad temporal periods and subperiods must be tracked across the Chesapeake region. As is traditional, the Archaic and the Woodland periods are further subdivided with Early, Middle, and Late qualifiers denoting smaller increments of time in each. Within these two periods I also define *eras* that are based on common lifeways persistent for significant amounts of time across the study area. One such era joins the Early and Middle Archaic and a portion of the Late Archaic. Another era links subsequent events in the Late Archaic with most of the Woodland period.

At the next level of abstraction, I employ a relatively conservative and, again, almost boilerplate system focused initially on a discussion of sites and components

Table 1.1. Temporal Periods and Subperiods

Paleoindian period: circa 11,000 to 10,000 yrs ago
Archaic period: circa 10,000 to 3,000 yrs ago
  Early Archaic: 10,000 to 8,000 yrs ago
  Middle Archaic: 8,000 to 5,000 yrs ago
  Late Archaic: 5,000 to 3,000 yrs ago
Woodland period: circa 3,000 yrs ago to European settlement
  Early Woodland: 3,000 to 2,300 yrs ago
  Middle Woodland: 2,300 to 1,050 yrs ago (2300 BP to AD 900)
  Late Woodland: 1,050 to 343 yrs ago (AD 900 to circa AD 1607)

within sites. The definition of archaeological *sites* is based on the recovery of significant deposits of artifacts within a discrete or bounded area. If the deposit represented an aboriginal occupation of some duration it is viewed as a site. Smaller deposits, perhaps representing minimal occupation or simple resource extraction activity, are referred to as *off-site* locales. A *component* is identified through the presence at a site of a stratigraphically discrete cultural episode, often containing one particular diagnostic artifact type or assemblage. In the absence of stratigraphy at surface manifestations, components are also defined on the presence of certain well-established diagnostic artifact types. Many archaeological sites within the study area are multicomponent sites. Most will recognize much of this analytical protocol as a simplified derivative of that advocated by Willey and Phillips (1958). The terms above will be used explicitly throughout this research.

The final level of taxonomic abstraction involves the identification of diagnostic artifact types and assemblages. Archaeologists working in the Chesapeake region have been engaged in this task since at least the nineteenth and early twentieth centuries and they continue to do so today (e.g. Custer 1984, 1989; Evans 1984; Griffith 1982; Hranicky 1991; L. C. Steponaitis 1986). In this research, a diagnostic artifact *type* should not be viewed as a single or absolute real artifact. A type consists of recurring groups of artifacts having constellations of similar attributes. Their diagnostic value has been verified by independent nonartifactual data. These data could include common stratigraphic position or isolated spatial distribution within the regional archaeological record or sometimes within related sites outside this area. Various types of relative ordering and/or chronometric dating techniques are also commonly used in their definition. For the Chesapeake region, diagnostic types are almost always distinctive forms of projectiles or ceramic wares. A diagnostic *assemblage* is an extension of the type concept in that it is sometimes possible to identify sets of associated artifacts that define specific portions of the archaeological record.

To conclude, the taxonomic/descriptive system I employ in this book is hopefully simple and relatively straightforward. The definitions cited above no doubt appear, to most prehistorians, as almost common sense and probably already inhabit their subconscious mind as an archaeological *lingua franca*. While this taxonomic protocol is not always universally applauded, it is at least widely understood. It has another advantage in that a similar system, by acclamation, has been used extensively in the Chesapeake region for a number of years. As such, when balanced against the scope of this undertaking, I hope it will be viewed as an effective system of communication within the present context.

Interpretation: The Explanatory Menu

Archaeological interpretation must go from the particulars of the description of the archaeological record to generalizations about the meaning of this same record. Meaning or interpretation are now seen as almost universally synonymous with explanation. Nevertheless, a number of trends relevant to the present undertaking are evident at this point in the ongoing explanatory revolution. The situation as it relates to regional archaeologies such as this is as follows.

The first apparent tendency is that the discipline does not seem to produce as many studies as it once did that concentrate on expansive periods of time over large areas—what I call regional archaeologies. While there certainly are notable exceptions, two factors appear to mitigate against such studies. Today we are more likely to trumpet our knowledge of more temporally and often spatially restricted realms from early populations to complex society, and everything in between. At the same time, the range of knowledge and expertise required to do archaeology has led to increasing specialization in this or that archaeological method. Many of our colleagues are just as likely to identify themselves with some specialty—geoarchaeology, floral or faunal analysis, lithic technology, ceramic studies, dating techniques, and the like—as they are to adopt some particular geographic region. In the end, archaeology as a whole tends to know more and more about less and less. Even when books are published on the archaeology of a particular region, they often are edited volumes of papers on very selective topics.

The second tendency, one that I feel is even more troubling, is symptomatic of what is happening vis-à-vis theory and practice. Our theoreticians, to whom we turn for guidance, have increasingly engaged themselves in an industry that has become almost an end in itself. The result is that theoretical arguments are often either hypothetical, reactionary, or so generally divorced from practice that the realms of theory and application often appear virtually unrelated. Theory seems increasingly divorced from the vicissitudes and reality of doing archaeology. I do not know exactly why this has happened. Perhaps the trends mentioned in the last paragraph have something to do with this situation.

Whatever the case, the production of regional archaeologies has not been at the top of the discipline's agenda for a good while. I am obviously arguing that this trend should change. While such archaeologies need not be at the very top of our agenda, they do serve a real need. I do not think that I am alone in believing this. Accepting that, one impediment to the production of effective regional archaeologies—and this returns us to the second tendency—is the current divorce of theory and practical application.

There needs to be more debate and consensus on effective ways to examine and interpret the archaeological record of regions—ways that can still complement the goals of contemporary archaeology and anthropology. Lack of such explanatory frameworks dictate a revisitation of relatively recent thoughts on explanation in general. The obvious goal is to mine our various ideas about interpreting the past for help with the problem at hand. Begging the reader's indulgence, this book is aimed at a relatively broad spectrum of archaeologists, both amateur and professional. Those who are saturated in such reviews of explanatory archaeology, or who are nauseated by them at this point, may just wish to rejoin this introduction where I come back to the direct interpretation of Chesapeake prehistory.

Before starting, practical parameters for the review must be set. First, the revisitation in this context will be selective. It is rather myopic in addressing only those elements of our explanatory arsenal that may be useful in illuminating an archaeological record of the type and nature recovered in the Chesapeake region. The peoples that inhabited the past in this region did not leave behind a record as rich and spectacular as that recovered in some other areas of the world. I see little sense in pretending they did. Second, this is certainly not the venue for an extended discussion of the polemics and philosophical nuances of the totality of archaeological theory. This review is a relatively quick look at some of the pluses and minuses of relatively recent attempts at explaining the past. It is tempered by the problem at hand.

I also want to say a word about my intentions in this review. I have avoided citing specific examples of what I see as less than positive aspects of past and present efforts at explaining the past. This was done for two reasons. First, it is easy today to find fault with almost any research undertaken even a few years ago, much less decades ago. Second, the comparison of one way of explaining the past with a different way of doing the same thing can become almost satirical. In print and at our conferences, for example, salvos are regularly launched back and forth between the so-called processual and postprocessual camps. To make and advance ideas in an epistemological repartee is understandable. It is, at least, good theater. Nevertheless, most folks actually engaged in working with archaeological data, while listening intently, do still remember to run the occasional reality check. Afterwards they take the best of what is out there and go about their business, even if their decisions force them into a state of paradigmatic homelessness. The following review is not undertaken to advance any particular agenda. It is only a search for help in the matter at hand.

To start, we are all aware that our explanations of the past change as new sets of ideas about the nature of the past are entertained. If these ideas about the past gather some momentum within the discipline as a whole, either through broad consensus, or through advocacy of a vocal minority, they are then increasingly used by us all to assign meaning to the archaeological record. Concurrent attempts are made at developing appropriate methodology. Dominant ideas about the past, spanning the past two or three generations of archaeologists, form the foundations of what are often labeled the cultural historical, processual, and postprocessual paradigms. Each will be briefly addressed in turn.

Setting the stage, an exploration of the explanatory potential of the culture history paradigm may at first appear futile. During the heyday of this archaeology its practitioners spilled little ink over the debate of such matters. And after the processual assault, there is no need once again to slay the slain. But as Dunnell (1986:33) has recently reminded us, the culture historians did produce explanations of a certain kind. Issues of chronology were paramount, and the archaeological record was analyzed in internally homogeneous and externally contrastive units. All significant change was to be found and thus explained at the boundaries separating identified units on the time–space chart. Independent invention, diffusion, trade, migration, and the like became standard explanatory favorites. While the explanations were limited and cultural historians seldom strayed far from the immediate experience of a rather inert archaeological record, it was, perhaps for the first time, possible to do archaeology and be wrong (Dunnell 1986:29).

Another lasting legacy of cultural historical archaeology that should be acknowledged is the robust methodology it developed to rationalize and support its assumptions about the past. In the Chesapeake region, this methodology has certainly been employed successfully by a variety of archaeologists over the years to produce a fairly accurate and detailed culture history. I want to acknowledge that we all still depend on this tool. However, the explanations that emerge from this protocol, here and elsewhere, have remained rather limited and ignore a wide range of internal and external factors. The significant successes of cultural historians toward one end seemed to insure other neglects. This opened the door for a new archaeology.

The challenge, processual archaeology, had certainly arrived in full force by the early 1960s. With it, a new set of ideas and assumptions about the past became preeminent. Archaeologists went into the field to look at human adaptation to both the social and natural environment. In all too many cases, especially early on, the latter was deemed the principal causal agent of change. Over long periods of time, what often emerged was a picture of different but periodically stable past ecological episodes separated by abrupt transitions or discontinuities. The discontinuities isolated in the paleoecological record were then correlated with discontinuities in the archaeological record. On a more temporally restricted scale, archaeologists looked for and found adaptation to a series of discrete niches or resources across the landscape. In both cases, ecological factors were given status as agents of change that stimulated perturbations in the archaeological record. The archaeological record thus became littered with artifacts of adaptation and readaptation: human prehistory effectively became to various degrees a proxy of ecological history.

There is much to be said for such an idea about the nature of the past, in the Chesapeake region and elsewhere. The ecology of this region, for example, has changed dramatically since the late Pleistocene. Early hunters and gatherers and later incipient horticulturists were obviously affected by these changes. By the time that processual archaeology piqued the interest of local prehistorians, regional culture history had been reasonably well documented and the time was ripe for exploring new explanations. The most vocal early advocate of processual archaeology, Binford (1964, 1991), had even left us his dissertation that applied some of these new ideas to the local archaeological record.

Aside from some of the paradigm's more pernicious aspects, it would be foolish not to argue that the discipline as a whole has benefited from the efforts of the processual archaeologists. Adaptation has not been difficult to find in the archaeological record. Processual archaeology also perceptively matured and gained sophistication throughout the decades of the 1970s and 1980s through its development of an increasing variety of new ideas about human behavior; optimal foraging strategies, information processing, risk management, and the like offered new ways to understand past behavior. Its maturation coherently linked diverse sets of archaeological data into rational human adaptational systems. We could see how societies once functioned within their environmental contexts. The old, inert archaeological record faded away as processual archaeologists vigorously pursued explanations from a variety of sources external to the artifacts themselves. Many new techniques were concurrently developed to recover data relevant to this goal.

At the same time, like before, efforts toward one set of goals brought about disappointments in other realms. To my mind two are the most damning. First, in attempting to understand how a prehistoric society functioned within its environmental context, processual archaeology, again especially in its early formulations, often sank into a vulgar materialism of sorts. Human choice and action all too often disappeared from the equation as the winds of ecological change became paramount. Even in mature processual archaeology, people seldom are seen as true agents of change. Instead, they appear, at best, to take advantage of change and, at worst, to materialize as victims of change. Only after change is delivered by the environment do they arrive to satiate systemic needs for procurement scheduling, risk management, information processing, or the like.

Second, while few challenge processual archaeology's cherished goal of isolating laws of human behavior, most are less than sanguine with the results thus far. Bruce Trigger (1978:7) rightfully points out that "appalling trivialities have been disguised as laws." Colin Renfrew (1982:7) expands on this when he states that the metaphysics of processual archaeology is "difficult to refute but impossible to use." In the interest of fairness, some of the criticisms above relate more to practice by some archaeologists and not to the good—even noble—intentions of processual archaeologists overall. Nevertheless, few can help but occasionally cringe at some of what has been produced under the processual banner. As before, tensions again opened the door for change.

A so-called postprocessual archaeology began to stir emotions by the early 1980s. This label, postprocessual, represents an inclusive term for a not-so-unified undertaking. There are a variety of often diverse movements—from the radically aggressive to the truly different—under this larger banner. And in its formative stages much of what it produced was either harangue against processual archaeology or homilies on how archaeology should be practiced backed by very selective examples. This situation is only now beginning to change with actual postprocessual studies beginning to appear in the corpus of literature (see Duke 1991; J. Thomas 1991). At the local level, only very limited attempts have been made to apply postprocessual archaeology to the Chesapeake region (e.g., J. Haynes 1984; Jirikowic 1990; Williamson 1979). If the postprocessual agenda can be characterized at all, it in many instances seems to seek what a number of people have labeled (albeit tongue-in-cheek) a kinder, gentler archaeology.

Several recurrent themes within postprocessual archaeology offer alternatives to dominant archaeological interpretation. To my mind, perhaps the cornerstone of the postprocessual challenge is that it questions the tendency of its nemesis to give precedence to systemic adaptation to the natural environment while neglecting, at the very least, equally important human social agency. As noted earlier, people in the past, under the processual protocol, more often than not disappear as they fade into larger dehumanized eco-evolutionary adaptational systems. Postprocessual archaeology strongly asserts that we need once again to see people as active agents in the creation of a social world, separate from and only conditioned by the natural world. It is difficult to dismiss such a plea.

Next, from my reading, postprocessual archaeologists want to see a fundamentally different type of archaeological record. Processual archaeologists most often seek a continuous record of coherence and efficiency. One challenge after the other, presented to system maintenance by the environment, is overcome in a slow, progressive march through time. The system of one era is understood as a rationally altered state of its predecessor, as its successor will ultimately be to it. If the processual archaeological record appears continuous, the archaeological record postprocessual archaeologists expect is more discontinuous. No rationality is necessarily sought, given that none may be found. Continuity is rare since people as prime movers of change make a wide variety of choices. And their choices, tempered by a variety of immediate and historical contingencies, are not always necessarily rational or with precedent.

Last, postprocessual archaeology holds out the hope for a discovery of the "other" in the archaeological record. Artifacts are not linked as systems of adaptation; instead, efforts are made to challenge the notion of a system's absolute functional coherence in an effort to recover native meaning and culture. While artifacts may have a behavioral context, they also occupy a discoverable symbolic space. Postprocessual archaeologists attempt to arrive at an understanding of another, probably very foreign, way of thinking that should often appear qualitatively different from what came before and after it.

Postprocessual archaeology is certainly not immune to its own set of criticisms. Some of these derive from the problem of the development of a theory with no accompanying adequately articulated methodology. First, there is at present no widely accepted means to unequivocally distill native meanings from artifacts. There have, however, been some interesting suggestions made in isolated and relatively restricted studies. Second, postprocessual archaeology has expressed a profound mistrust of positivism. Yet it has not provided a rational and logically sound way to demonstrate the validity of its interpretations over alternative challenges. Most rest on the principle of competitive plausibility. Third, one branch of this diverse undertaking, namely, so-called critical theory, in its most extreme manifestation, holds out little hope that it is even possible to do archaeology as we know it. Under this formula, all that can be hoped for is to use archaeology's reconstructions of the past as a vehicle to reflect on ourselves in the present. I sense an outright rejection of this particular premise by much of the discipline and even a softening of such a perspective by the critical theorists themselves.

I do not propose even to begin to answer the questions raised about all three paradigms discussed above. This is well beyond the scope of undertakings such as this book. I do, however, feel that a review of each of the three archaeologies was important for two reasons. First, it is beneficial to systematically outline both the merits and limitations of the various sets of ideas that have been advanced to explain the archaeological record. Precedent is important to the interpretation of the archaeological record of this or any region. Second, it is important to acknowledge that all past and present efforts to understand the archaeological record fit into a larger continuum with a larger purpose. On this grand continuum the limitation(s) of any one point plants the seeds of the next.

Culture history, as an explanatory alternative, has now been effectively laid to rest, yet our current explanations often depart from its chronological and spatial reconstructions of the past. Processual archaeology is still perhaps dominant, but it is increasingly being challenged by postprocessual archaeology. Processual archaeology, to its credit, is even challenging itself. A distinct loss of innocence is in the air. I cannot begin to suggest which way of doing archaeology will eventually prevail. With a fondness for axioms, I suspect that the archaeology of the near and distant future will probably not be a case of "either-or," but more likely consist of "both-and." All sides will no doubt eventually claim victory. But for now, regardless of labels, it is important to work with the strengths of our existing explanatory repertoire.

INTERPRETING CHESAPEAKE PREHISTORY

In the chapters that follow, I will attempt to offer explanations of the patterns and processes isolated in the known archaeological record of the Chesapeake region. The preceding review of explanatory archaeology has hopefully identified at least some of the pluses of the discipline's current perspectives on explanation. While there have also been minuses to each approach, it does not make sense to sink into cynicism over them or to become polemical about the crossing of boundaries between camps. A pragmatic approach, without resorting to a hyperrelativism and its fondness for everything, offers the greatest hope for a broad understanding of regional prehistory.

The following is the situation in the Chesapeake region as I see it. From what we now know, the first approximately 7000 or so years of prehistory was marked by hunter-foragers operating at the band level of sociocultural integration. These peoples fall into what archaeologists would label the Paleoindian period and into much of the subsequent Archaic period. I do not mean to imply that there were not significant and very interesting variations on this basic way of life. There certainly was diversity, but within the parameters of the broader theme. After circa 4200 years ago, sometime in the Late Archaic, people began to transform their traditional ways of life. This transformation had a significant impact on human societies in the Chesapeake region and is graphically reflected in the archaeological record. I generically label this change an *intensification* effort. Changes wrought in this era culminate by the end of prehistory, in the Late Woodland, with the establishment of chiefdoms across much of the region.

The interpretations I offer to explain this sequence of events are dependent on only one major assumption. This assumption, which is a hybrid of both processual and postprocessual archaeology, will appear very obvious. But it needs to be restated for the record. My interpretations rest on the premise that people in the past lived under influences from both their social environment and their natural environment, although the degree of influence of either variable on life in the past may have fluctuated depending on circumstances. Make careful note of this fact. If I am absolutely sure of anything about the state of Chesapeake archaeology today, it is that we have overemphasized the natural environment field of the nature–culture equation. We must remain mindful of the impact of the environment on human society, but it is also time to move in the direction of a more balanced equation. Leaving the specifics for the subsequent chapters, the general outline of what I hope to present is as follows.

I want to view regional prehistory as representing a record of peoples in the past who changed from *accommodating* nature to socially *appropriating* or transforming nature (follows J. Thomas 1991). In other words, I see the approximately 7000 years of regional hunter-foragers as being tightly bound to the constraints and opportunities of the prevailing natural environment at any given point in time. Because the natural environment changed dramatically over the 7000-year period, it surely exerted a great influence on these peoples. The archaeological record directly registers this influence. At the same time, I feel that we can also read instances in at least some of these same artifacts whereby society actively used material culture to reproduce and maintain this lifeway.

Following this earliest period of Chesapeake prehistory, after about 4200 years ago, the region witnessed the beginning of what I have labeled an intensification effort. Such transformations are traditionally interpreted as economic phenomena: acceleration of wild food resource procurement or adoption of agriculture becomes fuel for social elaboration. While such factors are important, they are only part of the story. I would argue they are only a small part of the story. Given this, I feel it is important to move in the direction of seeing intensification and its subsequent developments less as an economic phenomenon and more as being driven by a set of social relations and the new ideas that sustained these relations (J. Thomas 1991:77).

During this era, in a radical break with their pasts, societies began to actively transform and appropriate nature for their own ends. Attempts to understand this transformation should focus on what triggered such a change after so many thousands of years of prehistory, and how such a change was sustained after the threshold was crossed. The answer to the former question rests more with people as agents of change in the past than it does with the environment. It is *not* suggested that we seek an individual responsible for this act. It would be impossible to find such an individual in the archaeological record if one ever really existed. It *is* suggested that we acknowledge that we are studying societies of individuals that for the first time created the conditions for the active transformation of their former ways of life through an invention of a new way of social reproduction. What is really remarkable is that this transformation required such a lengthy prelude and perhaps even that it happened at all. In this sense, the preceding 7000 years of what was essentially social sameness becomes all the more intriguing.

Archaeology is equipped to isolate the artifacts that provide answers to the question of how society initiated and maintained this new way of social reproduction. Chesapeake prehistory of this era is littered with artifacts of the invention and development of this new way of life. The archaeological record is a witness to a container revolution, expansion of infrastructure at sites and across the landscape, development of new portable technologies and new subsistence and storage practices, an elaboration of mortuary rituals, as well as the creation of new and very different social and political systems. The evidence is available to track the invention, reproduction, and subsequent development of a different and regionally unique way of life.

To accomplish this goal, I also want to add something further about two assumptions that tend to polarize the processual and postprocessual protocols as they relate to any understanding of prehistory. They specifically relate to the way in which I want to explain Chesapeake prehistory. One assumption relates to the very nature of the archaeological record. The other assumption concerns questions of explanatory adequacy. Each is addressed below in turn.

In terms of the first, I want to make mention of processual archaeology's tendency to see the archaeological record on somewhat of a continuous eco-evolutionary trajectory, while postprocessual archaeology seeks a more discontinuous phenomena. Current thinking, even within broader evolutionary theory, points to the latter instance as a better approximation of reality in the past. Archaeologists need to at least remain vigilant on this matter. There is also the question of interpreting artifacts as rationally functional elements of an adaptational system versus attempting to discover their meaning vis-à-vis the people that produced them. These are overlapping and not mutually exclusive means of understanding the archaeological record. There should be room for both perspectives in our interpretations. Artifacts are certainly a part of both larger economic and social dramas. My interpretations of Chesapeake prehistory incorporate these conclusions.

In terms of the second assumption, we come to the sensitive question of how the interpretations or explanations of Chesapeake prehistory will be constructed. It is my intention, as stated previously, to consider a broad range of factors—both social and ecological—that may have been relevant to the occurrence of events in the past. Inspiration for these factors typically originates from any number of sources: from anthropology, ethnohistory, and ethnoarchaeology, from actualistic and experimental studies, and from other disciplines such as ecology. These factors are used to produce what are conceptualizations of particular ways of life that may have existed within contexts similar to those at one time present in the prehistoric Chesapeake region.

I employ these conceptualizations, like many prehistorians, to create sets of expectations about the potential archaeological residues of such ways of life. These expectations are then compared with the actual known archaeological record of the Chesapeake region. Interpretations that result are based on both the meeting of expectations as well as ambiguity between the same expectations and the reality of the archaeological record. The latter process holds out the hope for the discovery of the truly unique and different. This methodology is similar to what is currently known as middle-range research.

This raises the question of explanatory adequacy. My answer to the question is basic and general. Explanation or interpretation should be viewed as adequate if it seeks to answer certain types of "why" questions. These represent the links between the particular phenomena to be explained in the archaeological record and the factors that produced them. Positivism, part of the ambitious theoretical package of processual archaeology, is but one answer to the search for explanatory meaning. It insists on the production of a final and universal understanding of the particular event under examination. To some, the search for and discovery of general laws represents a litmus of sorts. There are, however, other ways to produce legitimate explanations. Many archaeologists, by acclamation at least, have long endorsed a much wider range of acceptable explanations.

The nature and form of the explanatory methodology employed herein is dictated by the characteristics of this particular undertaking. I can ill afford to narrowly focus on the many elements of every minute segment of the archaeological record throughout 11,000 years of prehistory. The project has a regional scope and depends on a vast amount of data collected for a wide variety of different purposes. Explanations must therefore remain broad. They are expressed in a qualitative and textually narrative fashion. They represent interpretive scenarios that hopefully have explanatory value vis-à-vis certain long-term patterns and key disjunctures in the archaeological record of the Chesapeake region.

This brings us to a consideration of checks that could potentially monitor my perceptions of Chesapeake prehistory. First, while I may represent a minority opinion, I feel there is still room in archaeology and in science in general to acknowledge an investigator's ability to recognize worthwhile explanations. Part of what we do is still craft. We should not deceive ourselves into thinking that the use of any one particular explanatory protocol automatically guarantees total objectivity and final answers.

While I have attempted to remain as objective as possible through this research, an investigator's biases and predispositions always inhabit the final product. This need not be all bad. Merrilee Salmon and Wesley Salmon echo this opinion when they state:

> Recognition of satisfactory explanation does not depend on a set of carefully detailed criteria. . . . It is philosophically satisfying and theoretically important to have such criteria. Yet in the last analysis, the development of adequate theory of

explanation for anthropology and any other science depends on a delicate balance between the invocation of logical principles and the considered judgments of scientists. (1979:72)

I have attempted to follow the spirit of this argument, by considering as many different points of view as exist in this region in the construction of my interpretations of Chesapeake prehistory.

From a perspective external to this study there is one other ultimate check on my conclusions. What has been presented thus far illustrates how I want to go about offering an interpretation of the archaeological record. I have made my argument, as it were. Perhaps my rationalization has been lengthy, but the subject of explanation is, after all, still a rather inflammatory issue in archaeology. My final observation about this matter is therefore simple and short. It applies to both this research and to all other such undertakings.

Scholarly discourse is always ultimately dialectical. It involves a larger process external to any single study. And it manifests itself through critical tension and debate between old interpretations, new directions, and future rethinking. The very title of this volume recognizes two of these domains and one of my specific research goals anticipates the latter realm. The community of scholars interested in Chesapeake prehistory in particular and archaeology in general will have the final word on the interpretations offered herein through their reactions to my arguments. This is how it should be. Books such as this are no more or less than a part of a much longer conversation.

Last, it occurs to me that it is necessary, probably healthy, and, at the very least, honest to admit that there are some silences in any archaeological record that will answer to no currently known or even anticipated way of interpreting the past. Chesapeake prehistory, no doubt, has it share of such instances. In those cases, I can only promise to mark the limbs I will inevitably have to crawl out on through a language set in the conditional and the subjunctive, if not by direct statements noting these instances as my own informed speculation. Let us all not forget the ultimate nature of what we attempt to study.

PROSPECTUS

This volume is organized in the following manner. First, this introductory chapter has made a case for the purpose of this effort and the general research goals. It serves to introduce the reader to the geographic boundaries of the study area through time. Finally, it has outlined how I intend to go about constructing Chesapeake prehistory. This latter section includes a guide to the data employed, taxonomic description, and interpretation.

Moving forward, the second chapter presents what is in essence a history of ideas: how Chesapeake prehistorians have looked at the region's archaeological record during the nineteenth and twentieth centuries. It surveys the principal ideas about the past that have influenced the interpretation of archaeological data by a variety of investigators working throughout the region. I argue that a great deal of thought has already been put into regional prehistory. It would be unwise to move blindly into a new synthesis without understanding where we, as a discipline, have been and how we have arrived at our present state. This is not a new argument.

In the third chapter, I offer a paleoecological reconstruction of the Chesapeake study area. This chapter outlines the dramatic changes that have taken place in the regional landscape since the end of the Pleistocene. Employing the contemporary biophysical environment as a datum of sorts, this section includes a discussion of geologic history, marine regression, Late Pleistocene paleoecology, marine transgression, and subsequent Holocene paleoecological evolution. The chapter draws on contemporary and historical floral and faunal analyses, estuarine biology, oceanography, geology, palynology, and various other sources of information. Subsequent issues of prehistoric adaptation in the study area depend on this overall paleoecological reconstruction.

The fourth chapter examines the Paleoindian period (circa 11,000 to 10,000 years ago) in the Chesapeake study area. I first briefly review Paleoindian studies in eastern North America and then turn to Paleoindian manifestations recovered within the study area. Data patterning is described in order to produce a comprehensive understanding of Paleoindians in the region, and then an interpretation is offered as a new and expanded perspective on Paleoindian lifeways. I argue that this interpretation may ultimately be applicable to Paleoindian manifestations in other, similar unglaciated contexts.

A chapter on the Archaic period (circa 10,000 to 3000 years ago) in the Chesapeake study area follows. This section briefly reviews the creation of the idea of an Archaic period in broader eastern North America and then outlines extant knowledge of similar Archaic manifestations in the study area. The cultural historical synthesis is followed by a critical rethinking of the Archaic period within the study area, including an examination of the initial specialized adaptation to the newly formed temperate ecosystem and the rapidly forming estuary. What is referred to as an intensification effort, leading to a transformation of aboriginal lifeways approximately 4200 years ago in portions of the Chesapeake region, is also closely examined. I argue that this is a story of both adaptation and human agency in a redirection of lifeways.

Following this, the last increment of regional prehistory, the Woodland period (from circa 3000 years ago up to the Contact era), is addressed. This chapter, like those for the two earlier archaeological periods, begins with a brief examination of the Woodland period in broader eastern North America. Included is a discussion of outside influences on the region, both native and eventually European. The chapter then moves to a synthesis of our current knowledge of the Woodland period within the Chesapeake study area. Again, the chapter ends with the presentation of a more current and comprehensive interpretation of this period. The record of technological development and social elaboration evident during the Woodland period in the local area is presented as further elaboration of the intensification process begun some 1200 years earlier. The epitome of these changes is the appearance of chiefdoms across the region late in prehistory. Possible scenarios for the development of these chiefdoms are reviewed.

Finally, in the last chapter I return to the theme that a contemporary understanding of Chesapeake prehistory requires consideration of both old traditions and new directions. In particular I reflect on the expression of this theme in the various focal points that constitute my discussion of regional prehistory. Prospects for future research and analysis are addressed, followed by a brief concluding statement.

Chapter 2

The Idea of the Past

INTRODUCTION

Archaeology, as a discipline with its eye on the past, is itself increasingly coming under historical scrutiny. General histories by Gordon Willey and Jeremy Sabloff (1993) and Trigger (1989) are perhaps some of the more visible artifacts of this process. More focused studies have been produced by a number of other scholars. Archaeological research in the Chesapeake region has a remarkable tenure in its own right, and local prehistorians, albeit most often from the perspective of individual states within the broader region, have likewise begun to reflect on the history of archaeology in this area (e.g., Bastian 1980; Custer 1989; MacCord 1990; Porter 1981, 1983; Weslager 1968).

There is good reason for this historical examination of archaeology. Some of the reasons are self-evident; some are not. Through this chapter, I hope to contribute to this tradition by presenting an historical overview of archaeology's endeavor to understand Chesapeake prehistory. Many now-existing local histories are factual, chronologically oriented examinations written from the perspective of archaeology in one of the three states that make up the region. The perspective I take here is instead a regionally based history of ideas; that is, I intend to examine how archaeologists have constructed local prehistory. My reasons for approaching the history of Chesapeake archaeology in this manner deserve some brief elaboration.

In attempting any archaeological history it is now almost obligatory to recite R. G. Collingwood's (1939:132) proclamation "that no historical problem should be studied without studying . . . the history of historical thought about it" (cited in Dunnell 1986; Trigger 1989). This is, of course, the self-evident reason for this section of the book. Even though, as Trigger (1989:4) points out, historical examinations are notoriously subjective, such research does offer a unique datum from which to view the accomplishments of a discipline. While such a perspective admittedly does little to stop new desecrations of the past, historical reflection might at least help present researchers avoid the repetition of old abuses.

Several specific reasons for producing this particular history can also be cited. First, I see this book as part of a greater tradition. Attempts at understanding Chesapeake prehistory effectively extend beyond the boundaries of my research into the past. They likewise will continue into the future. It is today impossible to accurately anticipate this future. At the same time, however, it is important to understand the specifics of the existing foundations of our knowledge of Chesapeake prehistory. The history presented in this chapter serves to acknowledge what has been accomplished to date, and it helps to set a point of departure for the present analysis. It will further serve to expand on some of the thoughts presented in the previous chapter.

Second, I think it is time to recognize that everything accomplished in the past is not an impoverished preface to the present. In my opinion, Willey and Sabloff's (1993) now almost standard history of American archaeology errs to a certain degree in setting up the discipline's past as an essentially atheoretical gestation toward the archaeology of today. This is probably an unintended artifact of the widely adopted Kuhnian (Kuhn 1970) notion of disciplinary shift. As Philip Duke (1991:5) notes, we often seek to identify modes of thought as rigidly defined and absolute paradigmatic camps. The dominant received view of the moment is science, and everything before it, or currently challenging it, is not. Yet objective studies of early phases of research often reveal a much richer and more comprehensive explanatory perspective than many believed existed (see Dunnell 1986; Trigger 1989).

Third, and finally, historical overviews remind us that what is ultimately learned about the past is relative to the system of inquiry. The archaeological record remains a constant in the equation, and the system of inquiry becomes the dependent variable. It is important in this analysis that recognition be granted to alternative modes of explanation. Much of what I aim to accomplish fits within the confines of contemporary archaeology as it is practiced in the Chesapeake region, but some ultimately goes in other directions. Archaeology should be flexible enough to allow alternative ways of looking at the same archaeological record. In its extreme form this approach could lead one into relativism. But in another sense, considered historical analysis will often confirm that some diversity is healthy and is indeed a positive part of the discipline's tradition.

While what I have stated above does represent specific goals of this history, it is important to note what is *not* on my agenda. I do not present this history to argue that nothing is new in archaeology in general or in Chesapeake archaeology in particular. The old adage that "the more things change, the more they remain the same" should not be induced from what follows. I do argue that there are benefits to taking a moment to look back, but only as a tool toward moving forward.

PREFACE TO A HISTORY

This history focuses on what I see as key disjunctures in the more than a century-long tradition of archaeologists' attempts to understand Chesapeake prehistory. It identifies and examines what are argued to be changing perceptions of the region's archaeological record. It is, simply put, a history of ideas about the nature of the prehistoric past in the Chesapeake region.

This history looks at these ideas in roughly the chronological order in which they originated. It is not, however, designed to be an exhaustive historical survey, nor does it aim to examine in any great detail the much broader social and intellectual milieus that stimulated these new ways of looking at the past. On the first score, the history must remain selective. Little purpose would be served through the citation and discussion of nearly every example in the small mountain of archaeological literature that has accumulated on this region. It seems more realistic to be selective and focus on what can be argued to be landmark studies that in their own way and time stimulated new directions in thinking. I aim for a history of significant changes, not details.

On the matter of the second score, Chesapeake prehistorians, in completing the research now under scrutiny here, were certainly influenced by, and reacted to, much broader forces stimulating new ideas about the nature of the past. And it would be interesting in this history to detail both the larger social milieu as well as the forces internal to the broader discipline of archaeology that were affecting the ways Chesapeake prehistorians approached the past. These matters, unfortunately, are beyond the scope of what is primarily a regional archaeology. This history is therefore, for the most part, less a history of ultimate causes and more a history of specific consequences.

A HISTORY OF CHESAPEAKE ARCHAEOLOGY

The history that follows focuses specifically on the definition and discussion of five periods within the overall tradition of Chesapeake archaeology. Labels chosen for each period reflect general theme or direction. The specific research cited, while selective, hopefully further illustrates each period's tenor in more detail. The periods discussed often do have some sort of rough chronological integrity, although the divisions by no means represent an interval scale of time. As with most histories, boundaries are occasionally porous, and specific trends that were developed in some of the periods defy tight chronological closure. This is especially true of the first period in this history. I have generally attempted to appreciate developments within each of the five periods from the perspective of their own era. I have tried to demonstrate that at least some of these earlier periods have a unique implicitness and more internal consistency than we have sometimes wanted to believe. Each subheading below labels one of the five periods of the general history.

Antiquarianism

A curiosity about objects from the past antedates the formalization of archaeology as a discipline in this region as it did elsewhere. I have therefore found it necessary, like others producing archaeological histories, to include an initial period that is characterized by activities centered mainly around little more than the acquisition of artifacts. Such historical periods are sometimes created to address what motivated people to collect artifacts, but more often such periods are constructed to herald just how far we have come as students of the past. I will admit to both tendencies.

To chronologically delimit periods dominated by antiquarian interests is especially difficult. Much of this activity was restricted to the early years of regional Euro-American history, up until about the mid-nineteenth century. Yet this activity even slips back into prehistory itself, and it continues up until today. In fact, it is probably better to view this particular period as characterizing an outlook rather than as being a temporally bounded entity.

Definition of this outlook is rather simple. People and institutions sought to amass collections of prehistoric artifacts from sites across the Chesapeake region. Objects were also collected from native groups still living in the region at the time of early colonization. To understand the reasons for the collection of these objects is quite another matter; often one can only speculate. I will come back to this matter after a brief review of what is known about the early participants in this activity in the Chesapeake and a discussion of the very few artifacts still surviving from early in this era.

The collection of artifacts is a pursuit that has no definable genesis. There is ample evidence that during prehistory native peoples themselves sometimes collected and kept objects attributable to earlier times. One does not have to excavate too many sites in the Chesapeake region before coming across an instance of a much older artifact appearing in isolation within a significantly later context. Lacking any physical evidence for natural redeposition, curation of the object by subsequent peoples becomes the likely alternative explanation.

It is certainly evident that the first European colonists to settle in this region likewise indulged in collecting various relics. Historic documents indicate that fossils and artifacts from the region were being shipped back to Europe from the early seventeenth century onwards. Most are now lost. A spatially discreet cache of prehistoric artifacts, no doubt someone's early collection, was recently discovered during the excavation of the ruins of the eighteenth-century John Hicks house along the middle reaches of the Chesapeake Bay. Similar collecting of artifacts, often for no apparent reason other then to collect them, has persisted until today.

On an institutional basis, artifacts from the Chesapeake tidewater area were put on display in Europe from at least as early as the seventeenth century. Objects from the region appeared by at least 1638 in the Tradescant collection, now part of the Ashmolean at Oxford, England. Other artifacts undoubtedly arrived in similar repositories across Europe. Collections of artifacts from the lower Chesapeake region originally formed part of the Sloan collection (Bushnell 1906). This collection, now held by the British Museum, Museum of Mankind, was severely impacted by bombing during World War II, and the artifacts from the Chesapeake region were apparently destroyed or lost (Jonathan King [Keeper of North American Collections], personal communication, 1986). Two artifacts from the lower Chesapeake in the Tradescant collection, the so-called Powhatan's Mantle (Figure 2.1) and a skin pouch with beadwork (Figure 2.2), however, are miraculously still in existence (MacGregor 1983). While there is some reluctance to associate the former item with Powhatan himself, few doubt that both objects date to the very early seventeenth century. As such, they deserve some discussion in this context.

The most well known surviving object from the Chesapeake from this era, or for that matter any era, is Powhatan's Mantle, now curated by the Ashmolean Museum in Oxford, England. The object can be historically traced to a collection amassed by John Tradescant, the elder, and his son, John Tradescant, the younger. This early collection, originally known as "The Ark," was on display to the paying public by 1634. In 1638, Georg Christoph Stirn noted that he had visited the collection and viewed "the robe of the King of Virginia" (Feest 1983). Current opinion seems to be that the younger Tradescant may have acquired the object on one of his three collecting trips to Virginia. His 1637 journey appears to be the most likely candidate for this particular acquisition. Alternatively, the elder Tradescant is known to have had many contacts, and the object could conceivably have been presented directly to him through an unknown intermediary. For example, Captain John Smith, the early well-known English explorer of the Chesapeake, did bequeath part of his library to Tradescant. Whatever the case, in 1656 his son listed it in his *Musaeum Tradescantianum* as "Pohatan, King of Virginia's habit all embroidered with shells, or Roanoke." Later, in 1662, the entire collection was deeded to Elias Ashmole and eventually formed the foundation for the museum that today bears his name.

The following brief description of the mantle is a synopsis of the official description written for the Ashmolean Museum by Christian Feest (1983). According to Feest, the mantle is made up of four tanned hides of white-tailed deer (*Odocoileus virginianus*) that are each cut straight on two adjacent sides and sewn together with sinew thread to form a larger, almost rectangular piece of leather. Attached shell beadwork of prepared *Marginella roscida* forms a standing human figure flanked by two upright quadrupeds and surrounded by 34 disc designs. The two animals resemble one another in outline, yet are clearly different based on tail and foot details. They could represent some sort of presumably mythical composite creatures, but a number of investigators believe the right figure to represent a white-tailed deer and the left to be a mountain lion (*Felis concolor*).

Two questions naturally come to a viewer of this object: Did it belong to the historical figure Powhatan, and what does the design mean? The answer to either question is, of course, problematic. Most do not see the object as having come, so to speak, directly off Powhatan's back. If it was collected in 1637 by the younger Tradescant, then the historical figure known as Powhatan had been dead for close to two decades. It also does not fit the surprisingly numerous mentions of Powhatan's dress that survive in ethnohistorical documents. There is even serious question as to whether the object was actually made to be an item of clothing (see Feest 1983:133–134). Some see it more as a sort of decorative banner.

Symbolic meaning of the iconography on the object is another difficult, but

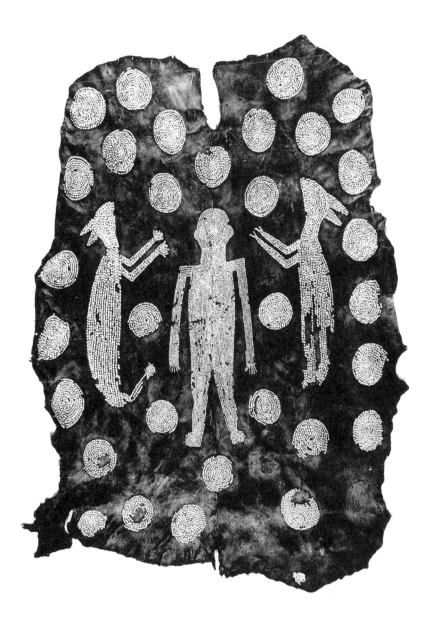

Figure 2.1.   Powhatan's Mantle, originally part of the Tradescant collection. Placed on display circa 1638. Ashmolean Museum, Oxford.

Figure 2.2.   Decorated skin pouch from Virginia, originally part of the Tradescant collection. Placed on display circa 1656, Ashmolean Museum, Oxford.

interesting, question. Feest (1983:135) feels that the human and two animal figures may be representations of the sentinel figures documented as having been erected at Powhatan's "treasure house" at Orapakes. In fact, he believes the object under discussion may originally have been looted from that location around 1622 and later sold to the Tradescant collection. Randolph Turner (1976:133) has suggested that the numerous round designs that cover the background of the mantle may each be symbolic of the individual districts under Powhatan's control. There is a rough correlation between the numbers of the former and the latter.

In addition to Powhatan's Mantle, there is one other object in the Ashmolean—a decorated skin pouch—that is thought to have originated in the Chesapeake region (Figure 2.2). It too was originally a part of the Tradescant collection. Again, following a detailed description by Feest (1983:135–137), the pouch is constructed from a piece of tanned animal skin, probably deer. This single piece has been folded together and sewn with another smaller piece of animal skin added to form a bottom. On each end of this pouch close to 6,000 specimens of prepared shell are attached. Species include *Oliva nana*, *Saxidomus aratus* or *S. graciles*, and *Marginella* sp. This object appears to have been an asymmetrically folded pouch, sometimes referred to as a slit pouch, that was worn folded over a belt. An existing central crease on the pouch, apparently original, lends credence to this interpretation. This particular pouch is the last known surviving example of four similar objects listed in the 1656 *Musaeum Tradescantianum* as "Virginia purses embroidered with Roanoke." Although seldom discussed, it is the second important item from the Chesapeake region that ended up in an early European collection and has survived until today.

An early corollary interest in collecting similar objects probably also existed here within the Chesapeake region. In 1814, Rembrandt Peale opened his "Peale's Baltimore Museum and Gallery of Fine Arts." Exact details on the collections held in this museum remain sketchy. It is known from contemporary advertisements that the curiosa on the first floor of the museum included prehistoric antiquities and ethnographic objects (Hunter 1964:9). It would be surprising if local objects were not included in this display. We do know that one of the mastodons (*Mammut* sp.) recovered in 1801 through the famous Peale family excavations in Ulster, New York, was displayed in the Baltimore museum, and that many duplicates from the more well known and earlier Peale Museum in Philadelphia were also on display. Surviving records and illustrations of the interior of the Philadelphia museum indicate an evolutionary sequence to the displays: geologic exhibits were followed by preserved flora and fauna, which yielded to aboriginal artifacts, which were then topped by artifacts of contemporary society. A similar display scheme apparently was employed in the new Baltimore museum. Unfortunately, a fire in 1833 destroyed a significant portion of the collections from the Peale Baltimore Museum, and remaining items were dispersed to a number of parties. Surviving written descriptions are likewise not numerous. The Maryland Academy of Science and Literature, established in the same city by 1844, may have kept similar collections of local antiquities (Bastian 1980:2).

Whatever the ultimate motives, an understanding of the antiquarian interest in collecting various aboriginal objects from the Chesapeake region is by necessity general. Such an understanding is probably best approached from both the perspective of the individual collector and from an institutional perspective. In terms of the former, the comprehension of prehistoric peoples holding an artifact from an earlier era can only be speculative. Trigger (1989:28), for example, assumes such kept objects were viewed as having supernatural power, thereby offering the potential of some collateral benefit to the keeper.

Artifact collecting by individuals from early historic times until today probably exists for any number of reasons. At least three general explanations come immediately to mind. First, people are curious about the past. And the possession of artifacts, as tangible reminders of what are generally perceived to be purer and simpler times, may at a deeper level offer collectors some psychological escape from the complexities of their own world. Second, artifacts are sometimes collected for direct economic reasons. More than a few sites from the Chesapeake region have been plundered to fuel the antiquities market (see Dent and Jirikowic 1990:32; MacCord 1990:1). Finally, archaeology is itself generally an artifact of the middle class (see Trigger 1989). Activity within that enterprise, collecting being the prime example, potentially can be seen as a vehicle for the acquisition or reaffirmation of that status.

Reasons for display of objects of antiquity at early museums or similar institutions were, at least, less idiosyncratic. On the surface, such displays in Europe and in the United States helped to satisfy the public's curiosity about the past. Public curiosity, in turn, provided sponsors some hope of a monetary return on their efforts and investment. At a deeper level, however, a concept of aboriginal savagism was being employed to ideologically define contemporary culture and its perceived destiny (Hinsley 1976:10; Sheehan 1980:1–8). Native populations and, by extension, displays of their material culture were convenient reminders of what civilization had left behind; the apparent technological simplicity of these artifacts reinforced progressivist faith in technological progress. The past was being used to rationalize the present.

As a postscript to this period, one cannot fail to mention Thomas Jefferson's early excavations of a mound on his Monticello property located not far to the west of the Chesapeake Bay. The remarkable nature of this undertaking has been commented on by many (e.g., Willey and Sabloff 1993:31–33) and need not be recounted here. Suffice it to say that this endeavor was an early and unfortunately unique event in regional prehistory and, indeed, in archaeology in general.

Emerging Regional Archaeology

By the last quarter of the nineteenth century a new, more scholarly interest in the past begins to emerge and crystalize. A growing cadre of individuals begin the sustained study and debate of the regional archaeological record. This period further represents the roots of an alliance between a number of dedicated and industrious local citizens and the staffs of the nearby Bureau of American Ethnology (BAE) and Smithsonian Institution. But more important, it marks the origins of a new perspective on the archaeological record of the Chesapeake region, wherein, for the first time, it is more than just a curiosity or source of primitive relics. There is a new awareness that the local prehistory represents a unique and important past that is worthy of study in its own right.

An example of this new study and debate of local prehistory can be seen in the activities of the Anthropological Society of Washington (ASW). This society, formally established in 1879, brought together interested parties, both amateur and professional. Local prehistory was often a focus of their deliberations. Otis T. Mason, Smithsonian ethnologist and a vice president of ASW, introduced a symposium held on April 13, 1889, in the following manner:

> The vice-president of the section of technology, despairing of accomplishing unaided all that is to be desired with reference to the human fauna of the Potomac and Chesapeake tide-water region, a few months ago devised the plan of inviting the co-operation of members of our Society. The gentlemen responded promptly to the call, and it was decided to prepare first a series of short papers to be read before the society, and afterwards make them exhaustive so as to form a monograph . . . (Mason 1889:226)

At this meeting, papers were read by W. J. McGee (geologist/BAE ethnologist), Thomas Wilson (Smithsonian, Department of Antiquities), S. V. Proudfit (collector from Falls Church, Virginia), William Henry Holmes (BAE archaeologist), Elmer Reynolds (collector and Federal pension examiner), and James Mooney (BAE ethnologist). None other than Frederick Ward Putnam, from the Peabody Museum of American Archaeology and Ethnology in Cambridge, served as discussant. A special publication in the July 1889 issue of the *American Anthropologist* offered revised and illustrated versions of these papers.

Two themes run through this early collection of papers on regional archaeology. First, there was a multifaceted effort to gain a better understanding of the archaeological record as it was then known to exist. The papers of Proudfit and Reynolds, for example, represent reports on the known distributions of regional archaeological sites. There was a definite interest in understanding prehistoric technology. Holmes's paper is the best example of this interest, and it anticipates his later published work on the aboriginal pottery of eastern North America. In addition, there was a strong interest in gaining an understanding of how a knowledge of local geology may aid in interpreting the archaeological record. McGee was called on to tackle this issue.

Second, there was great interest in the potential of a so-called North American "Paleolithic." Regional archaeologists were responding in two ways to Charles C. Abbott's claims of deep antiquity for the archaeological record of North America based on his discoveries at Trenton, New Jersey. Wilson, for example, had lived in

France and studied its antiquities. He was also well aware of the research of Abbott and others. The conclusion of Wilson's article states:

> . . . when I review all these facts I am forced to the conclusion that the implements I exhibit from the District of Columbia are of the same paleolithic type as those found in the gravels at Trenton and elsewhere, and that they tend to prove the existence of a paleolithic period in the United States. (1889:241)

This statement, while still leaving some room for qualification, helped to push open the door for an extension of the notion of a Paleolithic period into the Chesapeake region.

At the same time, Proudfit seized historical precedent in what soon would become a debate of epoch proportion and presented an unqualified dissenting opinion by stating that:

> My own conclusion as to the relics found at these points is that they are the resultant debris of Indian workshops, where material was roughly blocked out, to be afterward fashioned into knives, spearheads, &c.; and that no good reason is yet apparent for attributing their origin to paleolithic man. (1889:245)

Holmes, at this particular forum, focused on pottery and remained remarkably silent on the matter of antiquity. This is somewhat curious, perhaps purposefully so, given his ultimate stand on the question. Just seven months later, in November 1889, he would deliver another lecture at the same venue that would represent the opening BAE salvo formally challenging Abbott and his notion of a North American Paleolithic. Both Mason and Putnam, for their parts at this particular forum, simply expressed guarded opinions on the conclusions of Wilson's paper.

I view this collective activity as representing an example of a unique, albeit short, transitional era in Chesapeake archaeology for two principal reasons. First, in juxtaposition to the earlier antiquarian period, individuals were actually beginning to look to the local archaeological record in terms of what it might tell them about prehistory. While some were overly influenced by ultimately false evidence of deep antiquity, a climate had been established where a growing number individuals were presenting and debating ideas. And the archaeological record itself was increasingly seen as the ultimate arbitrator.

Institutions were at the same time beginning to curate substantial collections of local antiquities. From the mid-nineteenth century on, large collections of regional artifacts have been kept and displayed at the Smithsonian Institution. Artifacts were held and displayed by the Maryland Academy of Sciences starting in 1875, and the Maryland Historical Society joined in this practice by 1880 (Bastian 1980:2). Johns Hopkins University apparently began to acquire local antiquities beginning in 1888 (Bennett 1989:5).

Second, the critical tension of conflicting views caused this nascent interest in Chesapeake prehistoric archaeology to lurch forward. No matter which side of the debate one chose, the consensus was that more evidence and a rigorous methodology for interpreting that data were needed. The activity of this period was a prelude to an unprecedented era in the study of local prehistory that would ultimately propel regional archaeology onto the national stage.

Early Chesapeake Archaeology

The expanded alliance between the BAE and amateurs that forms the defining attribute for this period represented a true florescence in the study of Chesapeake prehistory. Based on the initial publication of its seminal literature, this period began at the start of the last decade of the nineteenth century, although the roots of this period admittedly extend back into the era just discussed. This period technically closes by about the middle of the third decade of the new century with the appearance of a different set of ideas about the past. Nevertheless, some of the ideas advanced during this period continued to influence local prehistorians well into the 1950s and beyond. I want to begin by looking at the BAE's use of Chesapeake prehistory as part of a broader national agenda.

Some of the most informative research on this period of American archaeology in general, to my mind, has been produced by David Meltzer (1983). An article by Meltzer and Robert Dunnell (1992) provides additional details. Readers are referred to these essays for a discussion of many of the larger issues as well as the details involved in the early debate over human antiquity on this continent. There is no need, in the present context, to repeat a description of the battles being waged. Following a discussion of the part that local archaeology played in the BAE's challenge of claims for a North American Paleolithic, I do, however, want to focus particularly on the local consequences of the BAE's interest in Chesapeake archaeology.

In terms of the national issue, Abbott's claims for his "paleoliths" had been well advertised. A growing number of followers were now seeing similarly ancient artifacts at a wide variety of locations across the country. The Paleolithic question within the context of Chesapeake prehistory was first raised in 1878 when W. J. Hoffman read a paper to the ASW comparing local implements to Abbott's finds near Trenton, New Jersey (Holmes 1890:2). It had been left simmering for over a decade. Wilson (1889, 1890) reopened the issue at the 1889 ASW symposium and through a subsequent publication of the National Museum.

Protagonists of the issue had literally delivered the North American Paleolithic to the BAE's back door. A more critical look at the issue seemed unavoidable. Several other factors may have been influential in provoking the BAE into action. First, BAE scientists, and indeed some other local archaeologists, were justifiably skeptical of the arguments from which Abbott and others had drawn their conclusions. Alternative explanations seemed possible, especially given the lack of consensus on the geologic age of the paleolith-bearing deposits. Second, the BAE had just succeeded in settling the Moundbuilder controversy. Indians had been linked to the mounds, and to the BAE the whole of the rest of the archaeological record was therefore now likewise associated with the direct ancestors of those peoples. As Meltzer (1983:14–15) comments, to accept a much earlier Paleolithic race on the continent during the Pleistocene would introduce a massive temporal and cultural chasm into the BAE's view of the archaeological record. Finally, the BAE was consciously trying to create a professional science of anthropology and archaeology, preferably in its own image. Institutional *esprit de corps* and perhaps even a tinge of nationalism, given that the archaeological record of the United States was increasingly being presented as less unique and more like that of Europe, may have helped urge them into the fray.

The BAE's response was delivered by Holmes. It was based on research undertaken at the Piney Branch Quarry site in Washington, D.C., and it ultimately proved devastating to Abbott and the notion of a North American Paleolithic. In 1889 Holmes was formally transferred by John Wesley Powell from the United States Geological Survey (USGS) to the position of archaeologist at the BAE. The Piney Branch Quarry site had already been strategically selected by Powell as a starting place for Holmes's research given the light it might cast on the Paleolithic controversy. Lithic implements that were very similar to Abbott's paleoliths were found among cobble deposits at the site. This fact had been known for some while to the local archaeological community.

Claiming total objectivity on the issues, Holmes began excavations at Piney Branch in the autumn of 1889 (Figure 2.3). By the time fieldwork had to stop for the winter, Holmes could no longer contain his conclusion. He delivered a paper to ASW on November 16, 1889, that began with a rather sober discussion of the site, its artifacts, and its geology. The particular artifacts in question were linked to the Cretaceous stratum and at the end of the paper Holmes focused in on the Paleolithic controversy. Based on replicative research and the assemblage recovered at Piney Branch, Holmes argued that every implement passes through certain common stages of development during manufacture (Figure 2.4). At early stages of this sequence implements do appear very crude. Nevertheless, Holmes correctly concluded that a relative crudeness in appearance was not a reliable chronological indicator. He then went on to suggest that the so-called paleoliths, at least from this site, were rejects from the various stages of manufacture and were not of paleolithic age.

The paper that he read to ASW was published just two months later in the January 1890 issue of the *American Anthropologist*. It essentially substantiated Proudfit's earlier conclusions concerning the so-called local paleoliths delivered at the ASW symposium of the year before. It is also possible that Holmes's conclusion reflected his own earlier experiences at Obsidian Canyon in Yellowstone where, while studying the geology of the area in 1878, he had pondered the meaning of various artifacts found among the debris at that location (Meltzer and Dunnell 1992:xv).

Shortly after the publication of this paper, Abbott was anxiously soliciting a reprint from one of his contacts in Washington. Abbott eventually even visited the Piney Branch Quarry (Meltzer and Dunnell 1992:xvi). While he predictably left unconvinced, the case for the North American Paleolithic had nevertheless been dealt a substantial blow by Holmes under BAE auspices. Holmes then went on to methodically expand his conclusions by broadening his research to include the direct exam-

ination of many of the so-called paleoliths across the rest of the continent. Between 1890 and 1903, "Holmes personally visited—and criticized—nearly every North American site" reported to be assignable to the so-called Paleolithic (Meltzer and Dunnell 1992:xvi). His original conviction was not altered. Holmes would ultimately remark that all Paleolithic finds had been "prematurely announced and unduly paraded" (cited in Meltzer 1983:22). While proponents and opponents of the North American Paleolithic would continue to bitterly talk past each other for some time, the question of deep antiquity had been effectively settled by Holmes and the BAE; the flow of paleoliths would be effectively curtailed by the turn of the new century.

The BAE's interest in local archaeology during the late nineteenth century had at least two important long-term consequences for Chesapeake archaeology. First, the BAE promised a larger program in regional prehistory that would go beyond the initial focus on the Paleolithic controversy. They did deliver on that promise. In doing so, BAE archaeologists helped forge the methodological and analytical foundation on which Chesapeake archaeology would continue to rest for many years. Second, BAE archaeology created and ultimately left a legacy of a unique view of the past. This idea about the nature of the past in this region had distinct consequences of its own, ultimately dictating the way data were collected and explained for many years to come. Of course, BAE dominance in early archaeology had a profound impact on all of the discipline. Nevertheless, in this context, I want to focus on these two consequences in relation to Chesapeake archaeology. Each will be addressed in turn below.

Holmes was ostensibly transferred from the USGS to the BAE in July of 1889 to begin archaeological investigations along the Atlantic Coast. His initial research assignment was to focus on the Paleolithic issue at the Piney Branch Quarry site. After this he did return to a more general concern with Chesapeake prehistory while occupying a variety of positions within and outside the BAE (see Meltzer and Dunnell 1992). The most direct artifact of Holmes's interest in Chesapeake archaeology was his volume *Stone Implements of the Potomac-Chesapeake Tidewater Province*, completed in 1894 and published in 1897 as the BAE's Fifteenth Annual Report.

This volume is both a detailed expansion of his study of manufacturing processes at quarry sites and an effort to further determine the final disposition, form, and context of the implements once removed from the quarries (Holmes 1897:13–14). Much attention is given to illustrating initial manufacturing processes at quarries. This is undertaken in the context of an expanded discussion of the Piney Branch Quarry and other quarries across the region. Holmes then goes on to trace the quarry products to outside sites where further reduction into finished implements was accomplished. This expansion forces a discussion of almost the entire range of

←──

Figure 2.3. William Henry Holmes at Piney Branch Quarry, Washington, D.C., circa 1890. A notation in pencil at the bottom of the photograph—"Holmes in an ocean of the 'paleoliths' of Abbott, Putnam, Wilson and the rest of the early enthusiasts of American antiquities"—was apparently added by Holmes, himself. Courtesy of the Library of the National Museum of American Art and the National Portrait Gallery, Smithsonian Institution.

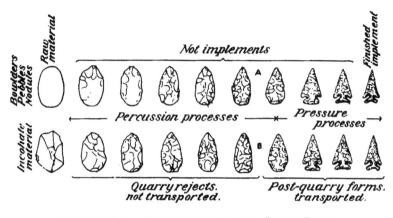

DIAGRAM II.—MORPHOLOGY OF THE SPEAR POINT

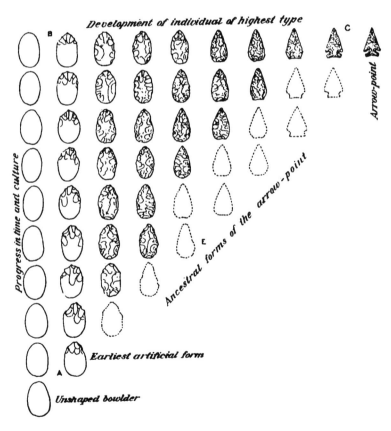

Figure 2.4. Holmes's reduction sequence as illustrated in an 1894 publication prepared for the International Congress of Anthropology in Chicago. Originally captioned, "steps in the evolution of a species."

prehistoric lithic implements found at local prehistoric sites. The book ends with a survey of the distribution of lithic materials and implements across the region. The volume today still stands as a monument to Holmes's pathfinding experimental studies, lithic tool analysis, and classification of the local archaeological record. It also can be seen as a BAE prescription for archaeological methodology.

A plate included in the 1897 volume (Figure 2.5) graphically summarizes the research agenda as carried out through that volume, and Holmes's accompanying notes about the scene add the rest of the picture (1897:150–151). The plate shows three aboriginal figures that artists had been called on to create for the World's Columbian Exposition at Chicago in 1892. On the return of the figures to Washington, Frank Hamilton Cushing, also of the BAE, had them taken out to Piney Branch Quarry on Holmes's behalf. Cushing, never known for any sense of restraint, literally recreated Holmes's research in situ. A small lodge was constructed, a drying rack built, and other appropriate artifacts scattered about. One aboriginal figure is depicted quarrying raw material from the ground, another is shown starting initial reduction, and the third figure is creating the final preform. Overall, this illustrates the very processes Holmes had established as having taken place at numerous quarry sites across the region.

In the accompanying notes describing the scene, Holmes laments that a fourth figure had not been created to illustrate the final steps of the process (1897:150). This figure would have been shown undertaking the further modification of the quarry preforms through pressure flaking into finished implements. Most of this particular activity would have taken place at actual habitation sites across the region. Together with the comments by Holmes, this plate literally illustrates the conclusions of this important early research. The re-creation was eventually installed as a diorama at the National Museum and remained on display until very recent times. Holmes's 1897 volume, itself, would soon be awarded the prestigious Loubat prize for the best recent work in archaeology.

This BAE interest in local archaeology was not limited to Holmes's initial volume on stone implements. For example, Gerard Fowke, of the BAE, had been dispatched to expand surveys up the James and Potomac river valleys as part of the larger program (Fowke 1894). He would often serve as a proxy of sorts for Holmes in defending established doctrine. Holmes also included a substantial discussion of what he referred to as Potomac–Chesapeake Ware in his later more ambitious book, *Aboriginal Pottery of the Eastern United States* (Holmes 1903). This was published as the Twentieth Annual Report of the BAE. The volume covered the one major class of material culture that Holmes had neglected in his earlier work and presented Chesapeake archaeology with one of the first surveys and discussions of local pottery. Together with the earlier volume on lithic implements, this second volume would stand for many years as a standard reference on the archaeological record of the Chesapeake region. At the same time, given the greatly expanded geographic focus of this later volume, this research foreshadows an eventual BAE movement away from active research in the Chesapeake region. Holmes, himself, was certainly soon des-

Figure 2.5. Life-size quarry group in plaster set up on the Piney Branch site, with construction or placement of various accessories by F. H. Cushing. This scene illustrates most of the Holmes research agenda in the Chesapeake region. Smithsonian Institution.

tined for other responsibilities. His own archaeological fieldwork was largely over by 1902 (Hinsley 1981:279).

No matter where one places the chronological end of direct BAE research on Chesapeake archaeology, one important consequence of that era would continue to actively influence local prehistory for many years. In fact, the basis of that legacy probably had much to do with the eventual BAE exit from the region. As mentioned previously, the BAE had consciously created what has been labeled a "flat past" (Meltzer 1983:38–40). Given their hard-fought battles over the Paleolithic and Moundbuilder issues, the past and present were not now perceived as being distinct. In other words, the archaeological record was firmly linked to the direct descendants of historic Indian groups, effectively becoming a mirror of sorts of the ethnographic present. If variability was to be found, it would be along the spatial and not the temporal axis. There can be little doubt that this belief was a major force in the BAE interpretation of local prehistory.

The preeminent archaeologist of the era articulates this position with great assurance in the following passage. Holmes states:

> As to the present state of the evidence, I hold that there can be but one opinion. It is impossible to show that there exists the slightest trace of any other race than the American Indian as he is known to us, and I am convinced that if the great Powhatan should at this late day rise from the dead and claim for his people all the stone implements of the Potomac Valley no reasonable objection could be made to the claim. (1890:24)

These lines ended his initial article on research at Piney Branch Quarry. The essence of this conclusion was to be repeated again and again by Holmes and the BAE.

As just mentioned, the interest in linking the past to the ethnographic record was probably one of the factors that caused the BAE to expand its research to the West and to other areas. Ethnographic cultures after all remained substantially more intact in those locations. Whatever the case, BAE archaeological activity in the local area was effectively over soon after the turn of the century, creating an archaeological vacuum of sorts in the Chesapeake region (follows Porter 1983). Into this void would step an active cadre of amateur archaeologists. In fact, one can make an argument that this amateur community represented an early constant in Chesapeake archaeology. They were present at the beginning of a real interest in Chesapeake prehistory (see previous section). And while they were somewhat subsequently eclipsed by government archaeology in the last decade of the nineteenth century, they were again poised to step in and continue research when the BAE ceased its active program.

A complete honor roll of individuals engaged in this activity would be quite lengthy (see Bastian 1980; Custer 1989; Holmes 1897, 1903; MacCord 1990; Porter 1981, 1983). Some of the more prominent members of this list would certainly include David I. Bushnell, E. Ralston Goldsborough, Talbot D. Jones, J. D. McGuire, William B. Marye, S. V. Proudfit, Elmer R. Reynolds, and Joseph Wigglesworth. While most of these individuals were active in other professions, their real calling appears to have been archaeology. The other interesting fact about many of these investigators is that most were influenced by various BAE scientists, some directly, others indirectly. Their private collections had often been called on in the past to provide evidence of this or that BAE position. These individuals often arrived at the BAE to use the library and discuss their thinking on various subjects (see Judd 1967). The BAE, Smithsonian Institution, or other organizations friendly to the cause, in turn, sometimes published the results of their subsequent research.

The other important point to be made in this context is that the BAE party line on the so-called flat past continued to profoundly influence the amateur community. One need only turn to a sample of the archaeological literature produced in the first half of the twentieth century to find the impact of this legacy. Marye, a respected Maryland amateur archaeologist, is a good example (Figure 2.6). During his long fascination with local archaeology, Marye investigated a wide variety of seemingly atemporal archaeological phenomenon, from actual sites to notations in colonial records about native groups to petroglyphs and Indian trails. Much of his published research is on the Contact era (e.g., Marye 1935, 1936, 1938a,b, 1939). Such topics, couched in a shallow antiquity, were in line with the BAE's view of the past. It is known that Marye had active ties with the BAE, including connections to Holmes himself. It would not be until very late in the span of his archaeological investigations

Figure 2.6.   William B. Marye (far right) with (from left to right) Richard Stearns, Howard MacCord, Sr., and an unidentified individual at a site near the head of the Anacostia River. William B. Marye Collection, Maryland Historical Society, Baltimore.

that Marye began to cautiously entertain any real notion of time depth for Chesapeake prehistory (e.g., Marye 1963).

Figure 2.7 represents a tangible artifact of the impact of a limited past on local archaeology. This early map was apparently printed by the Maryland Academy of Sciences in 1938. The makers of the map became blatant in their attempts to equate ethnographic groups with archaeological data. In fact, even at that time, there was enough debate over the map's apparent conclusions to prevent its widespread circulation (Bastian 1980:4). Still, the mapmakers' simple formula of equating an archaeological site or feature with a known historic aboriginal group was in the spirit of the times.

Finally, Alice Ferguson's research at the Accokeek Creek site on the Maryland shore of the Potomac River provides a particularly pointed example of the impact of the flat past on regional archaeology. In 1923 Ferguson (Figure 2.8) had purchased a farm that bordered the river. In the later words of her husband, "archaeology became a surprising and disturbing by-product of agriculture" (H. Ferguson 1960:5). After looters excavated a hole in her alfalfa field, penetrating a refuse pit, Ferguson did some excavation on her own and began to realize that a major archaeological site was located in the river fields of her farm. Appeals for help were made to various individuals and institutions, but little real help was forthcoming. In Ferguson's own words, "since nobody wanted it and it was in my front yard, the development seemed up to me" (cited in Stephenson and Ferguson 1963:iv).

And develop it she did. The major feature of the site, actually a whole complex of sites, was the remains of a large stockaded village. Three large ossuaries were contained within the stockade lines. I want to reserve the more detailed discussion of this site for later in this chapter and subsequent chapters (also see Dent 1984). In this context, however, I would like to discuss the immediate problem that faced Ferguson in interpreting the site. This problem relates to the ever-present flat past that still dominated regional archaeology.

While Ferguson did excavate a remarkable assemblage of prehistoric artifacts at Accokeek Creek, no European trade goods were ever recovered on the site during her years of excavations or during subsequent more localized testing that has since taken place at the site (Thurman 1972; Gary Hume, personal communication, 1989). The presence of European trade goods on Chesapeake sites has long appeared to be an accurate register of sites occupied during the Contact period. Yet, given the prevailing limitation of the flat past and the associated tendency to link the archaeological record to historically known tribes, she had little choice but to proceed in that direction.

Ferguson went straight to the premier surviving ethnohistorical document of the Contact era, Captain John Smith's 1608 map of the Chesapeake region. Smith had placed symbols on this map noting the locations of two different classes of Indian villages along the Bay and its major tributaries. Ferguson states:

> During the past three years the writer has been excavating the site of an Indian village on the south bank of the Potomac just below Piscataway Creek. The village

Figure 2.7. Map titled "The Indian Tribes of the State of Maryland as Seen by Capt. John Smith, His Party of Twelve Men and More Recent Observers." A direct effort is made on this map to link prehistoric archaeological sites with known historic Indian groups. Courtesy of Enoch Pratt Free Library, Baltimore.

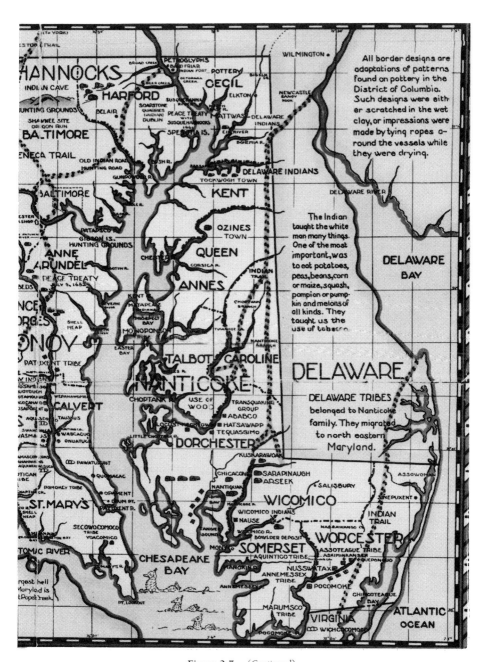

Figure 2.7. (*Continued*)

Figure 2.8.   Alice Ferguson, excavator of the Accokeek Creek site along the Potomac River below Washington, D.C., circa 1920. Courtesy of the Ferguson Foundation, Accokeek, Maryland.

can be identified with considerable certainty as the Moyaone mentioned by Captain John Smith as the site of a king's house. (1937:3)

It is now generally agreed that the Ferguson's Accokeek Creek site actually dates to the late prehistoric period, possibly to sometime around the early to mid-sixteenth century. It had been long abandoned by the time of Smith's arrival and actually does not even match the exact location of his Moyaone.

This misinterpretation of the site does not detract from the importance of Ferguson's research. Chesapeake archaeology was still in its formative stages at the time of her excavations, and it was to be greatly enriched by her labors at the Accokeek Creek site. It does illustrate that the influence of the BAE view of the past extended well into the 1930s. Perhaps it was no coincidence that the first person to suggest to her that she had found the village of Moyaone on Smith's map was Henry Collins, the last director (acting) of the BAE (cited in Stephenson and Ferguson 1963:v).

Aside from being burdened by a limited temporal vista bequeathed to them by BAE archaeology, the active and expanding amateur community did move forward to continue archaeological investigations in the Chesapeake region. This long tradition of amateur involvement would have to sustain local archaeology, for the most part, for over the next 50 years. Large-scale, sustained institutional support would not arrive again until the influx of federal funding to local universities starting in the mid- to late 1960s. During this extended interlude, regional archaeology could count on only sporadic institutional support. In 1905 the Phillips Academy of Andover, Massachusetts, did carry out the systematic excavation of the stratified Bushey Cavern site near Hagerstown, Maryland (Peabody 1908). This site is well west of the Coastal Plain, but the data recovered have direct bearing on Chesapeake prehistory. That institution's Susquehanna River Expedition, conducted between 1916 and 1919, also collected data on shell middens in the northern Chesapeake and on the famous petroglyphs of the lower Susquehanna River (Moorehead 1938). Beyond that, the Maryland Academy of Sciences, Maryland Historical Society, and the Natural History Society of Maryland became active in the curation, collection, or display of local antiquities.

There is one last closely related research interest of this period that deserves some discussion. This is the development of an active ethnographic interest in people or groups thought to be maintaining aboriginal traditions: that is, the study of what were essentially cultural survivals. Much of this research was being undertaken independent of archaeology for the ethnological purpose of attempting to understand the tenacity of lifeways many had thought to be extinct. Nevertheless, there was also a corresponding direct archaeological interest in such surviving traditions. Much of this almost naive interest is another artifact of the flat past. In short, if the archaeological record was linked to historic aboriginal groups, then a study of their survival and accompanying material culture might offer additional clues to the interpretation of the past. Brief examples of each area of interest, ethnographic and archaeological, follow.

One of the earliest attempts to document ethnographic survivals was James Mooney's 1889 questionnaire polling local physicians on the locations of people within the region who might be of native heritage. While at the BAE, Mooney (1890, 1907) eventually published two articles on the Powhatan. More comprehensive fieldwork, albeit it of limited duration, would come with the arrival of Frank Speck, an anthropologist at the University of Pennsylvania. Speck (1915) visited and wrote about surviving Nanticoke populations in Delaware. Later he undertook more extensive research (Speck 1925, 1928) with Powhatan-related groups. Speck's research has always been a favorite among archaeologists because of his focus on cultural survivals as registered through material culture.

From the archaeological perspective, there was clearly always an interest in what the material culture of these living descendants might reveal about the past. The notion of the flat past naturally led to the direct historical approach as a means of investigation. Holmes (1903), for example, included a discussion of contemporary Pamunkey ceramics in his discussion of aboriginal wares from the Chesapeake region. Even with his desire to link past and present—the Powhatan with the Pamunkey—Holmes was forced to admit that the contemporary potters of Pamunkey appeared to be quite unaware of aboriginal methods (1903:153).

As a postscript to the discussion of this period, I want to point out one last area of interest. Local archaeologists naturally became very interested in surviving ethnohistorical documents and the information that they might contain about local native groups at the time of contact and beyond. Edward Arber (1884, 1910) had recently

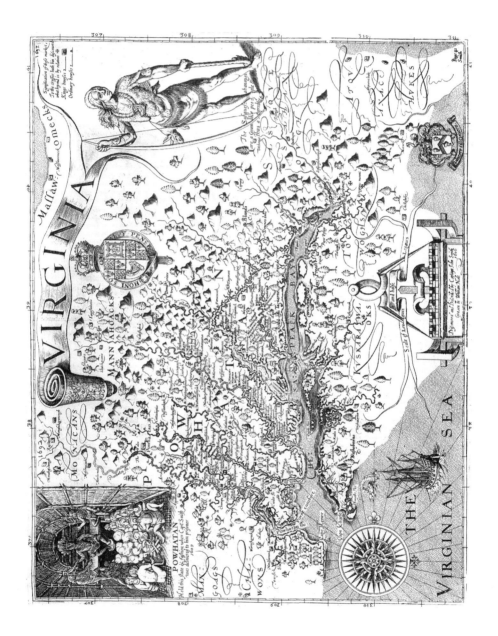

published his *Travels and Works of Captain John Smith*. For the first time a detailed collection of Smith's writings and a sober discussion of his activities were assembled and available to local scholars. A substantial number of these writings contained information about Chesapeake native populations of the early seventeenth century. Smith's 1612 map (Figure 2.9) is certainly the premier example of the information bequeathed to us by this remarkable individual.

Local investigators, many of them amateurs, expanded on a search for related records in both national and international archives. Marye's (e.g., 1936, 1937) interest in colonial records and Bushnell's (e.g., 1907) research in England are examples of these efforts. No stone was being left unturned in the pursuit of information about local native groups. This intensive search of the documentary record is another important artifact of the period.

Expanding the Past

In the decades leading up to the middle of the twentieth century, significant changes were in store for Chesapeake archaeology. Change often comes to archaeology from a number of directions; change can be stimulated by broader external social forces, by the internal development of new theories or methodologies, and, of course, by new discoveries from the archaeological record itself. All three of these forces had an impact on Chesapeake archaeology beginning in the late 1930s and early 1940s. I would extend the terminal boundary of this period up until the mid- to late 1960s. Throughout this era the received view of the previous period was challenged and ultimately changed.

During this time, the amateur community began a remarkable expansion of its activities within the region. One of the most tangible outcomes of this process was the formation of regional and state archaeological societies. The Eastern States Archaeological Federation, including many members from the Chesapeake region, was formally established in 1934. It has continued since that time to promote archaeological research by both amateur and professional archaeologists.

Because the Chesapeake region is contained within the boundaries of three separate states, a number of active organizations were eventually created across the local area. The honor of being the first such state society so formed goes to Delaware. H. Geigor Omwake was the driving force behind the formation of that society in 1933 (Weslager 1944). The *Bulletin of the Archaeological Society of Delaware* has been issued regularly by that organization.

Further south, in the winter of 1940, a small group of individuals organized themselves as The Virginia Indian Relic Collectors' Club. By 1941 the name had been

---

Figure 2.9. Captain John Smith's Map of Virginia illustrating native settlements. At least ten different states of this map, first published in 1612, have been documented by historians. Original is based on information collected by Smith between 1607 and 1608. Engraved by William Hole. Courtesy of Maryland State Archives.

changed to the Archaeological Society of Virginia (ASV). One year later Volume 1, Number 1 of the *Quarterly Bulletin of the Archaeological Society of Virginia* was issued. Aside from no further publication until after the war, this journal has appeared at regular intervals since that time. A history of the ASV, on the occasion of its fiftieth anniversary, has recently been issued (MacCord 1990). The longevity and the activity of this organization as well as the sustained quality of its journal make the society a landmark, in its own right, in regional archaeology.

Archaeologists in Maryland followed suit and formed their own state society, the Archaeological Society of Maryland, in 1954. This organization has likewise been very active in local archaeology. It too issues a publication, *Maryland Archaeology*. In addition to these major state societies, several other even more localized organizations had sprouted within the region. One of the earliest was the Sussex Society of Archaeology and History formed in 1948 in Delaware. It soon issued its own publication, *The Archeolog*. All of these various archaeological organizations represented crucial elements in the promotion and investigation of regional prehistory during this period. Chesapeake archaeology owes a great debt of gratitude to the initial and continued efforts of these societies as well as to the people who have participated in them.

As Chesapeake archaeologists were engaged in organizing themselves, great changes in the way they were to eventually perceive the past loomed on the horizon. The stimulus for this change had taken place in 1926 in western North America. The breakthrough alluded to was the unequivocal linkage of the remains of Pleistocene fauna to stone tools in Folsom, New Mexico (Figgins 1927). The presence of early populations before the end of the Pleistocene had finally been documented. This particular association would soon be widely accepted by archaeology, and other data to provide additional support would not be long in arriving.

In many regions of North America these events almost immediately opened up sweeping and vast temporal vistas for archaeologists: what is herein referred to as deep time. For the Chesapeake tidewater area, and the entire Atlantic Coast in general, the shift to such a perception was slow in coming about. Many archaeologists in the study area curiously remained cautious in commenting on the possible presence of similarly early regional populations. For one, the flat past of the previous era had become a virtual "taken-for-granted," and it was not going to disappear quickly. Holmes, himself, who was still alive at the time of the Folsom discoveries, did not challenge the new evidence, nor did the rest of the old BAE alliance. Yet, at the same time, Holmes did not enthusiastically embrace these new discoveries in any tangible way. A nod from him, even though he was no longer active in Chesapeake prehistory, would have carried great weight with local archaeologists.

There was also the problem of the absence of an effective dating mechanism for such very early sites in the Chesapeake region. Most potential artifacts that were candidates for early status were surface discoveries. Western Paleoindian sites, for all practical purposes, could be unequivocally dated to before the end of the Pleistocene by their direct association with extinct megafauna. While there was not any real shortage of megafaunal remains in eastern North America, no similar associations between these remains and artifacts could be demonstrated. This remains the case today.

Given all this, it would take some time for Chesapeake archaeologists to sort out the question of deep time in the region. Almost a decade after the original Folsom discoveries, Bushnell took the first step and published a report on purported Paleo-indian artifacts from the Chesapeake region. His article was published in *Literary Digest* (Bushnell 1934) and carried the title "Stone Relics of Oldest Americans?" The punctuation at the end of this title reveals Bushnell's caution. Nevertheless, in this two-page article he did illustrate two fluted specimens that had been discovered in Virginia within the Chesapeake Bay drainage area. These were compared to Folsom projectiles reported from western North America. Even six years later, in another article (Bushnell 1940:Plate 2), he still appeared reluctant to come out and claim a Paleoindian period for the Chesapeake region. This caution was undoubtedly not unique to Bushnell.

Additional evidence, however, would soon arrive to buttress the notion of a Paleoindian period in the Chesapeake region. Ben C. McCary, of Williamsburg, Virginia, began the active solicitation of information on what he at the time referred to as "Virginia Folsom." The ASV would serve as a primary conduit for his efforts. A call for information was issued and a questionnaire requesting data on fluted point finds as well as context was mailed to "members and friends" of the ASV (MacCord 1990:9–10). A meeting was called in 1947 in Richmond, Virginia, especially for the display of many of these finds. In the September 1947 issue of the *Quarterly Bulletin*, the first of many continuing reports on the results of this survey was published. C. A. Weslager (1944), in his early volume on Delaware's past, also reported similar early artifacts in that state.

If there was still any doubt, one additional discovery would seal the matter of the Paleoindian occupation of the Chesapeake region. This discovery, the Williamson site in Dinwiddie County, Virginia, was reported by McCary and two associates in 1949 (McCary, Smith, and Gilliam 1949). Shortly thereafter, McCary (1951) reported the site to the entire discipline through a summary article in *American Antiquity*. The Williamson site, over the years, would prove to be one of the richest Paleoindian sites identified thus far in all of eastern North America. There could now be little doubt of deep antiquity in the Chesapeake region. The bottom had fallen out of the flat past.

These cumulative events, in effect, finally succeeded in opening up the temporal dimensions of Chesapeake tidewater region prehistory. With the knowledge that human populations had been in the study area by the terminal Pleistocene, along with the data that had already been collected in what was now seen as late prehistory, one of the challenges of the era became to recover and explain the long developmental sequence between these two extremes of time. This new opportunity sent Chesapeake archaeologists into the field with a different perception of their data and the past.

I would like to briefly cite and discuss four studies that typify this era. While each study was a regional landmark in its own right, together they share a number of common elements. First, each example illustrates the new interest in both space *and* time, an interest stimulated by a newly expanded temporal vista. Second, each study reflects a new concern with cultural change rather than stasis. This change is implicitly presented as a gradual phenomenon wherein small changes over time eventually produce new cultural forms. Third, each example is concerned with the development of a reliable regional culture history. Finally, some of this research introduced new analytical techniques to the region. Articles or monographs by Karl Schmitt (1952), Clifford Evans (1955), Robert Stephenson and Alice Ferguson (1963), and Henry T. Wright (not published until 1973) will be discussed in turn.

Schmitt's article, "Archaeological Chronology of the Middle Atlantic States," appeared in Griffin (1952). That book, often called the "green bible," was an initial attempt to discuss and illustrate data on the whole of eastern North American prehistory. Schmitt (see Eggan 1953; Stewart 1990) had worked on a number of early excavations in the Chesapeake region and then went on to complete his doctorate at the University of Chicago. His master's thesis at that institution, written under the direction of Fay Cooper-Cole, reported on the excavations at the Patawomeke site along the Potomac River. Schmitt (Figure 2.10) eventually assumed a teaching position at the University of Oklahoma, but was tragically killed in an automobile accident before his article appeared in 1952. The article, while ostensibly focusing on the entire Middle Atlantic, employed a great deal of data from the Chesapeake region. It had been completed by Schmitt in 1947.

Schmitt's article is a very early example of an attempt to produce a culture history applicable, at least in part, to the Chesapeake region. In this article it is still possible to see the residual impacts of the old flat past on regional archaeology. Much of the paper focuses on the Woodland period and recent discoveries about the development of the associated ceramic sequence. Nevertheless, there is a short discussion of the newly established Archaic period. For example, he defines the Archaic with negative traits— "prepottery" and "preagricultural"—but its importance as the foundation that would eventually give birth to the more extensively discussed Woodland period is noted (Schmitt 1952:70). In short, there is an unprecedented interest in both time and space in the archaeological record as well as the implicit notion of a gradual transformation taking place throughout prehistory. While the Paleoindian period is relegated to a single footnote noting the discovery of the soon to be well-known Shoop site, there is at least a hint of even deeper antiquity.

Clifford Evans's (1955) monograph, *A Ceramic Study of Virginia*, has long been recognized for its contribution to Chesapeake archaeology. After joining the faculty at the University of Virginia, Evans (Figure 2.11) received funding to survey and excavate prehistoric sites in Virginia during the summer months of 1950. The eventual result of this research was the above-named monograph, which included a study of Virginia ceramics by Evans and an appendix containing an analysis of projectile points and large blades by his collaborator, C. G. Holland (Figure 2.12). With Evans accepting a position with the Smithsonian Institution, the monograph was issued as Bulletin 160 of the Bureau of American Ethnology.

Figure 2.10.   Karl Schmitt at the Shepard site in Montgomery County, Maryland, circa 1937. Photo and information courtesy of Richard "Gates" Slattery.

The stated goal of the research was to study the cultural development of aboriginal groups from a temporal and spatial standpoint (Evans 1955:2). This effort was pathfinding in the Chesapeake region for at least two reasons. First, Evans demonstrated, through ceramic analysis, that there was a time depth to the local archaeological record that could be discovered and documented. In the process he established a typology of ceramic wares that would guide regional classification studies for years to come. Second, Evans showed archaeologists how to overcome one of the basic limitations of many regional sites: that is, how to address the issue of change at the mixed component surface sites that are a fact of life in this area. Based on the ceramic sequence recovered at the stratified Potts site, he was analytically able to produce a seriation of like ceramics at other nonstratified sites. At the time,

Figure 2.11. Clifford Evans and Betty Meggers on Fields Island in the Roanoke River in Virginia, circa 1950. This island, now submerged by a reservoir, was surveyed and some test excavations were completed for Evans's monograph on Virginia ceramics. Courtesy of Virginia Department of Historic Resources. Reproduced with permission of Betty Meggers, Smithsonian Institution.

Figure 2.12. C. G. Holland at ASU meeting in the mid-1940s. Courtesy of Virginia Department of Historic Resources. Reproduced with permission of C. G. Holland.

this was an important demonstration of an unexplored technique in regional archaeology.

As an appendix to this same publication, Holland (1955) produced a similar study of lithic remains. This addition to the monograph was especially important in that it attempted to do for projectiles and blades what Evans had done for ceramics. The result was a complementary taxonomy of selected diagnostic lithic implements from the same geographic area. I want to point out that Holland deserves special credit for his earlier efforts to define the Archaic period in the region (e.g., 1949a,b, 1953). Through his research, it is possible to trace the working out of the questions crucial to its establishment as a formal entity in regional archaeology. Evans's monograph, with the appendix by Holland, still stands as a useful source of information on Chesapeake prehistory.

Another major accomplishment of the period was the publication of Stephenson's reanalysis of the Ferguson excavations at the Accokeek Creek site. The resulting monograph, published by the University of Michigan, carried both Stephenson and Ferguson (1963) as authors. Ferguson's original interpretation of a large stockaded village found on her property was discussed in the previous section.

In the late 1950s, for his dissertation project, Stephenson (Figure 2.13) undertook the task of analyzing the 71,000-plus artifacts from what was actually a complex of sites originally excavated by Ferguson. The complex included two stockaded late prehistoric villages (one of which Ferguson had chosen to label as Moyaone), another small multicomponent site, and a historic fort built and occupied by fleeing members

Figure 2.13. Robert L. Stephenson at the 16th Plains Conference, Lincoln, Nebraska in 1958. This photograph was taken at about the time Stephenson completed his analysis of the Accokeek Creek site collections. Photograph by Herman Harpster, negative on file at South Carolina Institute of Archaeology and Anthropology. Photo courtesy of Albert Goodyear, University of South Carolina.

of the Susquehannock tribe (see Dent 1984). Stephenson, employing what he called a comparative approach (Stephenson and Ferguson 1963:84), used the excavation data to create various cultural periods and foci spanning from the Archaic through historical periods. He also made a concerted effort to relate this sequence to the greater Middle Atlantic cultural province. This study has taken its place among the most important pieces of research yet produced on the region. Its emphasis on the broader issues of space and time as well as developmental sequence still causes local prehistorians to consult this important study.

Last, between 1956 and 1964, Wright (Figure 2.14) had completed a survey of the Severn River and its environs. It did not appear in published form until sometime later (Wright 1973). Nevertheless, the research on which it is based is another early example of the attempt to produce culture histories for the region. Wright's study, of particular applicability to the middle Chesapeake area, defined a series of diagnostic artifacts, components, and phases within the archaeological record.

Certainly one innovation of Wright's research was the publication of a series of four radiocarbon assays to support the chronology being proposed. Radiocarbon dating was not completely unheard of in the region by this time, but it was typically used as a tool to date particular sites. Wright's study is a good early example of using

Figure 2.14. Henry T Wright at the Sang Run site in Maryland, west of the study area Photograph by St. Clair Wright. Courtesy of Henry T. Wright, University of Michigan

the technique to support the validity of a broader developmental sequence that goes beyond the bounds of any one site. Wright's monograph also stands out for its identification of faunal remains from various increments of the sequence, anticipating a future interest of eventual great concern to regional archaeologists. The small monograph would likewise take its place as an example of often-cited literature in the years to come.

To briefly summarize, the four studies discussed above are notable examples of the research undertaken during this era. None of this research would have been possible just a few decades earlier, with regional archaeologists still under the influence of the now-dismissed flat past. And while each study focuses on different parts of the archaeological record, they all are linked by a number of newly shared concerns. These concerns, listed previously, typify the archaeology of this era. The other remarkable fact about all four examples is that they still occupy the reference shelves of any serious student of Chesapeake prehistory. In a discipline where literature is often outdated before its publication, such longevity is a testament to the quality of this research and the continuing necessity for archaeologists to be concerned with issues of both time and space.

Beyond traditional archaeological research, physical anthropologists also began to be drawn to the archaeological record of the Chesapeake region. Regional mortuary practices, especially late prehistoric ossuary burials, had for a good while piqued the interest of a number of individuals. Scholars were well aware of the descriptions of rather unique local burial customs in the ethnohistorical documents of the Contact era. By the nineteenth century various individuals (e.g., Fowke 1894; Huffington 1838; Mercer 1897) were beginning to describe the discovery of aboriginal interments at various locations across the region. By the following century, archaeologists started to actively excavate ossuary burials (e.g., Ferguson 1937; Graham 1935).

Certainly, the general interest in burial practices extends beyond only a focus on ossuary burial, and admittedly overlaps into both earlier and later periods of this history. I would argue, however, that the real beginning of the purposeful analysis of regional mortuary practices is an artifact of the period under discussion. I would also argue that the effects of this interest have had a great impact on regional archaeology. The driving force behind the analysis of regional ossuaries was T. Dale Stewart of the Smithsonian Institution (Stewart 1940a,b,c; Stewart and Wedel 1937). As a result of his research, archaeologists began to have a greater understanding of many aspects of Native American lifeways. Furthermore, Stewart always made himself available to lend a hand in the identification of human remains from almost any local site. He also did more than most people realize to nurture Chesapeake archaeology through an era of little sustained institutional support (see MacCord 1990:49–50). At the same time, he conducted a remarkable series of archaeological excavations at the Patawomeke site, a substantial Contact period village site along the Potomac River. Stewart rightfully stands today as a legend in Chesapeake archaeology (Figure 2.15).

To close the discussion of this period of the history, I think it is safe to say that the

Figure 2.15.   T. Dale Stewart, Curator of Physical Anthropology at the National Museum of National History. Smithsonian Institution.

very nature of the Chesapeake's past had been changed. A new foundation had been set and archaeologists were hard at work creating the culture histories necessary for the further investigation of the regional archaeological record; developmental sequences were proposed and issues of culture change were being addressed. In fact, the basic periodic sequence that still dominates regional archaeology today was invented and refined during this period. Much effort was also devoted to further work out the methodological rules and techniques for the excavation as well as analysis of archaeological data. The arrival of a relatively affordable and reliable chronometric dating technique would further enhance the quality, as well as the validity, of archaeological research being undertaken during this period.

Given the scope of this history, I have only discussed a very few examples of the activity of this period. Many of these examples were the results of professional archaeologists taking an active interest in the region. In most cases they completed their particular study, and were unable to continue working in the region. Sustained archaeological research, by default, fell into the capable hands of the amateur community. Occasionally, someone such as C. A. Weslager (1944) would synthesize the efforts of the archaeological community. Nevertheless, the active cadre of amateur archaeologists who undertook research during this period deserves some individual recognition. Special mention is made of the efforts of Howard MacCord, A. F. Johnson, Carl Manson, Richard Slattery, and Richard Stearns. There are undoubtedly others that belong on this list. While the few mentioned above are buried here in my history, their contributions are immense.

Contemporary Archaeology and Beyond

As any history, even a history of ideas, draws nearer the present, clear synthesis becomes more elusive. This is certainly the case with contemporary archaeology in the Chesapeake region. Nevertheless, if there is a dominant paradigm guiding archaeology in the region today it is more or less associated with the new, or processual, archaeology. The ascendancy of processual archaeology, however, was not without resistance and certainly exhibits its share of irony. In the previous chapter, I outlined the conceptual foundations of processual archaeology. This archaeology, and its assumptions about the nature of the past, is also well known through any number of other reviews, case studies, criticisms, and rejoinders to these criticisms. It is therefore unnecessary, in this context, to spend any more time on a discussion of its agenda.

In this section of the history I instead want to discuss the path by which processual archaeology arrived in the Chesapeake region and eventually became widely embraced by local archaeologists. To do this, I focus my examination on the two major conduits of its ascendancy: what, for lack of better terms, could be labeled university-promoted archaeology and governmental archaeology. A few examples will be discussed to illustrate these two vectors of processual archaeology. This history will open with a discussion of a somewhat remarkable event whereby regional archaeology once again played a role, albeit one that has never been widely heralded, in the larger national debate over the nature of the past. This section of the history will conclude with a look at what might be termed challenges to the prevailing state of affairs. This period of the history spans the most recent three decades of the present century.

It is fitting to begin a discussion of processual archaeology with Lewis Binford's (1964, 1991) dissertation research in northeastern North Carolina and southeastern Virginia. The latter area is within the Chesapeake region and the former neighboring area may be considered directly related. (I will cite exclusively from the new, slightly revised edition of this dissertation [Binford 1991]; it varies from the original version only in the deletion of some outdated descriptive sections and examining committee polemics.) In the interest of chronology, Binford (1991:vi) notes that the basic research for the project had been completed by 1956 in anticipation of taking a master's degree at the University of North Carolina. After his acceptance into the doctoral program at the University of Michigan, Binford (1991:vi) began to "rethink the earlier work in light of a different set of problems" and completed it to his satisfaction in 1959. It was not finally accepted by his committee at the University of Michigan until 1964.

Binford's research in the Chesapeake region represents a cauldron of interests and ideas. On one level, the study clearly illustrates the genesis of a new archaeology, with the regional archaeological record serving as the development laboratory. While many scholars point to Binford's 1962 article as the seminal statement on processual archaeology, his dissertation predates that paper and contains all the ingredients for a new way of looking at the past. The first part of the research established a natural history of the region, and much of the remainder of the dissertation was concerned with investigating a systemic relationship between available resources and emerging cultural complexity. A number of specific propositions were created as part of a processual model to explain the overall evolutionary trajectory of late regional prehistory. All the key words and phrases that would eventually come to typify the processual agenda inhabit the final product. While reserving a detailed discussion of his overall research for later in this volume, it is clear that Binford (Figure 2.16) was advocating a new way of looking at the past using Chesapeake archaeology as a test case.

In the end, Binford succeeded in producing a dissertation that built on existing archaeological traditions, yet at the same time presented a very different understanding of regional archaeology. The irony of this important step forward is that it was immediately ignored by regional archaeologists. For example, a citation search of the *Quarterly Bulletin* of the ASV for the first five years immediately after the release of Binford's dissertation reveals that in 118 published articles his research was cited a total of only four times. And those particular citations were all a case of Binford citing himself. Chesapeake prehistory had just helped to serve as an incubator for a theoretical tidal wave that would soon impact the wider discipline of archaeology, but scarcely a ripple of this process was felt at the time on the local shores. This would not, however, be the case for long. And, indeed, local archaeologists did finally

Figure 2.16. Lewis R. Binford in 1955 at the Gaston site, North Carolina. This photograph was taken at about the time Binford completed the research on local prehistory that would form the basis of his later dissertation written at the University of Michigan. Photo courtesy of the Research Laboratories of Anthropology, the University of North Carolina at Chapel Hill. Reproduced with permission of Lewis Binford, Southern Methodist University.

resurrect and celebrate Binford's dissertation in the 1970s when they themselves became interested in issues of developing sociocultural complexity.

If Binford's research had little direct early impact on local archaeology, other events would eventually deliver the gospel of processual archaeology to the Chesapeake region. As mentioned in the previous section, sustained institutional support for regional archaeology had evaporated with the BAE's departure from the scene around the turn of the century. While the BAE and Smithsonian would indirectly continue to do what they could to assist local archaeologists, the direct financial backing once reserved for Chesapeake archaeology had quite literally moved west. Only occasionally would a professional archaeologist be able to complete a research project in the area. Amateur archaeologists were largely left with the task of sustaining research efforts in local prehistory.

By the mid- to late 1960s, however, changes were on the horizon. A number of factors stimulated this change. First, while the amateur community was doing archaeology, it was also lobbying for archaeology (see Bastian 1980; MacCord 1990; Weslager 1968). Second, regional demographics were changing. A large urban and suburban middle class had come to call the area home. Many residents eagerly connected with the region's sense of place and history. Their children were also destined to attend university in the region. Third, federal funding poured into the area to create or expand institutions of higher learning. Some of this funding was in response to this demographic growth, and some can be linked to other national priorities. Whatever the reasons, anthropology departments, by now a traditional unit of the American university system, began to spring up across the region. Archaeologists, often with an interest in local prehistory, joined the faculties of these expanding institutions. As an example of this phenomenon, at the end of World War II there were no archaeologists to be found on the permanent academic staffs of local universities. Some four decades later, over 12 major educational institutions supported a faculty that included at least one archaeologist and often more. This sequence of events would have a significant impact on local archaeology and on the way it was done.

A second conduit of change in Chesapeake archaeology would be the creation of what could be called, for lack of a better label, government archaeology. By this time federal, state, and sometimes even local governments were recognizing their obligations to support their constituent's interests in the past. Two basic facts fostered this now-mutual interest. First, there was little doubt by this point that the region contained a significant record of the past. Second, development pressures in the local area were beginning to have a greater and greater impact on this record. It was increasingly evident that the region's cultural resources, like its natural resources, would require protection and conservation. Ensuing government intervention would eventually help create what is today known as cultural resources management (CRM). Early in this period, initial government reaction focused around the creation of what were essentially, by today's standards, very small state archaeologist's offices.

In Virginia, MacCord was employed by the Virginia State Library starting in 1963 and served almost as a de facto state archaeologist. The state of Delaware had created a State Archaeological Board in 1953, and in 1965 it was able to employ Ronald Thomas as Delaware's first state archaeologist (Weslager 1968:176). The state of Maryland soon followed and through the Department of Natural Resources appointed Tyler Bastian as its state archaeologist in 1968. While the legacy of these three early programs today now forms the tip of much larger government archaeological programs, the establishment of state archaeologist's offices represented a start.

The net effect of the creation of this program of university and government archaeology was the cultivation of a new view of the past, a view that would increasingly project the processual agenda into Chesapeake archaeology. This was especially true of the new generation of archaeologists that would arrive to fill various recently created university positions. It was less true early on of government archaeology, although the Delaware program may have been an exception. And, in any case, all state offices soon expanded and employed a substantial number of individuals that would identify with processual archaeology.

Focusing first on the university front, perhaps the earliest truly local effort to directly transfer the processual program of analysis to Chesapeake archaeology can be seen in the establishment of the Potomac River Archaeology Survey (PRAS) in the very late 1960s. PRAS was created through a research consortium originally involving American University, Catholic University of America, and George Washington University. Charles W. McNett, William Gardner, and Robert Humphrey had at the time recently assumed faculty positions as archaeologists in the anthropology departments at these three Washington D.C. institutions. They were soon successful in obtaining two National Science Foundation grants, in 1969 and 1970, to analyze existing material and conduct new excavations within the Potomac River basin. Some of their concerns, such as refining the existing culture history, were traditional. In another sense, however, their research included a direct interest in the systemic relationship between prehistoric culture and the changing natural environment of that area.

An explicit goal of PRAS was to recast approximately 11,000 years of Potomac Valley prehistory in light of the new interest in prehistoric adaptation to the changing environment. Aside from Binford's fairly well ignored earlier effort, this interest in cultural adaptation was new to local archaeology. For the totality of Potomac Valley prehistory, a beginning was made in this regard through an unpublished manuscript produced by McNett in the early 1970s. McNett's (1974) unpublished volume looks at cultural adaptation throughout the 11,000 or so years of local prehistory. At more specific points in the regional sequence, PRAS archaeologists employed processual archaeology to examine a series of individual sites.

The study PRAS conducted at the Rowe site (Gardner and McNett 1970) is a good example of this new way of looking at regional prehistory. This site is a multi-component Archaic surface site located in southern Maryland. The study can be seen as an example of how local archaeologists would increasingly seek to understand the archaeological record. Even a cursory look at the resulting publication reveals a litany of different interests that clearly separates this archaeology from the archaeology of earlier periods. While the authors chose to ignore Binford by tracing their intellectual inspiration to Walter Taylor (1948), Gardner and McNett still clearly attempted to disassociate themselves from an exclusive interest in only time and space. They then went on to discuss ecological setting, cultural systems, intrasite distributions, behavioral significance, and so on. Quantitative methods for pattern recognition were tested, and the authors actively searched for hypotheses that could be further tested on other regional sites. In short, their analysis of the Rowe site illustrates that processual archaeology had finally made its appearance on the local front in the Chesapeake region.

From this early PRAS base, American and Catholic universities, in particular, would continue to push the processual agenda through research, the training of a new generation of archaeologists, and the further organization of a community of scholars with interests in processual archaeology. Victor Carbone, then one of Gardner's graduate students at Catholic University, subsequently produced a much-cited dissertation that delivered what he labeled the "episodic approach" to regional archaeology. Carbone (1976) advocated that discontinuities isolated in the paleoecological record through time be given causal status in stimulating prehistoric cultural change. Jay Custer (1984, 1989), another of Gardner's students at Catholic University, subsequently went to even greater lengths to apply this basic premise to the archaeological record of Delaware and the Eastern Shore of the Chesapeake region.

Another tangible effect of PRAS activity was the formation of the Middle Atlantic Archaeological Conference starting in 1970. Middle Atlantic, as it is known, quickly became a forum for processual archaeology. Even cursory examination of its early published proceedings, by now fourth-generation photocopies, reveals the ongoing struggle to apply the tenets of processual archaeology to regional prehistory. Its first real publication (Moeller 1982), literally a "best of" collection of papers given at Middle Atlantic over its first decade of existence, is aptly titled *Practicing Environmental Archaeology: Methods and Interpretations*. Processual archaeology, albeit modified for local purposes, had become the predominant way to explain Chesapeake prehistory, and university-based archaeology served as a major conduit.

While the activity discussed above relates to PRAS or second-generation archaeologists trained by its founders, there are other good examples of research interests that relate to processual archaeology's becoming the vehicle to understand the Chesapeake's past. One such notable example is Turner's 1976 dissertation focusing on the evolution of ranked societies on the Virginia Coastal Plain. This particular study rekindled the interest in late prehistoric sociocultural complexity that Binford had pondered over a decade earlier. That subject has continued to evoke a steady stream of published literature on the origins and evolution of chiefdoms along the shores of the Chesapeake Bay and it tributaries.

Another major conduit for the advancement of processual archaeology in the Chesapeake region was the continued growth of government archaeology programs. The small offices of the state archaeologists of the 1960s evolved into much larger programs throughout the 1970s and 1980s. Delaware's programs are consolidated under the Bureau of Archaeology and Historic Preservation. The Virginia Department of Historic Resources coordinates that state's activities in archaeology. In Maryland, all archaeology has recently been reorganized under a greatly expanded Maryland Historical Trust. Beyond these lead programs, archaeologists in all three states inhabit a host of other agencies.

My goal in this context is not to offer a description of every service these government archaeology programs provide. While individual mandates and priorities vary, each provides a host of services to its constituents in general and to the archaeological community in particular. I do want to argue that the subsequent development of these programs throughout the period under consideration has done much to promote the processual agenda. I would add that, while I am specifically addressing state programs here, much the same can be said for other government programs at both the national and local levels that deliver services to the Chesapeake region.

To begin, the expansion of these programs in the region was in concert with the ascendancy of processual archaeology as the dominant paradigm within archaeology as a whole. This expansion likewise occurred during the development of CRM as a major element of archaeology in the United States. Almost all archaeologists that now occupy leadership positions or staff the various state programs in the region were trained as processual archaeologists during the 1970s and 1980s. Indeed, a significant number of them are second- or third-generation processual archaeologists who received their graduate degrees from the very university programs just discussed. It was only natural that they sought to transfer the archaeology they had studied to the various problems of regional prehistory.

The fact that processual archaeology is a major element of state CRM today is codified in the various documents emanating from those very programs. For example, *The Maryland Comprehensive Historic Preservation Plan* (Maryland Historical Trust 1986:279), in the very first point of its recommended research questions for archaeologists, urges exploration of "the role of environmental change in the process of prehistoric culture change." Another example can be cited from the recently released guidelines for CRM studies in Virginia. These guidelines (Virginia Department of Historic Resources 1992:5) state that "for archaeological research, relevant information might include changes in the post-Pleistocene climate and biota and the manner by which cultural systems adapted to those conditions." The two examples cited, very much in keeping with the processual agenda, are mirrored over and over in the policies and procedures of all local government archaeology programs. If there is still any doubt about the scale of the processual impact on local CRM, a quick look at the mountain of project-specific studies completed to date should dispel any question of this fact.

I want to add one further comment about the linkage of processual archaeology to government archaeology programs. While certainly beyond the scope of this history, it is probably time to begin to explore the degree to which the alliance of processual archaeology and CRM was used as a tool to counter and control earlier cultural historical archaeology and its practitioners. If the construction of culture histories was a very empirical undertaking and dependent on the continual recovery of data from the archaeological record to advance its cause (see Dunnell 1986:30–32), then CRM, with its new emphasis on conservation, was a distinct control mechanism that actively promoted the programmatic goals of the new archaeology over those of the old.

It can be argued that, in the Chesapeake region at least, CRM archaeology was used as an effective way to promote processual archaeology and its interests at the expense of other ways of looking at the past. One can debate the virtues of that fact from a variety of different perspectives. And while no serious archaeologist would today urge a return to culture history, I do have to wonder if CRM and its now rather homogeneous theoretical stance will ultimately hinder the development of newer ways of looking at the past. Everyone agrees that we need to conserve our diminishing data base, but hopefully we can achieve that and still not legislate the way that it is understood.

In addition to this widespread activity in processual archaeology, I want to take a moment and acknowledge other concurrent topics of interest in Chesapeake archaeology. For example, physical anthropology has continued its tradition of investigating regional mortuary practices. Douglas Ubelaker's monograph (1974) on an analysis of ossuaries along the Potomac River is an example of this interest. Scholars likewise continue to be fascinated by regional ethnographic cultures of the seventeenth century and beyond. Helen Rountree (1989, 1990, 1993) has recently published a trilogy on the Powhatan of Virginia, and Paul Cissna (1986) has completed a similar study of the Piscataway in Maryland. I also want to make special mention of the experimental studies by Errett Callahan (1976, 1981, 1985), including everything from lithic replication research to the reconstruction and habitation of a small re-created Late Woodland village.

Returning to government archaeology, those programs also pursue a variety of ancillary interests. Delaware's Island Field Museum, built around a site of the same name, led the regional effort to bring archaeology directly to the public beginning as early as 1967. Recently the state of Maryland established the Jefferson Patterson Park and Museum to interpret local archaeology. Virginia, through the Council of Virginia Archaeologists, has initiated a most welcome publication of a whole series of volumes on archaeological research within its borders. It goes almost without saying that all of this activity has been healthy for Chesapeake archaeology.

To complete this history of Chesapeake archaeology, I want to close with a discussion of some research that begins to challenge, or at least tweak, the current domination of processual archaeology. These studies, of course, reflect broader trends within all of archaeology. The received view of processual archaeology is increasingly being challenged by a variety of perspectives that have more or less united under what is now known as postprocessual archaeology. Some of the local research discussed below could comfortably be included under that heading, while other examples are more concerned with redirecting or overcoming limitations of processual archaeology vis-à-vis the specific data base of the Chesapeake region. In the interest of not extending this section of the history much further, I will leave it to the reader to decide if the local variant of processual archaeology is just hemorrhaging at this point or beginning to sustain more ultimately fatal wounds.

To begin, the explanatory protocol of processual archaeology as it is practiced locally, where paleoenvironmental discontinuities are often seen as having stimulated prehistoric cultural change, presents some problems with the archaeological record, especially during the latter stages of prehistory. A number of regional archaeologists have had difficulty isolating the perturbations in the paleoecological record, which processual archaeology presupposes, to match with the significant changes they see in the archaeological record. The challenge to this camp is to find an alternative mechanism to provide a stimulus for culture change. In a number of cases migration leading to widespread population displacement has been suggested in place of ecological adaptation as the prime vehicle of change in regional prehistory after about 2600 years ago.

The fountain of this approach has been a paper published by Alvin Luckenbach, Wayne Clark, and Richard Levy (1987). They examine what they believe to be significant population disturbances late in prehistory. While it is admittedly somewhat difficult to completely assess the approach they advocate for a number of different reasons, there is no problem in saying that their ideas have had an impact on Chesapeake archaeology. Archaeologists do express discomfort with the foundation of the paper being based on a glottochronological analysis of linguistic data. It is difficult to ignore the fact that there is no widely held consensus within linguistics itself (see Bergsland and Vogt 1962; Campbell 1986; Weiss and Woolford 1986) on the validity of this analytical technique and that the actual linguistic data analyzed are by necessity scant. And at the same time the approach advocated is clearly reminiscent of an archaeology abandoned in the region three decades ago: that is, culture history. The use of terms like "migration," "adaptive radiation," "divergence," "diffusion," and so on recalls an era almost forgotten. At the same time, Luckenbach, Clark, and Levy (1987:27–28) are arguing for a consideration of historical and social processes as well as a return to a more balanced view of explanatory possibilities than is possible under the processual protocol. In the end, I cannot help but see their paper as a challenge to the dominance of processual archaeology in regional prehistory (see also Custer 1989:308–311).

While the ideas expressed in the above paper are being quite actively debated, three other rather unique studies are being ignored. Two of these analyses, one by Margaret Williamson (1979) and another by John Haynes (1984), represent potentially new interpretations of the Powhatan. The third paper, by Christine Jirikowic (1990), offers a different explanation for the ossuaries excavated along the Potomac River. Each of these studies, in its own right, has landed with somewhat of a resounding "thud" in the corpus of literature on local archaeology. I briefly want to sketch what each has to say and then come back to their collective lack of significant impact.

Williamson (1979) employs ethnohistorical descriptions of the Powhatan to present a structural and symbolic model of their worldview. The article presents a thought-provoking analysis of Powhatan gender construction embedded in a series of primary cultural oppositions such as east/west, gardening/hunting, friend/enemy, female/male, life/death, and so on. While such oppositions inspired by structural anthropology are possibly foreign to many prehistoric archaeologists, the basic implications of her analysis are imminently testable using archaeological data. Haynes (1984) looks at the origins of the Powhatan chiefdom. The chiefdom, in his analysis, results from human invention and agency rather than being a byproduct of external forces. Jirikowic (1990) sees prehistoric and early historic ossuaries in a new light—as artifacts of political and social forces within culture rather than inert cultural traits.

Death and resulting mortuary ritual become a venue for group definition and the negotiation of status, wealth, and power.

I see each of the studies discussed above as containing the potential seeds of change in the ways that archaeologists will interpret Chesapeake prehistory in the future. The ideas of Luckenback, Clark, and Levy (1987) have already found a waiting audience. They offer to fill an existing vacuum where processual explanations have clearly been questioned. The latter three studies, by Williamson (1979), Haynes (1984), and Jirikowic (1990), have had less of an impact perhaps because they rest on an epistemological foundation that is still somewhat foreign to regional archaeologists. I suspect, however, that each will soon be resurrected as local archaeologists begin to react to the tremors of the current debate in the wider discipline of archaeology and begin to look at their data in different ways.

CONCLUSION

While the practical constraints on histories such as this are many, I feel that this history was successful in suggesting a demonstrable pattern to the ways in which countless individuals have sought to understand Chesapeake prehistory. There are discernable redirections in thought that mark the periods of this history over the last century or so. In the larger scheme of things these may represent mostly small revolutions in ideas. And while they certainly were inspired by a wide variety of greater influences, each does lend a little appreciated richness and integrity to the broader trajectory of local archaeology itself. Perhaps the history also has some special value in that it focuses on the region as a whole rather than presenting a series of histories constrained by modern political boundaries. And while it is certainly my goal to contribute additional new ideas in the chapters that follow, I would be neglectful if I did not acknowledge this much larger struggle to understand the Chesapeake's prehistoric past. It does represent the point of departure for what is to follow.

Chapter 3

Natural History of the Chesapeake Region
Past and Present

INTRODUCTION

The Chesapeake tidewater area in its present state is the final product of dramatic change. Change is, in fact, perhaps the only constant in the region's ecological past. In this chapter I would like to detail what is known about the physical and ecological transformation of the Chesapeake region from late Pleistocene to Holocene times. The changes that took place during this era impacted all of the area's prehistory. To begin to assess these impacts it is necessary first to understand the magnitude and nature of these changes. That is the purpose of this chapter.

As a first step, it is important to appreciate the geologic and physiographic foundations of the region. The chapter will then turn to an examination of the natural history of the terminal Pleistocene riverine-dominated landscape that preceded the estuarine landscape of today. This ancient riverine ecosystem was created by glacially induced sea level decrease and associated climatic change. During this period there was no Chesapeake Bay. In its place was an extension of the Susquehanna River that flowed down through the region and out onto the exposed continental shelf. A cooler climate prevailed, greatly affecting floral and faunal communities.

Following the retreat of the last major North American glacial advance, both the continental shelf and the ancestral Susquehanna River were transgressed as sea levels began to rise. These transgressions began at 14,000 to 15,000 years ago and at 10,000 years ago, respectively. In concert with this process, post-Pleistocene climatic amelioration brought about a series of changes in regional floral and faunal communities. It was not until approximately 3000 years ago that the Chesapeake Bay, as it exists today, was essentially complete. This transformation is the last major concern of this chapter.

PHYSIOGRAPHY AND GEOLOGIC FOUNDATION

The study area is situated within the Coastal Plain physiographic province along the Atlantic slope of the North American continent. Highest-order drainage tends diagonally across the Coastal Plain toward the ocean. This pattern creates a natural subdivision of the region into what are commonly referred to as the Eastern and Western shores (Figure 3.1). The Eastern Shore, bounded by water on both sides, is distinctly peninsular. The Western Shore, with its greater area and more significant topographic relief, is generally subdivided into an inner and outer Coastal Plain. The former surrounds generally less saline but tidally influenced interior portions of tributaries and their associated freshwater feeder streams. The latter flanks the lower, estuarine portions of regional tributaries and the bay itself.

Total areas of emerged landmass on the Coastal Plain, of course, varied through time. In its greatest extent, the Coastal Plain within the study area ran laterally some 335 km from the western fall line marking the beginning of the Piedmont physiographic province to the eastern scarp of the continental shelf. Today only about two-thirds of this total area remains above sea level. For comparison, the distance from the fall line to the present strandline with the Atlantic Ocean is now approximately 184 km. This reduction of available landmass was a circa 12,000-year process, beginning about 14,000 to 15,000 years ago and ending only some 3000 years ago. More will be said about this soon.

The highest-order drainage feature in the region, originally the ancestral Susquehanna River and now the Chesapeake Bay, receives runoff from a large number of tributaries. At present, the major tributaries on the Eastern Shore include the Sassafras, Chester, Choptank, Nanticoke, Wicomico, and Pocomoke rivers. Along the Western Shore an even greater number of tributaries enter the estuary. The Susquehanna River still feeds into the northernmost end of the Bay, and the Northeast, Bush, Gunpowder, Patapsco, Magothy, Severn, South, Patuxent, Potomac, Rappahannock, Payankatank, York, and James rivers pay tribute to it laterally. Thousands of other smaller tributaries are also present. Three of these Western Shore rivers, the Susquehanna, Potomac, and James, today combine to contribute 80% of the fresh water entering the estuary. All of these tributaries—with the exception of the James River, which was a more recent capture by the estuary—once paid tribute to the ancestral Susquehanna River.

Topographic relief on the Coastal Plain of the study area is variable. The Eastern Shore is essentially a flat, low-lying plain. Its Atlantic shore is protected by a long line of barrier beaches backed by lagoons. Its opposite shore contains extensive estuarine wetlands. The Western Shore, averaging four times the elevation of its counterpart, has allowed substantial downcutting by its more numerous streams and therefore exhibits greater topographic relief. In many areas its shoreline is also low and contains extensive wetland areas. In a few locations, however, the coastline of the Western Shore is straight and rugged, rising to a height of 30 m or more. On both the Eastern and Western shores sometimes expansive interior wetland areas have been formed

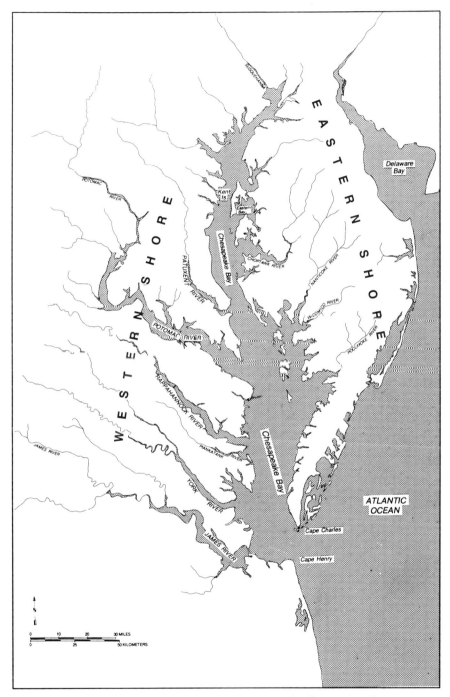

Figure 3.1. Map of Chesapeake Bay with major landforms indicated.

where water has perched on impermeable substrata. This phenomenon is especially pronounced after 10,000 years ago.

Geologically, the Coastal Plain in the study area is underlain by a series of southeasterly dipping layers of unconsolidated sediments. These sediments consist of sands and clays along with lesser amounts of gravel. They date from Triassic through Holocene times. All of these unconsolidated sediments rest on a crystalline basement. The brief description of these geologic formations that follows is drawn from H. E. Vokes and J. Edwards (1974:47–56). It is based on data collected on a geologic cross section running from the fall line of the Western Shore to the eastern edge of the continental shelf.

The ultimate foundation of the Coastal Plain province is a basement of mica gneiss or gabbro that dates to Precambrian or possibly early Paleozoic times. The surface of this crystalline basement has been heavily eroded and slopes steeply away from the fall line. In west to east cross section, this foundation is nearest the surface at the fall line, some 2400 m below the surface of the Eastern Shore, and up to 6000 m below the surface at the now-submerged scarp of the continental shelf (Dietrich 1970:175). More recent deposits that overlay this basement, the unconsolidated sand, clay, and gravel strata mentioned above, are therefore wedge shaped in cross section, thinner near the fall line and gaining thickness as one moves further east.

Many of these later unconsolidated deposits were either transported into the region by very ancient river systems or were laid down as shallow-water marine deposits. These former river systems transported gravels that have provided good sources of lithic materials for the prehistoric inhabitants of the region. The marine deposits often contain fossil inclusions. A series of well-known marine deposits are exposed at the Calvert Cliffs along the mid-Western Shore. Fossil-bearing strata in these formations include the remains of various marine or shoreline creatures that were alive between 10 to 20 million years ago. Prehistoric inhabitants of the region collected these fossils, and that pursuit has continued through colonial and modern times.

The most recent deposits on the Coastal Plain are of Pleistocene and Holocene age. Again, gravels have been transported into the tidewater area by a system of rivers that flowed through the Piedmont and slowed as it encountered the Coastal Plain. Much of this gravel was then deposited as alluvial fans or terraces. In more recent times the Coastal Plain has continued to receive sediments from the Piedmont to the north and west. Much of this redeposited material was originally glacial till. Windborne loess deposits also cap much of the Western and Eastern shores (Foss et al. 1978). Together all of these various episodes have provided the materials that constitute the geologic foundations of the study area as it exists today.

THE LATE PLEISTOCENE

The period of time included within the Pleistocene epoch was marked by great changes for all of North America. The most significant of these changes were associated with the period's glacial pulses. While the study area was well south of even the deepest of the glacial advances, it did not escape the indirect effects of these episodes. In particular, the Chesapeake area was especially susceptible to the impacts of these glacial advances on sea levels, as well as on climate, flora, fauna, and aquatic regimes. To a greater or lesser extent, the study area was subjected to these disturbances a number of times during the Pleistocene as the glaciers waxed and waned. It is the last such disturbance, brought about by the Wisconsin glacial advance, however, that is of particular relevance to prehistory. In this section of the chapter I would like to examine the changes that came to the study area during this time period. This discussion will start with an examination of sea level fluctuation and then turn to other changes in regional ecology.

Marine Regression

Estuaries, even large ones like the Chesapeake Bay, can be created or destroyed by eustatic changes in sea levels. As sea levels fluctuate, estuaries are liable to appear and disappear. It is apparent that a whole succession of Chesapeake Bays have been born, have matured, and have died as the Atlantic Ocean advanced on the coastline or retreated in response to interglacial and glacial episodes during the Pleistocene (Schubel 1981:6). Changes in eustatic sea level that control estuarine formation or removal were responses to perturbations ultimately affecting the entire planet's hydrologic cycle. As a significant portion of the world's total water budget becomes locked in the massive continental glacial ice packs, sea levels fall, coastal estuaries are drained, and oceans retreat from the continental shelf. During interglacial periods the opposite occurs. Glaciers melt and retreat, oceanic sea levels start to rise, and transgressions begin at the edges of landmasses. The present estuary is the latest in a series of such reincarnations that occurred during the last two million years.

This last cycle began approximately 40,000 years ago when eustatic sea levels were about what they are today. The Wisconsin glacial advance then commenced. More and more water gradually became trapped on land as ice accumulated. Sea level responded by falling slowly until about 21,000 years ago, and then receded rapidly from that point until about 16,000 years ago (Milliman and Emery 1968:1123). The maximum eustatic low was reached sometime between 18,000 and 15,000 years ago (Edwards and Merrill 1977:1). Figure 3.2 graphs the rate of marine regression for the Atlantic coastal area. At the point of maximum sea level drop, the Wisconsin glacial advance was covering some 15.6 million km^2 of the North American continent.

Effects of this series of events were substantial in the study area. The Coastal Plain is broad and exhibits little relative relief. Today, for example, a drop in sea level of a mere 10 m would lay bare more than 75% of the Chesapeake Bay (Schubel 1981:8). A significant portion of the continental shelf, now submerged, would likewise be exposed. Worldwide sea level drop reached up to -130 m during the late Pleistocene. Sea levels on this particular portion of the mid-Atlantic coast are projected at about -83 m during this era (Dillon and Odale 1978). As a result, by

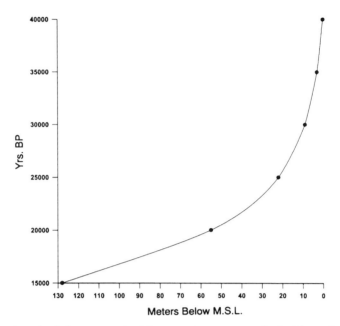

Figure 3.2. Generalized Pleistocene sea level drop—marine regression—for the Atlantic Coast of eastern North America (after Edwards and Merrill 1977).

between 18,000 and 15,000 years ago, the entire Chesapeake Bay had disappeared and the continental shelf off the present Atlantic coast was exposed.

This sequence of events had important implications for the earliest-known inhabitants of the study area. Landscape was dramatically different; by 18,000 years ago and until 10,000 years ago, the Chesapeake Bay and its embayed tributaries were gone. The region instead contained the ancestral Susquehanna River that flowed down and out onto the continental shelf where it emptied into a reduced Atlantic Ocean. For almost the same period of time, the continental shelf was exposed with the strandline up to 152 km east of its present location. This shelf area was relatively flat and contained its own mostly undeveloped drainage system (Edwards and Merrill 1977:34).

Recent research within the region undertaken by the USGS in cooperation with the Maryland Geological Survey and Virginia Institute of Marine Science has added significant detail to our understanding of the ancestral river system (Colman and Halka 1989a,b; Colman and Hobbs 1987, 1988). These organizations have recently completed an extensive geophysical survey of present-day subaqueous landforms. Much of their findings are based on the collection of some 2771 km of high-resolution seismic reflection profiles of the strata that are now submerged beneath the Chesapeake Bay.

Based on the seismic analysis, it was possible to identify and map three fluvial paleochannels of the ancestral Susquehanna River; all three are now partially or completely filled with sediments. These three paleochannels all tend seaward under the now-existing southern tip of the Eastern Shore. Each paleochannel is informally named for the town nearest that feature's location on the Eastern Shore—Exmore, Eastville, and Cape Charles. The former two paleochannels are ancient, having been active some 200,000 and 125,000 years ago, respectively. While they are not of direct concern to this research, their positions vis-à-vis the later Cape Charles paleochannel do indicate a steady shift of the channel of the ancestral Susquehanna River to the southwest over time.

The Cape Charles paleochannel is clearly what remains of the fluvial channel of the late Pleistocene ancestral Susquehanna River. The first known human inhabitants of this area, appearing about 11,000 years ago, occupied the banks of this river and its tributaries. Remnants of this channel are the most westward of the three paleochannels, and its course closely matches the dominant bathymetric feature—the deep midshore trough—running under the present estuary. The Cape Charles paleochannel is seismically registered as a fluvial erosional unconformity cut some 54 m into older underlying Tertiary marine-deposited strata. Today this paleochannel is partially filled with sediments that have been collecting in it since the post-Pleistocene marine transgression of the ancestral river system. These sediments in the mid- to upper portions of the present estuary are still charged with biogenic gases (primarily methane) released through the breakdown of organic matter trapped within them.

Combining these data on the Cape Charles paleochannel with a recent USGS reconstruction (Escowitz, Hill, and Bowen 1988) of the continental shelf it is possible to visualize the landscape configuration of the study area during the late Pleistocene. From Figure 3.3 it is possible to visualize the regional landscape during the point of maximum marine regression. This represents the study area between 18,000 and 15,000 years ago. Sometime after this the ocean began responding to eustatic sea level rise, and a reclamation or marine transgression of the continental shelf started at about 14,000 to 15,000 years ago. It would be another 5000 years before ocean water had completely transgressed this feature and arrived at the portions of the Cape Charles paleochannel within the present limits of the Chesapeake Bay. The first known inhabitants of the region and their immediate ancestors were witnesses to this dramatic process as they settled and began to populate the region.

Late Pleistocene Ecology

The same larger forces that were disturbing sea level had a substantial impact on other regional ecological regimes. The local pollen record is perhaps the most direct line of evidence available for reconstructing those aspects of the past ecology of the study area. The formula for such a pollen-based reconstruction is straightforward. Though seldom acknowledged, the Blytt–Sernander system (see Zeuner 1952) developed by the Danes for a similar purpose in northern Europe forms the armature of the

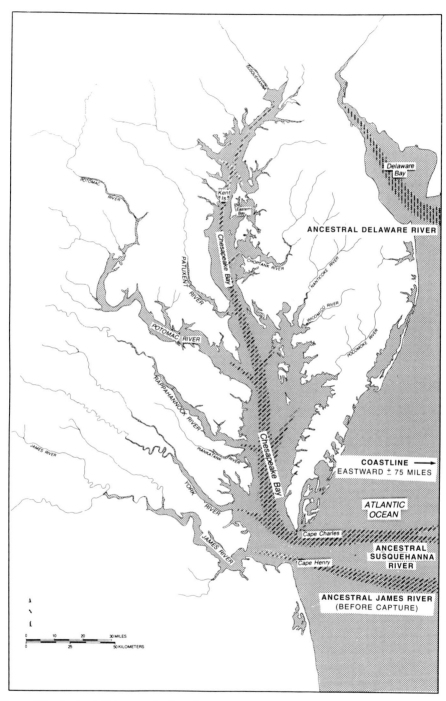

Figure 3.3. Regional Pleistocene land configuration with channel of ancestral Susquehanna River indicated.

logic employed by most paleoecologists. In this system the percentages of various floral species, as fossilized in the pollen record, are employed to suggest dominant vegetative communities through time. In a comparison of these past vegetational communities to modern analogues, a relationship between vegetation and climate is then established. Finally, the third variable, associated faunal communities, can then be implied based on the complete floral and climatic reconstruction. All three elements—flora, climate, and fauna—are viewed as inextricably intertwined.

It is known that contemporary ecological zones were displaced southward, by as much as 1040 km, by the Wisconsin glacial advance. Within the Chesapeake study area prevailing forest during the late Pleistocene was of a boreal type with spruce (*Picea*) as a primary arboreal dominant. To the north and at higher elevations to the west full tundra conditions existed. Further south, pine (*Pinus*) replaced spruce as the dominant arboreal species. For the Chesapeake area it is possible to be more specific based on the pollen record recovered at a number of locations across the region. Figure 3.4 maps all pollen sampling stations discussed in this chapter. Six of these sites yielded samples dating to the late Pleistocene. Two of these six locations are at the mouth of the present estuary, another three are on the Eastern Shore, and one is reported from the Western Shore. Each sampling station is discussed below.

W. Harrison, R. J. Malloy, G. A. Rusnak, and J. Teresmae (1965) were able to collect sediment samples from test boring at the Chesapeake Bay Bridge and Tunnel Crossing at the mouth of the estuary. Two concentrations of plant and peat fiber were analyzed. This organic matter was probably the result of water ponding in the area between about 15,000 and 8000 years ago. The chronology is supported by a series of six radiocarbon assays. Based on the analysis, vegetation at this site during late glacial times was composed mostly of coniferous species including spruce, pine, and fir (*Abies*), along with a few deciduous species, birch (*Betula*) and alder (*Alnus*), recorded in very small amounts. About 10,000 years ago, pine reached a maximum at the expense of spruce. Unfortunately, pollen from nonarboreal species was not reported for this site.

Pollen cores from the Dismal Swamp, also near the mouth of the Chesapeake Bay, have been analyzed by D. R. Whitehead (1965, 1972). These are some of the most comprehensive pollen data available for the study area. Clay, below peat deposits radiocarbon dated to 7670 ± 60 (Y-1146) and 8900 ± 160 (Y-1320) years ago, provides evidence of late glacial conditions. This stratigraphically lower clay stratum is thought to date between 12,000 and 10,700 years ago (Whitehead 1965:428). High percentages of pine and spruce along with birch and alder are reported. Significant quantities of herb pollen were also recovered. For the southern portions of the study area, the pollen assemblages reported by both Harrison et al. (1965) and Whitehead (1965, 1972) are in close agreement.

On the central Eastern Shore, L. A. Sirkin, C. S. Denny, and M. Rubin (1977) undertook a rather extensive study of the Parsonburg Sand mantles. These formations are exposed in parts of southern Delaware and adjacent Maryland. Based on a series of 21 samples, all rich in organic matter, a dated pollen assemblage has been isolated that stretches from 30,000 to 9000 years ago. In the latter portion of this sequence,

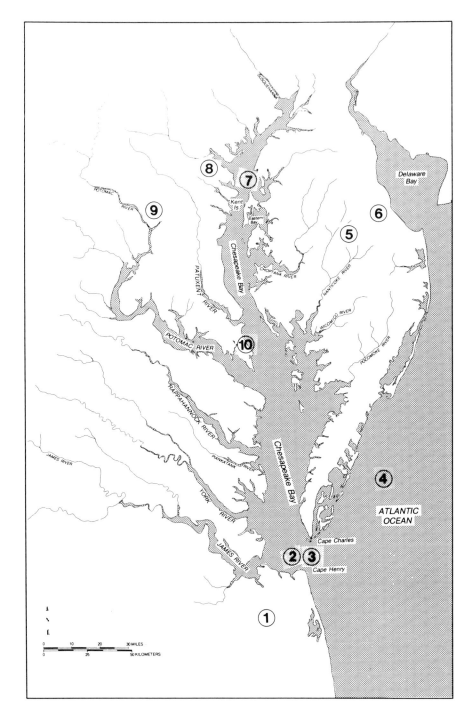

radiocarbon assayed at 13,420 ± 300 (W-3105) years ago, a boreal forest consisting of spruce, pine, birch, and alder is indicated (Sirkin, Denny, and Rubin 1977:142). Recovered pollen from various aquatic plants indicates standing fresh water in the area at that time.

Another isolated peat sample from the now-submerged edge of the Coastal Plain on the Eastern Shore has been reported by K. O. Emery et al. (1967). This sampling station is currently submerged some 63–70 m below mean sea level. The sample itself was radiocarbon assayed to 13,500 ± 350 (W-2014) years ago. Pollen within that sample is identified as being dominated by spruce and pine with lesser amounts of fir and oak (*Quercus*). Water lily (*Nymphae*) and sedges (Cyperaceae) were also present along with various fern and sphagnum spores as well as arrowhead (*Sagittaria*) and club moss (*Lycopodium*) pollen (Emery et al. 1967:1304). A measurement of stable carbon isotopes links the sample to a former freshwater environment. The analysis of this sample is especially important in that it extends the prevailing boreal ecosystem well out to the eastern margins of the continental shelf during the late Pleistocene.

At a more interior and northern location, Custer (1989:50) has reported on an early sample from the Dill Farm site in Delaware. The sample of relevance to the problem at hand is radiocarbon assayed to 9890 ± 140 (I-6045) years ago. It is somewhat later than the two samples just discussed. Analysis of this sample reveals pine dominance with associated hemlock (*Tsuga*), birch, and oak. A strong nonarboreal component is also noted. The ascendancy of pine at the expense of spruce in this case may be a marker of the beginning of early Holocene changes in the area.

Moving to the Western Shore, a pollen core has recently been obtained from an abandoned stream channel near the Indian Creek V archaeological site in Maryland (LeeDecker 1991). Indian Creek, a nearby stream, is a tributary of the Northeast Branch, which in turn flows into the Anacostia River, itself a tributary of the Potomac River. The sample site, once an active channel of Indian Creek, is on the inner Coastal Plain very near its boundary with the Piedmont physiographic region. Analysis of the core reported here was undertaken by Grace Brush of Johns Hopkins University for archaeologists with Louis Berger & Associates, Inc. The research was completed in conjunction with an excavation of the nearby Indian Creek V site in anticipation of the site's destruction for a rail storage and maintenance yard.

The core was recovered from black organic peat that had collected in the channel. C. H. LeeDecker (1991:31) remarks that pollen preservation was excellent. A suite of five radiocarbon assays with intervening pollen zones calculated based on sedimentation rates provides a complete record of local late Pleistocene and Holocene vegetation. An assay of 10,800 ± 200 (Beta-42668) years ago marks the lower zone

Figure 3.4. Pollen sampling sites in the Chesapeake region. Numbers indicate the following sites: 1, Dismal Swamp; 2, Chesapeake Bay Bridge-Tunnel at mouth of bay; 3, second sampling of Chesapeake Bay Bridge-Tunnel at mouth of bay; 4, submerged Eastern Shore site; 5, Parsonburg Sands on the central Eastern Shore; 6, Dill Farm, Delaware; 7, Upper Bay Bridge; 8, Magothy River; 9, Indian Creek; 10, St. Marys City.

of the core. Vegetation in that zone was dominated by pine and spruce with alder becoming more abundant toward the end of the period. Principal nonarboreal taxa recovered include madder (Rubiaceae), milkwort (*Polygala*), and composites (Compositae). These data are especially important given the paucity of other such similar research on the Western Shore.

Based on all these late Pleistocene assemblages, climatic conditions during the period were obviously cooler and moister. Techniques have been developed to mathematically transform pollen data into quantitative estimates of past environments. Such transformations have been undertaken in the Shenandoah Valley to the southwest of the study area by Carbone (1976) and to the north in the Upper Delaware Valley by the author (Dent 1985). While both climatic reconstructions are in close agreement, factoring out differences in latitude, Carbone's reconstruction is perhaps more applicable in this instance given its closer geographic proximity.

For the late Pleistocene, Carbone (1976:104–105) postulates a 5° F mean July temperature difference between late glacial times and today. Annual precipitation, especially snowfall, was also much higher with a 25% increase in overcast days during the late Pleistocene. The projected increase in precipitation and cloudiness was probably due to extreme frontal activity in the area, while the decrease in temperature was a result of a 50% increase in the duration of arctic air over the region. These climatic parameters are based on the frequencies of pollen rain reported by A. J. Craig (1969) from Hack Pond in the Shenandoah Valley. Whitehead (1972:312) has commented that the Hack Pond pollen record compares favorably with his Dismal Swamp data, thereby adding some additional validity to the comparison of the two areas. Table 3.1 compares Carbone's late Pleistocene and Holocene reconstructions with modern parameters.

Terrestrial and aquatic faunal species within the study area during late Pleistocene times are difficult to unequivocally reconstruct. There is simply little direct evidence, and the faunal remains that have been recovered are often not temporally fixed by radiocarbon assay or clear early artifact association. With this state of affairs, the only line of evidence open is to use terrestrial and aquatic faunal data outside the immediate study area to suggest a general picture of these communities within the study area during the appropriate period.

Late Pleistocene aquatic communities are especially difficult to suggest. With an extension of the Susquehanna River flowing down through the region, it is evident that the late Pleistocene aquatic regime was riverine and correspondingly contained more species diversity than the estuary of today. This species diversity, however, was offset by the absence of many prolific and economically valuable species. For example, estuarine organisms such as the oyster (*Crassostrea virginica*) and the blue crab (*Callinectes sapidus*) that were harvested in large numbers by later prehistoric inhabitants were unavailable. Anadromous fish runs, presenting another set of aquatic species for human exploitation, were also likely not as well established. One is left to assume that the ancestral Susquehanna River was much like any freshwater ecosystem at a similar latitude.

Table 3.1. Reconstructed Climatic
Parameters for Various Increments
of the Late Pleistocene and Holocene[a]

B.P.	Temp[b]	Precip[c]	Snow[d]	Hrs. sun[e]	Arctic air[f]
435	23.8	26	137.9	2585	1.75
1305	23.6	21	131.6	2624	1.49
2175	23.8	23.2	134.6	2607	1.22
3045	23.9	24.1	134.6	2615	1.63
4350	24.5	15.2	126	2654	1.50
5220	24.2	16.2	126.5	2656	.80
6090	24.3	16.9	127	2658	1.22
7395	23.4	25.6	141	2535	1.36
8265	22.9	33.4	153.4	2427	1.93
9135	22.3	44.3	170.2	2288	3.38
10,105	22.3	44.5	168.9	2311	3.04
11,175	21.9	48.9	179.8	2190	3.82
12,245	21.9	49.4	178	2200	3.69

[a]After Carbone 1976.
[b]Mean July temperature in degrees C.
[c]Centimeters precipitation minus potential evaporation.
[d]Centimeters annual snowfall.
[e]Annual hours of sunshine.
[f]Number of months of arctic air mass duration annually.

Reconstruction of terrestrial fauna must be viewed in almost the same light. Late Pleistocene fauna is known to have consisted of a combination of (1) now extinct megafauna, (2) extant temperate megavertebrates and microvertebrates, and (3) disjunct large and small northern boreal species (Semken 1983:192). Again, in terms of species diversity, the area was much richer during this period in terms of total variety of species. This disharmonious faunal community is typical of the late Pleistocene in many regions of North America.

The remains of extinct megafauna have been recovered in the study area. R. L. Edwards and K. O. Emery (1977:251) report the discovery of four mammoths (*Mammuthus primigenius*) and four mastodons (*Mammut americanum*) on the continental shelf off of the Eastern Shore. Although no dates are available on these finds, I would generally suspect the former to be chronologically older than the latter. R. L. Edwards and A. S. Merrill (1977:9–11) add another mammoth from this same area and also report seven walrus sites (*Odobenus rosmarus* and possibly another species). O. P. Hay (1923:344–354), in his classic compilation of Pleistocene faunal remains east of the Mississippi River, reports numerous other mastodont and mammoth fossils as well as the remains of other extinct species from the Coastal Plain of the study area. Most recently, a subadult mammoth (*M. columbi*) has been recovered by the Smithsonian Institution in a buried stream channel on the inner Coastal Plain of the

Western Shore. Bone collagen from the creature was radiocarbon assayed to 20,070 ± 265 (SI-5357) years ago.

These extinct Pleistocene megafauna continue to fascinate archaeologists. As one can see from the above listing, chronological resolution is a significant obstacle to their linkage with early humans in the Chesapeake region and elsewhere in eastern North America. And of course there is the additional fact that archaeology has been unsuccessful in recovering artifacts in clear association with these remains. Comparing the handful of secure radiocarbon dates on eastern Paleoindian sites with dates on megafaunal remains (Martin and Kleine 1984) in the same area might lead one to believe that at the time of human entry into the region these species had already vacated the area and were therefore not available for human exploitation (see Dent 1985:157). Alternatively, human subsistence strategies in eastern North America may not have favored these creatures. Whatever the case, the nearest well-documented association of early humans and megafauna (*M. americanum*) occurs on the far western border of eastern North America in present-day Missouri (Graham et al. 1981). Paleoindians also probably dispatched an extinct species of giant land tortoise (*Geochelone crassiscutata*) at the Little Salt Spring site in Florida (Clausen et al. 1979). Other unequivocal associations are unknown.

The remainder of the late Pleistocene faunal community included many of the temperate species that still inhabit the area along with disjunct boreal species (Graham 1979:52; Lundelius et al. 1983:312–314; Semken 1983:192). It is evident that faunal communities of the late Pleistocene, in comparison with today, were disharmonious. Temperate species and glacially displaced boreal species seemed to have lived side by side in the study area. This indicates that affected faunal species, at least, were more individualistic in their response to climatic changes and displacements of the period. The nearest data available to suggest the actual range of species inhabiting the study area are to the southwest (e.g., Guilday 1962; Guilday and Hamilton 1973; Guilday, Parmalee, and Hamilton 1977; Wetmore 1962) and to the north (e.g., Guilday, Hamilton, and McCrady 1966; Guilday, Martin, and McCrady 1964; Leidy 1889) of the Chesapeake region. These analyzed faunal assemblages generally contain both boreal and temperate fauna. This same phenomenon is also seen at Meadowcroft Rockshelter (Adovasio et al. 1978) to the northwest.

Data discussed above present a *general* picture of flora, climate, and faunal populations during the late Pleistocene in the study area. It is important to remember that any number of other factors must be taken into account at specific sites within the study area to evaluate these data vis-à-vis the early archaeological record. This will be a matter of concern for the subsequent chapter on the Paleoindian period.

THE HOLOCENE

The chief instrument of the forces delivering great change to the study area during the late Pleistocene eventually began to undergo changes. Beginning about

15,000 years ago the Wisconsin glacier had started the slow process of downmelt and retreat. With the water once locked within the ice mass now beginning to return to the ocean, eustatic sea levels began to rise. The ocean responded by advancing and the birth of the present Chesapeake Bay soon began. The process of estuarian formation essentially dismembered the old late Pleistocene drainage system dominated by the ancestral Susquehanna River. Climatic amelioration likewise began to impact regional late Pleistocene flora and fauna. In this section of the chapter I would like to look at the ensuing process of estuary formation and then turn to other changes in regional ecology during the Holocene.

Marine Transgression

Eustatic sea levels were responding to water returning from the melting ice mass starting along the entire Atlantic coast approximately 14,000–15,000 years ago. Sea level rose fairly rapidly from this point in time until about 7000 years ago when the rate declined and became more gradual (Milliman and Emery 1968:1123). The rate of eustatic sea level rise for the earlier 7000-year period is projected at up to 1.6 m per century. It is estimated that for every .3 m that sea level rose, the ocean would transgress the dry continental shelf approximately 510 horizontal meters. These calculations are generalized curves for the entire Atlantic continental shelf, and local isostatic adjustments are not included. Figure 3.5 graphs the transgression sequence described above for the Atlantic coast.

More specific sea level data are available for the Chesapeake study area. Until recently, a composite curve based on the research of John Kraft (1977) in the nearby Delaware Bay, Kraft and Brush's (1981) work along the St. Mary's River, and the report of Harrison et al. (1965) at the mouth of the estuary presented the best available evidence in this regard. Fortunately, S. M. Colman, J. P. Halka, and C. H. Hobbs (1991) have offered another, more detailed transgression curve specifically for the Chesapeake Bay. Figure 3.6 presents their data.

In terms of the numbers, relative sea level directly in the evolving Chesapeake estuary rose an average of 1.3 m per century between 10,000 and 6000 years ago. The transgression continued at a reduced rate of about .2 m per century after this, between 5000 and 1000 years ago. It is interesting to note that the pre-10,000-year rate of sea level rise, which submerged the continental shelf to the east, may have been up to 1.4 m per century. Furthermore, relative sea level rise appears to have accelerated in this last century, doubling from about 1.5 mm per year to more than 3 mm per year.

As a footnote to these quantitative data, Colman et al. (1991:14) add that the submergence of the ancestral Susquehanna River by the estuary is the result of a combination of both local sea level rise and local subsidence of the earth's crust. Harrison et al. (1965:224) also earlier raised the question of tectonic movement in the region. If nothing else, the possibility of such landform adjustment reminds us as archaeologists that these processes may not be as simple as we all want to believe.

Turning to a more qualitative account of the effects of relative sea level rise on the

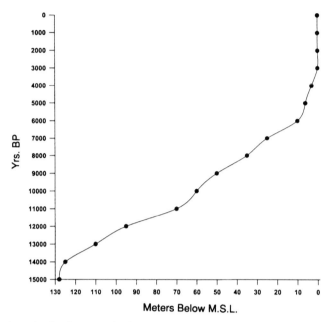

Figure 3.5. Generalized Holocene sea level rise—marine transgression—for the Atlantic coast of eastern North America (after Edwards and Merrill 1977).

Chesapeake region, one can envision the following scenario. Starting by about 14,000–15,000 years ago the Atlantic Ocean began to rise and started its march across the continental shelf. The lower portion of the ancestral Susquehanna River, out on the shelf, began to be inundated. This stage of transgression proceeded rapidly and probably did not allow for the formation of coastal lagoons, embayments, or other relief features (Edwards and Merrill 1977:33). Aqueous loading may have had some impact on landform. By 10,000 years ago the advancing ocean had reached the mouth of the present Chesapeake Bay. Several thousand years later, at 7000 years ago, seawater was lapping at the mouth of the Anacostia River, a tributary of the Potomac River, at about the midpoint of the present estuary. This information is based on core samples taken for the Washington, D.C., Metro System. At some point during this same era the nascent Chesapeake Bay must have captured the formerly independent James River. By 6000 years ago, the transgression had reached Annapolis, Maryland, marking the beginning of the northern reaches of the extant estuary. And it is estimated that the entire Chesapeake Bay was essentially complete by approximately 3000 years ago, even though sea level rise continues today. From the standpoint of human exploitation of estuarine resources, it is evident in some locations that estuarine-based human subsistence processes were operating even before the final completion of the Bay.

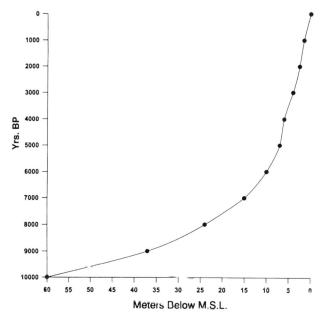

Figure 3.6. Sea level rise—marine transgression—specific to the Chesapeake region (after Colman, Halka, and Hobbs 1991).

A secondary, yet important, consequence of this local marine transgression was its influence on regional subterranean water tables. As inundation progressed, water tables likewise rose, and extensive interior wetland areas were formed inland of the Chesapeake Bay. These interior wetlands, commonly referred to as swamps, are a direct result of rising sea level forcing subterranean water tables to appreciably rise. A net effect was that standing fresh water could collect in poorly drained areas or perch on impermeable sediments. Whitehead (1972:313) documents this process in his discussion of the formation of the Great Dismal Swamp in the lower portion of the study area. This and other similar Holocene wetlands, themselves secondary effects of the transgression sequence, soon presented unique interior habitats that became important foci for prehistoric settlement and subsistence systems.

Holocene Ecology

Regional floral and faunal communities began to undergo dramatic changes starting approximately 10,000 years ago. Once again, the pollen record provides a direct line of evidence for assessing these changes. The data available are fairly extensive, and, of course, cover a much greater time range than that discussed for the late Pleistocene.

For these reasons, I have chosen first to discuss the complete Holocene pollen records of two particularly well documented sites: the long-term pollen records from the Dismal Swamp and Indian Creek. I will follow this with an examination of three more temporally restricted pollen reconstructions and, in another case, a more chronologically expansive yet less detailed pollen analysis. These discussions will lead to a general summary portrait of changing vegetation in the region between about 10,000 years ago and the present. Pollen sampling locations within the study area were noted on Figure 3.4. Analysis of a set of actual botanical specimens collected from the Chesapeake region in the late seventeenth and early eighteenth centuries will be employed to enrich this portrait of the local Holocene vegetational community. The section then turns to a discussion of wetland formation, climate, and prevailing fauna.

Whitehead's (1965, 1972) research at the Dismal Swamp at the southern margins of the region presents a comprehensive picture of local vegetational change during the Holocene. At that site, between 10,600 and 8200 years ago, the pollen record indicates the presence of a beech (*Fagus*), hemlock, and birch forest. A radiocarbon assay of 8900 ± 160 (Y-1320) was employed to project the duration of this association. As this forest established itself, pine decreased while oak increased in importance. Whitehead (1972:308) sees this association as a transition between the former pine–spruce late Pleistocene forest and the soon to appear oak–hickory association.

This oak–hickory association was established at about 8200 years ago. Three radiocarbon assays chronologically define the formation and establishment of this association: 7670 ± 60 (Y-1146), 4210 ± 160 (Y-1322), and 3580 ± 100 (Y-1321). The forest consisted of high percentages of oak and hickory along with a relative abundance of many other deciduous genera. This forest persisted until approximately 3500 years ago when changing conditions created a locally unique vegetational community.

The pollen record recovered during the mitigation of the Indian Creek site on the inner Coastal Plain just above the midpoint of the Chesapeake region is likewise one of the more complete pollen records known for both the late Pleistocene and the Holocene. The descriptions of it below are drawn from the report produced by Louis Berger & Associates (LeeDecker 1991:31–34). From the end of the Pleistocene to about 7660 years ago an increase in birch at the expense of both pine and spruce is noted at this sampling site. Alder likewise decreases, but remains plentiful. At the same time oak, while still less abundant than birch, is increasing. Goldenrod (*Solidago*) and arrowwood (*Viburnum*) are represented as major nonarboreal taxa. The termination of this association and the beginning of the next is supported by a radiocarbon assay of 7660 ± 160 (Beta-42667) years ago. Warmer conditions marking the onset of the Holocene are evident.

From the end of the association above until about 5000 years ago, a warmer and moister environment leads to the reduction of pine and birch and the virtual disappearance of spruce and fir. Oak, hazelnut (*Corylus*), and alder begin to dominate, accompanied by maple (*Acer*), black gum (*Nyssa*), beech (*Fagus*), ash (*Fraxinus*), and walnut (*Juglans*). Cinnamon fern (*Osmunda*) is the dominant herbaceous species. Succeeding this, starting about 5000 years ago, drier conditions altered local vegetation. Oak becomes the dominant species. Pine, hickory, and walnut also increase, while alder, birch, and hazelnut accordingly decrease. Major nonarboreal taxa again include cinnamon fern along with blueberry (Ericaceae) and elderberry (*Sambucus*). The end of this community and the beginning of the next is supported by a radiocarbon assay of 3860 ± 110 (Beta-42666) years ago.

Starting at that date and lasting until 1770 years ago, the pollen record indicates a major reduction of arboreal pollen and corresponding expansion of herbaceous species. Oak is the major arboreal species, but in significantly reduced frequency. An influx of legumes (Leguminosae) along with significant quantities of elderberry, blueberry, and arrowwood are noted. The end of this vegetational landscape is marked by a radiocarbon assay of 1770 ± 140 (Beta-42020) years ago. After 1770 years ago, the site witnessed a return to cooler and moister conditions. The reestablishment of mixed deciduous forests is projected across the region even though nonarboreal species continue to dominate this particular landscape.

From a more temporally limited perspective, Robert Rogers (1992) has recently reported on two dated pollen samples taken from boreholes for the proposed second, parallel Chesapeake Bay Bridge and Tunnel Crossing at the mouth of the estuary. The oldest sample, radiocarbon assayed at 9290 ± 100 (Beta-54285) years ago, is dominated by oak and grass pollen. A hardwood forest situated near wetland areas is suggested. The sample was recovered 8.0–8.3 m below the bottom of the Chesapeake Bay. Above that, the pollen record indicates that the wetland may have been expanding but that significant hardwood stands were still nearby. This sample was radiocarbon assayed at 8520 ± 70 (Beta-54284) years ago and it was taken 5.4–5.9 m below the bottom of the estuary.

At St. Mary's City, the original colonial capital of Maryland, geologists (Kraft and Brush 1981) have completed a reconstruction of the vegetation near the midpoint of the Western Shore of the Bay over the last 5000 years. This analysis is based on a core extracted from what is locally referred to as St. John's Pond. The pond is actually a small, open tidal embayment off of the St. Mary's River, a tributary of the Potomac River. The basal sample from this core is radiocarbon assayed at 4580 ± 100 (JCK-SMC-79-4) years ago.

The entire pollen profile from this location represents a mixed deciduous forest with some coniferous admixture. Oak and hickory are dominant, followed by maple, birch, beech, ash, sweet gum, and chestnut. The latter species is poorly represented, but this may be due to chestnut's general tendency to produce restricted amounts of pollen. Pine is represented in significant quantities and typical nonarboreal taxa were reported. Kraft and Brush (1981:11) add that they see no indication of a response of vegetation to climatic variation over the period in which the sampled sediment was being deposited.

J. P. Owens, K. Stefansson, and L. A. Sirkin (1974), as part of a larger study of a series of Atlantic coast estuaries, have reported on the limited palynological analysis of a series of borehole samples from the northern one-third of the estuary. These samples were obtained incidental to the construction of the second bridge crossing between the Eastern and Western shores near Annapolis, Maryland. Analyses of restricted samples from four of the eight widely spaced boreholes are reported in their paper.

A single radiocarbon assay of 9800 ± 250 (W-2300) established the minimum age of the fill. On the basis of pollen content, an oak–hickory association is reported throughout the entire period (Owens, Stefansson, and Sirkin 1974:392). This rather blanket assessment does tend to ignore what appears to be significant changes in the frequencies of various species throughout the composite column. For example, in basal samples, based on a visual examination of the pollen profile, oak does not appear to dominate. I suspect a continuous, completely analyzed core based on adequate samples would present a picture much like that seen in the Dismal Swamp and Indian Creek profiles. Unfortunately, the pollen analysis reported in this paper was only a small part of a study primarily undertaken for other purposes.

To extrapolate from the pollen profiles of the various sites discussed above to the vegetational history of the entire Chesapeake region is no easy task. It can be accomplished in only the most general manner, and complicating factors must be recognized. Perhaps the most striking illustration of the caution necessary can be seen by looking at the present vegetational diversity existing in the region. The modern vegetational pattern is distinctly ecotonal. Along the north–south axis of the Chesapeake Bay three distinct forest regions can be isolated (Braun 1950). In the northern reaches of the region the Oak–Chestnut Forest edges out onto the Coastal Plain. On both the Eastern and Western shores, at latitudes running from present-day Baltimore, Maryland, to the James River further south, the Atlantic slope portion of the Oak–Pine Forest dominates. Below this, the Southeastern Evergreen Forest stretches up into the study area. Figure 3.7 illustrates this pattern. There is little reason not to believe that similar diversity was present throughout the entire Holocene. Local conditions, such as moisture, exposure, soil, lithology, and so on, combined in the past, as they do today, to create a regional mosaic of vegetational types.

At a general level, indications are that changes associated with the Holocene began to impact the nature of regional vegetation beginning after approximately 10,000 to 9800 years ago. These changes may have occurred somewhat earlier in the southern reaches of the Chesapeake study area. During this time, the late Pleistocene predominantly coniferous vegetation (mainly a spruce–pine association with significant percentages of birch and alder) began to be displaced. Its initial replacement appears to have been locally variable and somewhat transitional. In the southern portions of the region this consisted of a beech–hemlock–birch forest association with oak, at the same time, beginning to rise significantly. Further north, oak appears to have more quickly increased in a community complemented by both birch and alder. This new post-Pleistocene transitional forest appears to have sustained itself for somewhere on the order of 1000 to 2000 years.

After about 8200 to 7600 years ago, oak becomes a clearly dominant species

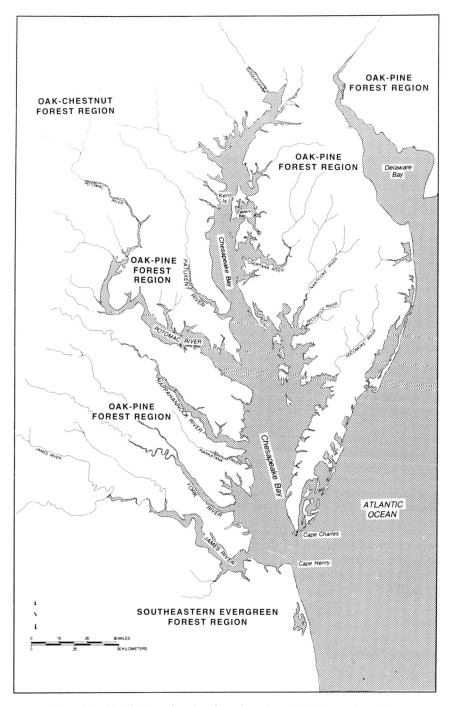

Figure 3.7. Distributions of modern forest formations in the Chesapeake region.

across the region. Other associated taxa vary, however, depending on location. Across much of the region hickory becomes the primary codominant. On the inner Coastal Plain of the Western Shore an oak–hazelnut–alder association prevailed. In all cases, a number of other deciduous genera along with significant percentages of pine provided variation to this larger essentially oak–hickory association.

Percentages of more mesic arboreal species likewise rise in some locations between 5000 and 3800 years ago. After this the fairly typical mixed deciduous association reestablished itself and persists until recent times. Pine remains present in significant quantities. Even with these last possible small perturbations, a number of researchers remark (e.g., Brush 1986; Kraft and Brush 1981; Stenger 1982) that they see little in the pollen profiles to indicate any real regional vegetational change over the past 5000 years. Vegetationally, for all practical purposes, the region had effectively stabilized by about 5000 years ago.

It may be possible to present a more specific picture of this post-5000-year-old regional vegetational community. M. Brown, J. L. Reveal, C. R. Broome, and G. F. Frick (1986) have undertaken some fascinating botanical research that focuses on historical voucher specimens. These preserved plant specimens are now curated at the British Museum in London as well as at the Lindley Herbarium and the Fielding–Druce Herbarium in Cambridge and Oxford, respectively. The collections were placed in these repositories primarily by the Reverend Hugh Jones between 1696 and 1700 and by Dr. David Krieg and William Vernon in 1698. This early plant-collecting activity was apparently the result of efforts by the Royal Society to acquire exotic plants from the far reaches of the British Empire.

Preserved specimens in the collections represent 626 species distributed among 353 genera (Brown et al. 1986:743). Most of the specimens were collected in modern-day Anne Arundel, Prince Georges, Calvert, and St. Mary's counties. All of these Maryland counties are just above the Potomac River on the Western Shore of the Chesapeake Bay. Some collecting also appears to have taken place within Talbot or Dorchester County on the Eastern Shore of Maryland. One of the collectors, Krieg, may have ventured up the Chesapeake Bay as far north as the Susquehanna River.

In their analysis, Brown et al. (1986) use the historic plant specimens they were able to examine to reconstruct native flora. A number of obstacles to this goal are readily acknowledged. For one, it is obvious that no where near the whole flora of the region was gathered by these pioneer collectors and that the forest had, even at this early time, already suffered impacts through land clearing and the introduction of nonnative species. For example, by 1753 some 60 introduced species have been documented. The lack of exact provenience data on the historical plant specimens are also worrisome. Nevertheless, the researchers felt that a combination of the careful identification of the historic specimens supplemented by available pollen data and known ecological principles would allow a fairly accurate conceptual reconstruction of native flora.

Brown et al. (1986) reconstruct a whole series of habitats across the Coastal Plain. For the purposes of this chapter, I will concentrate on their ideas about the nature of the precontact forest ecology. They believe that the regional pristine forest contained well-defined oak–hickory, oak–gum, and oak–pine associations. The presence of each association would have been determined by local conditions. This diversity is in keeping with the present diversity seen across the region.

Being more specific, higher well-drained sites would have been dominated by various species of oak and hickory. Species would have included white oak (*Quercus alba*), chestnut oak (*Q. prinus*), Spanish oak (*Q. falcata*), black oak (*Q. velutina*), blackjack oak (*Q. marilandica*), post oak (*Q. stellata*), and willow oak (*Q. phellos*). The hickory component of this association would include *Carya cordiformis*, *C. ovata*, and *C. tomentosa*. An occasional pine might also have been found among these deciduous species. At lower locations where more moisture was available an oak–gum association thrived. Willow oak would have been joined by water oak (*Q. nigra*), basket oak (*Q. michauxii*), pin oak (*Q. palustris*), and swamp oak (*Q. bicolor*). These species were likely associated with sweet gum (*Liquidambar styraciflua*), beech (*F. grandifolia*), tulip tree (*Liriodendron tulipifera*), red maple (*A. rubrum*), and sour or black gum (*N. sylvatica*). Understory plants included at least some 63 other species.

The oak–pine association is more difficult to suggest, with members of the latter species seldom being collected by the early naturalists. Willow oak was certainly a major tree in these forests and it was undoubtedly accompanied by loblolly pine (*P. taeda*), scrub pine (*P. virginiana*), and possibly pitch pine (*P. rigida*). A total of 44 other species can be documented or suggested as growing around or under this arboreal overstory. Local edaphic conditions played a large part in selecting for this association over the two previous deciduous associations. In any case, Brown et al. (1986:753) do not see pine as a major arboreal species in native forests. They suggest that its increased presence across the region today is a direct result of the historic clearing of the native hardwood forests as well as plant succession processes in abandoned agricultural fields.

In addition to terrestrial flora, tidal wetland vegetational communities were being formed during the Holocene at the edges of the expanding estuary. Kraft (1977:46–48) has demonstrated that this process was evolutionary in nature: wetlands forming as the transgression began, then becoming inundated themselves, and reforming again at the new margins of the water. Extant wetlands along the edge of the Chesapeake Bay are therefore approximately 2000–3000 years old. Before contact these tidal wetlands covered some 300,000 ha within the region. They provided food and protection to a wide variety of faunal species. Migratory waterfowl traveling the Atlantic Flyway in particular are drawn to these wetlands for winter habitat.

It is important to note the variation within these tidal wetlands across the region. Freshwater wetlands have formed along the more limnetic upper reaches of the Chesapeake Bay, while estuarine wetlands dominate the more saline portions. Within the freshwater wetlands the dominant vegetation consists of various species of sedge (e.g., members of the genera *Scirpus*, *Carex*, and *Eleocharis*) and grass (e.g., members of the genera *Phragmites*, *Panicum*, *Dichanthelium*, *Zizania*, etc.). Cattail (*Typha*) is also conspicuous. In the estuarine wetlands three species of cord-grass (*Spartina cynosu-*

roides, S. alterniflora, and *S. patens*) dominate. Brown et al. (1986:758–761) offer an extensive listing of the various plant species found within each ecosystem.

At the same time, interior wetlands were formed or expanded as the marine transgression began to cause regional water tables to rise into low-lying areas or perch on impermeable sediments. These so-called swamps dot the landscapes of both the Eastern and Western shores. The arboreal overstory dominants in these wetlands vary from cypress (*Taxodium*), to white cedar (*Chamaecyparis thyoides*), to various other mixed deciduous species. Understory species are diverse and varied (see Brown et al. 1986:762–765). These interior wetlands, like their tidal counterparts, are unusually productive habitats and were favored centers of human subsistence activities throughout prehistory.

Last, it is important to mention the subaqueous vegetation of the Chesapeake Bay. These vegetational communities, literally submerged meadows, were established during the Holocene concomitant with estuary formation. While not directly exploited by humans to any great extent, these vegetational communities are vital to the overall health of the estuary. Their presence in the estuary does translate into higher numbers of aquatic fauna that are of direct importance to human habitation of the region. The meadows in areas of higher salinity consist primarily of eelgrass (*Zostera marina*) and widgeon grass (*Ruppia maritima*). In areas of lower salinity the number of species of submerged plants become more plentiful.

Given the history of vegetational change just discussed, it is evident that the Holocene was a period of overall climatic amelioration. As Whitehead (1972:312) has commented, the documented changes in vegetation throughout the Holocene suggest unidirectional climatic amelioration from the cooler and moister conditions of the late Pleistocene to conditions roughly comparable to the present starting approximately 8200 years ago. As outlined in an earlier section of this chapter, techniques have been developed to derive quantitative estimates of past climatic parameters via mathematical analyses of the fossil pollen record. The reconstruction offered by Carbone (1976:104–107) for an area just to the west of the Chesapeake region is briefly discussed below.

Based on that research, changes in atmospheric circulation initially began to disturb the prevailing late Pleistocene climatic regime after about 10,500 years ago. A second dramatic shift in circulation patterns is indicated at around 8700 years ago. Climatic conditions after that time are characterized as relatively warm and humid with temperature eventually continuing to rise, accompanied by increasingly drier conditions. This trend culminated around 4350 years ago. A return to cooler and moister conditions is projected as starting shortly thereafter. Table 3.1 included reconstructed climatic parameters at various times within the Holocene with late Pleistocene and contemporary parameters.

The changes that came to the study area during the Holocene had profound effects on faunal communities. Climate had ameliorated. Marine transgression dismembered the riverine drainage system of the late Pleistocene replacing it with a great estuary. An earlier distinctly boreal forest ecosystem had yielded to subsequent

Holocene forests. The new ecological regime dictated that aquatic species would now be estuarine and terrestrial populations were to consist of temperate species. The paragraphs below discuss the general characteristics of the regional fauna of the Holocene.

Aquatic communities underwent significant changes as the ancestral Susquehanna River was replaced by the new estuary. The exact timing of the concomitant replacement of freshwater aquatic fauna with estuarine species remains largely unknown. In fact, the replacement of one community by the other, in the case of aquatic populations, was almost certainly an extended process rather than a distinct event. There are perhaps two lines of evidence that are currently available to suggest a temporal window for this process. First, the physical establishment of estuarine conditions was an obvious prelude to the complete transformation of aquatic communities. Based on available transgression curves, the ancestral Susquehanna River was not completely transgressed, within the boundaries of the Chesapeake Bay, until about 5000 to 6000 years ago. Second, the presence of the oyster, a prolific and well-preserved member of the estuarine ecosystem, in datable contexts may serve as somewhat of a marker species for the establishment of estuarine conditions. The fact that substantial oyster beds have been dated in the northern third of the estuary to 5000 -6000 years ago may suggest that era as the threshold of an established estuarine aquatic ecosystem.

The establishment of estuarine aquatic communities had important implications for prehistoric subsistence practices. Estuaries, in general, are among the most productive bodies of water on the planet. The potential biomass offered by an estuary is astounding. Modern catch data can be employed to illustrate this fact. The Georges Bank, arguably some of the best fishing ground off the Atlantic coast, today yields slightly less than 3 metric tons of fish per 2.6 km^2 per year. In comparison, the Chesapeake Bay yields about 11 metric tons of fish per 2.6 km^2 per year (Schubel 1981:18). The reasons for this productivity at first appear contradictory.

Estuaries are considered relatively harsh environments for aquatic species. An estuary plays host to constant changes in salinity rates, temperature, suspended sediment, and dissolved oxygen. As a result they are what is termed biologically monotonous; that is, they do not contain the species diversity, in terms of total number of species, that would be found in either a purely freshwater or purely marine ecosystem. Only a limited range of species can tolerate the conditions that estuaries present.

It is a fact, however, that what an estuary lacks in terms of species diversity, it more than makes up for in terms of the sheer population sizes of the species that can tolerate its environment. Aquatic species that can establish themselves in an estuary find that life-sustaining resources are especially abundant. Most of the species that call an estuary home were ultimately of a marine origin. On making the transfer to an estuary these species leave many of their natural predators behind. These two factors allow the limited number of species within an estuary to flourish in often astounding numbers.

In the Chesapeake Bay today, microscopic plankton, including phytoplankton, zooplankton, and bacteria, forms the base of the aquatic community. These organisms float or drift with the water current, but to a certain degree can move up or down in the water to take advantage of the light or to avoid being washed out into the ocean. While these tiny aquatic organisms are not directly exploited by human inhabitants of the region, they do form the base of the food chain for other economically important aquatic species.

Benthic organisms constitute the bottom dwellers of the estuary. Salinity and sedimentation are the two major determinants of the distributions of this aquatic community. Principal members of the group include barnacles, sponges, worms, shrimp, clams, crabs, and oysters. The best-known benthic animals in the Chesapeake Bay are certainly the blue crab and the oyster. These two aquatic species reproduce in large numbers and have been exploited extensively by prehistoric peoples in the region.

The swimmer community consists of approximately 200 different species of fish. This group can be further divided into resident and migratory populations. As the labels imply, some of these species remain permanent residents of the Chesapeake Bay and others leave to reproduce or, conversely, enter the estuary and its tributaries to spawn. The anadromous members of the migratory group appear each spring. These migratory fish, in particular, provided a third abundant and easily exploitable seasonal aquatic source of protein to the prehistoric inhabitants of the study area.

Emerging terrestrial faunal communities generally contained fewer total species when compared to the high species densities characteristic of the late Pleistocene. This reduction of the total number of extant species causes zoologist to regard the Holocene land fauna as depauperate (Martin 1967) or impoverished (Semken 1974) relative to its predecessor. The timing for the transition from the late Pleistocene to the Holocene terrestrial faunal community is considered to have been rather abrupt, occurring between 9500 and 10,000 years ago (Semken 1983:202).

While the new Holocene land fauna was, relative to the previous late Pleistocene fauna, impoverished, it is evident that the population sizes of those species that did remain could rise—a situation where fewer individual species were present but in greater overall numbers. With late Pleistocene megafauna becoming extinct and boreal species returning to more northern latitudes, those temperate species that remained were free to expand their numbers across the recently established Holocene ecosystem.

White-tail deer (*O. virginianus*), wapiti (*Cervus elaphus*), turkey (*Meleagris gallopavo*), and bear (*Ursus americanus*) were standard temperate dominants. Wapiti, or elk, has now been extirpated from this region. These animals were, of course, associated with many other species of small mammals, avifauna, reptiles, and amphibians. Total mammalian fauna includes some approximately 121 different species (Webster, Parnell, and Biggs 1985). About 301 different species and subspecies of birds, including over 37 species of waterfowl, were common to the region (Cooke 1929). The waterfowl travel the Atlantic Flyway in great numbers each year to winter in the study area. These species have traditionally played a large seasonal role in regional human subsistence practices. Approximately 28 species of amphibians (Conant 1945) and 37 species of reptiles (McCauley 1945) roundout the Holocene fauna of the Chesapeake Bay region.

LOOKING FORWARD

As discussed throughout this chapter, the Chesapeake region has seen dramatic changes in both landscape configuration and ecology from the time of first human occupation to the end of prehistory. My portrait of these changes within the context of this chapter has been quite linear; a rather broad record of floral, faunal, and climatic change from the terminal Pleistocene through much of the Holocene has been presented. Such a portrayal, of course, tends to ignore many important specifics, such as the spatial pattern of natural rhythms within ecosystems, matters of seasonality, and the biogeographical distribution of resources across the landscape at any particular point in time.

Hopefully, however, this chapter has created the necessary baseline for an appreciation of the magnitude of the unique transformation that occurred in the region as background to the prehistoric habitation of the study area. With that accomplished, it is now possible to address the more specific questions of human adaptation to the regional natural landscape at selected points in time. Here the perspective will become more oriented to the spatial distribution of resources and questions of these resources' potential human economic importance. These specifics are more appropriately set within the context of the individual chapters that follow pertaining to the major periods of Chesapeake prehistory.

Chapter 4

The Paleoindian Period
Deep Time and the Beginning of Prehistory

INTRODUCTION

The discussion of the earliest populations to inhabit North America is almost guaranteed to stir the emotions of any archaeologist. In the sometimes acrimonious debate over early populations, strong opinions are cast, boundaries are quickly drawn, and the polemics often overshadow the real evidence. It was the early debate over the timing of the human entrance into the New World, in fact, that helped the archaeological record of the Chesapeake region gain its first real identity late in the nineteenth century. Even though archaeology has matured as a discipline, it still reserves a certain fascination for the earliest materials.

Currently, there appear to be two foci of controversy within contemporary archaeology on this matter. First, archaeologists are still actively debating the question of exactly when humans first entered the Americas. One camp sees ample evidence of pre-Paleoindian populations, while adversaries remain skeptical of data presented thus far. Second, although few, if any, archaeologists now question the authenticity of Paleoindians, there is still significant debate over many features of their lifeways. In this chapter I will ignore the controversy over the matter of pre-Paleoindians since there is no known evidence from the Chesapeake region that addresses this problem. Instead, I will focus on reviewing the evidence for the Paleoindian occupation of the region after about 11,000 years ago. I will then discuss what these data might offer in terms of a further understanding of Paleoindian lifeways.

This chapter will be organized along the following lines. I first want to present a general overview of what archaeologists have discovered about Paleoindians in eastern North America. I will then turn to the Paleoindian period within the Chesapeake region. I offer a review of known regional Paleoindian sites followed by a discussion of the distributions of what might be termed the off-site (Binford 1980; Thomas 1975) or isolated Paleoindian artifacts recovered across this same region. This section of the chapter closes with a summary of the various site and off-site data. Third, I will present a new interpretation of all these data, actual sites and off-site isolates, within the Chesapeake region. This will be a story of Paleoindian lifeways within the context of the late Pleistocene ecology of the region.

PALEOINDIAN STUDIES IN EASTERN NORTH AMERICA

The Chesapeake Bay area is but one small part of greater eastern North America. The study area is within the Middle Atlantic region directly between the Northeast and Southeast archaeological regions. To begin to understand Paleoindian lifeways in the study area it is important to appreciate associated archaeological research on this early period in the broader surrounding region.

Data Base

Available data on eastern Paleoindians fall into one of two categories, definable sites and so-called isolated diagnostic projectile point discoveries. Over 50 major archaeological sites in eastern North America are now assigned to the Paleoindian tradition (see Anderson 1990:173; Meltzer 1988:8). Some of these sites have yielded buried Paleoindian assemblages while others are primarily surface manifestations. Many of the buried sites are located in the Northeast, but a number of exciting new, stratified sites have recently been reported from the Southeast (see Anderson, Sassaman, and Judge 1992). In terms of isolated Paleoindian projectile point discoveries, the most comprehensive recent survey puts their number at approximately 11,000 specimens (Anderson 1991:3). This is no doubt a conservative count.

Typology

While the Paleoindian tradition is often discussed as an almost homogeneous entity, there is every indication that it includes a suite of various diagnostic projectile point types. Prehistorians working with Paleoindian materials from the Northeast have long commented on the variability in projectile point styles exhibited at various sites in the region (e.g., see Haynes 1983:25). In the Southeast, however, typological variability has been even more precisely documented. A brief overview of this situation would be useful.

For the Northeast, archaeologists have generally been content to note stylistic differences between the projectile points recovered at various sites. Here the classic Clovis fluted form is often seen as having been modified in both dimension or form. With the chronology of the sites where these various forms have been recovered being rather uniform, observed variation is viewed as more of a functional or geographic phenomenon than a temporal indicator. One exception to this situation is the recovery of a distinctive notched projectile point type at the Shawnee Minisink site in Pennsylvania (see McNett 1985). The projectile was discovered at that site in a discrete stratum above the level yielding a Clovis fluted projectile, but below upper strata containing traditional Early Archaic forms. This notched variety, named the Kline point, dates stratigraphically to about 10,000 years ago. It is at least a first hint of temporally significant typological diversity in the Paleoindian period of the Northeast.

Further to the south, archaeologists recognize a distinctive tripartite sequence of Paleoindian projectile point forms (see Anderson 1990:164–166). The earliest forms are similar to classic western Clovis projectiles. These are large lanceolate bifaces, basally ground with concave bases, and flutes extending about one-third of their total length. A later middle grouping contains a variety of forms, both fluted and unfluted. Included in this grouping are the Cumberland, Simpson, Suwannee, and Quad types. Late portions of the Paleoindian period in the Southeast are dominated by the ubiquitous Dalton type, in both fluted and unfluted varieties.

Chronology

A growing number of Paleoindian sites within eastern North America have been radiocarbon dated. In the following discussion of Paleoindian chronology I will concentrate on such sites well east of the Mississippi River within the general proximity of the Atlantic and Gulf coasts. Some of these Paleoindian sites have yielded rather extensive suites of radiocarbon assays. Often a small number of these reported assays are clearly equivocal, for one reason or another, when compared with other dates from the same site. This is not unexpected given the realities of the radiocarbon dating technique itself and the very early dates of these sites. I generally ignore these aberrant determinations in this discussion. All available assays, however, are cited on tables included with this section.

Within the Northeast, eight dated Paleoindian sites have been reported. From north to south these include the Debert site in Nova Scotia (MacDonald 1968), the Vail site in Maine (Gramly 1982), the Whipple site in New Hampshire (Curran 1984), Bull Brook (Byers 1954, 1955) and Bull Brook II (J. Grimes et al. 1984) in Massachusetts, the Templeton Site in Connecticut (Moeller 1980), Dutchess Quarry Cave in New York (Funk, Fisher, and Reilly 1970), and the Shawnee Minisink site in Pennsylvania (McNett 1985). Radiocarbon assays for each site are listed in Table 4.1. Meltzer (1988:15), in his analysis of these assays, considers the determinations from the Debert, Vail, Whipple, Templeton, and Shawnee Minisink sites to be the most accurate for the Paleoindian tradition in this region. This would generally place the Paleoindian occupation in the Northeast—as typified by sites containing various forms of Clovis-derived projectiles—at about 10,600 to 10,200 years ago.

Radiocarbon assays from Paleoindian sites in the Southeast are sparse, yet, when available, they are very intriguing. A Paleoindian assemblage that includes Clovis projectile points has recently been recovered at the Johnson site on the south bank of the Cumberland River in Tennessee (Borster and Norton 1992). Three radiocarbon assays have now been reported for this site (see Table 4.2). The 11,980 ± 110

Table 4.1. Radiocarbon Assays on Northeastern Paleoindian Sites[a]

RCYBP[b]	Lab number	Comments[c]
Debert, Nova Scotia		
10,466 ± 128	P-743	
10,656 ± 134	P-739	
10,545 ± 126	P-741	
10,641 ± 244	P-967	
10,572 ± 121	P-966	
10,518 ± 120	P-970	
10,467 ± 118	P-970A	
10,773 ± 226	P-971	
10,511 ± 120	P-972	
10,652 ± 114	P-973	
10,837 ± 119	P-974	
11,026 ± 225	P-975	
10,128 ± 275	P-977	
Vail, Maine		
10,300 ± 90	SI-4617	
11,120 ± 180	Beta-1833	
10,500 ± 400	AA-117	AMS
10,600 ± 400	AA-114	AMS
10,550 ± 800	AA-115	AMS
10,040 ± 390	AA-116	AMS
Whipple, New Hampshire		
11,400 ± 360	AA-150C	AMS
10,300 ± 500	AA-150A	AMS
9600 ± 500	AA-149A	AMS, equivocal
9400 ± 500	AA-149A	AMS, equivocal
9700 ± 700	AA-149B	AMS, equivocal
Bull Brook I, Massachusetts		
9300 ± 400	M-807	Equivocal
8720 ± 400	M-808	Equivocal
6940 ± 800	M-809	Equivocal
8940 ± 400	M-810	Equivocal
Bull Brook II, Massachusetts		
8565 ± 284	GX-6279	Equivocal
Templeton, Connecticut		
10,190 ± 300	W-3931	
Dutchess Quarry Cave, New York		
12,580 ± 370	I-4137	Equivocal
Shawnee Minisink, Pennsylvania		
10,590 ± 300	W-2994	
10,750 ± 600	W-3134	
9,310 ± 1000	W-3388	Equivocal
11,050 ± 1000	W-3391	Equivocal

[a]Radiocarbon assays obtained from Curran, 1984; Funk *et al.*, 1970; Gramly, 1982; Grimes *et al.*, 1984; MacDonald, 1968; Meltzer, 1988; Moeller, 1980; and McNett, 1985.
[b]RCYBP, radiocarbon years before present.
[c]AMS, accelerator mass spectrometry used in age determination.

Table 4.2. Radiocarbon Assays
on Southeastern Paleoindian Sites[a]

RCYBP[b]	Lab number	Comments
Clovis		
Johnson, Tennessee		
12,660 ± 970	TX-6999	Equivocal
11,980 ± 110	TX-7454	
11,700 ± 980	TX-7000	Equivocal
Little Salt Spring, Florida		
13,450 ± 190	TX-2335	On tortoise shell
12,030 ± 200	TX-2636	Wooden stake in tortoise
Later Paleoindian		
Rogers Shelter, Missouri		
10,530 ± 650	ISGS-48	Dalton
10,200 ± 300	M-2333	Dalton
Graham Cave, Missouri		
9700 ± 500	M-130	Dalton
9470 ± 400	M-1928	Dalton
9290 ± 300	M 1889	Dalton
Arnold Research Cave, Missouri		
9130 ± 300	M-1197	Dalton
8190 ± 400	M-1496	Dalton
Stanfield-Worley, Alabama[c]		
9640 ± 450	M-1152	Big Sandy & Dalton
9440 ± 400	M-1346	Big Sandy & Dalton
9340 ± 400	M-1347	Big Sandy & Dalton
9040 ± 400	M-1348	Big Sandy & Dalton
8920 ± 400	M-1153	Big Sandy & Dalton
Dust Cave, Alabama		
10,490 ± 360	Beta-40681	Big Sandy
10,330 ± 120	Beta-41063	Big Sandy
Puckett, Tennessee		
9790 ± 160	Beta-48045	Dalton

[a]Radiocarbon assays obtained from Borster & Norton, 1992; Clausen *et al.*,
 1979; Driskell, 1992; and Goodyear, 1982.
[b]RCYBP, radiocarbon years before present.
[c]See comments of Goodyear 1982:385.

(TX-7454) determination, given its small sigma, is considered the most accurate (John Borster, personal communication, 1993). That assay was run on material recovered from a small hearth yielding a Clovis preform and carbonized spruce scales.

The Little Salt Spring site in southwest Florida has produced a similar early date. At this location a now-extinct species of giant land tortoise (*Geochelone crassiscutata*) was apparently dispatched with a wooden stake and cooked in situ. Charring is evident, and fire-hardened clay was discovered in the general vicinity. A radiocarbon assay of 12,030 ± 200 (TX-2636) years ago was obtained from the wooden stake. In isolation such an early determination once appeared perplexing, but it can now be interpreted as in line with the assay just cited from the Johnson site. The episode discussed above at the Little Salt Spring site, however, cannot unequivocally be assigned to the Clovis subtradition in the Southeast given a complete lack of diagnostic stone tools in this component of the site.

Other early radiocarbon dates from the Southeast are attributable to the latter portion of the Paleoindian period (see Table 4.2). Most of these assays were run on components yielding Dalton projectiles. Currently available evidence suggests a temporal range for Dalton of between 10,500 to 9900 years ago (Goodyear 1982:389). The early beginning date for this temporal range is based on the two radiocarbon assays, averaging around 10,500 years ago, on Dalton components reported from the Rogers Shelter in Missouri. Recently, Big Sandy projectile points, another late Paleoindian type, have been recovered at Dust Cave on the north side of the Tennessee River in Alabama (Driskell, 1992). The two radiocarbon assays on this component at Dust Cave average around 10,400 years ago.

In summary, a number of trends can be noted regarding the chronology of the Paleoindian period across all of eastern North America. Based on available evidence, the earliest material is appearing in the Southeast. The predictions made by any number of archaeologists that fluted points in the Southeast may turn out to be surprisingly early appear prophetic based on currently available evidence. Clovis projectiles, albeit from only one dated site in the Southeast, are almost 12,000 years old. This slightly predates comparable Clovis sites even in western North America (Haynes 1987:84). It certainly predates Clovis sites in the Northeast, where similar material is dated 10,600–10,200 years ago. If anything, the later northeastern Clovis material is chronologically more comparable to Folsom in the West and to the later Paleoindian material such as Dalton and related forms in the Southeast.

Site Structure

The corpus of data on Paleoindian site structure within eastern North America is not enormous, but a significant number of sites have been investigated to some degree. Several patterns can now be noted on the structure of such sites within both the northeast and southeast regions.

Site visibility, the nature of the signature of the site in the archaeological record, is a function of a host of factors, both natural and cultural. Everything from geologic processes to long-term (or repeated) versus short-term use of the site by Paleoindians to modern-day land uses (see Lepper 1983, 1985) can be a factor in site visibility. Meltzer (1988:14) has noted the differences in the potential for site creation, preservation, and discovery across eastern North America. Buried sites, for example, seem more prevalent in the Northeast, while many sites in the Southeast appear as surface manifestations. This can be attributed to regionally specific factors such as depositional processes and regional ecological structures and concomitant subsistence patterns.

Data on site infrastructure is admittedly sparse. Even so, some tantalizing glimpses into features of a Paleoindian camp have been reported. It is obvious to everyone that structures must have been a necessary component of most settlements. Although there is not universal acceptance of these data, William Gardner (1983:56) maintains that there is evidence of structures at the Thunderbird site in the Shenandoah Valley of Virginia based on a series of postmolds that he believes are present within the Paleoindian stratum. Richard Gramly and Robert Funk (1990:14) likewise argue for the presence of structural remains at the Adkins site in Maine. These two investigators also claim that they have recovered evidence of small stone structures used by Paleoindians for meat caching.

Paleoindian hearths exhibit a near universal pattern. These features appear to have been what might be better termed descriptively as fire-floors. The informal nature of these fire-floors can be seen as an indication of a highly mobile lifeway. The building of a fire during the late Pleistocene seems to have been an expedient task that left little evidence of formal definition and no evidence of pit excavation or rock lining. This may be one reason why the resulting charcoal is so difficult for archaeologists to recover on such sites. Excavators are left to collect only the small flecks that have been scattered across the site by the forces of nature. If the site was buried, such collection still might be possible. It is probably for this reason that more sites have been dated in the Northeast than in the Southeast, as buried sites in the former region outnumber those in the latter.

Finally, many archaeologists have commented on the discontinuous distributions of artifacts across Paleoindian sites. Artifacts are often recovered at loci or in discrete clusters within site boundaries. As early as 1952, John Witthoft (1971) observed that the distribution of artifacts at the Shoop site in Pennsylvania clustered in 11 loci, each less than 10 m in diameter. Since that time many others have echoed similar conclusions about Paleoindian sites in both the Northeast and Southeast. The only point of contention one can find on this phenomenon relates to meaning. Archaeologists speculate that loci were the result of everything from individual family units occupying particular areas of the site to functionally specific work areas to evidence of reoccupation of the site at various intervals. All explanations are plausible.

Settlement Strategies

For many years prehistorians were content just to discover and excavate a Paleoindian site in eastern North America. If thought was given to larger patterns, it was most often through a rather myopic lens whereby everything else was related back to the favorite Paleoindian site of that particular archaeologist. Ronald J. Mason's 1962 paper, which looked at the total universe of available Paleoindian data for eastern North America, was perhaps the premier early exception to this trend. Following in his footsteps, a few archaeologists are now once again returning to this type of broad synthetic research.

A good example of this reemerging trend can be seen in a recent paper by Meltzer (1988). Through this paper Meltzer draws a distinction between two major late Pleistocene environmental regions within eastern North America, a periglacial tundra or open spruce parkland to the north and the complex boreal–deciduous forest at lower latitudes. These two paleoecological zones are divided by the line of maximum Wisconsin glacial advance, and each area selected for distinct adaptive strategies on the part of Paleoindians.

Meltzer views Paleoindians in the north as having been specialized, highly mobile pursuers of caribou. Repeated use of locations along migration routes resulted in sites that are now more visible being preserved in the archaeological record. Tool kits recovered at these sites are dominated by formal implements including projectile points, scrapers, bifacial knives, and drills. Few utilized flakes are recovered, and tools often were heavily modified and exhausted before discard. Isolated Paleoindian projectile points are not as numerous in the Northeast given this reuse of specific sites and a propensity to use all lithic material to the fullest possible extent.

Meltzer argues that in southern forests below the line of maximum glacial advance Paleoindians assumed the adaptive role of generalists. Here the reuse of locations was less frequent, and fewer visible sites were thereby fossilized within the archaeological record. This has made actual sites in the Southeast less abundant and isolated projectile points more so. The few highly visible sites in this region appear to have been focused around specific sources of lithic materials. Use of lithic material in the Southeast was more indulgent, and expedient tool forms appear frequently in the archaeological record. Many of the so-called fluted projectile points in these assemblages appear to have been used as hafted knives. The conclusions of Meltzer's paper, essentially an exegesis of his dissertation (Meltzer 1984), are buttressed by a broader array of data from across eastern North America than can be discussed herein.

David Anderson (1990) has produced an interesting paper that likewise examines Paleoindian settlement strategies across all of eastern North America. Anderson attacks the problem from a slightly different perspective than Meltzer, focusing less on adaptive strategies and more on the origins as well as the diffusion and subsequent regionalization of the Paleoindian tradition. The first important pattern highlighted by this research is the dense concentrations of Early Paleoindian projectile points (Clovis) in the central Ohio, lower Cumberland, and central Tennessee river valleys. These areas are projected as major early points of entry for Paleoindians into the eastern Woodlands. Such a view fits well with the early radiocarbon assays now beginning to appear from Southeastern sites.

As populations in these initial staging areas expanded, Anderson contends, group fissioning launched splinter groups into new areas. This is projected to have begun after 11,000 years ago during what is known in the Southeast as the Middle Paleoindian subperiod. Eventually the entirety of eastern North America was populated from this Southeastern river valley heartland. After colonization of most of the eastern Woodlands was complete, regional diversity in tool forms began to incubate as groups adapted to specific areas. For example, after 10,800 BP, in the Southeast lanceolate forms gave way to notched Dalton types, and in the Northeast modifications were made to the original classic fluted point. Again, available radiocarbon assays can support such a perspective.

The two papers briefly examined above (Anderson 1990; Meltzer 1988) are good examples of the recent attempts to look at Paleoindians across all of eastern North America. Both efforts are especially laudable for their attempts to escape the parochialism of views that see the Paleoindian tradition from the perspective of only one particular site or a few sites within a restricted area. While the conclusions reached in the two papers are, of course, not immune to challenges or future modifications, both pieces of research are particularly valuable for their suggestions of readily testable expectations for Paleoindian data in specific areas of the broader region.

Subsistence Practices

Watching Paleoindian artifacts being recovered at site after site in western North America in direct association with late Pleistocene megafaunal remains has had a definite effect on prehistorians working on the opposite shore of the Mississippi River. Yet similar associations in eastern North America, at least between Paleoindians and extinct proboscideans, remain at best equivocal. This has led archaeologists into subscribing to one of three positions. One camp, adhering to the belief that "absence of evidence is not evidence of absence," still seeks to lump all Paleoindians into a pancontinental big-game hunting tradition (e.g., see Dragoo 1976; Funk 1978; Stoltman 1978). Following Mason (1981:98) they view the onetime connection between Paleoindians and megafauna in the East as ultimately having been more than platonic. Another group of archaeologists takes a wait-and-see attitude. One such prehistorian, writing in apparent frustration several years ago, suggested that the hard evidence indicated that eastern Paleoindians "ate nothing and lived primarily as isolated individuals" (Brose 1978:729). A third position, seemingly gaining in strength, appears open to projecting a more diverse subsistence base for eastern Paleoindians (e.g., see Dent 1985; Dincauze 1981; Meltzer 1988). I want to look at what archaeology has discovered, in both faunal and floral remains, to support this latter position.

Unequivocal linkages between Paleoindians and late Pleistocene proboscideans east of the Mississippi River remain elusive. Within the Southeast, in Florida, James Dunbar and Benjamin Waller (1992) claim to have documented ivory foreshafts in submerged contexts that suggest an affinity to other Paleoindian artifacts. Every so often other indirect evidence is advanced to make a linkage between eastern Paleoindians and, usually, mastodon, but none has really passed muster (see Meltzer 1988:22–24). In point of fact, the nearest unquestioned *direct* association between a Paleoindian tool assemblage (Clovis) and megafauna (mastodon) is found at the Kimmswick site in Missouri just west of the Mississippi River (Graham et al. 1981).

Direct association, however, has been established between Paleoindians and nonproboscidean faunal remains at three Southeastern sites. The giant tortoise dispatched with a wooden stake at the Little Salt Spring site in Florida has already been mentioned. At the Wacissa River site, again in Florida, the very tip of a projectile point of an unidentifiable type was found embedded in the skull of an extinct species of bison (*Bison antiquus*). This bison cranium was radiocarbon assayed to 9990 ± 200 (Beta-5941) years ago (Webb et al. 1984:390). Both aquatic and terrestrial shell and bone along with fish scales have very recently been recovered at Dust Cave in Alabama (Driskell 1992). While the taxonomic identification of this faunal material is in progress, two radiocarbon assays are available on the component and date it to about 10,400 years ago. This site may prove to be one of the more remarkable recent discoveries.

Faunal remains at Paleoindian sites in the Northeast have likewise been reported. The association of Paleoindian artifacts with caribou has long been debated at Dutchess Quarry Cave in New York. General consensus appears to question this association. More recently, however, caribou have been identified in the faunal remains from Bull Brook (Spiess 1984:280) and at the Whipple site (Curran 1984:13; Spiess 1984:280). Caribou bone from both these New England sites are assigned to the species *Rangifer tarandus* (Spiess, Curran, and Grimes 1985:147). Beaver (*Castor canadensis*) has also been identified within the Bull Brook faunal assemblage. Calcined bone of caribou (*Rangifer tarandus groenlandicus*), hare (*Lepus* sp.), and arctic fox (*Alopex lagopus*) has recently been recovered within a good context at the Udora site in southern Ontario (Storck and Spiess 1994:126–128). At the Shawnee Minisink site in Pennsylvania, charred fish bone (species unidentifiable) has been recovered from a hearth in direct association with Paleoindian artifacts. The hearth itself yielded a radiocarbon assay of 10,590 ± 300 (W-2994) years ago.

Floral remains from Paleoindian sites in eastern North America are unfortunately still scarce. Scarcity of these remains is as much a matter of archaeologists failing to consistently employ adequate recovery techniques as it is attributable to a generally poor preservation environment (Dent and Kauffman 1985). From the same hearth just discussed above at Shawnee Minisink, the carbonized remains of acalypha (*Acalypha virginicus*), blackberry (*Rubus* sp.), chenopod (*Chenopodium* sp.), hawthorn plum (*Crataegus* sp.), hackberry (*Celtis* sp.), and wild grape (*Vitis* sp.) have been recovered. Most recently, at Dust Cave in Alabama, another set of floral remains has been reported from a Paleoindian site (Driskell 1992:278). These remains include charred hickory nut shell, walnut, wild grape, and chenopod. Precise taxonomic identification is in progress. The two radiocarbon assays on this floral material from Dust Cave average around 10,400 years ago, making its occupation very close in time to Shawnee Minisink. Both sites demonstrate that Paleoindians were foragers of plant material and that archaeologists can collect these materials with appropriate recovery techniques. Intensive use of flotation at both sites is responsible for the recovery of these floral remains.

Based on the data discussed above, it is difficult to link eastern Paleoindians to subsistence practices based on the pursuit of late Pleistocene proboscideans. A different and more diverse subsistence base is indicated. There is even reason to believe that archaeology may eventually be able to differentiate Paleoindian economic systems unique to various regions within broader eastern North America. As Meltzer

(1988:43) comments, the traditional notion that Paleoindian subsistence "was uniform throughout the continent is ecologically improbable and cannot withstand close empirical scrutiny."

CHESAPEAKE PALEOINDIANS: THE UNIVERSE OF DATA

It is now appropriate to focus on the Paleoindian period within the Chesapeake region itself. This section of the chapter is largely descriptive and draws together a diverse array of data on the period. First, I examine what can reasonably be seen as actual Paleoindian sites reported from the study area. All of these sites yield discrete, bounded concentrations of artifacts including diagnostic Paleoindian types. In two cases, because of their size and/or geographic proximity, I have chosen to lump together a group of sites into what has been labeled a complex. Second, I want to discuss what has been discovered about the nature and distribution of off-site or isolated Paleoindian artifacts scattered about the region. Finally, a discussion of patterning evident in the combined site and off-site data closes this section. It is important to remain cognizant of both what archaeology has discovered as well as how much it has yet to discover about the Paleoindian period of the Chesapeake region.

Paleoindian Sites

There are at present a total of 25 known Paleoindian sites from the Chesapeake region; seven of these sites are combined into one larger complex and four form another such complex. Almost all of these sites, as single entities or complexes, appear as surface manifestations, although a number may eventually prove to have buried components. Definite exceptions include the buried Paleoindian components recently discovered at the Higgins and Paw Paw Cove sites in Maryland as well as a few partially buried components on Virginia sites. Figure 4.1 maps the locations of these sites and the two complexes. In brief synopses of each below, I describe the circumstances of discovery, report on artifacts recovered, discuss site context in terms of local environment and possible relationship to other nearby sites, and make note of any unique features. Samples of artifacts from some of the larger sites are illustrated with photographs. The discussion below first concentrates on the inner Coastal Plain area of Virginia, turns next to the outer Coastal Plain of Virginia, and then moves to the more northern sites in both Maryland and Virginia.

Williamson

The Williamson site represents the most extensive Paleoindian site located within the study area, and it is one of the major such sites thus far identified in eastern North America. This site was first reported in 1949, and a summary article was subsequently published in *American Antiquity* by the site's founder and long-time

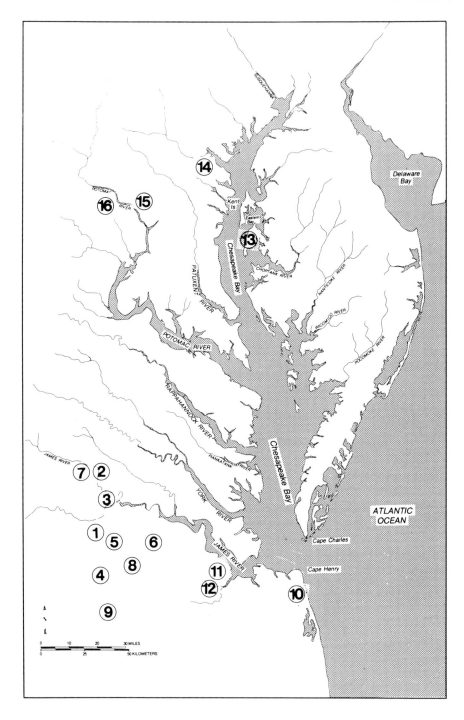

advocate, Ben McCary (1951). Since this early report, many other articles have been published on various aspects of this important site. Much of this literature has been reissued in a compendium (Peck 1985). Joseph McAvoy (1992) has also published a short reanalysis of the site in his study of Clovis settlement patterns. The Williamson site and the massive artifact collection it has yielded will no doubt continue to stimulate research for years to come. This site's importance is only mitigated by the tragic fact that most of the artifacts it has yielded have been collected by a variety of people over the years in a completely unsystematic fashion.

It is estimated that the Williamson site has produced approximately 175 fluted bifaces and over 2000 end- and side-scrapers (McCary 1983:43). Errett Callahan (1979) includes a detailed analysis of many of the bifaces from the site in his monograph on the Eastern fluted point tradition, and McCary (1983) has added a description of both bifacial and unifacial tool assemblages from the site. The overall assemblage includes fluted bifaces, cores (in various forms), preforms, knives, drills, gouges, wedges, end-scrapers (both spurred and nonspurred), side-scrapers, spoke-shaves, gravers, perforators, denticulates, beaks, hammerstones, and anvils. McAvoy (1992:45–47) makes an argument that chisel-wedges, or *pieces esquillees*, are prolific on the site. Much of the lithic material employed at the site is locally known as Cattail Creek chalcedony, technically a chert.

Given the apparent artifact densities at the site, the Williamson site was probably occupied on repeated occasions by Paleoindians. The discontinuous nature of artifact concentrations across the site is frequently mentioned in the literature. Some of these clusters appear to yield functionally specific tool types, and others consist of discards (McAvoy 1992:45). A nearby source of chert as well as potable water were probably important elements in the selection of this location. The site's location in an ecotonal setting near the western edge of the Virginia inner Coastal Plain may have influenced settlement choice. Unobstructed southern exposure and topographic protection from winter winds appear to have been additional attractive factors of this site (McAvoy 1992:48). Major known artifact collections from the site are in the possession of McCary, McAvoy, and the College of William and Mary, Department of Anthropology. A sample of artifacts from the latter collection is illustrated in Figure 4.2.

Richmond

The Richmond site, reported by Edward Bottoms (1966, 1972), is located along the James River in Virginia. This site, like the Williamson site, is near the western margins of the inner Coastal Plain. The site has yielded both Paleoindian as well as

---

Figure 4.1. Nominal locations of Chesapeake Paleoindian sites and complexes. Numbers indicate the following sites: 1, Williamson; 2, Richmond; 3, Point-of-Rocks; 4, Petrified Wood; 5, Conover; 6, Carpenter; 7, Marine Spring Branch; 8, Nottoway River Complex; 9, Meherrin River Complex; 10, Quail Springs; 11, Isle-of-Wight; 12, Dime; 13, Paw Paw Cove; 14, Higgins; 15, Pierpoint; 16, Catoctin Creek.

Figure 4.2. Sample of artifacts from the Williamson site in Virginia. Artifacts illustrated include a variety of fluted bifaces of different materials, end- and side-scrapers, utilized flakes, generalized bifaces, wedges, and various perforators or drills. Courtesy of Ted Reinhart and Norman Barka, the College of William and Mary, Department of Anthropology.

Archaic components, and artifacts are reported as scattered over approximately 1.5 ha. Nearby springs and streams as well as locally available lithic material may have been principal factors in site location.

At present, 25 fluted bifaces have been recovered from this site (Bottoms 1972:119). In addition to these artifacts, 26 other Paleoindian tools are reported. These include end-scrapers (both spurred and nonspurred), side-scrapers, drills, perforators, gravers, and knives. Artifacts from the site, including the fluted bifaces, were manufactured from a number of lithic materials. Quartz and quartzite, both of which are locally available in cobble form, were utilized in about 42% of the fluted bifaces. Silicified wood and silicified slate were also used. In fact, chert was employed in only 7% of the fluted bifaces. As a postscript, it is the collector's opinion that the recovered artifacts represent only a small fraction of the site's total number.

Point-of-Rocks

The Point-of-Rocks site is located on the inner Coastal Plain along a swampy area of the Appomattox River in Virginia. It has been surface collected for a number of years and was reported by McAvoy (1965, 1979). Unlike many of the Paleoindian sites within the Chesapeake region it appears to represent a single-component occupation. McAvoy (1979:98–100) reports the recovery of fluted bifaces, preforms, cores, end-scrapers, side-scrapers, knives, spokeshaves, gravers, and an awl, as well as a denticulate. A wide variety of lithic materials were used, and tool rejuvenation as well as reuse of debitage is evident.

It should be noted that the site's five fluted bifaces are fragmented and that the one additional complete specimen appears to be heavily reworked. Fluting on all the bifaces is notably minimal. Based on this feature, McAvoy (1979, 1992) views the bifaces as distinctive enough to include them in a new classification that he refers to as the Appomattox River type. He suggests that this type occurs late in the Paleoindian sequence, around 10,400 years ago, and may be the local equivalent of the Dalton type (McAvoy 1992:140). The latter type, while prevalent over much of the Southeast, is relatively rare in the Chesapeake region.

Petrified Wood

Little has been published on the Petrified Wood site located on the inner Coastal Plain in Virginia. According to Bottoms (1972) the site is situated on a high ridge near a wetland area. This pattern of site location is duplicated at many Virginia Paleoindian sites within the interior region. The site has yielded five fluted bifaces and a larger number of end-scrapers as well as one side-scraper and two spokeshaves. There appears to have been a parsimonious use of raw materials at this site, and Bottoms (1972:129) remarks that all the artifacts made of silicified wood appear to have been struck from a single core. Little else can be said about this site at this point in time.

Conover

The Conover site is a multicomponent Paleoindian and Archaic site discovered on the property of Harold Conover. Conover and his friend Melvin Lilley made the first collections from the site. This site is again on the inner Coastal Plain of Virginia 11.2 km from the Williamson site. Subsequent surface collection has been undertaken by the Virginia Department of Historic Resources. E. R. Turner (1983), of that state agency, has published a report on the site, as has McAvoy (1992). Limited test excavations appear to have established that the site is strictly a surface manifestation.

Over 1,100 artifacts, both formal tools and debitage, have been recovered from the Conover site. In addition to nine fluted bifaces and preforms, the assemblage includes end-scrapers, side-scrapers, gravers, awls, modified flakes, perforators, chisel-wedges, generalized bifaces, and cores (McAvoy 1992:107). Much of the raw material used is similar to the chert recovered from the nearby Williamson site. Tool production and maintenance was apparently taking place at the Conover site. Four distinct clusters of material each about 18 m apart were recovered within an area approximately 150 m in diameter. The site is situated on elevated ground above two small tributaries of the Nottoway River and has the typical southern exposure noted for some of the previous sites.

Carpenter

The Carpenter site is near the Blackwater River on the inner Coastal Plain of Virginia. All that is known about the site can be credited to the efforts of McAvoy (1992:75). This apparently small site covers an area of about 180 m². While the known artifact assemblage is minimal at this point, two extensively reworked fluted bifaces have been recovered along with a perforator, some end- and side-scrapers, utilized flakes, and cores. Artifacts were manufactured from both chert and quartzite. The Paleoindian occupation of this site may be due to a nearby springhead and the not-too-distant wetland areas along the Blackwater River. Again, the site possesses an unobstructed southern exposure and a ridge to the northwest that may have served as a windbreak.

Marine Spring Branch

The recovery of 102 Paleoindian tools, including numerous fluted bifaces, has been reported by Wilson Crook (1992) at this site on the inner Coastal Plain below the James River. Clovis, Dalton, and what appear to be Appomattox types appear in the assemblage from this site. Other artifacts include scrapers (types unspecified), knives, gravers, drills, hammerstones, and a grinding stone. The site appears not to have yielded utilized flakes, but they may have been lumped by the author into the scraper category. Approximately 77% of the tools recovered at the site, some apparently from a buried context, were manufactured from quartz or quartzite (Crook 1992:127). This site, another exciting recent discovery, is located near a small tributary of the James River.

Nottoway River Complex

The discovery and publication of the Nottoway River Paleoindian sites can be attributed to the efforts of McAvoy (1992). His research on the Paleoindian period should serve as a model for all archaeologists. Between 1980 and 1992, he and his family along with ASV members surveyed adjacent areas along about 64 km of the Nottoway River. This river is a tributary of the Chowan River, which feeds Albemarle Sound. Most of the survey area is on the inner Coastal Plain, but part of it extends up into the Piedmont. During the survey seven Paleoindian sites were recorded and four of these were tested further through excavation. Six of these sites are located on the floodplain of the Nottoway River below the fall line, and one additional site is above that division (McAvoy 1992:72). Another site that McAvoy believes to contain a Paleoindian component, the Harris Creek site, is not included within the complex as defined herein because no fluted bifaces have as yet been recovered from it. By definition, I have more cautiously chosen to include only sites that have yielded such artifacts.

Paleoindian sites recorded through the survey include the Baskerville, Ridge, Fannin, Slade North, Sunflower, Hill Farm, and Hollowell sites. In the publication resulting from this survey, McAvoy (1992:75–100) offers complete descriptions of each site. All of the sites mentioned above have yielded fluted bifaces and examples of the typical associated Paleoindian assemblage, along with artifacts from subsequent periods of prehistory. It should be noted that the Paleoindian artifacts were collected from discrete areas of concentration on most of these sites. The tools were manufactured from locally available cherts and a variety of other lithic materials. Each site is situated near at least one spring, and many are located on elevated terraces or ridges overlooking wetland areas. The locations of four of the seven sites offer at least some protection from the elements, but three are situated so that inhabitants would have been completely exposed. McAvoy (1992:152) believes this exposure may be indicative of a summer occupation of those sites.

Meherrin River Complex

The Meherrin River Complex consists of four sites, the largest of which is the Greensville County site. All four sites are located on the inner Coastal Plain of Virginia. Published reports on this complex emanate from McAvoy's (1992) research on Paleoindian settlement patterns.

A local collector, J. H. Boney, discovered the Greensville County site in 1981. McAvoy (1992:117) views the site as one of the most significant recent discoveries on the Paleoindian period in the lower Chesapeake region. The site is situated on a sandy terrace with good southern exposure, adjacent to a wetland area just south of the Meherrin River. Nine fluted bifaces along with over 100 end-scrapers have been recovered to date. These are accompanied by preforms, generalized bifaces, side-scrapers, awls, spokeshaves, gravers, cores, utilized flakes, and debitage (see McAvoy 1992:124). The artifacts were collected from seven distinct loci within a linear distance of about 180 m. The site is certainly one of the larger Paleoindian sites in this part of the Chesapeake, and McAvoy (1992:139) feels that it might represent a single occupation by a number of individuals drawn to the wetland area for the purpose of hunting.

The three smaller sites, the Otterdam Swamp, Three Creek, and Meherrin River sites, may be related to the more substantial site discussed above. All of these sites have produced fluted bifaces accompanied by small amounts of other tool types. All are located a short distance to the north of the Greensville County site, on the opposite shore of the Meherrin River. A fifth site, the Brunswick Quarry Site, may have been one source of chert for the occupants of these sites. I am reluctant to formally include it in this complex, however, because it has apparently not as yet yielded any fluted bifaces.

Quail Springs

The Quail Springs site, unlike the sites above, is located on the outer Coastal Plain. It is the easternmost Paleoindian manifestation in Virginia yet discovered. This site was first reported by J. G. Pritchard (1964), and since that time others have published details on the site (McAvoy 1968, 1979, 1992; McCary 1983). The site contains components from all periods of Chesapeake prehistory.

Paleoindian artifacts were isolated on the basis of raw material and tool morphology. McAvoy (1968:62) reports three fluted bifaces from the site, two of these manufactured from quartzite and one of chalcedony. Other artifacts include preforms, drills, awls, gravers, knives, side-scrapers, end-scrapers (spurred and nonspurred), denticulates, utilized flakes, and cores. The overall assemblage includes about 60 tools.

Isle-of-Wight

The Isle-of-Wight site is another small Paleoindian site located on the outer Coastal Plain of Virginia. Site location is on a small rise adjacent to a swampy tributary of the Blackwater River. R. M. Peck (1969) published the first report on this site, and McCary (1983) has provided some additional details.

To date, some 23 fluted bifaces manufactured of quartzite, quartz, chert, and silicified slate have been recovered. Over 100 additional tools accompany these implements. These include end-scrapers (spurred and nonspurred), side-scrapers, gravers, knives, and spokeshaves. The numbers of artifacts suggest that the site may be rather extensive. Peck (1969:9), noting a good deal of variation within the fluted bifaces, suggests multiple occupations of the site.

Dime

The Dime site is located along the Nansemond River on the edge of the Dismal Swamp. It is the third site that has been located on the outer Coastal Plain of Virginia. All reports on the site have been published by Bottoms (1964, 1974, 1985). The site appears to be relatively extensive, and there is some indication that a sealed component may be present.

In Bottoms's most comprehensive report (1974) he refers to the site as a two-stage Paleoindian site. The initial stage includes Clovis fluted bifaces and other associated tool types. A later component is similar, but the bifaces are only minimally fluted and appear similar to the Appomattox types reported by McAvoy (1992). However they are classified, a large number of fluted bifaces have been reported from this site.

Paw Paw Cove

Moving to the upper Chesapeake, Darrin Lowery (1989, 1990) has recently reported on the Paw Paw Cove Paleoindian site. This site is now located directly on the Chesapeake Bay and is the only reported Paleoindian site on the Eastern Shore of the estuary. In view of the documented marine regression, during the late Pleistocene the site would have been in a more upland setting at the headwaters of two small tributaries that emptied directly into the ancestral Susquehanna River (Lowery 1990:29).

Over a number of years a total of 14 fluted bifaces have been recovered by Lowery at the site. Preforms, gravers, end-scrapers, side-scrapers, utilized flakes, cobble tools, denticulates, *pieces esquillees*, spokeshaves, perforators, knives, cores, and some debitage have also been recovered (see Figure 4.3). Both high-grade chert and other materials such as quartz and quartzite were utilized to manufacture the assemblage. Even small, locally available cobbles were used by the site's inhabitants. Lowery (1989:161) makes special note of the high degree of utilization and curation evident in the tool kit. All artifacts were collected from three distinct localities along about 450 m of shoreline. Many of these artifacts are precipitates of the erosion process, but further excavations have now revealed sealed deposits situated back from the strandline (Lowery 1990).

Higgins

The Higgins site was discovered during mitigation activities by the Maryland Geological Survey, Division of Archaeology, under the direction of Carol Ebright (1992). This site is located on the inner Coastal Plain of the Western Shore. It contains one of the few completely buried Paleoindian components yet reported for the Chesapeake region. Paleoindian artifacts were recovered in a stratified context below temporally later layers. These artifacts were distributed across approximately a 14-m^2

Figure 4.3. Sample of artifacts from the Paw Paw Cove Paleoindian site on the Eastern Shore of Maryland. Artifacts illustrated include fluted bifaces, a generalized biface, a small core, utilized flake tools, end-scrapers, side-scrapers, a *pieces esquillees*, and flakes from bifaces. Courtesy of Darrin Lowery.

area. Three basal fragments of two quartz fluted projectile points were recovered (Ebright 1992:235). Of the 26 chipped-stone tools recovered, 16 of the associated bifaces, scrapers, gravers, and retouched flakes were manufactured from chert (Ebright 1992:240). Unfortunately, no charcoal was preserved for dating purposes. Ebright (1992:255) believes Higgins was a small, short-term site where game was processed near a small nearby stream.

Pierpoint

The Pierpoint site is located along the Potomac River at its confluence with Seneca Creek on the Maryland shore. This location is just above the fall line of the Potomac River. The site has been surface collected for a number of years and has yielded three fluted bifaces and an associated assemblage of typical Paleoindian tool forms. Its assemblage, now in collections kept by the Maryland State Highway Administration, was manufactured from a number of diverse materials. Tool forms show heavy usage. A formal report on the material is being prepared by Richard Ervin, but it is not yet available.

Catoctin Creek

The Catoctin Creek site is located on a small peninsula of land along the Virginia bank of the Potomac River near the mouth of one of its tributaries, Catoctin Creek. Upstream from the Pierpoint site, this location is on a second terrace formation above the floodplains of both streams. I have recently published two reports on this site (Dent 1991, 1993). The site was originally investigated by the Potomac River Archaeology Survey in the early 1970s.

Major portions of two fluted bifaces were recovered from the site along with spokeshaves, generalized bifaces, a backed knife, end-scrapers, side-scrapers, utilized flakes, cores (tabular, polyhedral, and discoidal), cobble tools, and hammerstones. These tools and an enormous amount of debitage were all collected by exact provenience. The predominant lithic material was locally available jasper (chert), with only small amounts of another gray chert appearing in the assemblage. This latter material was acquired at some as yet unknown source. It is evident that tool manufacturing was taking place at the site. The recovery of cores, cobbles of raw material, large quantities of primary flakes, a number of bifaces in the process of being reduced, and hammerstones supports this conclusion. It is very apparent that many of the formal tools recovered were discards at the end of their usable life as implements. This again can be seen as evidence of the site's function as a place for, among other things, tool manufacturing. Some of the raw material and tools also appear to have been thermally altered. Figure 4.4 illustrates a sample of the artifacts recovered at the Catoctin Creek site.

Off-Site Paleoindian Artifacts

Archaeologists are most content when they can discover and discuss archaeological sites. The site, as David Hurst Thomas (1989:246) remarks, is for the most part the smallest unit of space dealt with by archaeologists and remains the discipline's primary existential unit. And indeed, I have gone to considerable lengths to produce the previous descriptions of the known Paleoindian sites within the Chesapeake region. It is not my intention to diminish the importance of such site-related data. Nevertheless, it is a mistake to conclude that archaeological sites per se are necessarily the smallest unit worthy of our consideration (Thomas 1975:62). I therefore do want to discuss another very important element of the universe of data on the Paleoindian period of the study area—what I refer to as off-site data.

The overwhelming majority of the artifacts that constitute this off-site data base are the fluted bifaces recovered in isolation across the study area. Given the context of their discovery, these fluted bifaces are traditionally referred to as isolates. In my opinion, however, that label may be somewhat of a misnomer. Calling them isolates effectively diminishes their analytical usefulness relative to actual sites; it becomes somewhat of a discriminatory label. In the end, many see these so-called isolates as artifacts that offer little information beyond standing as examples of a particular

Figure 4.4. Sample of artifacts from the Catoctin Creek site on the Potomac River in Virginia. Artifacts illustrated include two fragments of fluted bifaces, generalized bifaces, a backed knife, spokeshaves, combination end-/side-scrapers, and end-scrapers. All objects shown were manufactured from jasper with the exception of one gray chert end-scraper.

technology. Instead, I see these artifacts as analytically important and as one of the keys to understanding the Paleoindian period in the Chesapeake region.

Over the years a variety of people and organizations have reported finds of off-site Paleoindian artifacts across the Chesapeake region. Certainly the longest-term effort to record these artifacts can be attributed to McCary. Starting in 1947, McCary began to record and publish all fluted bifaces reported to him from the state of Virginia. By 1990, when he was no longer personally able to continue this activity, McCary had published information on 845 individual specimens. The survey is now continued for the ASV under the direction of Michael Johnson, Fairfax County Archaeologist. At the time of writing, 920 fluted bifaces have been recorded under what has now become known as the Dr. Ben McCary Virginia Fluted Point Survey.

For the state of Maryland, M. D. Dilks and G. M. Reynolds (1965) published an early survey of fluted bifaces. With the establishment of the Division of Archaeology at the Maryland Geological Survey in 1968, this cumulative record was formalized and continued. Lois Brown (1979) maintained that catalogue for a number of years, and the task is now under the direction of Richard Ervin, Archaeologist with the State

Highway Administration. A total of 106 fluted bifaces have now been reported from Maryland. For Delaware, Ron Thomas (1966) published the first comprehensive overview of the Paleoindian period in that state. A fluted biface data file is currently maintained at Delaware's Island Field Museum. As of the last published report there were 52 specimens recorded from that state (Custer 1984:17–18). Records at the Smithsonian Institution are the only source of information on Paleoindian material from the District of Columbia. Several bifaces, a Dalton and two unfluted specimens, have been reported from that location (Dennis Stanford, personal communication, 1994). These data from Virginia, Maryland, and Delaware are most often provenienced at the county level and contain other miscellaneous metric information and commentary.

In considering the magnitude of these off-site data, I will restrict my discussion to just those artifacts recovered on the Maryland–Virginia Coastal Plain of the Chesapeake Bay, the focus of this study. By political unit, these data break down as follows. A total of 159 fluted bifaces have been reported on the Coastal Plain of Virginia, on both its Western and Eastern shores. In Maryland, 58 fluted bifaces are recorded from the Coastal Plain, again on both shores. Together, as best as I can determine, a total of 217 fluted bifaces have now been reported from the entire Coastal Plain surrounding the Chesapeake Bay. Table 4.3 tabulates these artifacts for the entire study area based on a less geopolitical division of the Coastal Plain. It will be important to return to a consideration of the meaning of these off-site data when an interpretation of the Paleoindian period within the study area is offered later in this chapter.

Data Patterning

The previous two subsections of this portion of the chapter have described the 25 known Paleoindian sites within the study area as well as reported off-site data. My goal now is to look at the patterning that might be evident in that data. In this regard, interesting patterns are evident in the distributions of sites and off-site artifacts within

Table 4.3. Paleoindian Isolate Densities in Chesapeake Region

Subregion or shore	Reported bifaces	Land area (km²)	Bifaces/km²[a]
Subregion[b]			
Southern: below James River	127	10,936	1:86
Midregion: James River to Potomac River	32	16,814	1:525
Northern: above Potomac River	58	16,710	1:288
Western	177	35,162	1:199
Eastern	40	9,298	1:232

[a]The number of Paleoindian bifaces per square kilometer in each subregion or shore is calculated as an even distribution across landscape for the purposes of illustration.
[b]The three subregions include relevant areas of land on both shores of Chesapeake Bay.

the region, in aspects of site structure, and in the characteristics of the lithic industries recovered at sites and nonsites. Finally, I will offer a few additional comments about chronology and subsistence systems. All of these patterns will form the armature for my interpretations of Paleoindian lifeways presented in the next section of this chapter.

Distribution of Sites

The distribution of definable Paleoindian sites across the Chesapeake region is by no means even (see Figure 4.1). Of the 25 known sites, 21 are located in the southern area of the region below the James River. These include the Richmond, Point-of-Rocks, Petrified Wood, Williamson, Conover, Carpenter, Marine Spring Branch, Nottoway River Complex (seven individual sites), Meherrin River Complex (four individual sites), Dime, Isle-of-Wight, and Quail sites. The distribution of these sites below the James River can be further subdivided into those on the inner Coastal Plain (n = 18) versus those on the outer Coastal Plain (n = 3). The Dime, Isle-of-Wight, and Quail sites fall into this latter location.

The next cluster of Paleoindian sites, a total of four individual sites, is located in the more northern reaches of the Chesapeake Bay, on or above the Potomac River. These include the Catoctin Creek, Pierpoint, Higgins, and Paw Paw Cove sites. Catoctin Creek and Pierpoint are located on the Potomac River just above the fall line. The Higgins site is on the inner Coastal Plain of the Western Shore, and the Paw Paw Cove site is the lone reported Paleoindian site from the Eastern Shore of the Chesapeake Bay.

Looking at all these data together, reported sites cluster in both the more southern (below the James River) and more northern (above the Potomac River) areas of the Chesapeake region. Paleoindian sites in the middle latitudes of the study area have not as yet been reported. A critical observer might wonder if this pattern is more apparent than real. The complete answer to such a question is unknown at this time, but some commentary can be offered on the matter.

To begin, Paleoindian sites are certainly prevalent below the James River in the southern portions of the study area. This situation is the result of at least three general factors. First, an active cadre of archaeologists, both amateur and professional, have completed extensive site surveys in that region. Their specific interest has often been the location of Paleoindian sites and artifacts. Second, much of the land below the James River remains free of development and is still in cultivation. As a consequence, site visibility is generally very high relative to other portions of the study area. Third, there is some indication that sedimentation processes are not as active in this area and that fewer sites may therefore have been deeply buried.

A variety of factors, including luck, relate to the location of the four sites in the northern reaches of the Chesapeake Bay. Archaeologists were able to discover the Catoctin Creek and Pierpoint sites given their locations at significant elevations above the Potomac River and due to adequate surface collecting conditions. Paw Paw Cove was found when shoreline erosion exposed artifacts near the home of one archaeologist. Paleoindian material at the Higgins site was discovered buried beneath later components through CRM activities.

On the whole, I have no doubt that there are many more Paleoindian sites yet to be found in the Chesapeake region. At the same time, however, I would not be surprised if the basic patterning noted above remains valid. Paleoindian sites are prolific below the James River and even more will be discovered. There may be an ecological reason (to be discussed in the next section of this chapter) for such sites being numerous in this area. The absence of similar sites above the James River but south of the Potomac River is curious, but it may reflect the reality of Paleoindian settlement choices. As Turner has noted:

> The sharp drop in presumed Paleoindian occupation . . . north of the James River in Virginia is not likely to be merely a result of various forms of collector or survey biases, but rather should have some basis in a combination of sociocultural and environmental factors not yet fully identified. (1983:115)

In short, the perceived absence of Paleoindian sites in the middle latitudes of the region may be real.

I believe that additional sites will also eventually be discovered in the northern portion of the study area. I strongly suspect that a significant number of other sites will soon be located on the Eastern Shore. At the same time, the sites we have already located in this area, situated as they are from the fall line to the Coastal Plain, likely represent an adequate sample of the total universe of such sites. Until additional sites are located, therefore, it appears reasonable to base conclusions on the existing sample.

For the southern, central, and northern portions of the study area, it is certainly safe to assume that many Paleoindian sites along the course of the ancestral Susquehanna River and on the banks of its lower tributaries are now underwater. Post-Pleistocene marine transgression has removed them from view, and the further development of underwater archaeology is the only hope for learning about these sites. This is a matter for the future.

Distribution of Off-Site Artifacts

These data, as discussed previously, consist of isolated fluted bifaces recorded at various locations across the study area. A total of 217 such fluted bifaces have now been reported from the Coastal Plain surrounding the Chesapeake Bay. And while the number of these artifacts continues to grow, there is reason to believe that the currently known quantities possibly reflect an adequate sample of the total universe of data. Relying on the same geographic subdivisions of the region employed in the discussion above, patterning is apparent. A total of 127 fluted bifaces have been reported below the James River in the southern portions of the study area. Above the Potomac River, in the northern reaches of the region, a total of 58 specimens have been reported. Within the middle latitudes of the study area, 32 fluted bifaces have been recovered.

In a more qualitative sense, most agree that the known fluted biface quantities are dense south of the James River and more moderate above the Potomac River. In the same sense, such artifacts are significantly less dense in the middle latitudes of the study area. To quantitatively compare the densities of these off-site artifacts across the region, Table 4.3 also lists the surface areas of the various divisions of the Coastal Plain, numbers of fluted bifaces per division, and density ratios based on the amount of land per single artifact if one assumed an even distribution. These density figures are revealing and support the observations of many archaeologists over the years.

Site Structure

Three elements of patterning at the intrasite level on Chesapeake Paleoindian sites deserve mention. First, it is important to recognize patterning in what I have labeled site signature. Second, archaeologists have noticed that artifact distributions within the boundaries of any one site often are discontinuous. Artifacts are frequently recovered at discrete loci or in clusters. Third, a number of regional Paleoindian sites appear to have been situated in such a way as to minimize exposure to prevailing winter winds and to maximize solar warming. Each observation will be addressed below in turn.

Site signature, in the context of this research, primarily concerns the depositional context within which artifacts were recovered at the various sites under consideration. For the Paleoindian period within the Chesapeake region, surface manifestations are the general rule. Of the 25 sites reported herein, 19 appear to consist solely of surface deposits. Two sites in the northern portion of the study area, the Higgins and Paw Paw Cove sites, contain buried components. The Higgins site Paleoindian component is completely sealed, and the Paw Paw Cove site appears sealed, though suffering from the effects of lateral shoreline erosion. Three sites within the Nottoway River Complex (Fannin, Slate Farm, and Ridge sites) and the Marine Spring Branch site have yielded artifacts both from the surface and from a buried stratum. There is, of course, always the chance that some of the other regional sites may yet be found to contain undisturbed buried deposits. Table 4.4 offers summary details on the matter of site signature.

As mentioned in the first section of this chapter, archaeologists working at Paleoindian sites across eastern North America have long commented on the tendency of artifacts at many of those sites to cluster at discrete loci. This pattern was noted early on for the Williamson site within the Chesapeake region. Since that time a number of other regional Paleoindian sites have been reported with similar discontinuous distributions of artifacts. Eight of the currently known sites (see Table 4.4) definitely fit into this category, and there is a very good chance that others, if fully explored, would exhibit this pattern. Some of the reported clusters are no doubt the result of multiple occupations, but the presence of discrete activity areas or areas

Table 4.4. Summary Data on Region Paleoindian Sites[a]

Site[b]	FBI	PRF	BIF	ESC	SSC	UFL	SS	GR	PE	DE	WED	COR	TT	LOCI	W	WTLD	PROT	SUR	BUR	ICP	OCP
Williamson	175	1000	500	1500	1000	500	50	40	30	30	1500	10,000	6000	Y	Y	Y	Y	Y	?	Y	
Richmond	28	6	2	14	4			1	1				50	?	Y		?	Y		Y	
Pt-of-Rocks	6	6	5	12	2		2	2	1	1		4	37	?	Y	Y	?	Y		Y	
Petr Wood	5			27	1		2						35	?	Y	Y	?	Y		Y	
Conover	7	15	28	37	9	13		1	3		1	13	114	Y	Y	Y	Y	Y		Y	
Carpenter	2			2	1	2			1			2	8	?	Y	Y	Y	Y	Y	Y	
Marine SB	44		12	36				12	3				102	?	Y	?	?	Y	Y	Y	
Not Comp	19	12	5	66	49	35	6	4	6		10	15	212	4 of 7	Y	5 of 7	4 of 7	4 of 7	3 of 7	Y	
Meh Comp	18	14	9	166	33	41		9	1			1	291	1 of 7	Y	2 of 4	1 of 4	Y		Y	
Quail	3	2	4	7	6			3	3				28	?	Y	Y	?	Y			Y
I-of-Wight	21	3	4	6	9		2	6	2				53	?	Y	Y	N	Y			Y
Dime	2	1		6	2			3	5				19	?	Y	Y	?	Y			Y
Paw Paw	14	6	6	6	1	16	2	7	2	2	1	5	64	Y	Y	Y	N		Y	Y	Y
Higgins	2		3	4	1	9		1			3	11	23	N?	Y	N	N		Y	Y	
Pierpoint	3			13	11	25	10	3				11	65	N?	Y	Y	Y?	Y		Y	
Catoctin	2	3	5	5	4	32	3	3	3	1	1	9	65	N	Y	Y	Y	Y	Y	Y	

[a]Definitions of heading abbreviations are as follows: FBI, fluted bifaces; PRF, preforms; BIF, generalized bifaces; ESC, end-scrapers; SSC, side-scrapers; UFL, utilized flakes; SS, spokeshaves; GR, gravers; PE, piercing implements; DE, denticulates; WED, wedges; COR, cores; TT, total tools; LOCI, indications of discontinuous artifact distributions within site boundaries; W, nearby fresh water; WTLD, nearby wetlands; PROT, topographic relief to shield site; SUR, surface manifestation; BUR, buried site; ICP, on inner Coastal Plain or beyond; OCP, on outer Coastal Plain. *Note:* All counts are nominal and were based on best available evidence at the time this chapter was written. Data are, however, still being collected from these sites and final publications were not available on a number of locations summarized in this table. In addition, artifact categories vary greatly in relevant literature.

[b]Marine SB, Marine Spring Branch site; Not Comp, Nottoway River Complex; Meh Comp, Meherrin River Complex.

relating to particular social units within the settlement are also a distinct possibility. Combinations of all three causal mechanisms are likely, especially at large sites like Williamson.

Gardner (1977:259), working at the Flint Run Complex of Paleoindian sites west of the Chesapeake, was the first to mention the potential impact of prevailing climatic conditions on Paleoindian site location. McAvoy (1992:153) further investigated this subject in relation to a number of sites directly within the study area. At least 10 of the recorded sites discussed herein appear to have been located to maximize the effects of solar warming while at the same time using some nearby feature of topographic relief to shelter the site from prevailing winter winds (see Table 4.4). Again, other regional sites may eventually be seen, with a second look, as having similar settings. If not, location with a disregard for such features may be indicative of those sites' season of occupation. Warm weather settlement may be the case in those particular instances.

Tool Assemblages

Paleoindian tool assemblages, at a very general level, are notoriously homogeneous. Fluted bifaces of one sort or another are the major diagnostic artifacts, and these are accompanied by a variety of generally uniform types of bifacial and unifacial implements. Flake and cobble implements round out the tool kit. In addition, investigators frequently add that various cryptocrystalline lithic materials were preferred for the manufacture of this tool assemblage. Looking at the literature, one can almost sense a late Pleistocene fetish for such lithic materials. In the paragraphs below I would like to describe patterns seen in the Paleoindian technological system as recovered on Chesapeake sites. This discussion will focus on fluted point typology, overall tool kits, and lithic material choice.

Fluted Biface Typology. Archaeologists have long speculated on variability within fluted bifaces, even within the Chesapeake region (e.g., Fitting 1965). Perhaps the most frequently cited example of this endeavor for the study area was proposed by Gardner and one of his students (Gardner and Verrey 1979). They divide the fluted bifaces of the period into three subphases: Clovis, Middle Paleo, and Dalton. The Clovis subphase is comparable to western North American counterparts. The Middle Paleo subphase is assigned fluted bifaces that are smaller, thinner, and generally less bulky than Clovis types. Dalton types are smaller still and triangular in outline. This typology is based on a stratigraphic sequence of specimens recovered at the Flint Run Complex to the west of the study area, and although no radiometric dates are available, a chronology is suggested.

This typology has gathered its share of advocates over the years. Brown (1979) and Custer (1989) claim it to be a valid typology for Chesapeake Paleoindian sites. Some dissent, however, is becoming evident. There appears to be little question that the beginning and the end of this typological sequence work well on regional sites. Clovis bifaces would appear to be the earliest diagnostic type to typify the Paleoindian period within the region. And Dalton bifaces, based primarily on their stratigraphic position and radiometric-backed chronology at sites in the Southeast, can reasonably be seen to be late. At the same time, it should be noted that Dalton types are relatively rare in the Chesapeake region. Out of a total of 217 fluted bifaces examined from off-site locations within the study area, only 11 Daltons (about 5% of total sample) were counted.

It is the Middle Paleo type, a more gracile yet hypothetically later version of the classic fluted form, that generates the most comment. McAvoy (1992:38) has suggested that his Appomattox type may be a good candidate for an intermediary between Clovis and Dalton. This biface is lanceolate in shape, but is only minimally fluted. In many ways it is reminiscent of the similar unfluted mid-Paleoindian types recovered in the Southeast. Appomattox types have been recovered in quantities on local Paleoindian sites below the James River. Nevertheless, we still must remain aware that its temporal position between classic Clovis and Dalton is yet to be demonstrated either stratigraphically or by radiometric dating techniques.

Regardless of this, and returning to Gardner and Verrey's Middle Paleo type, Lowery (1989:161) has questioned if the type as proposed is itself valid for the Chesapeake region. Based on a general scarcity of quality lithic material, he suggests that the so-called Middle Paleo types that other investigators identify in the region may often be the simple result of not having substantial pieces of lithic material from which to manufacture such implements in the first place. There is some logic to this assumption. I would suggest that a typological sequence based on fluted bifaces in the Clovis form, followed by unfluted or minimally fluted bifaces, and finally Dalton bifaces be given our serious attention in the Chesapeake region (see Figure 4.5).

Tool Kit.   Paleoindian tool kits at sites within the Chesapeake region almost always contain a fairly consistent range of standardized tool forms. Much the same can be said for many other Paleoindian sites outside the region. The typological categories into which archaeologists place these tools, however, do vary somewhat. One investigator's wedge is often another's *pieces esquillees*. In evaluating the assemblages recovered on the various regional sites there is an additional problem. Many sites are surface manifestations that have been collected by a variety of people with various intents. Some finds are reported and others, sadly, are not. In addition, every collector is not consistent in what he or she retrieves.

Nevertheless, most Paleoindian tool forms typically discussed in the literature do appear in significant quantities on study area sites. Table 4.4 lists frequencies by type for the various sites discussed in this chapter. The type categories included in this table are purposefully broad. The more substantial sites that have been systematically collected, like Conover or Catoctin Creek, are probably the best indication of the relative frequencies of various tool types at a typical regional site. Paw Paw Cove and the Higgins site likewise fall into this category. The Williamson site, while genuinely enormous, should be approached with caution as the counts are often estimates based on tabulation of various people's collecting activities at that location.

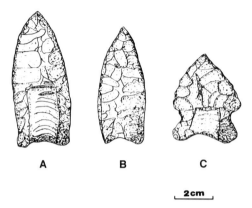

A   B   C

Figure 4.5.   Illustration of major Paleoindian biface types: A, Clovis; B, unfluted lanceolate; C, Dalton.

As stated before, the importance of this site is only surpassed by the irony of its collection.

Being mindful of all this, regional Paleoindian sites, by definition, always contain fluted bifaces. The next most prolific artifact type, and this will come as no surprise, is the ubiquitous end-scraper. On sites where it is possible to be reasonably sure that an accurate tool count is available, end-scrapers account for approximately 25–35% of the formal tool assemblage. They are joined by various numbers of side-scrapers, generalized bifaces, spokeshaves, gravers, piercing implements (awls and drills), denticulates, wedges, and cores. Special note should be made of the informal flake tools, labeled utilized flakes, that appear in sizable quantities (approximately 20% of all tools) on carefully collected sites.

Lithic Materials.   The use of cryptocrystalline lithic material—fine-grained silicious rock given a variety of colloquial names—is often seen as a hallmark of the Paleoindian period. Within the Chesapeake region, like everywhere else, the fluted biface chipped from almost translucent chert represents the epitome of prehistoric lithic manufacturing traditions. Archaeologists marvel at these artifacts' exquisitely thin cross sections, their remarkably straight edges, and their long, parallel flake scars interrupted only by deep, basal flutes. Reading the region's corpus of literature on the Paleoindian period leaves one with the impression that the use of cryptocrystalline material was almost exclusive. Was this the case?

Based on my research, I suggest that archaeologists working within the Chesapeake region have gone a bit overboard in their propensity to link Paleoindians to this type of lithic material. We tend to see Paleoindians as having been almost tethered to sources of cryptocrystalline lithic material. While there are certainly many Paleoindian artifacts recovered from the region that were manufactured from this lithic material, at the same time, a wide variety of other lithic materials is also recovered. I would like to look at this matter in some detail.

I see an interesting pattern in terms of lithic choice for the Paleoindian period in this region. At actual Paleoindian sites, a wider variety of different materials were employed in the manufacture of the tool assemblage than one might believe from reading much of the literature. In many cases this includes both cryptocrystalline and noncryptocrystalline types. For example, at the Williamson site, slightly over 25% of the known fluted bifaces that have been reported from the site were manufactured from quartz or quartzite (McAvoy 1992:145). Neither material falls within the cryptocrystalline category as traditionally defined. Of the 28 fluted bifaces reported from the Richmond site (Bottoms 1972:116–119), 42% are of quartz or quartzite, 51% were manufactured from silicified wood or slate, and 7% were chipped from jasper. Quartz and quartzite were used in 58% of all artifacts recovered from the Clovis component at the Dime site (Bottoms 1974:104). Quartz and quartzite again appear as the dominant (77% of all artifacts) lithic materials at the Marine Spring Branch site (Crook 1992:127).

My point here is not to imply that cryptocrystalline lithic material was used infrequently by regional Paleoindians. That material does appear at every site, and, in fact, was almost exclusively employed at some sites. Catoctin Creek and Conover, for example, exhibit an almost total reliance on cryptocrystalline lithics. At many other sites, however, a wide variety of various lithic materials, including noncryptocrystallines, were often employed in the manufacture of those sites' assemblages. Let us not ignore that fact.

The choice of lithic materials employed to manufacture off-site artifacts provides an interesting contrast to these site data. As discussed above, a wide variety of lithic materials appears on regional Paleoindian sites. In contrast, for the isolated bifaces that make up the universe of off-site data, cryptocrystalline lithic material clearly does dominate. Providing precise and exact percentages of cryptocrystalline versus noncryptocrystalline material usage in off-site artifacts is somewhat difficult. McCary's long-term survey of Virginia fluted bifaces is sometimes difficult to interpret in terms of each artifact's definite point of origin as well as other details. His three locational categories became essentially site, isolate, or a question mark. Lithic material employed to manufacture each artifact, especially with early listings, is also sometimes unclear. Taking a conservative approach and just counting the fluted bifaces from the Coastal Plain that are clearly designated as isolates, approximately 83% of the 159 specimens were manufactured from cryptocrystalline materials. Moving north, on the Maryland portion of the Coastal Plain, 83% of the reported 58 isolated fluted bifaces are again of that material. In an independent survey of fluted bifaces just from the Eastern Shore of the Chesapeake (Custer 1984:17–18), 97% of those artifacts were made from cryptocrystalline lithic material.

In short, I feel that this contrast between the employment of a wider variety of lithic materials at actual sites versus a more exclusive reliance on cryptocrystalline materials at off-site locations is not without significance. This pattern may, in fact, be an important key toward understanding regional Paleoindian settlement systems. This matter will be explored in the next section of this chapter.

Chronology

Radiometric dating has unfortunately not been possible at regional Paleoindian sites. Most of these sites are surface manifestations. In the few cases where buried deposits have been located, sufficient material for radiocarbon assay has not been recovered. One can only turn to the chronologies formulated outside the study area for fixing the temporal position of local Paleoindian sites.

Based on external data, Clovis material in the Chesapeake region should range in the extreme between about 12,000 and 10,400 years ago. This is based on the very old, albeit sparse, dates on Clovis in the Southeast and an average date for that material in the Northeast. With the study area located between both of these regions, and assuming some time lag from the early Southeast dates, perhaps an estimate of around 11,200 years ago for the earliest Clovis material in the Chesapeake region may eventually prove to be correct. Later diagnostic types, either the unfluted Appomattox type or the so-called Middle Paleo type, may fall in behind Clovis somewhere around 10,800 years ago. This would be followed by Dalton somewhere around 10,400 years ago. Let me be honest enough to state, however, that this chronology, like *all* others without radiometric support, should be approached as tentative.

Subsistence

Direct evidence for regional Paleoindian subsistence systems is absent. It is only possible, by inference and comparison to sites from other areas, to make a few broad statements on such matters. At a general level, it appears safe to assume that local Paleoindians followed a broad-based subsistence pattern as discussed in the first section of this chapter. Most local sites yield a range of implements appropriate for a variety of tasks. The fact that sites are located in a variety of physiographic settings may be seen as additional evidence for this suggestion. Based on floral and aquatic remains found at sites like Dust Cave to the south and Shawnee Minisink to the north, foraging was no doubt part of the subsistence system as was fishing and shellfish gathering. With so many local Paleoindian sites located near wetlands (see Table 4.4), cervids, which congregate in such locations, may have been a major item of consumer choice.

As a final note, hickory phytoliths have been recovered from a fluted biface at the Higgins site in the northern Chesapeake (Ebright 1992:410). While no one wants to suggest that Paleoindians were harvesting hickory trees, these remains suggest that this biface may have been hafted either to a hickory foreshaft or handle. If many fluted bifaces were in fact employed more often than not as knives, the latter may be the case. Finally, some charred nut fragments of an unspecified species have been recovered from a buried context at the Williamson site (Benthall and McCary 1973:130).

PALEOINDIAN LIFEWAYS IN THE CHESAPEAKE REGION: AN INTERPRETATION

In light of what has been discussed thus far in this chapter, it is now appropriate to offer a general interpretation of Paleoindian lifeways in the Chesapeake region. Some meaning must be attached to the empirical observations that have been made about the archaeological record. My interpretation of the Paleoindian period is predicated on the accommodation of hunter-foragers to the prevailing boreal landscape of the study area during the late Pleistocene. It is about the interrelationship of local Paleoindian social systems and the environment.

Within archaeology today there are a variety of ways in which scholars study the remains left behind by hunter-foragers. I have found Robert Bettinger's (1991) recent characterization of these ways to be particularly cogent. Approaches currently in vogue include various types of neofunctional cultural ecology, so-called middle-range theory, optimal foraging theory, Marxist and structural Marxist perspectives, and neo-Darwinian theoretical ecology. In my opinion, each perspective has its own unique advantages as well as disadvantages. Each seems to arise out of the limitations of its predecessor or its current competition.

In the interpretation of the Paleoindian period of the Chesapeake region that follows I am drawing much of what I say from the body of literature employed by middle-range theorists. The reason for this is straightforward and follows many of the critical arguments already expressed by Bettinger (1991). Middle-range theory, first and foremost, is what might be called *grounded*; it is most interested in directly interpreting the archaeological record. While there are many limitations to what we know about the Paleoindian period in the study area, I feel that this chapter has demonstrated that we are on our way to accumulating a significant body of data on local Paleoindians. It makes sense to start directly with what so many have worked so hard to discover.

While middle-range theory is not without its drawbacks, the same can also be said of its competition. Much of cultural ecology is deterministic and mired within old "man-the-hunter" ideas. Optimal foraging theory has been applied with greatest success to ethnographic settings. It produces elegant explanations of living people in contemporary environments. While its findings can be heuristically applied to the past, problems arise when one's knowledge of the people or their environment is constrained. Such is the case for the study area. Marxist-inspired approaches face obvious obstacles with classless hunter-foragers (see Leone 1978). The panacea is then to postulate Althusserian-inspired contradictions between people instead of classes (Bettinger 1991:137). One ends up looking at tensions between individual hunting or foraging versus group hunting or foraging. While I feel that such tensions no doubt existed in the past, it appears that Paleoindians found a way to keep them in check during the late Pleistocene when voting with one's feet was still an ever-present option. Finally, neo-Darwinian theoretical ecology has a great deal to offer hunter-forager archaeology. Even so, I remain uncomfortable with explanations that in their lowest common denominator filter down to arguments of genetic fitness. While the boundary between hunter-forager culture and nature is porous, I am not sure it is totally absent. To be fair, however, Bettinger (1991:221–223) would not agree with this last characterization, and he does makes some interesting counterpoints to it.

Hunter-Forager Worldview

I want to briefly characterize what might be called the worldview of hunter-foragers. There is no need to be exhaustive in rehashing the description of a way of life that is by now well known to many. A quick listing of basic characteristics will suffice. And I do want to make special note of one basic assumption that is a key to my interpretation.

To begin, there is no reason not to believe that Paleoindians were anything other than hunter-foragers. The structure of the sites they left behind, their technology, their settlement and subsistence patterns, as well as their temporal position within prehistory all converge on this fact. It is also common practice to see them at the band level of social organization. Fitting's (1977) argument to the contrary is the only exception that I am aware of that questions this assignment.

Scholars generally agree that hunting-and-foraging bands, regardless of time or place, exhibit certain universal characteristics (follows Service 1962). Bands are composed of groups of nuclear or extended families and are subject to periods of both aggregation and dispersal. Some of this fluctuation in group size is due to seasonal cycles and some is attributable to social and ritual obligations. Overall population densities are low. In both interpersonal and societal relations, individuals possess a high degree of flexibility and fluidity, although kin networks may be prescribed. Politically, bands are what is termed egalitarian. This is not to say that everyone was equal. As Morton Fried (1967:33) stated, in juxtaposition to stratified societies there are in fact as many positions of prestige in band society as there are people capable of filling them. Even though resources crucial to a band may be owned, all members are generally given undifferentiated access. The band economic system is likewise not institutionalized, but is one based on generalized reciprocity. Marshall Sahlins's (1972:1) observation that if economics is the dismal science, then the study of hunting-and-foraging economics must be its most advanced branch, rings true. Religion is not institutionalized. Technology is simple but effective. Exogamic prescriptions are often employed by hunting-and-foraging societies to extend the breeding, alliance, and exchange range of the band. All of this is fairly well accepted at this point.

I do, however, want to reinforce one particular point that concerns each of the various elements stated above. My point is that all of these various elements of band-level, hunter-forager society are systematically interrelated. Each element of band society forms a reciprocal bond with the others, and each is adaptive and responsive to the nature of the others. As Sahlins (1972:87) long ago suggested, each element of band society by its own modesty of scale is adapted to the nature of others, and if any one of the elements showed an inclination to develop, it would meet an increasing resistance from the others. A system of checks is built into the social construction.

Given this logic, it is a basic assumption of the interpretation I will offer that behavioral variability in any one element of Paleoindian society will be coupled with or reflected by variability in other elements. The implication being, for example, that an understanding of technology or settlement patterns often has something to say about social organization. This precept of interrelationship is what allows archaeology to say things about matters that leave no distinct trace in the archaeological record. It is also the faith that spawned processual archaeology from its predecessor, and, for the most part, separates it from the archaeology that hopes to succeed it.

With that said, my interpretation considers four elements of regional late Pleistocene society, all related to and constrained by one another. These elements—settlement organization, technology, subsistence economy, and social organization—constitute what I have chosen to call Paleoindian lifeways. All of these elements are examined within the ecological context of that era. My coverage of each element unfortunately cannot be consistently equal. Some can only be discussed indirectly given the existing evidence. It is, nevertheless, important to make a start.

Ecological Context

Before returning to a direct discussion of Paleoindian lifeways, it is important to outline the nature and structure of the regional ecology of the late Pleistocene. General characteristics of this ecology were outlined in the previous chapter. In quick summary, Paleoindians inhabited a boreal landscape. Based on an analysis of six pollen-sampling sites across the region, dominant arboreal vegetation consisted of spruce and pine, comprising a mostly coniferous overstory, along with birch and alder. Spruce was the primary arboreal dominant over much of the study area, but pine appeared to prevail in southern portions. Climate was cooler and moister than today. Regional rivers and streams, dominated by the ancestral Susquehanna River and its major tributaries, were fresh water. Wetland areas near these rivers and at interior locations appear to have been numerous. Faunal communities were effectively disharmonious, including both temperate and boreal species.

On another level, this broad late Pleistocene boreal regional landscape needs to be seen more in terms of its structural properties. It is important to understand potential resource distribution patterns within that landscape. In the present instance, this becomes somewhat complicated. Normal procedure would be to use modern analogues for purposes of comparison. As stated in the previous chapter, given the unique series of events that created this landscape, contemporary boreal forests are, unfortunately, not completely analogous. Nevertheless, some generalizations can still be made, albeit based on somewhat different modern boreal ecosystems.

Most boreal ecosystems, at first glance, feign monotony over both space and time (Winterhalder 1983:9). One tends to see a dense coniferous canopy with little understory plant growth. It appears to be an almost closed, impenetrable forest. On closer examination, however, boreal landscapes are rather complex and dynamic mosaics. They consist of many different habitats, or what might be labeled patches. The patches, which are usually small and dispersed, are created by edaphic conditions. Such factors as soil, lithology, exposure, and the like come into play. Blow-downs and lightning strikes have a major impact on the formation of these patches. In addition, an internal rhythm of disturbance and succession endemic to the ecosystem itself is in operation (Winterhalder 1983:32). In sum, a boreal ecosystem is not so much a seasonal ecology as it is a *periodic* ecology; changes occur on a longer-term basis. One can reasonably expect all of these various forces to have been continuously impacting the late Pleistocene boreal landscape of the Chesapeake region. On top of this, the ecosystem was exposed to the gradual impacts of climatic amelioration. Climate was shifting toward more modern conditions throughout the period. All of these forces were no doubt having their effect on the boreal flora as well as on the associated fauna inhabiting this landscape.

Making the axis of the ancestral Susquehanna River a datum of sorts, I would now like to address potential areas of diversity along an east–west transect of the region. The two distinct landmasses of the study area, the Western and Eastern shores, will need to be discussed separately. I will assume that the ancestral Susquehanna River was a deterrent to practical movement between these two landmasses. This may or may not be a safe assumption, as little is really known about the ability of Paleoindians to cross significant bodies of water. At the same time, however, even if Paleoindians did have watercraft, the ancestral Susquehanna probably was at least an effective impediment. Why cross a large body of water for resources that can more easily be obtained elsewhere?

Starting with the Western Shore, significant concentrations of economically important resources were present on the outer Coastal Plain near the banks of the ancestral Susquehanna River and along the nearby banks of its tributaries. It is evident that the ancestral Susquehanna had for many years meandered and braided along its length in the soft, unconsolidated sediments of the Coastal Plain. The wide valley that it created in the process would eventually be a factor in its transgression. During the late Pleistocene, as old channels were abandoned by the shifting river, extensive wetland areas developed. Escaping biogenic gas, still being released from sediments now covering the once extensive wetlands, is evidence of their onetime existence and substantial size. In addition to these wetland areas, the river itself offered aquatic resources. All of the resources offered by this zone would be attractive to the late Pleistocene residents of the area.

Unfortunately, because the subsequent marine transgression of the Holocene inundated this zone, almost all record of Paleoindian occupation was lost. The Paw Paw Cove site, once situated on two small tributaries of the ancestral Susquehanna River (Lowery 1990), is the one known exception to this rule. The artifacts that watermen today pull up from the bottom of the estuary in their dredges and oyster tongs are small additional reminders of the many sites that at onetime existed in this area.

Moving inland to the interior Coastal Plain region, ecological resources were certainly present, but they were much more diffuse. Concentrations would no doubt be found near the banks of tributaries as they flowed out of the Piedmont through this zone on their way to the ancestral Susquehanna River. Interior wetland areas were numerous, and in addition to containing floral resources, they provided important habitats for game. In addition, it would have been possible to encounter resources at the many small patches mentioned earlier that were interspersed across this entire zone. A number of regional Paleoindian sites are in fact located in this zone.

The last zone of significant resources on the Western Shore was located in and beyond the transition zone at the western margins of the inner Coastal Plain. Ecotones are traditionally areas of abundant and diverse ecological resources, and this zone would be no exception. Furthermore, with the unconsolidated sediments of the Coastal Plain feathering out here, many sources of high-grade lithics are exposed for exploitation. This would have provided an additional incentive for Paleoindian settlement in this zone. Most known Paleoindian sites are in fact located in this zone.

In all, I see three major zones on the Western Shore that provided significant and exploitable resources. Moving from east to west, the first zone is near the ancestral Susquehanna River itself. Next, another zone was located within the interior of the Western Shore. Finally, a third distinct zone would have presented itself as an ecotone between the Coastal Plain and Piedmont physiographic provinces. All three zones, and the much smaller patches throughout each, had resources to offer the late Pleistocene inhabitants of the region. Again, however, with some exceptions, the resources within each of these zones were not spatially and temporally differentiated given the nonseasonal nature of the boreal ecosystem. This is a very distinct feature of the study area during the late Pleistocene.

In addition to this east–west tripartite zonation, ecological diversity varied with latitude (north–south) on the Western Shore. I want to particularly focus on the differences between the very southern portions of the region, below the James River, and the more northern locales. Even today, the area below the James River is somewhat ecologically distinct from the rest of the region. As discussed in the previous chapter, the great Southeastern Evergreen Forests extend up into the area below the James making it distinct vis-à-vis contemporary forest types to the north. There is evidence from the pollen record that this area was also different during the late Pleistocene. Pine was the principal arboreal species there, replacing the spruce that dominated to the north. It appears likely that other temperate species made their appearance in that location earlier than in the rest of the region. The James River was, in addition, a late capture. It was only after the ancestral Susquehanna River began to feel the effects of marine transgression that the James River lost its own distinct lower channel directly to the ocean (see Figure 3.3, Chapter 3). The area below the James River was once effectively cut off from the region as it is known today.

Finally, although wetland areas certainly do dot the interior Coastal Plain of the entire region, they are more extensive below the James River. Extending up into the lower portion of the Chesapeake region, the Great Dismal Swamp is the premier example of extant interior wetlands today. As one moves north of the James, elevations increase on the Coastal Plain and the sediments are therefore thicker and better drained by a larger series of tributaries. These wetlands below the James River no doubt felt the effect of rising water tables earlier given that this area was the first to be transgressed.

In short, these early changes that came to the southern portion of the Western Shore below the James River may in part account for why so many Paleoindian sites have been discovered in that area. While there are no doubt other reasons for this phenomenon, it does appear that Paleoindians found a more diverse ecosystem in that region and exploited it earlier and more fully than other areas in the Chesapeake region.

Moving across the ancestral Susquehanna River, the Eastern Shore during the late Pleistocene was unique in its own right. The relatively low-lying peninsula had increased in area with the marine regression. By the time of Paleoindian occupation, however, the inundation of the eastern margins of the expanded landmass by the now-encroaching Atlantic Ocean had begun. Transgression was apparently rapid enough—up to 1.4 m per century—to forestall the development of coastal lagoons or embayments. This situation would somewhat circumscribe resource diversity on the Atlantic Ocean side of the peninsula. Nevertheless, it has been demonstrated that wetland areas were located on the now inundated portion of the Eastern Shore. The extent of such wetlands is unknown. If such features were extensive, they would have greatly increased coastal resource diversity.

Aside from the era's transitory Atlantic coast, the remainder of the Eastern Shore was covered by the same patchy boreal ecosystem as described for the opposite shore. Wetland areas today run the length of the Eastern Shore at midpeninsula. The late Pleistocene, with the transgression of the continental shelf area influencing groundwater levels, must have seen the development or expansion of many of these interior wetland areas. Such areas, like those on the Western Shore, would have presented significant exploitable resources. Moving further west, the next zone of important resources would have been the ancestral Susquehanna River itself.

In sum, the Eastern Shore represented a more laterally compact, yet certainly inhabitable, environment. I suspect that interior wetland areas as well as the resources near the ancestral Susquehanna River were the most heavily exploited. Patches of ecological diversity across the landscape would have provided additional resources. There is ample evidence of Paleoindian occupation of the peninsula, and I suspect even more sites will be found in the near future.

As a final note on the Chesapeake region's late Pleistocene boreal landscape, ecologists today sometimes calculate what is known as the effective temperature (ET) of an ecosystem. This quantitative measurement has been used in recent analyses of hunter-foragers to predict various elements of their lifeways relating to subsistence and settlement patterns (see Binford 1980). The calculation of ET places an ecosystem on a scale of floral and faunal productivity as well as relative seasonality. Prehistoric human adaptive strategies can then be predicted based on known ethnographic examples situated in settings with a similar ET. The ET of the boreal landscape discussed above, based on a reconstruction of regional climatic parameters from the late Pleistocene, is approximately 13° C. I will return to the implications of this measurement shortly.

Chesapeake Paleoindian Lifeways

At the beginning of this interpretation section of the chapter, I listed four elements of Paleoindian lifeways in the Chesapeake region. While the four are separated for the purpose of analysis and discussion, all are in fact closely coupled, and patterns isolated in any one ripple throughout the others. These elements include settlement systems, technology, subsistence economy, and social organization. They are arranged in this discussion by what might be called their degree of murkiness relative to the local archaeological record. We clearly have more direct data to address settlement systems and technology than we do to specify subsistence economy and social organization. Be that as it may, faith in a direct interrelatedness of elements allows some comment on even the least visible aspects of Paleoindian lifeways. Many of the interpretations that follow are drawn from what has become known as middle-range theory in hunter-forager studies.

Settlement Systems

Archaeology has made great strides in understanding both prehistoric settlement systems and the resulting settlement pattern of sites. In the last 30 or so years our vision has shifted from a series of individual excavation units across one's favorite site to a perspective that links together many such sites across entire regions. Chesapeake prehistorians have joined in this effort. I want to mention briefly two such sets of ideas on the nature of local Paleoindian settlement systems and then go on to my own interpretation of the same.

As Daniel Mouer (1989:185) has commented, Gardner's work on Paleoindian settlement systems represents the null hypothesis in terms of regional studies. Gardner's (1977, 1981, 1989) model is based on his long-term excavation project at the Flint Run Complex in the Shenandoah Valley of Virginia. While that complex is located well west of this study area, he and others (e.g., Custer 1989) have applied his ideas to Paleoindian data in the Chesapeake region and elsewhere. In a nutshell, the armature of this model is based on the contention that the use of geographic space by

Paleoindians was conditioned primarily by the status of their tool kits and the concomitant need for high-quality cryptocrystalline lithic material. Lithic resources therefore would have provided fixed points in the Paleoindian settlement system (Gardner 1977:258). The six types of sites that form the various components of the settlement system are as follows: quarry-related base camps, base camp maintenance stations, outlying hunting sites, isolated point sites, quarry sites, and quarry reduction stations (Gardner 1981:55–59). Few think about regional Paleoindian sites without considering this model.

More recently, McAvoy (1992) has published a monograph on Clovis settlement patterns based on his own survey of a portion of the Nottoway River located on the inner Coastal Plain of the lower study area. McAvoy (1992:142–145), mindful of Gardner's research, divides a significant number of Paleoindian sites near that river into 10 site types. The types include all of Gardner's and several more. Greater site diversity along the Nottoway is attributed to less emphasis on the so-called quarry-related base camp as a center of activity (McAvoy 1992:145). McAvoy adds that along the Nottoway River settlement choices were probably often made for reasons other than lithic procurement. In McAvoy's settlement system there are a number of base camps and quarry sites, but the largest number of sites are small and directed toward exploitation of food resources. At a microband level, the typical Paleoindian settlement territory is postulated to have been somewhere on the order of approximately 6,500 km^2 (McAvoy 1992:157). The description of the Paleoindian exploitation of this territory is rich in detail and supported by a wide variety of data.

I would like to build on the accomplishments of these two archaeologists in relation to Paleoindian settlement studies. A total of 25 known sites and a variety of off-site data are now available for the Chesapeake region. It would be tempting to just put each of these into the existing site types and leave it at that. I do, however, see the situation as being much more complex. Let us remember that in looking at these site and off-site data we are, more likely than not, seeing various elements of a number of different Paleoindian settlement systems over both time and space. In my opinion it is therefore more reasonable to work at delineating what a typical generalized settlement system must have included and then see how what has been discovered might fit into that system.

It has been established that Chesapeake Paleoindians inhabited a boreal landscape. Exploitable resources across this landscape, while broadly located in three distinct zones, occurred as both point and randomly distributed resources. Occupation of any one zone would not necessarily allow access to particularly unique resources. And with the carrying capacity of boreal ecosystems being what it is, it certainly would be possible to deplete resources in any one zone by extended occupation. I might also qualify this by saying that sources of high-quality lithic materials at the western margins of the interior Coastal Plain were perhaps somewhat unique and that they may have been a crucial element for *one part* of the seasonal round. I will come back to this matter shortly.

With all this in mind, and following Binford (1980), hunter-forager adaptive strategies can be arrayed along a spectrum moving between two end points that he labels foragers and collectors. In terms of mobility strategies, foragers generally move consumers to resources while collectors do quite the opposite. In one sense, I doubt that regional Paleoindians were truly typical of either extreme. And this is the point. Binford (1980:18) does not intend for the two types to be opposing; each merely occupies the extremes of a larger spectrum. Based on the nature of the late Pleistocene boreal ecosystem, including its ET, I feel that regional Paleoindians were relatively close to what Binford would label foragers, with perhaps some variation at certain times of the year.

Elaborating further (follows Binford 1980), based on ecological context and ET, about 61% of ethnographically known hunter-foragers in similar situations would be classified as seminomadic. These groups move in small bands for at least one-half of the year while occupying fixed settlements at some season or seasons. Such peoples typically settle on two types of sites, what have been labeled residential bases and locations. The size of each type varies. Residential bases would be larger and located in zones of more homogeneous resources. Locations, in contrast, would be smaller and situated in zones of less predictable resources. Consequently, site signature would be high in the former sites and low in the latter. Binford (1980:18) also uses the term "grain" to characterize these two types of sites. Grain is a function of the degree of mobility inherent in each situation. Few activities taking place at a site makes that site fine-grained, while more activities or repeated occupations would make it coarse-grained. Residential bases would be coarse-grained, given the longer term of occupation and the variety of activities taking place. Locations would be fine-grained for the opposite reason. Translating this scenario to the Chesapeake region is relatively straightforward. Archaeologists may expect to encounter two types of sites within Paleoindian settlement patterns, each variety with certain unique characteristics. Regional residential bases would be larger, have a higher signature and a coarser-grained assemblage, and be located in the most productive ecological zones. Locations, in contrast, would be exponentially smaller, have a weaker signature and a finer assemblage grain, and be found in less ecological productive zones. These locations could be the result of extractive tasks to maintain the residential base, or they could reflect the disintegration of the group into smaller social units at certain times of the year.

It is impossible to unequivocally assign each of the 25 known sites to one of the two site categories. Information on a number of sites is incomplete, and a few have been destroyed. In addition, the Paleoindian settlement strategy probably included periods of coalescence followed by periods of fission into smaller social units. Nevertheless, some definite examples can be cited, and it is, of course, possible to speculate.

In terms of possible candidates for residential base status, the Williamson site would be anyone's natural first choice. Its size, its signature, the coarse grain of its assemblage, and its location at the western margin of the inner Coastal Plain point to this conclusion. Other potential residential base sites on the inner Coastal Plain include the Richmond and Conover sites along with the recently discovered Greensville County site. The last site is a part of the Meherrin River Complex as I have defined it. One interesting feature about most of these sites is that they appear to offer their occupants protection from the elements (McAvoy 1992). This may indicate that inner Coastal Plain residential base sites were cold weather occupations. It may also indicate that the colder portions of the year were times of congregation.

The only two known potential candidates for residential base status on the outer Coastal Plain are the Paw Paw Cove site and possibly the Dime site. Such an assignment for either, however, cannot be totally substantiated based on what we now know. I suspect that most of the true residential base sites in this portion of the region were located very near the ancestral Susquehanna River and are now inundated. It is interesting that the location of Paw Paw Cove does not appear to offer much protection from the elements, and this may be an indication that sites near the ancestral Susquehanna were occupied during periods of warmth.

Almost all other known sites appear to have been locations rather than residential base sites. Most are small sites, have a low site signature, yield relatively fine-grained deposits, and are scattered about the three ecological zones. Many of the sites are located near wetlands, which would have been attractive to game. Seven offer protection form the elements, eight of them do not, and five are unknown in this regard. Some of these sites could be a part of the universe of small sites that were attached to residential bases, and others could be linked to periods of the year when groups dispersed into smaller social units to harvest resources over a broader area. Perhaps the sites with protection from the elements fall into the former category and sites without such protection were the latter.

The most extreme examples of locations in the regional Paleoindian settlement strategy would be represented by the off-site artifacts. In this perspective, a single artifact becomes the ultimate example of a fine-grained assemblage. Mobility dictates grain, and isolated fluted bifaces can be seen as the result of very high mobility. Given this, I view the off-site data as representing actual behavioral episodes that served as an important component of local Paleoindian adaptive strategies. I rather suspect that these off-site data were the result of Paleoindians attempting to exploit the before-mentioned many small patches that dotted the boreal landscape. The type of lithic material employed to manufacture most of these off-site artifacts will be cited as additional evidence of this strategy in the discussion of technology that follows shortly.

To conclude this discussion of Paleoindian mobility, I would like to offer a model of the regional settlement system. This model predicts residential base sites at the western margin of the inner Coastal Plain and along the ancestral Susquehanna River on the outer Coastal Plain. These sites were accompanied by a variety of associated locations. I suspect that sites on the far western edge of the inner Coastal Plain were occupied during colder periods, and those along the ancestral Susquehanna River in warmer periods. In between these extremes, evidence indicates that local Paleo-indians dispersed into smaller social units thereby broadcasting themselves across much of the region. Perhaps the zone between the western edge of the inner Coastal Plain and the ancestral Susquehanna River to the east was exploited most heavily during the periodic migration between major sites.

Technology

In the paragraphs below I want to look at the nature of the local Paleoindian tool assemblage, consider how it might have been structured by social relations, and examine patterns of lithic raw material utilization. It is especially important to recall that the nature of the period's technological system reflects all the other various elements of Paleoindian lifeways. All elements can additionally be related back to ecological context.

Percentages of various tool types at Chesapeake Paleoindian sites, as best as can be determined from the literature, have already been offered (Table 4.4). And at some point a detailed technological analysis of each assemblage, including use-wear study, needs to be undertaken. This is unfortunately well beyond the scope of the present effort. Nevertheless, it is evident that the Paleoindian tool kit on regional sites is a nonspecialized assemblage oriented toward undertaking a wide variety of subsistence activities. It is also an assemblage that can quickly and reliably be recast or modified for unexpected contingencies. I base these assertions on the nature of the regional ecology, the technology of ethnographically known foragers (Binford 1980), and on a more detailed knowledge of the assemblages recovered at other similar sites across eastern North America (Meltzer 1988).

Because boreal ecosystems offer a variety of subsistence resources often on a less than predictable basis, a highly portable tool kit capable of performing a wide variety of tasks is necessary to exploit this ecosystem. Ethnographically known hunter-foragers at low population densities in similar environments manufacture tool kits that are likewise typically generalized and often quite expedient. This expediency is echoed at actual Paleoindian sites both within and outside the immediate study area. Utilized flake tools, when collected by archaeologists, appear on Chesapeake sites in significant numbers. In many ways I feel that we have underestimated the importance of this less formal aspect of the overall tool kit. In terms of beginning to engender the Paleoindian tool kit, I have made the argument that at the very least many utilized flake tools and other cobble tools may be viewed as candidates for female tool manufacture and use (Dent 1991).

Moving forward, archaeology has made significant progress in understanding stone tool manufacturing processes and in deciphering how these finished tools might have been used. This is certainly commendable, but at another level we also need to begin to see material culture as a more active agent in both the production and reproduction of social relations. Put another way, in any truly complete technological analysis an understanding of the relationship between tools and users is just as important as analysis of the tools themselves (Sahlins 1972:79). Dolores Root (1984) has recently pointed out some ways that it might be possible to look at tool assemblages in a less technologically oriented or functionally specific way. I want to briefly address this issue in regard to regional Paleoindian tool assemblages.

To begin, mention has been made of what might be called the overt homogeneity of regional Paleoindian tool kits. A fluted biface or end-scraper from one site, all things being equal, more often than not closely resembles the same tool type from a different site. While we often discover that tools that look the same sometimes had radically different uses in the past, the "sameness" that seems to be built into the standard Paleoindian tool assemblage remains remarkable. Archaeology needs to begin to think about what this sameness might mean.

From one perspective, the overt homogeneity of the Paleoindian tool kit could suggest that technology was not individualized, but was in fact group centered. Items of material culture did not function to socially mark or draw attention to a tool's user. By extension, and at a larger level, it may also mean that tools did not even advertise group identity. The lowest common denominator of these implications would be that the Paleoindian means of production was solely extended to individuals, and not to specific social or kin units within a group or even to specific groups within a region.

The consequences of all this in the past are difficult to fathom. From a symbolic standpoint, a number of investigators comment that stylistic variation in technology is most common with potentially competing kin groups within a social unit or between socially distinct groups in close contact. The former scenario might offer some insight into Paleoindian social organization, and the latter could mean that there was effectively little or no contact between groups. I do eventually want to talk more about social organization and will come back to this idea. From an adaptive standpoint, however, everyone using the same technology could serve to cement and maintain ties between groups in an expansion-oriented society. This could very well have been important, for obvious reasons, during the Paleoindian era. There are, without a doubt, alternative explanations. Whatever the answer, however, I feel it is important for archaeologists to begin to entertain these questions. Let us not forget that at least one important element of the Paleoindian assemblage, the fluted biface, no doubt had both an adaptive *and* an unprecedented symbolic significance. In this latter realm, it may be seen as the only truly universal pancontinental symbol of the entire prehistoric era.

Finally, a closer look at lithic raw material utilization patterns is necessary. A dichotomy has been established between site and off-site data. In terms of actual sites, I have already made the case that a wide variety of lithic materials, including both cryptocrystalline and noncryptocrystalline rock, was employed to manufacture site-specific tool assemblages. Significant amounts of many materials, including chert, quartz, jasper, quartzite, silicified wood and slate, and quartz crystal, appear in quantity on local Paleoindian sites. It would, however, be difficult to recognize this fact from a reading of much of the frequently cited literature on the Paleoindian period. A common theme of that literature is a relentless focus on the myth of an almost exclusive Paleoindian reliance on cryptocrystalline lithic material. I do not find such a reliance to be true on actual sites within the Chesapeake region.

Off-site data, however, are another matter. At off-site locations the recovery of fluted bifaces made of cryptocrystalline material is very high. A survey was made of lithic material usage for fluted bifaces reported as being isolates on the Coastal Plain of the study area. As discussed earlier in this chapter, out of a total of 217 fluted bifaces reported as being isolates, about 83% were manufactured from cryptocrystalline lithic materials. Custer (1984:17–18), in an independent survey of fluted bifaces from just the Eastern Shore, reports 97% of the artifacts he examined as having been made from cryptocrystalline material. These percentages in off-site data appear significant, and I think the tendency to use that material for such artifacts says something about the nature of Paleoindian off-site adaptive strategies.

Albert Goodyear (1979, 1989) has published a thought-provoking analysis that examines the adaptive advantages of a reliance on cryptocrystalline lithic materials. His observations are pertinent to the off-site situation in the Chesapeake region. According to Goodyear, Paleoindians encountered a good deal of resource variation on a daily basis as a result of the ecological context within which they lived. He adds that although there might be suitable raw material of some type in the vicinity of any given resource encounter, the search time involved and the likelihood of failure to find suitable raw material would insure the efficiency of a curated technology. In short, the problem of geographic incongruity of suitable lithic material is alleviated with portable technologies, and the problem of situational contingencies is mitigated with a flexible technology. Flexibility in technology involves creating tool kits with appreciable life spans. It also includes designing tools that can be continally and reliably rejuvenated or recast into a needed tool. In Goodyear's opinion, cryptocrystalline material served as the best answer to these needs.

Cryptocrystalline material allows a flint knapper to fashion cores and tools with a high degree of control over the reduction process. The end product is an assemblage that possesses an extended life span because it can be easily and reliably rejuvenated. Given this, a curated tool assemblage manufactured of cryptocrystalline lithic material offers the greatest advantage in offsetting the geographic incongruity between lithic sources and the resources to be exploited. It gives consumers needed flexibility in handling the situational contingencies that occurred frequently in the everyday lives of Paleoindians.

Extending this to the Chesapeake region, extractive tasks carried out on or near actual sites could rely on a varied and often expedient tool assemblage. Local sources of many lithic materials were well known and their qualities understood. Off-site locations were another matter. These off-site locations represented small, highly mobile groups of hunter-foragers traveling across the landscape at certain times of the year in an attempt to encounter and harvest resources in the small patches of the boreal ecosystem. A curated cryptocrystalline-based tool kit was therefore dictated in these instances by the nature of the circumstances. Such a tool kit, as Goodyear (1979, 1989) suggests, would be very beneficial in the context of off-site locations to insure flexibility to cope with any resource, and to offset the potential absence of local suitable lithic materials for use on a more expedient basis.

Subsistence Economy

From the outset, it must be acknowledged that there is an almost total absence of direct evidence from Chesapeake-region Paleoindian sites on the subject of subsistence economy. Surface sites seldom, if ever, offer such data, and the few buried components discovered to date have yet to yield any floral or faunal remains. There is one possible exception to this rule. Charred nut fragments of an unspecified species have been reported from the Williamson site (Benthall and McCary 1973:130), but I do not have absolute confidence in the reported association. Therefore, in terms of regional subsistence practices, one can only rely on inference and data reported from elsewhere in eastern North America.

Starting with negative evidence, it now appears clear that Paleoindians in the Chesapeake region, despite a persistent mythology to the contrary, were not the hunters of now-extinct Pleistocene megafauna. These animals were probably unavailable in the area at the time of Paleoindian occupation. Even if available, specialized hunting is a high-risk venture. While caloric payoffs can offset this risk, such activities do not make much sense in ecosystems like that found during the late Pleistocene in the Chesapeake region. Effective hunting of such creatures is just the first problem. After a successful kill, the perishable products of that labor need to be processed and stored. Little evidence is available to suggest that local Paleoindians had either the technological capability to store such quantities of meat or the luxury of remaining close to these stores until exhausted. Yearly variation in temperatures may have also precluded such storage practices.

This returns archaeology to the albeit not so romantic position of viewing Chesapeake Paleoindians as basic hunters, foragers, and fishers of a wide variety of locally available species. Direct evidence of such Paleoindian subsistence practices has been cited from other sites, such as Shawnee Minisink and Dust Cave, across eastern North America. As Meltzer (1988:8) states, such strategies are low risk and appear to be the best available adaptation to the context of the lower-latitude eastern North American ecosystems.

Elements of the archaeological record in the study area indirectly support this assumption. Artifact assemblages within the region contain a wide range of multipurpose tools adaptable to many different subsistence activities. Regional settlement systems, with site and off-site activities broadcast across a variety of resource zones, likewise reflect the generalized nature of the Paleoindian subsistence economy. It is time to accept the nonspecialized nature of this subsistence economy as the norm for Chesapeake Paleoindians.

Social Organization

Last, I would like to offer some thoughts on the social organization of regional Paleoindian bands. As stated before, there is little doubt that Paleoindians were organized into some sort of band-level social organization. Population densities were low as the study area was being settled during the late Pleistocene. While his estimates appear rather liberal to me, Turner (1989:84) suggests a population density of about .0325–.065 individuals per km². Based on ethnographic analogies, it is probable that Paleoindian populations also went through periods of group coalescence and dispersal at various times of the year.

Going further, a few archaeologists have even commented on the particular type of social organization characteristic of these Paleoindian bands. Almost all who wade into such murky waters see the patrilocal band as having been the sine qua non of Paleoindian social organization, both here and elsewhere. The fascination archaeologists express for patrilocal bands can be related to the ideas advanced by Service (1962), which in turn trace their intellectual heritage to the earlier writings of A. R. Radcliffe-Brown and Julian Steward. Based on the notion that the patrilocal band was widespread in prehistory, it is given the additional status of being the primogenitor of all subsequent forms of social organization.

Patrilocal bands do make sense in many situations. This type of social organization functioned to keep men in territories they grew up in and presumably know well. Women marry out, and men remain in home areas. Service felt that intimate knowledge of a local area and the bonds of kin-based cooperation that developed between men as they matured were theoretically important to strategic group hunting and thus would dictate such a social organization through much of prehistory. The other side of this reasoning would be that women's foraging activities did not require close cooperation, and knowledge of foragable resources in a different area could be easily learned. This all appeared logical to archaeologists who have long seen hunting as the more important subsistence activity of Paleoindians. Service (1962:38) even added a simpler alternative explanation for the patrilocal band; men are dominant, they make the rules, and women have to leave.

There is, however, some reason to question this blanket belief in patrilocal bands during the Paleoindian period in the study area. Based on a barrage of counterarguments, Service (1971:x) even retreated from the ever-present patrilocal band in prehistory in a later edition of his book. My point here is that we should remain open to doing the same. If all that archaeologists look for is evidence of the patrilocal band, it logically follows that this is all we will see. Toward this end, I think that the archaeological record of the Paleoindian period in the Chesapeake region can be used just as well to support the argument that another type of social organization was dominant in the prevailing ecosystem.

The bilateral band type deserves some attention in this regard. Bilateral bands are characterized by a more fluid social structure allowing a high degree of mobility and flexibility among its members. Instead of stipulating the virilocal postmarital residence rules associated with the patrilocal type, bilateral bands allow various combinations of neolocality, ambilocality, and bilocality. Multiple residence options are open to conjugal pairs. Such practices allow an easy adjustment of group size to available resources, the leveling out of demographic variance, and the resolution of conflict by fission. The bilateral band represents a strategic type of social organization that recognizes the value of a fluid and flexible response to many different adaptational contingencies.

Evidence can be garnered to support such a social organization in the Chesapeake region during the Paleoindian period. From an ecological perspective, the prevailing boreal ecosystem was less than totally predictable, and flexibility in adaptational responses might have been very important. If this same boreal ecosystem was more periodic than seasonal, as I have argued, a good general knowledge of such an ecosystem may have been more beneficial than a detailed knowledge of one particular area of that environment. In other words, there may have been no particular advantage for certain members of the group to stay amongst their kin in the area of their birth and maturation. While I am in a clear minority among regional archaeologists, I would argue that foraging activities, presumably undertaken by women, were at the very least just as important as male hunting during the Paleoindian era. Bilaterality would preserve the option for movement toward the home range of either partner. It is not inconceivable that access to good foraging areas could have been at times just as important as access to hunting territory. Last, based on ethnographic evidence, a number of groups in Binford's (1980) foraging category are in fact bilateral bands.

From an archaeological standpoint, two additional sources of evidence can be cited. For one, the settlement system of regional Paleoindians appears to have been based on a flexible adaptational strategy. Movement was frequent, and periodic aggregation followed by group dispersal appears to have been likely. This would require not a small degree of social fluidity. For another, I come back to the overt homogeneity of the technology. It was argued that the mode of production was at the level of individuals and not at the level of smaller internal kin groups or the larger group as a whole. If the patrilocal band was the norm, one might reasonably expect the all-important kin-based male hunting groups to distinctively mark their weaponry. This did not appear to be the case. Technological sameness was instead dictated and as such would not advertise any particular group identity. All people could move at will, as one would expect within a bilateral social organization.

Again, all of this is difficult, if not impossible, to unequivocally prove. Social organization, bilateral or otherwise, is an element of hunter-forager lifeways that is problematic to address archaeologically. If time allowed, it would be possible to cite sound arguments in support of patrilocal bands being the norm in prehistory. Nevertheless, I still hope that the comments expressed above on this matter cause us to think about some of our "taken-for-granteds" in terms of local Paleoindian social organization. There is much work to be done in this regard that will result in a better understanding of these people. Perhaps what appears above is a start.

CONCLUSION

Through this chapter of the book I have attempted to accomplish a number of tasks. The first section presented a brief discussion of what we now know about Paleoindians across all of broader eastern North America. Lessons were drawn from these studies for consideration against the archaeological record of the regional Paleoindian period. The chapter then turned to our specific knowledge of Paleoindians in the Chesapeake study area. A total of 25 sites were described along with important off-site data. Efforts were made to characterize the nature of this data base. Last, the chapter presented a new and somewhat different interpretation of regional Paleoindian lifeways.

In regard to the totality of information that has been discovered on the Paleoindian period in the Chesapeake region, I suspect many are perhaps surprised by what has been unearthed. I know that I was. Through the labors of many we have managed to uncover a substantial body of information on this period in the study area. As to my interpretations, I equally suspect that some people will be less than sanguine with the direction in which I chose to move. Archaeology remains rather conservative when it comes to the Paleoindian period. There have, however, been recent calls in the regional literature for new ideas (e.g., Mouer 1989), and it seems likely that archaeologists are perhaps ready to reconsider some aspects of the period. I hope that at least some of the ideas expressed in this chapter might nudge us forward in this regard.

Chapter 5

The Archaic
Adjustment and Experiment

INTRODUCTION

The establishment of the Archaic as an archaeological entity in eastern North America is traditionally traced to William Ritchie's research undertaken during the 1930s at the Lamoka Lake site in central New York State. Since that time many others have reported additional details on the Archaic across eastern North America. By the 1950s, the Archaic period had become the subject of serious research within the Chesapeake region where it was recognized as the missing link between the then newly established Paleoindian period and the already well-known archaeological materials of the Woodland period. If debate on the earlier Paleoindian period has sometimes been acrimonious, study of the Archaic period has been comparatively sedate. To many, the Archaic period neither presented the intrigue of the earliest archaeological material nor matched the more spectacular remains of some later archaeological manifestations. Yet, in many ways, the Archaic period does represent an important key toward understanding all subsequent aboriginal lifeways, both here and elsewhere in eastern North America. Most now agree that it contains a remarkable record of cultural change that is of great interest in its own right.

As was previously discussed, there are many ways that archaeological periods can be defined. In this book the Archaic period covers an approximately 7000-year span of time, between roughly 10,000 and 3,000 years ago. This time period corresponds to the establishment of the temperate ecosystem across the local area and the corresponding formation of the Chesapeake estuary. The Archaic period was initially a time of adjustment to this rapidly changing landscape and finally a period that culminated in social experimentation and a redirection of human prehistory in this region. The archaeological evidence of this increment of regional prehistory is a record of hunter-foragers who, for the most part, left behind chipped- and ground-stone artifacts but maintained no ceramic tradition. In contrast to a number of recently proposed organizational schemes, the defining variable here is a negative

147

trait, the lack of ceramics. It is the traditional approach. Most archaeologists understand this system of organization, however, and I think that it works as well as any
for a large-scale regional study such as this one.

Given the extensiveness of archaeological data on the Archaic period, the first
section of this chapter will have to be organized somewhat differently from that of
the preceding chapter. Instead of summarizing most of what has been discovered in
neighboring areas to the north and south, here I want to take some time to trace the
historical development of the idea of the Archaic across eastern North America. I
argue that an understanding of archaeology's changing perceptions of this period
offers important lessons for the interpretation of its record in the Chesapeake region. Embedded within this examination I will present in more summary fashion
details on the Archaic in other nearby regions. The data are just too extensive to do
otherwise.

Following this beginning, a significant portion of this chapter will then turn to a
description of the culture history of the Archaic period of the Chesapeake region.
Particular areas of concern include diagnostic projectile point types and chronology,
associated tool assemblages, settlement strategies, and subsistence systems. Last, I
present an interpretation of the Archaic period based on the archaeological record of
the study area. This portion of the chapter will situate the Archaic period in its local
ecological context and I will ultimately suggest a rethinking of the important record of
culture change that occurred during this period. Particular emphasis is placed on the
dramatic changes that took place during the latter portion of the Archaic.

THE IDEA OF THE ARCHAIC

It is important in this context to appreciate the preconceptions that archaeology
has brought to its study of the Archaic period. It is apparent to me that our changing
ideas about the nature of the Archaic period have tinted archaeology's perceptions of
that period almost as much as have the actual data. Yet, in order not to neglect these
archaeological data, I will include a brief review of discoveries about the Archaic
period of broader eastern North America within this larger discussion. This appears
to me to be the most elegant and meaningful way to situate the Chesapeake region in
its larger context.

Origins

To appreciate the genesis of the Archaic is to understand Ritchie's early work in
New York State. Scattered throughout his report (Ritchie, 1932a) on what was then
called the Algonkin sequence in New York, one occasionally encounters phrases with
the word "archaic" qualifying various elements of the archaeological record. In this
context, the adjective "archaic" was used to further refine the "Algonkin/Iroquoian"
dichotomy created some years earlier by Arthur Parker (1920). At the time, earlier

materials in New York State were labeled Algonkin and the more recent were seen as Iroquoian.

Later, in another report, on the Lamoka Lake site, Ritchie (1932b) seemed more at ease with the idea of a formal "Archaic" designation, and in keeping with the times offered a list of traits to distinguish such an increment. While this list contained a number of distinctive artifacts, the real emphasis was on negative traits, especially the absence of horticulture and pottery. At the time of this research, these data appeared to be the earliest in the Northeast and thus quickly acquired the aura of great antiquity. This particular material soon came to define the Lamoka *focus* of the Archaic *pattern* in the terminology of the then widely used Midwestern Taxonomic System. Later Ritchie added the Brewerton and Frontenac foci to this pattern.

The notion of the Archaic was soon to spread. In the Southeast, William Webb (1938) had suggested the presence of yet undefined early cultures in eastern Tennessee. Further work (Webb 1939) in the Wheeler Basin of northern Alabama seemed to reinforce the idea. By the early 1940s, a relationship between materials in the Southeast and Ritchie's Lamoka Lake data was acknowledged in print (Webb and Haag 1940; Webb and DeJarnette 1942), and the Archaic was extended accordingly. This further recognition went hand in hand with the many archaeological projects related to the federal relief and development projects of the era. In a short time, the Archaic had rather quickly gone from a limited regional pattern in the Northeast to an archaeological manifestation across much of eastern North America.

Evolutionary Stage or Regional Sequence?

By the 1950s data on the Archaic had reached a critical mass. In the immediate future, studies of the Archaic would move in two different directions. For one, a number of archaeologists preferred to continue to approach the Archaic period on a strictly local, cultural historical level. Spatially restricted regional sequences defined by trait lists were to be the end product of this archaeology. For another, there were a number of archaeologists, including some soon to be very influential scholars, who had a grander vision for the Archaic. These archaeologists aimed to promote the Archaic as an evolutionary stage on a less local, more continent-wide basis. Each position had vocal advocates.

The focus on regional sequences is not surprising given the times. The existence of an earlier Paleoindian period had by then been established along with the acceptance of a distinctive accompanying suite of diagnostic artifacts. In the West, at least, the association of these artifacts at many sites with a unique Pleistocene fauna provided an indisputable chronology for the period. Although no such associated faunal material was unearthed east of the Mississippi River, the artifact half of the package was being recovered and it was seen as similarly ancient. At the other end of the temporal column, later Woodland materials could be more or less fixed in time via such methods as the direct historical approach linking written records with late prehistoric artifacts. The Archaic period, in contrast, enjoyed none of these benefits, and a reliable culture history seemed the first order of business. It should not be forgotten that a good deal of the early work on the Archaic period was also being done just before the revolution in radiometric dating techniques.

The establishment of a grander vision of the Archaic was more important to other archaeologists. Amercanists paid close attention when V. Gordon Childe modified the three-age system to include a notion of evolutionary development in the Old World. In this country a debate soon began on how to create an archaeological taxon with similar "developmental" implications. Given the then current political landscape of the United States, archaeologists carefully avoided directly discussing evolution. Yet Willey and Phillips (1958:107) felt compelled to appropriate the Archaic as the second stage of a general New World historical–developmental sequence. Would prehistorians working in eastern North America go along with this idea?

In 1955, a conference on the Archaic was called at the annual meeting of the Society for American Archaeology held that year in Bloomington, Indiana. It was hoped that such an effort might mirror the earlier success of a Woodland Conference and forge some degree of consensus on the Archaic. The larger goal was to convince archaeology that a continent-wide Archaic stage could be defined from the known archaeological record. Out of the meeting five papers on the Archaic across North America were assembled for publication in *American Antiquity*. A short passage from the introduction to these collected papers by Douglas Byers makes the larger agenda quite clear: "The Archaic stage is one step in man's upward climb: some never reached it, others were content to rest on its broad base, while others restlessly struggled on" (1959a:232). The Archaic was to be seen in a distinct evolutionary light. Nonetheless, many archaeologists working with Archaic materials, including those in eastern North America, still remained uncomfortable with such a notion of an Archaic stage. They said so at the conference and were left unconvinced by the resulting publication. One can read more than a little disappointment in this fact in Byers's (1959a) complete report on the effort.

And by the time Willey (1966) wrote his grand synthesis of New World archaeology, even he saw fit to abandon the notion of a broad evolutionary Archaic stage. Most of his colleagues in eastern North America, even before Willey's realization, had returned to the field with the more limited purpose of refining local sequences. Nevertheless, the debate had served to codify the Archaic as a legitimate taxon, and the task now at hand was to work out the specifics of the period in each and every region. If this was done well enough, then perhaps someday it would become possible to fit all the pieces together into a larger synthesis of sorts.

Until that day, the whole period was in need of chronological definition. Good culture histories demand beginnings and ends. Initial answers on the temporal depths of the Archaic came from the Midwest, at Modoc Rock Shelter in Illinois and from Graham Cave in Missouri. Melvin Fowler (1959a:268) was soon able to argue, aided by some of the first radiocarbon assays, that the Archaic extended back 10,000 years, presumably arising out of the Paleoindian tradition. A minority opinion (Bryan 1962; Byers 1959b) agreed with the early genesis of the period, but instead saw it as being spawned by an ancient unspecialized lithic industry that had managed to survive as a refuge tradition during the Paleoindian period. That position never seemed to gather many followers. With the threshold established, an arbitrary end to the Archaic period with the appearance of ceramics became the general consensus, never mind that this innovation's appearance across the region was hardly coterminous.

Archaeology had now effectively created a period that stretched across approximately seven millennia. Its temporal vastness and artifactual diversity seemed to demand subdivision. For a while archaeologists found it convenient to talk of early and late Archaic, but there was little real agreement on what these qualifiers were to mean (Willey and Phillips 1958:105). In 1956, by conference committee, a twofold subdivision of upper and lower Archaic, reminiscent of the Old World Paleolithic, was proposed. This terminology never made the transfer from conference proposal to common usage. Fowler (1959b), through his excavations at Modoc Rock Shelter, had subdivided the period into the Early (10,000 to 8000 years ago), Middle (8000 to 6000 years ago) and Late Archaic (6000 to 3000 years ago). This subdivision, partially based on artifact form and partially arbitrary in nature, became more or less codified in the literature. Perhaps this was fitting. The Archaic was, after all, about local sequences, and the answers would come from fieldwork instead of conferences.

Armed with some consensus on temporal range and internal subdivision, corps of archaeologists went into the field throughout the 1950s to provide the particulars. The Southeast was to yield tremendous evidence on this era. Special mention should be made of Joffre Coe's (1964) work at sites in the North Carolina Piedmont and Betty Broyles's (1966, 1971) labor at the St. Albans site in West Virginia. Thomas Lewis and Madeline Lewis (1961) unearthed three spectacular Archaic components at the Eva site in Tennessee. The Russell Cave site in Alabama (Miller 1958) yielded over 7 m of stratified deposits spanning 9000 years of prehistory.

In the Northeast, the very region that first piqued archaeology's interest in the Archaic, the earliest portions of the period seemed absent. In frustration, Fitting (1968) would ultimately suggest a post-Pleistocene population hiatus in the region attributable to a supposed low carrying capacity of the prevailing boreal ecosystem. With time, however, the gap between the already documented later portions of the Arachic and missing earlier components was somewhat filled. The lowest level of the Sheep Rock Shelter in Pennsylvania was radiocarbon dated to 9000 years ago (Michels and Dutt 1968). More significant in this regard were the excavations of amateur archaeologists at the Neville site in New Hampshire; Dena Dincauze (1976) would eventually publish these data. The Northeast indeed also had a more or less unbroken 8000-year Archaic sequence.

Trend and Tradition

With all these various data pouring in, larger questions of meaning could not be avoided. Joseph Caldwell (1958) produced a landmark monograph, *Trend and Tradi-*

tion in the Prehistory of the Eastern United States, and his ideas about the Archaic eventually proved popular as archaeologists began to grapple with larger issues. In this monograph, Caldwell first made clear his opposition toward attempts to portray the Archaic as an evolutionary stage on a continental scale, complete with apologies to both Willey and Phillips. As Brose (1973:106) comments, Caldwell likewise rejected the implications of the groupings proposed for the Archaic through the Midwestern Taxonomic System. What Caldwell did favor was the notion of the Archaic as consisting of broad economically based patterns cross cut by regional traditions. A new concept, the relationship between culture and environment, was mentioned as a part of this formula for understanding the Archaic.

Three trends were duly noted in the prehistory of the region. Caldwell (1958:71) saw the Archaic in eastern North America as representing the following: (1) the establishment of what he called "primary forest efficiency," (2) a dominance of regional differentiation and stylistic change, and (3) an increasing connection with Middle American civilizations. Primary forest efficiency—a phrase that if not directly echoed in much of the subsequent literature, at least was one that appeared ensconced in the minds of many archaeologists—represented the increasing efficiency and success in exploiting the resources of the Eastern Temperate Forest (Caldwell 1958:6). As an almost vitalist force, primary forest efficiency seemed ever present. It was, in this sense, very similar to Robert Braidwood's (1952, 1960) "settling in," which at about the same time was proposed as a stimulus to the rise of agriculture in the Old World's fertile crescent. Whatever the mysterious force behind primary forest efficiency in eastern North America, it did gain popularity as a way to explain changes that were by now very evident in the long Archaic column.

Caldwell's statements all made sense in terms of the dominant conception of the Archaic that had emerged after much debate. He managed to construct a unified idea of the Archaic that did not diminish any of its many smaller subregional parts; it was, in fact, a celebration of local diversity focused around primary forest efficiency. The notion of a diffusion of some traits from a more advanced Middle American source would help to explain some of the unprecedented innovations that culminated at the end of the period. Culture historians certainly understood diffusion. The post-Pleistocene ecological context of eastern North America was also now part of the formula. This fit well with emerging thoughts about the relationship between culture and nature. And finally, Caldwell offered one of the first widely accepted interpretations that regional prehistorians could call their own. It had come from this region, and it was an explanation that could be added as an afterthought to any carefully constructed local culture history.

While Caldwell had done everything in his power to resist the development of a grand evolutionary statement for all of North American prehistory, the very nature of his own scheme for the Eastern Woodlands did nevertheless have distinct evolutionary implications, albeit on a smaller scale. The 7000-year tenure of the Archaic period was particularly amenable to such a view, and the difference between the beginning and the ending of the period was explained based on a slow, steady, and progressive adaptation to the prevailing ecosystem via primary forest efficiency. In this view the environment was held constant and the engine of change was cultural as expressed primarily in local technological development and innovation, perhaps with some diffusion. In many ways, Caldwell's perspective stands as a good example of what within evolutionary theory is known as phyletic gradualism (Eldredge and Gould 1972) in that the history of the period was one of a steady almost stately unfolding by slow transformation.

The less desirable side of this type of interpretation was nevertheless soon evident. Within such gradualist explanations, change is most easily accounted for when one can see it as a sort of oscillation within the spectrum of possible states. Gradualism does begin to break down at the point of explaining something totally new and different (Eldredge 1985:145). In other words, its weak point for archaeology is evident when it is faced with explaining the eventual developments of the Late Archaic in relation to the Early Archaic. To be more specific, it is difficult, for example, to see Poverty Point in the Southeast as a gradual transformation of earlier portions of the Archaic (follows Smith 1986:32). Such matters would eventually present un-avoidable problems. In regional archaeology, the overuse of diffusion as an explana-tion for too much of what appeared suddenly would also eventually reach a point of diminishing returns. If everything of significance diffused into the region, one is soon left without a definable region.

All the while, data on the Archaic continued to pour in throughout the 1960s and early 1970s. From the site reports of the era one can almost feel a sense of relief in that archaeologists could return to what they did best—excavate and debate the details of the Archaic period's past. Caldwell, along with a number of others, had made the Archaic in eastern North America legitimate. The era's culture history was unfolding. Even if explanation was still viewed as almost an afterthought, primary forest efficiency appeared to be the answer. A long record of prehistoric culture change in the Archaic period driven by human innovation, efficiency, and some occasional strategic borrowing was the answer clearest to most.

Processual Archaeology

Enormous changes, however, were on the horizon. The impact of the new or processual archaeology would soon begin to ripple throughout eastern North Amer-ica and, inevitably, affect interpretations of the Archaic period. Established notions about the nature of the era would be inverted. Explanation was now to become paramount, and nature was to be given a more direct causal status. Diffusion was no longer de rigueur. Contempt between the old and new spilled out in print and at conferences.

The vanguard of new processual ideas was not to be found in either the Southeast or the Northeast, the two regions that had spawned the Archaic. It would instead come to eastern North America via a young, postwar generation of archaeolo-gists working in the Midwest. While Binford was certainly the leader of this movement, first as a student at the University of Michigan and then on the faculty at the University of Chicago, a whole corps of archaeologists that he either directly or indirectly influenced would deliver the gospel on the Archaic period.

All of a sudden, in the Midwest, Howard Winters (1969) was talking about Archaic settlement patterns in terms of how they might have reflected seasonal ecological diversity. Kubet Luchterhand (1970) produced a very different analysis of Archaic projectile points. Instead of talking about their diagnosticity, he was now more interested in functional diversity. Stewart Struever began to excavate an incredible sequence from the Koster site and talk about human adaptation to the Illinois River Valley during the Archaic. Much of that data would be published by his various students and colleagues associated with the Kampsville program. Clearly this all represented a different archaeology. This new or processual archaeology left a very different Archaic period in its wake. Processual archaeology nonetheless did seem to offer real hope of escaping some of the limitations inherent in the phyletic gradualism that typified its nemesis. It likewise appeared more in line with what had become a much more sophisticated knowledge of Holocene ecological change across eastern North America. Many archaeologists were now realizing that this ecology was never that constant, in a Caldwellian sense, during the Archaic period. These archaeologists saw the prevailing ecology as having been very dynamic, or what might be called *episodic*.

During the mid- to late 1960s archaeology had begun to become increasingly multidisciplinary. Prehistorians found themselves talking to and reading the literature produced by a number of palynologists (e.g., Bryson 1965; Sirkin 1967; Whitehead 1965). The message these scientists had for archaeology was that the past ecological history of the region was not constant, but had been characterized by a sequence of distinct climatic episodes. Over the long term, it appeared to an increasing number of prehistorians that these discontinuities in the paleoecological record might correlate with discontinuities in the archaeological record. Many of the so-called discontinuities under examination fell within the Archaic period. On a less temporally vast scale, the distributions of resources within any one of these past environments might also explain the distribution of Archaic sites across the landscape. This too, as Winters (1969) demonstrated, worked well with the Archaic.

From the long-term perspective, certainly a perspective the Archaic period had to offer, this new, episodic approach made it easier to appreciate the quantum changes of the era. The episodic perspective provided a definite series of ecological changes to stimulate a distinct series of responses on the part of prehistoric peoples. Where before there was only slow transformation within a constant environment, now there were distinct stimuli to induce change, even dramatic change. Within the episodic approach, archaeological entities were placed within an adaptive landscape that can be viewed metaphorically as having been a series of peaks and valleys (see Figure 5.1). With each recognizable archaeological entity occupying an adaptive peak, the problem was then to explain how the archaeological record reflects the movement, triggered by environmental discontinuities, from peak to peak (follows Eldredge

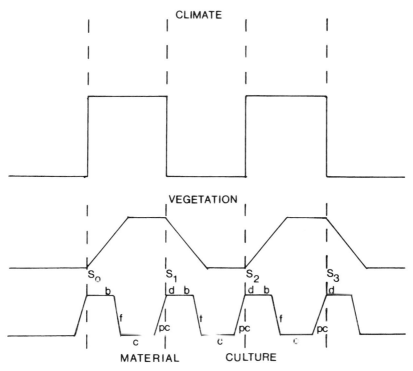

Figure 5.1. Square wave model as employed in the episodic approach. Schematic illustrates ideal relationship between changing climate, vegetation, and material culture. Abbreviations: S = various temporal states; d = death of cultural system; b = birth of cultural system; f = formative material culture; c = coherent material culture; pc = postcoherent material culture (after Carbone 1976:196).

1985). Archaeologists could study the adaptive peaks, in a temporally restricted sense across the landscape, or they could focus on the discontinuities and see long-term prehistoric cultural change. The Archaic was a natural laboratory for doing either.

As a postscript, I want to close by saying that this new way of interpreting the archaeological record, proclaimed under the banner of processual archaeology, also has costs of its own. Human action and choice were often removed from the equation, or at least ignored, as agents of change in the archaeological record. In many ways, by the early 1980s this forced a number of archaeologists to come full circle in questioning the role of the environment in cultural change and in reasserting human agency back into the formula. The very region that brought processual archaeology to the Archaic period, the Midwest, once again became an incubator of new ideas about the era. Barbara Bender's (1985a,b) distinctly postprocessual thoughts about Archaic hunter-foragers in the Midwest are an example of this fact. The points she raises have caused disquietude, at the very least, and perhaps even some reassessment in the world of Archaic archaeology. I think that her message should not go unheeded.

The Archaic Period Today in Eastern North America

To summarize our current knowledge of the Archaic period in eastern North America is no small task. In juxtaposition to the Paleoindian period, sites with significant Archaic components are far more numerous, as are the ideas about what these data mean. One thing that has not changed over the years is that the Archaic, by nature, is a period of many local sequences. Variability is the norm. And compounding this, processual archaeology, as the dominant paradigm through which the Archaic period is interpreted today, by its own nature, does not easily lend itself to such syntheses. While Bruce Smith (1986) has attempted to characterize the Archaic in the Southeast, similar summaries for the Northeast are absent or abysmal. Our knowledge of the Archaic in the Midwest is in somewhat better shape (see Phillips and Brown 1983), but good summary statements even on that region are still sparse.

The overview that follows is therefore derived from many diverse sources. It focuses for the most part on the Southeast region given that that region appears to have been the hearth of much of what is today called the Early and Middle Archaic. With the spread of those ways of life up through the Chesapeake region into the Northeast, it is then possible to see in situ regional diversification in the north during the Late Archaic. Given the general focus of this book, I only occasionally mention developments in the Midwest. In any case, this summary must remain very general.

Artifacts and Chronology

Formal biface typology is the very stuff of Archaic period archaeology. Coe's (1964) early research in the North Carolina Piedmont demonstrated that these particular artifacts were relatively sensitive chronological markers of the era. At the same time, a listing of all the various individual projectile point types named for the Archaic period would be impressive, yet probably impossible to produce and certainly meaningless. A style of projectile point called one thing in the Southeast is very often called something quite different not too many kilometers up the Atlantic coast. For this reason, I will discuss these various individual types in broad groupings linked in both time and in obvious common attributes. If labeled, I defer to the earliest or most prominent type name. Again, while I refer to them all as projectile points, many of these implements no doubt actually functioned as knives or other implements at various times in their use-life.

For the Early Archaic, a suite of side- and corner-notched projectile points typify the earlier portions of the subperiod, followed later by equally distinctive projectile points on bifurcated bases. Hardaway, Palmer, and Kirk types dominate the notched group. A number of other local types could be added to this group. Bifurcate types are usually classified as LeCroy, St. Albans, or Kanawha. In addition, Kirk-stemmed projectiles are often included in this early subperiod. This particular type is problematic, however, because it is apparently somewhat temporally long lived. It is placed by various investigators in either or both the Early and/or Middle Archaic subperiods.

For the Early Archaic, components with notched projectile point types are assayed to between 9850 and 8250 years ago. Bifurcate components range between 9380 and 7150 years ago. As stated before, they do appear to be somewhat later in time than the notched suite of projectiles. Kirk-stemmed points range from 9140 to 6960 years ago. I view them generally as a later phenomenon and dismiss the one very early date. See Table 5.1 for a sample of uncorrected radiocarbon assays on all types.

Tool assemblages associated with these two distinct suites of projectile points differ somewhat. For the temporally earlier notched group, the associated assemblages are very often similar to earlier Paleoindian assemblages. Most tools were formal implements, the result of a core–flake or blade manufacturing process. At sites in both the Southeast and Northeast it is typical to recover an assemblage including implements such as end- and side-scrapers, knives, drills, spokeshaves, perforators, gravers, utilized flakes, and so on. A ground-stone gouge was recovered in association with notched projectile points at the Shawnee Minisink site in Pennsylvania along with a significant number of rough-stone implements. At Early Archaic sites in the Little Tennessee River Valley, Chapman (1985a:147) reports the recovery of manos and metates as well as celts manufactured by bifacial percussion and then partially ground in association with these same projectiles. These latter tools represent the beginning of a more specialized tool assemblage out of the earlier Paleoindian base assemblage.

With bifurcate groupings in the Early Archaic, some changes in assemblages are evident. Less formal end-scrapers begin to appear, for example, and there is an increase in tools produced on bipolar flakes and a general reduction in the numbers of unifacial tools (Chapman 1985a:148). The employment of the bipolar manufacturing technique is generally interpreted to mean that materials were being employed that were too small to be effectively worked by more traditional reduction strategies. It results in flakes that are often small and irregular. One could argue that the assemblage associated with bifurcate projectiles is somewhat more expedient in nature.

A different suite of stemmed projectile points characterizes the Middle Archaic subperiod. Common types, again named by Coe (1964), include Stanly, Morrow Mountain I and II, and Guilford projectiles. Alternative type labels are again not in short supply. At the Neville site, in New England, Dincauze defines the Neville, Stark, and Merrimack types. In fact, however, Neville projectiles are very similar to Coe's Stanly type, and Stark projectiles look suspiciously like the Morrow Mountain type. Dincauze (1976) lumps all the look-alikes into what she calls the Atlantic Slope Macrotradition, stretching from at least North Carolina to New Hampshire. The side-notched Halifax, Otter Creek, and Brewerton types may also belong in this Middle Archaic typology along with various other local types.

For the Middle Archaic I group all projectile points into a stemmed grouping that contains a number of distinct types. I defer to the Coe (1964) classification and

Table 5.1. Radiocarbon Assays
on Early Archaic Projectile Points[a]

RCYBP[b]	Lab number	Location
Notched projectile points		
9435 ± 270	GX-4126	Icehouse Bottom, Tennessee
9350 ± 215	GX-4125	Icehouse Bottom, Tennessee
9175 ± 240	GX-4127	Icehouse Bottom, Tennessee
8715 ± 140	I-9138	Icehouse Bottom, Tennessee
8525 ± 355	I-9137	Icehouse Bottom, Tennessee
9410 ± 290	GX-4122	Patrick, Tennessee
9330 ± 250	GX-3564	Rose Island, Tennessee
9110 ± 145	GX-3565	Rose Island, Tennessee
9850 ± 500	M-1827	St. Albans, West Virginia
8930 ± 160	Y-1538	St. Albans, West Virginia
8850 ± 320	M-2294	St. Albans, West Virginia
8800 ± 320	M-2289	St. Albans, West Virginia
8250 ± 140	I-5330	Ward's Point, New York
9360 ± 120	I-4929	Richmond Hill, New York
7050 ± 250	M-1908	Sheep Rock Shelter, Pennsylvania[c]
8870 ± 320	M-1909	Sheep Rock Shelter, Pennsylvania[c]
Bifurcate projectile points		
8920 ± 325	GX-3597	Rose Island, Tennessee
8830 ± 700	M-1821	St. Albans, West Virginia
8820 ± 500	M-1820	St. Albans, West Virginia
8250 ± 100	Y-1539	St. Albans, West Virginia
9380 ± 100	DIC-261	Gardepe, New York
7390 ± 100	SI-451	Habron, Virginia[d]
7150 ± 500	M-357	Eva, Tennessee
7260 ± 125	I-4512	Ward's Point, New York
8250 ± 140	I-5331	Ward's Point, New York
7050 ± 250	M-1908	Sheep Rock Shelter, Pennsylvania[e]
8870 ± 320	M-1909	Sheep Rock Shelter, Pennsylvania[e]
Stemmed projectile points		
7520 ± 120	I-8315	Rockelein, New Jersey
7380 ± 120	I-6133	Harry's Farm, New Jersey
8160 ± 100	Y-1540	St. Albans, West Virginia
8585 ± 190	GX-8225	Johnsen No. 3, New York
8830 ± 210	GX-8223	Johnsen No. 3, New York
8880 ± 255	GX-8205	Johnsen No. 3, New York
9140 ± 260	GX-8204	Johnsen No. 3, New York
6960 ± 215	DIC-752	Russ Locus 2, New York
7880 ± 145	DIC-474	Russ Locus 2, New York
7960 ± 215	DIC-473	Russ Locus 2, New York
8220 ± 470	DIC-475	Russ Locus 2, New York

[a]Radiocarbon assays obtained from Broyles, 1971; Chapman, 1977; Funk, 1976; Kinsey, 1972; Kraft, 1975; Michels & Dutt, 1968; Ritchie & Funk, 1973; and McNett, 1985.
[b]RCYBP, radiocarbon years before present.
[c]In association with bifurcate projectiles.
[d]In association with Stanly types.
[e]In association with notched projectiles.

accordingly place the Northeastern Neville and Stark types into the appropriate Southeastern type headings. Stanly projectiles range in age between 8220 and 7015 years ago and Morrow Mountain types range between 8250 and 5380 years ago. Rejecting the one clearly very early assay for that type would present a range of between 7260 and 5380 years ago. Two Halifax projectiles have been dated to between 5440 and 4280 years ago. Table 5.2 presents all the assays discussed above for the Middle Archaic.

The trends started with the bifurcate portion of the Early Archaic continue into the Middle Archaic. Many types of lithic material were now employed to manufacture an assemblage that often contained a wider variety of bifacial tools along with many more ground- and rough-stone implements. Net sinkers more frequently appear in the earliest components of the Middle Archaic along with the first semilunar and tubular ground-stone atlatl weights. Such atlatl weights have been reported at various sites in the Southeast, and semilunar weights were first reported in the Northeast at the Neville site. Many Middle Archaic assemblages exhibit a trend toward the recovery of significantly higher percentages of projectile points versus other formal tool types. Middle Archaic sites in Florida yield the first direct evidence of a substantial

Table 5.2. Radiocarbon Assays
on Middle Archaic Projectile Points[a]

RCYBP[b]	Lab number	Location
Stanly		
7810 ± 175	GX-4121	Patrick, Tennessee
7790 ± 215	GX-4123	Icehouse Bottom, Tennessee
7390 ± 100	SI-451	Habron, Virginia[c]
7740 ± 280	GX-1746	Neville, New Hampshire
7650 ± 400	GX-1747	Neville, New Hampshire
7210 ± 140	GX-1922	Neville, New Hampshire
7015 ± 160	GX-1449	Neville, New Hampshire
7880 ± 145	DIC-474	Russ, New York
7960 ± 215	DIC-473	Russ, New York
8220 ± 420	DIC-475	Russ, New York
7695 ± 100	UGa-920	Hansford, West Virginia
Morrow Mountain		
6995 ± 245	GX-4124	Icehouse Bottom, Tennessee
5380 ± 140	I-1680	Peaks of Otter, Virginia
8250 ± 140	I-5331	Ward's Point, New York
7260 ± 125	I-4512	Ward's Point, New York
Halifax		
5440 ± 350	M-523	Gaston, North Carolina
4280 ± 350	M-522	Gaston, North Carolina

[a]Radiocarbon assays obtained from Chapman, 1977; Coe, 1964; Dincauze, 1976; Funk, 1976; Ritchie and Funk, 1973; and the Archives of the Virginia Department of Historic Resources.
[b]RCYBP, radiocarbon years before present.
[c]In association with bifurcates.

bone, wood, and shell technological tradition (Widmer 1988:66). A pointed oak digging stick dating to circa 7000 years ago was recovered at the Little Salt Spring site in Florida. It should be mentioned that a number of investigators (e.g., Coe 1964:122) see the direct origins of the Middle Archaic assemblage in the earlier, somewhat enigmatic but possibly homologous, Kirk-stemmed projectile point components.

By Late Archaic times, efforts at projectile point typology are made very complex by the apparent development of numerous subregional traditions. Archaeologists promote this complexity by becoming just as likely to coin a new label as they are to use an existing label for this variation. All in all, however, most projectile point types within the Late Archaic can be lumped together in two suites of either narrow-blade stemmed types or broad-blade stemmed types. In the interest of less cumbersome labels, I will hereafter just refer to these as narrow-blade versus broad-blade. Individual types within the narrow-blade grouping are too numerous to mention. The Lamoka types, employed by Ritchie to define the Archaic in the 1930s, are the first such designated types within this group in the Northeast. Broad-blade types of what might be called the Savannah River series, including other cognate types, blanket eastern North America from south to north.

In terms of developmental sequences, Dincauze (1976) argues the narrow-blade tradition was a result of in situ evolution out of a Middle Archaic base at various locations. A number of investigators have suggested Coe's Halifax type as a possible progenitor. Dincauze would probably prefer a more northern parent. Many also point to Midwestern influences. As for the broad-blade varieties, there appears to only be minor quibbling over a more southern source with subsequent diffusion up the Atlantic coast. Such types as Orient and Dry Brook may be later derivatives in the Northeast. The fact that broad-blade types originated to the south, however, may be the last point of agreement that can be cited for these types.

A list of assays for various Northeastern narrow-blade types is offered in Table 5.3. These assays span the entire Late Archaic subperiod from approximately 5000 years ago until 3000 years ago. The same is done for a sample of the broad-blade projectiles in both the Southeast and Northeast regions (Table 5.4). While these projectile types likewise span almost the entire Late Arachic subperiod, dates do tend to decrease in age as one moves from south to north.

Trends initiated in later portions of the Early Archaic and further developed in the Middle Archaic culminate by the Late Archaic when it is apparent that there is significant change occurring at the local level. Chipped-stone tools, often manufactured through biface reduction and bipolar techniques, were made from a wide variety of materials. So-called projectile points often appear to have served as more multifunctional implements, thereby somewhat reducing the number of other tool types in the assemblage. The ground- and rough-stone industry of the subperiod is well developed. Recovery of bone tools is frequently reported from Late Archaic sites across the region. Stone bowls, most often made from steatite but sometimes even from sandstone, appear in significant numbers on more than a few Late Archaic sites.

Table 5.3. Radiocarbon Assays on Late Archaic
Narrow-Blade Projectile Points[a]

RCYBP[b]	Lab number	Location
4920 ± 90	Beta-14431	Countryside, Virginia
4780 ± 100	Beta-10637	Countryside, Virginia
4730 ± 80	Y-1535	Sylvan Lake 2, New York
4560 ± 110	I-5234	Faucett, Pennsylvania
4474 ± 300	M-287	Bannerman, New York
4445 ± 130	I-5411	Faucett, Pennsylvania
4340 ± 100	DIC-221	Shafer 2, New York
4340 ± 120	Y-1664	Binette, New York
4160 ± 140	Y-1536	Sylvan Lake 3, New York
4140 ± 100	Y-1529	Hornblower II, Massachusetts
4130 ± 180	I-5236	Faucett, Pennsylvania
4110 ± 140	DIC-223	Shafer 2, New York
4000 ± 85	DIC-183	Sylvan Lake 3, New York
3920 ± 95	I-6598	Harry's Farm, New Jersey
3660 ± 120	Y-2342	Brodhead-Heller, Pennsylvania
3290 ± 95	I-4834	Whyte Field, New York

[a]Radiocarbon assays obtained from Funk, 1976; Kinsey, 1972; Kraft,
1975; Ritchie and Funk, 1973; and Rust, 1983.
[b]RCYBP, radiocarbon years before present.

They represent the beginning of the so-called container revolution (see Sassaman 1993).

Tool assemblages vary in association with narrow-blade Late Arachic projectile points and broad-blade projectiles. In terms of the former, the accompanying assemblage was likely to contain knives, drills, choppers, and some scrapers as well as ground-stone pestles, mullers, milling stones, net sinkers, atlatl weights, grooved axes, adzes, and celts (Kinsey 1977:376). Assemblages accompanying broad-blade projectiles are very similar (Cook 1976:346). Steatite bowls are certainly more common in these assemblages, although they also appear in the narrow-blade assemblages later in time. Chipped-stone artifacts in the broad-blade assemblage were more often than not made from locally available lithic materials.

Site Structure

Site visibility, what I referred to before as site signature, varies greatly throughout the Archaic period. As one would expect, sites within the 7000-year Archaic period run the spectrum from very large to very small. In a general sense, site revisitation appears to have been more common during the Archaic than during the Paleoindian period. By the end of the period, population densities seem to have risen significantly and mobility restrictions become apparent. Because of this situation, some Late

Table 5.4. Radiocarbon Assays on Late Archaic
Broad-Blade Projectile Points[a]

RCYBP[b]	Lab number	Location
Savannah River		
4865 ± 280	GX-2274	Warren Wilson, North Carolina
4700 ± 150	M-1279	Stallings Island, Georgia
4450 ± 150	M-1277	Stallings Island, Georgia
4390 ± 155	GX-5043	Bacon Bend, Tennessee
4175 ± 230	GX-2607	Harrison Branch, Tennessee
4070 ± 70	UGa-1879	Bacon Bend, Tennessee
3900 ± 25	M-524	Gaston, North Carolina
3820 ± 125	M-1111	Bilbo, Georgia
3780 ± 220	I-6810	Byram, Pennsylvania
3770 ± 200	M-236	Dulany, Georgia
3730 ± 150	M-1278	Stallings Island, Georgia
3730 ± 125	M-1112	Bilbo, Georgia
3700 ± 250	M-39	Sapelo Island, Georgia
3700 ± 125	M-1109	Bilbo, Georgia
3580 ± 225	GX-5044	Bacon Bend, Tennessee
Susquehanna		
3670 ± 140	Beta-12856	Corral, Virginia
3620 ± 110	Y-1373	Litchfield, New Hampshire
3600 ± 80	Y-2344	Zimmerman, Pennsylvania
3545 ± 100	I-7096	Kuhr No. 1, New York
3500 ± 105	I-6751	Kuhr No. 1, New York
3485 ± 90	I-7094	Kuhr No. 1, New York
3470 ± 125	GX-0568	Vincent, Massachusetts
3280 ± 90	I-7097	Fortin, New York
3220 ± 160	M-2085	Sheep Rock Shelter, Pennsylvania
3200 ± 100	Y-1274	O'Neil 2, New York
Perkiomen		
3670 ± 120	Y-2587	Miller Field, Pennsylvania
3590 ± 100	Y-2588	Miller Field, Pennsylvania
3570 ± 100	Y-2340	Brodhead-Heller, Pennsylvania
3450 ± 120	Y-2478	Faucett, Pennsylvania
3425 ± 95	I-6641	Camelot No. 1, New York
Koens-Crispin/Lehigh		
3830 ± 80	DIC-117	Enck No. 2, New York
3670 ± 100	Y-1826	Peters-Albrecht, Pennsylvania
3670 ± 90	DIC-264	Mattice No. 2, New York
3620 ± 130	I-6733	Kuhr No. 1, New York
3460 ± 100	Beta-11801	Countryside, Virginia
3420 ± 100	Y-1170	Snook Kill, New York
Orient/Dry Brook		
3230 ± 120	Y-2343	Zimmerman, Pennsylvania
3170 ± 120	Y-2589	Miller Field, Pennsylvania
3120 ± 120	Y-2339	Brodhead-Heller, Pennsylvania
2993 ± 300	M-586	Sugar Loaf Hill, New York

Table 5.4. (*Continued*)

RCYBP[b]	Lab number	Location
2994 ± 250	M-588	Stony Brook 2, New York
2894 ± 250	M-587	Stony Brook 2, New York
2894 ± 250	M-494	Orient No. 2, New York
2760 ± 100	Y-2477	Faucett, Pennsylvania
2713 ± 220	W-543	Jamesport, New York

[a]Radiocarbon assays obtained from Chapman, 1977; Coe, 1964; Funk, 1976; Gleach, 1985; Kinsey, 1972; Kraft, 1975; Michels and Dutt, 1968; Ritchie and Funk, 1973; Rust, 1983; and the Archives of the Virginia Department of Historic Resources.
[b]RCYBP, radiocarbon years before present.

Archaic sites will stretch for more than a few kilometers along various natural features. Even Early Archaic sites can be rather large. Because of the temporal duration of the Archaic, many sites from the period are multicomponent sites. Fortunately, a substantial number of deeply stratified sites have been located, and it is these locations that provide the best evidence of chronological subdivision of the period based on associated diagnostic projectile points. The best examples of such deeply stratified Archaic sites, like Koster and Modoc Rock Shelter, are found in the Midwest.

Site infrastructure becomes clearer during the Archaic and often stands in marked contrast to earlier Paleoindian sites. For example, hearths are generally more formal, even at Early Archaic sites. Evidence of Paleoindian-like informal fire-floors have been found at these sites, but more formally prepared, sometimes excavated hearths do begin to appear. A brief discussion of these features at both the Icehouse Bottom site (Chapman 1977) and the Rose Island site (Chapman 1975) in the Southeast is informative in this regard. Both unprepared and prepared hearth features were isolated in association with the earlier notched projectile point components at Icehouse Bottom. A significant number of the hearths at this level of that site preserve remarkable textile and basketry impressions (Chapman and Adovasio 1977). The former is interpreted as a part of netting possibly used in food procurement activities and the latter basketry specimens may have been a part of containers used for transportation or storage. At the Rose Island site, in the bifurcate levels, prepared hearths built in excavated basins appear even more common. Concentrations of nearby rock suggest baking, steaming, or container-boiling activities. It does appear that such formal, prepared hearths became more common in the bifurcate levels, and this may be seen as additional evidence of a shift in lifeways between the earlier and later portions of the Early Archaic.

In the same sense, small subterranean pits and basins have been noted at sites, beginning in the Early Archaic. The presence of these features increased throughout the Arachic and many appear to have been used in the cooking process. These features are often associated with deposits of fire-cracked rock. In the Late Archaic some similar features were possibly used to cache site furniture, apparently in anticipation of seasonal site abandonment. Finished projectile points or what were probably blanks are also often found cached in such features. There is, however, not much evidence to indicate that these early pit and basin features along the Atlantic coast served to store or hoard foodstuffs.

Domestic structures were no doubt present on Early Archaic sites, but hard evidence to indicate their exact form is unknown. Prepared clay floors, some surrounded by postmolds, have been reported for the Middle Archaic period in the Southeast (Smith 1986:27). There is definite evidence of structures from the Middle Archaic at the Koster site in the Midwest. One can assume that structures became even more prolific on Late Archaic sites across eastern North America.

Of course, the ultimate feature on many Archaic sites from the later portions of the period are the large nearby accumulations of shell. Aquatic resources, especially shallow-water molluscs, became heavily exploited in the Southeast by about 4200 years ago. Many sites at coastal and interior riverine locations in that region have substantial shell middens associated with them. These sites were important in the early definition of the Archaic in that region. Oyster middens may have been accumulating even before that time along the lower Hudson River in New York (Brennan 1974).

Definite evidence of mortuary practices is preserved at Archaic period sites. Two isolated burials from the Early Archaic have been excavated at the Icehouse Bottom site and represent green bone cremations (Chapman 1977:172). Such green bone cremations result from the burning of either partially decomposed or in-the-flesh corpses. A formal Middle Archaic cemetery consisting of over 100 individual interments was excavated at the Eva site. A smaller, but certainly remarkable, Middle Archaic cemetery, from which soft tissue was radiocarbon dated to circa 7400 years ago, has recently been uncovered at the Windover site in Florida (Doran et al. 1986). Other formal Middle Archaic cemeteries have been excavated at a number of sites in Florida (Widmer 1988:671). By the Late Archaic, grave goods are recovered at some locations in eastern North America and may be seen as evidence of increasing levels of sociocultural complexity. The very fact that archaeologists have been able to recover evidence of mortuary practices from Archaic period sites is itself an indication of the changing lifeways during this era.

Settlement Strategies

A quick scan of the literature on the Archaic period reveals many different ideas about the nature of settlement systems. In some ways this is to be expected given the diversity present over 7000 years of prehistory. In addition, this was a period of considerable ecological change that took place at different times as one moves south to north within eastern North America. It is perhaps not possible to hope for uniform patterning in regards to settlement systems; diversity is ever present during this period.

For the Southeast, Smith (1986) has presented the most cogent review of settlement strategies for the entire Archaic period. He suggests that the most we can say about initial Early Archaic settlement systems is that they may have been keyed toward residential base camps located in ecologically diverse floodplain areas supplemented by short-term occupation in less attractive floodplain and inter-riverine settings. This pattern is viewed as a carryover from the Paleoindian period. Later in the Early Archaic and throughout much of the Middle Archaic he proposes a similar dichotomous movement between riverine and upland locations, with perhaps some added opportunistic exploitation of aquatic resources contributing to increased occupation of sites near these resources. By the Late Archaic, more dramatic change is evident. In this subperiod, settlement systems shift to occupation of semipermanent dry-season residential base camps in river and stream valleys that are linked to a variety of smaller, short-term camps in upland locations. The base camps are situated in optimal settings to exploit both aquatic and nearby terrestrial floral and faunal resources.

Settlement systems in the Northeast are more of an enigma, especially for the earlier portions of the Archaic. The Early Archaic is sparsely represented in the region, and information on settlement strategies is therefore lacking. For the Middle Archaic, at least, settlement systems may have been oriented around large riverine or coastal base camps in warmer periods with dispersion to smaller interior camps during the winter and fall (see Dincauze 1976). For the Late Archaic, a similar settlement system of seasonal aggregation and dispersion appears to have continued. A higher degree of sedentism is evident, however, in zones of higher resource diversity.

Subsistence

Archaic subsistence strategies all appear to focus on the generalized exploitation of many available resources. The products of a more temperate ecology, especially items from the temperate forest mast, quickly became major elements of subsistence as those forests spread up the Atlantic coast. The same can be said for aquatic species that became prolific as sea levels rose and eventually stabilized. In many ways these subsistence systems followed the general pattern established in the earlier Paleoindian period. From an archaeological standpoint, however, perhaps the new variable is that a significant amount of subsistence remains from the Arachic period have survived for study.

Following Smith (1986:11–13), Early Archaic groups in the Southeast turned to the opportunistic exploitation of a broad array of floral, faunal, and aquatic resources. Various mast products such as acorn, hickory nut, and black walnut are recovered at regional Early Archaic sites. Seeds, including such species as chenopod and grape, have been recovered on these same sites. Evidence that a host of fish, amphibian, reptile, and small mammal species were also being exploited is available from the archaeological record. As one would expect, the favored large mammal appears to have been deer, but elk and even bison remains have been recovered on sites from this subperiod. Data are more sparse from the Northeast. While it is not possible to present such a complete list of exploited resources from Early Archaic sites in that region, the wide variety of seeds, including substantial amounts of chenopod recovered at Shawnee Minisink in Pennsylvania, is evidence of at least a portion of the local subsistence strategy (Dent and Kauffman 1985:67).

With the Middle Archaic subperiod, Smith (1986:21) indicates that shifts in subsistence systems were beginning to occur, but that it is difficult to determine the exact direction or intensity of these shifts. Perhaps subsistence strategies became more focused on certain resources within the total range available. Certainly, an increased utilization of hundreds of different species of riverine mollusc is indicated. In the Northeast, some have suggested an increasing adaptation to anadromous fish species that were beginning to establish themselves in large numbers. These specialized adaptations to aquatic resources in both regions were no doubt part of a continued reliance on many of the floral and faunal species discussed above for the earlier subperiod.

In the Late Archaic subperiod, all these tendencies continue. Settlement patterns broadcast sites throughout many ecologically diverse zones to facilitate more focused exploitation of certain floral, faunal, and aquatic resources. Estuarine, riverine, and sylvan settlements allowed this more intensive exploitation of seasonally available temperate species and species by-products. Certainly, anadromous fish were one such favored resource, and shellfish remained under intensive exploitation.

In addition, it is now fairly well documented that various newly domesticated plant species were under active cultivation in parts of eastern North America by the Late Archaic. There is substantial debate on the ultimate origins of the developmental sequence. Most of these plant domesticates were traditionally seen as introduced tropical cultigens. This process certainly accounts for the better-known later cultigens, such as maize. Nonetheless, Smith (1989) has recently proposed that eastern North America was an early independent center of plant domestication. While there is debate on this issue (see Riley, Edging, and Rossen 1990), it is still possible to appreciate such developments during the Late Archaic regardless of the path of introduction, diffusion, or in situ development.

Squash, both seeds and rind (identified as *Cucurbita pepo*), has been recovered at Late Archaic sites in Missouri and Kentucky dating to circa 5300 years ago (Chomko and Crawford 1978). Smith (1989:1567) appears to feel that some of these and other cucurbit remains might be better identified as domesticates of a *C. texana*-like indigenous wild ancestor. This is, of course, an argument for in situ domestication instead of introduced domesticates. Bottle gourd (*Lagenaria siceraria*) has likewise been recovered from sites dating to the same period. Other early domesticates are now being added to this list. Sumpweed or marsh elder (*Iva annua*) was brought under domestication at least 4000 years ago, and sunflower (*Helianthus annus*) was domesticated circa 3500 years ago (Smith 1989:1567–1568). The domestication of *Chenopodium* (*C. berlandieri* ssp. *jonesianum*) appears to have occurred also at about 3500 years ago. There is little doubt that at least these last three plant species were domesticated within eastern North America.

To support his ideas, Smith (1989:1568) provides a hypothesis to explain his proposed in situ sequence of domestication in eastern North America during the Late Archaic. He suggests that because regional populations occupied midden-bound settlements focusing on the increased exploitation of aquatic resources, they inadvertently provided anthropogenic disturbance and enriched habitats for these plant species. This was followed by increasing human intervention to encourage and replant these species in maintained gardens. Through this process the plant species were effectively domesticated. Such a perspective fits well with increased emphasis on the more focused exploitation of particular resources during the Late Archaic.

THE ARCHAIC PERIOD IN THE CHESAPEAKE REGION

The Archaic period was beginning to be recognized in the Chesapeake region by the early 1950s. Artifacts of the era, of course, had been recovered over a much longer period of time. The genesis of the recognition of the Archaic in the Chesapeake region can perhaps best be seen in the early research of Holland (1949a,b, 1953) on the archaeological record of Albemarle County in the central region of Virginia, slightly west of the study area. In an important early series of articles, Holland initially flirted with the definition of a preceramic period and then defined such a phenomenon. The Archaic period in the Chesapeake region had now become a reality within local archaeology.

Over the last four decades many regional archaeologists have labored to provide additional details on the Archaic period. The remainder of this section of the chapter will present a descriptive summary of the period within the study area. For each subdivision of the Archaic, I will discuss local diagnostic projectile point groupings and chronology, assemblages, site structure, settlement strategies, and subsistence patterns. Within this discussion I often focus on a site or series of sites that have yielded particularly good evidence of that subperiod. Discussion of social organization is deferred until the last section of this chapter given the changes that occurred within the Chesapeake region near the end of the Archaic period.

Early Archaic

Knowledge of the Early Archaic subperiod within the Chesapeake region is still somewhat dependent on information discovered at sites outside the area. Local prehistorians must depend heavily on a sequence of diagnostic projectile point types and an associated chronology developed elsewhere. Fortunately, however, a series of recent excavations at several regional Early Archaic sites have been completed, and each of these greatly enriches our knowledge of the subperiod within the study area. Exciting new data are now available on local Early Archaic assemblages, site structure, settlement, and subsistence strategies. In the paragraphs below I want to combine all these data into a description of the subperiod within the Chesapeake region.

Projectile Points and Chronology

The complete range of Early Archaic notched and bifurcate projectile points appears on sites within the region in both stratified and surface contexts. In general, the corner-notched grouping usually includes Palmer, Charleston, Amos, and Kirk types. Side-notched varieties include Hardaway, Kessel, Warren, and more local types. These are followed by such bifurcate types as St. Albans, MacCorkle, LeCroy, and Kanawha. The enigmatic Kirk-stemmed type is also well known on regional sites. It is often coterminous with bifurcate types (see Egloff and McAvoy 1990) but sometimes postdates those types (see Clark and Miller 1975). Figure 5.2 illustrates major projectile point types recovered on Early Archaic sites within the study area.

To date, the longest and most complete unbroken sequence of such Early Archaic types in the region has been reported by Egloff and McAvoy (1990). This is the result of McAvoy's excavations at the Slade site along the Nottoway River in Sussex County, Virginia. At this location, examples of the Hardaway type start a long stratigraphic column followed by small, Palmer projectiles that appear to be replaced by larger Palmer types and large side-notched projectiles labeled the Fort Nottoway type by McAvoy. Next in sequence, small, serrated corner-notched varieties, named the Decatur–Angelico type by the excavator, are followed by Kirk corner-notched projectiles. St. Albans and MacCorkle bifurcates appear next, followed by Kirk-stemmed types, which are in turn overlain by LeCroy and Kanawha bifurcate types.

Temporal placement of diagnostic projectile point groupings within the regional Early Archaic can be expected to follow the general time frames discussed previously for the broader Southeast region. In a general sense, notched types predate bifurcate types, and Kirk-stemmed appear at about the same time as the latter. Chronologically, notched types within the local area should date to between approximately 10,000 and 8500 years ago. Bifurcate types probably appeared as early as 9000 years ago and persisted until about 8000 years ago. Kirk-stemmed projectile points most likely were being deposited in the region by at least 8500 years ago, or even earlier, and may have lasted well into the subsequent Middle Archaic subperiod. McAvoy's stratigraphic sequence from the Slade site might enable cautious projection of a finer-scale chronology for individual types within the broader groupings (see Egloff and McAvoy 1990). As always, however, it would not be surprising to see variation depending on specific contexts.

Radiometric dates to support this chronology are very sparse from within the region. A feature at the Slade site containing carbonized hickory shell in association with bifurcate LeCroy and Kanawha types has produced an assay of 8300 ± 110 (Beta-16255) years ago. The series of unpublished radiocarbon assays on that site

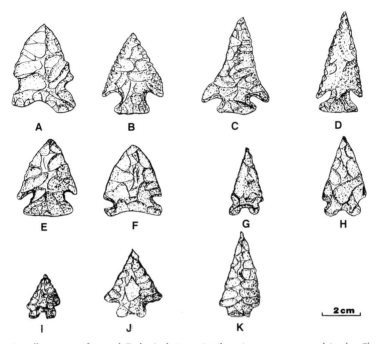

Figure 5.2. Illustration of typical Early Archaic projectile point types recovered in the Chesapeake region: A, Hardaway; B, Palmer; C, Charleston; D, Amos; E, Kirk corner-notched; F, Kessell; G, St. Albans; H, MacCorkle; I, LeCroy; J, Kanawha; K, Kirk-stemmed.

herein are courtesy of the Nottoway River Survey (McAvoy, personal communication, 1994). Readers are referred to that organization's forthcoming publication for the definitive discussion of these assays and that site. Radiocarbon dates to support the notched grouping chronology are not available directly from within the study area. To the west, Joseph Benthall (1979) does report an assay of 9790 ± 400 (FSU-330) on a notched projectile point recovered in the lowest component of Daugherty's Cave in Russell County, Virginia. The excavator identifies this projectile as a Lost Lake or Charleston corner-notched type. At the Thunderbird site in the Shenandoah Valley, Gardner (1974) reports a radiocarbon assay of 9900 ± 340 (W-2816) that may date corner-notched types at that site.

Assemblages

The assemblage recovered by Lowery at the Crane Point site on the Eastern Shore appears to be linked to notched projectile point types and is clearly reminiscent of the earlier Paleoindian assemblage (Lowery and Custer 1990:83). Information currently available from the Slade site (Geier 1990:89) indicates some departure from the earlier Paleoindian assemblage at the time notched projectile points were being deposited at that location. Scraper forms, associated with Palmer and Kirk notched types, are distinct from earlier Paleoindian scrapers. Not much else of any substance can be stated with certainly at this point.

It is possible to say more about tool assemblages accompanying bifurcate projectile points. A number of investigators comment on the increasing frequency of flakes and tools produced by the bipolar manufacturing technique. At the Slade site in Virginia bipolar wedges, flake knives, and split-cobble abraders appear in bifurcate levels (Geier 1990:88). In the northern reaches of the study area at the Higgins site (Ebright 1992:415–16), the assemblage associated with bifurcate projectile points (LeCroy type) is rather basic with only two formal tool types, projectile points and generalized bifaces. The latter were apparently used for a wide variety of purposes. There is little evidence for a unifacial tool industry here, but numerous utilized flakes were recovered.

The choice of lithic material to manufacture chipped-stone tools during the Early Archaic does present an interesting contrast between the notched and bifurcate tool assemblages. The recent excavations at the Indian Creek site illustrate a change in lithic material preference between the notched and bifurcate levels at that site. About 75% of the notched projectile points, Palmer and Kirk types, at that site are manufactured from nonlocal rhyolite and chert. By the time that bifurcate types were being deposited, local materials were being heavily utilized in about equal proportions to nonlocal materials. This trend has been noted at other sites, and it is generally interpreted as evidence of more restricted mobility during the latter portions of the Early Archaic.

Ground-stone tools definitely appear at regional Early Archaic sites. Lowery reports the recovery of a flaked and surface-ground celt and an axe as well as abraders from the Crane Point site (Lowery and Custer 1990:99). These tools are associated with notched projectile point types. Other types of ground-stone artifacts appear with bifurcates. A chipped-stone adz with surface grinding has been recovered at the Slade site in association with MacCorkle-like or St. Albans projectile points (Geier 1990:70). The presence of at least one pestle and a maul-like fragment has also been noted at the Higgins site (Ebright 1992:416). These three sites, given their Early Archaic notched and bifurcate components, currently represent the earliest available evidence for the beginning of a ground-stone tool industry in the local area.

Site Structure

Most known Early Archaic components in the region manifest themselves as palimpsests (to use a currently popular term) of multiple activities, likely the result of frequent reoccupation. And in most cases, local depositional processes were not active enough to insure significant vertical separation between such episodes. This unfortunately results in very coarse-grained deposits that are difficult to decipher. Such a situation, coupled with a general scarcity of stratified early assemblages, makes statements about site structure rather difficult. Some general trends, however, can be noted.

In the Early Archaic levels of both the Higgins (Ebright 1992) and Indian Creek (LeeDecker 1991) sites in Maryland, occupation areas appear to be marked by distinct clusters of fire-cracked rock usually less than 1 m in diameter. These features are identified by investigators at both sites as probable container dumps of boiling stones. Evidence of lithic tool use and maintenance activities often appears near these features. Based on her analysis of the Early Archaic assemblage at the Higgins site, Ebright (1992:411) adds that vegetable food processing and butchering were also taking place. At both sites, the areas of occupation are rather restricted. A hearth, in association with notched types, has been excavated at the Crane Point site on the Eastern Shore.

One important additional feature has been noted for the early bifurcate levels at the Slade site in Virginia. Egloff and McAvoy (1990:70) report the excavation of a cremated human interment at that site in association with MacCorkle-like or St. Albans projectile points. This duplicates similar treatment of human remains dating to the Early Archaic at the Icehouse Bottom site in Tennessee and represents a first glimpse into Early Archaic mortuary practices within the Chesapeake region.

Settlement Strategies

In any examination of regional Early Archaic settlement strategies, at least two factors must be recognized. First, evidence of subperiod settlement patterning, like that for the earlier Paleoindian period, has been truncated by the continuing sequence of local marine transgression. Laurie Steponaitis's (1980:20–22) observation that no notched or bifurcate tradition sites could be located through her survey of the transgressed portion of the Patuxent River speaks to this reality. Second, and possibly related, regional Early Archaic sites are not as prolific as those assignable to other subperiods. At this point in time, it is often possible to say more about even Paleoindian settlement patterns. In short, strong opinions about Early Archaic settlement strategies, based on currently available evidence, should be approached with caution.

It can be said with some degree of confidence that both notched- and bifurcate-bearing Early Archaic sites in the Chesapeake region are often small in size and widely distributed across the landscape. Larger subperiod sites do exist, but there is always the question of whether these sites were truly large or, rather, represented repeated occupations of the same location over many years. The Chance site on the Eastern Shore of the estuary represents such a potentially large Early Archaic site (Cresthull 1971, 1972). This site, whatever its exact nature, was oriented toward a local wetland area.

Exactly how known Early Archaic sites articulate into a settlement system is another matter. Many archaeologists simply argue that such sites were positioned to be near productive resource areas and leave it at that. Following a frequently expressed theme in Early Archaic studies, Gardner (1978:47) views notched tradition settlement patterns as similar to earlier Paleoindian settlement patterns. By 8500 years ago, changes in regional ecological structure stimulated the radiation of bifurcate groups into more numerous habitats, including inland wetland areas. Custer (1989) essentially reiterates this position in his study of the Early Archaic occupation of the Eastern Shore. In both cases, an Early Archaic settlement system based on the occupation of some large base camps and numerous associated procurement sites is the result.

There have been recent challenges to this position. Scott Parker (1990) questions the notion of resource availability as the sole determinate of Early Archaic settlement strategies. His model is instead based on the need for these early populations to mitigate the risk that was a fact of life in an unpredictable environment. In this perspective, the widespread Early Archaic settlement system of mostly small sites and a few larger sites is seen as an active effort not only to feed but also to integrate peoples. People moving between many sites are much more likely to interact than groups concentrated at a few more widely spaced larger sites. Contact between smaller units of that population leads to reciprocity, and risk can be pooled through information and resource sharing. Such a perspective could certainly be used to help explain the spread of nonlocal lithic materials across the Coastal Plain of the study area.

On a more empirical level, LeeDecker (1991:275) employs data from the Indian Creek site to challenge the idea that the notched settlement system was more similar to the Paleoindian settlement strategy and that the appearance of bifurcate-using groups marked a significant departure. While admitting that a new technology was being introduced with bifurcate projectile points, he adds that this introduction does not appear to be linked with any apparent change in settlement pattern. At the Indian Creek site a bifurcate assemblage is directly superimposed over an earlier notched assemblage. The same situation is likewise apparent at the Slade site in Virginia.

Subsistence Strategies

Most investigators, in both this region and others, believe that Early Archaic subsistence strategies were designed to exploit the wide variety of resources presented by the newly emerging Holocene ecology. Finding evidence of exactly what floral and faunal resources were being exploited has been another matter. Two lines of evidence that begin to suggest answers to this question—one direct (actual remains) and the other more indirect (residue analysis)—are now being reported from Chesapeake Early Archaic sites.

In terms of the direct evidence, carbonized nut fragments have been recovered at local Early Archaic sites. A feature containing carbonized hickory hulls has recently been reported at the Slade site (Egloff and McAvoy 1990:70). This feature, interpreted as a hearth, is associated with bifurcate projectile point types and has yielded a radiocarbon date of 8300 ± 110 (Beta-16255) years ago. On the Eastern Shore, Lowery has reported the recovery of charred hickory nut, butternut, and possibly acorns along with amaranth and chenopod from a hearth that is associated with notched projectile points at the Crane Point site (Lowery and Custer 1990:99). Through flotation, some 38 different species of charred seeds were recovered at the Indian Creek site (LeeDecker 1991:233). A large percentage of these seeds were from tuberous plants. Unfortunately, in this case, it does not appear possible to link particular species solely to the Early Archaic components at that site. Still, these data clearly indicate at least some focus on products of the forest mast and other tuberous and starchy seed-bearing plants during the Early Archaic subperiod.

A battery of new analytical techniques has recently been employed at both the Indian Creek and Higgins sites on the Maryland inner Coastal Plain. Resulting information on Early Archaic subsistence practices is at best unclear. Residue analysis, both presence/absence and family-level tests, has been undertaken on a suite of artifacts from the Indian Creek site (LeeDecker 1991:105–107). For the most part, however, Early Archaic bifurcate projectiles tested negative at the family level, and it is difficult to interpret the results of this analysis program on other artifact types with any degree of confidence. At the Higgins site, Ebright (1992) employed a range of analytical techniques, such as blood residue analysis, pollen-washes of tools, and phytolith and fiber analysis, to begin to decipher subsistence strategies. While these techniques did present useful information on local environmental context, little real data that can be confidently linked to Early Archaic subsistence practices are evident. In my opinion, while these analytical techniques perhaps do hold great promise for archaeology, at this point they have not revealed unequivocal evidence of Early Archaic subsistence practices at the two sites under examination. With that said, both LeeDecker (1991) and Ebright (1992) are still to be commended for exploring every avenue in the analysis of both sites.

Middle Archaic

The Middle Archaic within the Chesapeake region is broadly dated between 8000 and 5000 years ago. And of all the various increments of prehistory, both in the study area and in broader eastern North America, the Middle Archaic remains the most elusive. Students of local prehistory will, of course, recognize this cautionary note as similar to those that appear in almost all of the relevant literature on the subperiod. Various reasons, from imprecise taxonomies to inadequate survey to loss of sites as a result of continuing marine transgression, are usually advanced for this state of affairs. Nevertheless, it is now beginning to be possible to say more about the Middle Archaic within the local area. In many ways, however, what is now known about the subperiod makes it appear very similar to the preceding Early Archaic subperiod, especially the bifurcate phases of this increment. The same categories that guided discussion of the earlier subperiod will again be employed.

Projectile Points and Chronology

Projectile point groupings included within the Middle Archaic in the Chesapeake region include both stemmed and side-notched types. The former grouping consists of Stanly, Morrow Mountain I and II, and Guilford as dominant types. Side-notched types include Halifax, Otter Creek, and Brewerton types. Figure 5.3 illustrates major Middle Archaic projectile point types. While all of these various types are not evenly distributed across the study area, it is possible, by looking at a number of sites, to reconstruct a regional sequence of sorts.

Returning to the Slade site along the Nottoway River in Virginia, McAvoy and Egloff (1990:72–73) report that while Stanly projectile points are fairly rare, they do appear above earlier LeCroy types and below later Morrow Mountain I points at that site. Carbonized hickory shell and charcoal recovered under a mortar that is most likely associated with nearby Stanly projectiles have yielded a radiocarbon date of 7420 ± 160 (Beta-24427) years ago. Morrow Mountain I projectile points follow next in sequence. An associated pit containing carbonized wood and plant remains has produced a date of 6470 ± 90 (Beta-22838) years ago on this type. After that time period, Morrow Mountain II and Guilford types appear at the Slade site. Although what have been interpreted to be stone hearths are found in association with these

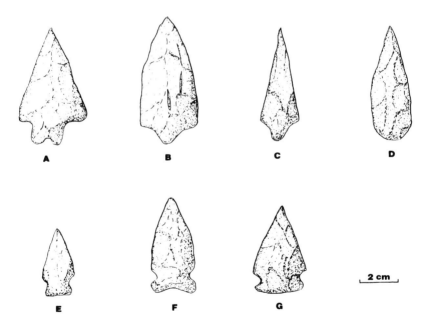

Figure 5.3. Illustration of typical Middle Archaic projectile point types recovered in the Chesapeake region: A, Stanly; B, Morrow Mountain I; C, Morrow Mountain II; D, Guilford; E, Halifax; F, Otter Creek; G, Brewerton.

point types along the Nottoway River, suitable amounts of charcoal could not be recovered for radiometric assay. A hearth in association with Morrow Mountain II types has been dated to 5380 ± 140 (I-1680) years ago at the Peaks of Otter site in Virginia, well west of the study area. Halifax side-notched types close out the Middle Archaic sequence at the Slade site. A fire pit evidently associated with Halifax projectile points was radiocarbon assayed to 5050 ± 400 (Beta-15529) years ago. In many ways, the Middle Archaic column described above for the Slade site essentially duplicates Coe's (1964) sequence for the North Carolina Piedmont.

All of the various projectile point types described above appear across much of the Chesapeake region. Some types, however, are not prolific. For example, Middle Archaic stemmed types become rarer as one moves north in the Chesapeake region. At the Indian Creek site in the northern study area, the Middle Archaic is practically nonexistent even though that site was intensively occupied during the Early Archaic and subsequently in the Late Archaic (LeeDecker 1991:269). This is somewhat perplexing. Part of the problem within the study area might be that stemmed Middle Archaic projectile point types appear to be candidates for frequent taxonomic mis-identification across the region. They are often collected and identified as Late Archaic broad-stemmed types.

Whatever the case, components probably dating to relatively late in the Middle Archaic have recently been excavated at the Higgins sites (Ebright 1991). Otter Creek and Brewerton side-notched projectile points are prolific at that site and should date to approximately 6000 years ago or possibly even earlier. This temporal assign-ment is based on Funk's (1988) identification of a Middle Archaic proto-Laurentian including these projectile point types. Unfortunately, not enough charcoal could be collected from those levels of the Higgins site to produce radiometric dates for those types. Both side-notched types, Otter Creek and Brewerton, appear to be more frequent in the upper reaches of the study area, perhaps serving somewhat as northern equivalents to the southern Halifax side-notched type.

In summary, the following broad incremental chronology for the Chesapeake region appears reasonable. Stemmed projectile point types in the earlier portions of the subperiod should date to between approximately 8000 and 6000 years ago. After this, subsequent side-notched types appear to dominate from about 6000 to 5000 years ago. Admittedly, however, there is a paucity of radiometric assays to support this last inference.

Assemblages

Trends initiated in the Early Archaic bifurcate components continue into this subperiod. Middle Archaic assemblages associated with both stemmed and side-notched point types are mostly bifacial. Unifacial tools, other than informal modified flakes, become rare. Projectile points and generalized bifaces represent the most notable tools of the Middle Archaic chipped-stone assemblage. Many of these bifacial tools were multifunctional. At the Higgins site, so-called projectile point specimens appear to have been used as knives and scrapers, given evidence of numerous margin spalls and polish on their lateral edges (Ebright 1992:418). Only a single formal unifacial scraper was recovered in the Middle Archaic levels of the Higgins site.

Lithic material preference during the Middle Archaic is variable depending on location. Certainly, there was an increasing preference for locally available materials. This is especially evident on the Eastern Shore (Hughes 1980) and in the southern areas of the Western Shore of the estuary where a near total reliance on quartzite is evident (Geier 1990). From the middle to upper reaches of the Western Shore, quartzite is heavily utilized along with nonlocal rhyolite (Ebright 1992; L. C. Steponaitis 1980). At the Higgins site, based on a low rhyolite debitage to rhyolite tool ratio, it is suspected that rhyolite tools were being manufactured from transported bifacial blanks (Ebright 1992:418).

Ground-stone tools appear to become more prolific during the Middle Archaic. An atlatl weight and a mortar have been reported in association with Stanly projectile point types along the Nottoway River in Virginia (Egloff and McAvoy 1990:72). Another atlatl weight in association with later Morrow Mountain II types is reported by the same authors along that river. The Higgins site has yielded mano and metate fragments, a pestle, and abraders from its Middle Archaic components (Ebright 1992:420). In general, Middle Archaic ground-stone tool types are completely pecked and/or ground, as opposed to tools reported for the earlier subperiod that are both flaked and ground.

Site Structure

Archaeologists have only recently begun to understand Middle Archaic site structure in the Chesapeake region. In general, trends initiated in the Early Archaic appear to continue in this subperiod. Formal hearths appear more common and sometimes are of substantial size. At sites along the Nottoway River in Virginia, however, charcoal is surprisingly rare in some such Middle Archaic hearths (Egloff and McAvoy 1990:72). The charcoal that remained may have been carried away by the elements or broken down and transported in solution through the sandy Coastal Plain sediments. Alternatively, these features may have had some altogether different function.

Recent excavations at the Higgins site on the upper Western Shore offer perhaps our most detailed view of Middle Archaic site structure (Ebright 1992). Various occupation zones of that site are dated to the subperiod based on the presence of Otter Creek and Brewerton diagnostic projectile point types. Middle Archaic deposits there appear to represent a series of reoccupations at that location. At least four different activity areas were isolated, each yielding evidence of tool manufacturing or maintenance as well as discrete concentrations of fire-cracked rock. There is additional evidence that each activity area was the focus of various subsistence and processing activities.

Settlement Strategies

Some data on Middle Archaic settlement patterns are available, yet these are admittedly sparse. Published statements on the subject tend to be either very general or overly optimistic in stating definite opinions based on less than extensive evidence. Most investigators note an emphasis on interior wetland areas as well as settlement near stream junctures, tributary floodplains, or other areas that might have offered resource concentrations (Hughes 1980; Rappleye and Gardner 1979; L. C. Steponaitis 1980). Sites are certainly prevalent in upland areas. Again, however, many Middle Archaic sites on the outer Coastal Plain have undoubtedly been lost to continuing sea level rise. The Higgins site, located on an inner Coastal Plain promontory between two small streams and not too distant from a wetland area, exemplifies subperiod settlement choices. In general, this occupation of many small sites scattered across the landscape repeats the pattern noted during the Early Archaic subperiod.

Subsistence Strategies

Based on available evidence Middle Archaic subsistence strategies appear very similar to patterns noted for the Early Archaic. Carbonized hickory shell has been reported in both the Stanly and Halifax levels of the Slade site along the Nottoway River in Virginia (Egloff and McAvoy 1990:72). Based on residue analysis, acorn and other nut processing as well as the utilization of various plant species, including sunflower, is linked to the Middle Archaic levels of the Higgins site (Ebright 1992:416). Exploitation of turkey, based on fiber analysis, is also suggested. While no other definite faunal remains can as yet be attributed to Middle Archaic sites in the study area, when such data are recovered it will most likely indicate exploitation of the typical suite of large and small temperate animal species. In many ways, the Middle Archaic subsistence strategy, like that in the Early Archaic, appears to fit well with Cleland's (1976) characterization of a diffuse adaptation.

The important question of shellfish exploitation during the Middle Archaic, especially in relation to the nascent Chesapeake estuary, has piqued the interest of archaeologists in the region. In the Southeast, increased exploitation of various species of riverine molluscs is evident by the Middle Archaic. Later in prehistory local groups were engaged in the intensive harvesting of Chesapeake Bay oyster reefs. Consequently, the Middle Archaic origin of shellfish exploitation in the study area remains a possibility.

Radiocarbon dates on oyster shell recovered on the Eastern Shore stretch back some 5000 to 6000 years into the Middle Archaic. The assays are the result of research undertaken on coastal adaptations by Steve Wilke and Gail Thompson in the early to mid-1970s. Sites dated by these two investigators are believed by them to be the earliest evidence of shellfish exploitation along the estuary (Wilke and Thompson 1977:99). Nevertheless, the assays appear particularly equivocal for a number of reasons including general problems in the radiometric dating of shell, not to mention the fact that the shell being assayed was not associated with artifacts or was associated with what were clearly much later artifacts. In fact, most now view this suite of radiocarbon dates as essentially useless (see Custer 1989:126–127).

At this point, there is no reliable evidence that *intensive* oyster exploitation had started in the study area by the Middle Archaic. Suitably old shell middens have not been found. Custer (1989:126) cites the absence of any large submerged shell reefs dating to this time period in the nearby Delaware Bay. Most feel that the marine transgression of the ancestral Susquehanna River was still progressing rapidly enough to preclude the establishment of sizable concentrations of oyster.

Late Archaic

The last subperiod of the Archaic to be discussed within the Chesapeake region, the Late Archaic, represents an extremely important increment of the prehistoric past. Chronological boundaries of the Late Archaic are drawn between approximately 5000 and 3000 years ago. This subperiod represents the culmination of trends begun during the Early and Middle Archaic as well as a time when important changes began to set the stage for many later developments in prehistory. It is a time that contains both the ends of one way of life and the beginnings of a significant subsequent redirection. The paragraphs below describe what archaeologists have discovered about the Late Archaic following the general categories employed for both of the previous two subperiods.

Projectile Points and Chronology

Archaeologists working within the study area have been debating Late Archaic projectile point sequences for some time. Early ideas on this matter were published by Holland (1955) and to a certain degree by Stephenson and Ferguson (1963). The thoughts of Ritchie (1961) and Coe (1964), working to the north and south, respectively, influenced the development of regional typologies. More recently, local archaeologists have begun to present their own formal typologies that include Late Archaic sequences (e.g., Gardner 1980; Gleach 1987; Hranicky and Painter 1991; McLearen 1991a; McNett 1974; Wesler 1985). Opinions on Late Archaic typological sequences differ along a spectrum ranging from subtle to radical.

In general, the distinction between narrow- and broad-blade Late Archaic projectile point types discussed previously does apply to the Chesapeake region. There is in addition, however, some overlap with earlier types and some regional variation that needs to be discussed. A number of generally narrow-blade projectile points appear to define the early portions of the Late Archaic in the study area. Some of these types overlap from the earlier subperiod into the Late Archaic. This appears to be especially true of both Brewerton and Halifax types, and it may likewise be true of Otter Creek. These are joined by a local variant labeled the Vernon type. Vernon points are morphologically very similar to Halifax. All of these various types, with the exception of some subtypes within the Brewerton series, are side-notched. Figure 5.4 illustrates all major projectile point types discussed for the local region.

These side-notched, narrow-blade varieties are joined by a series of stemmed, narrow-blade projectile points. Most of the latter are morphologically similar to Bare Island and Lackawaxen types as defined to the north by Ritchie (1961) and Kinsey (1959), respectively. In deference to both scholars, regional archaeologists usually refer to local specimens as the Bare Island/Lackawaxen type. Prehistorians in the Chesapeake region are also likely to talk about two additional slightly different projectile points, similar to Bare Island/Lackawaxen, but arguably unique. These are

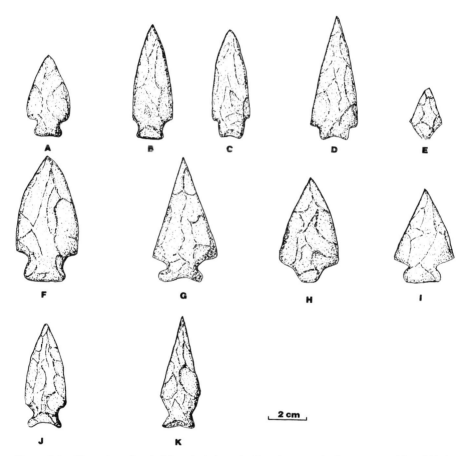

Figure 5.4. Illustration of typical Late Archaic projectile point types, both narrow- and broad-blade, recovered in the Chesapeake region: A, Vernon; B, Bare Island/Lackawaxen; C, Clagett; D, Holmes; E, Piscataway; F, Savannah River; G, Susquehanna; H, Koens-Crispin; I, Perkiomen; J, Orient; K, Dry Brook.

referred to as the Clagget and Holmes types. Both are stemmed and have narrow blades. The Clagget type was defined by Stephenson and Ferguson (1963) and the Holmes type, although a formal type description has never been published, is the result of research in the Potomac Valley by McNett (1974).

The Piscataway projectile point represents another indigenous narrow-blade type. My inclusion of this diminutive lozenge-shaped, contracting stem projectile in the Late Archaic sequence is likely to be debated. The type was originally defined by Stephenson and Ferguson (1963:195–196) from collections made at the Accokeek Creek site. In the report on that site it was assigned to the Late Woodland. Since that time it has variously been assigned to every subperiod of the Woodland as well as to the Late Archaic. While conceding that it may be a type of some temporal duration, I see its origins in the Late Archaic given its definite *stratigraphic* occurrence below or with other Late Archaic types at the Fraser and Ruppert Island sites in the Potomac Valley (McDowell 1972) and at the Katchef site along the Patuxent River (Boyd, Moore, and Dent 1990).

Subsequent to the various narrow-blade types discussed above, a suite of broad-blade projectile points are assigned to the Late Archaic. These are the so-called broadspears that dominate the end of the subperiod along much of the Atlantic coast. A number of investigators assign these types to a separate transitional stage between the Late Archaic and Early Woodland subperiods (e.g., Mouer 1991; Witthoft 1953). Given the fact that they are normally not associated with ceramics in this region, I assign them to the Late Archaic. In the Chesapeake region distinctive Savannah River, Susquehanna, Koens-Crispin, and Perkiomen types are recovered. At least two of these types, Susquehanna and Savannah River, appear in significant numbers across the region. Perkiomen types, by contrast, are less prolific and appear to cluster around the Dismal Swamp in the lower reaches of the study area (McLearen 1991a:104). Orient/Dry Brook types, apparently later derivatives of the broad-blade types discussed above, are also recovered across the region. In addition, many would argue that the Holmes type, placed by its founder (McNett 1974) in the narrow-blade tradition, should be viewed as a broad-blade type. I concur with this suggestion and would recommend that it henceforth be seen as the local small variant derivative of the Savannah River type.

Chronologically, Late Archaic narrow-blade types are generally earlier than broad-blade types within the Chesapeake region. While there is overlap between the two traditions, stratigraphic evidence and very limited radiometric assays from local sites support such an assertion. In an earlier section of this chapter I cited a sample of available radiocarbon assays on the various types assignable to each tradition across eastern North America. Using these data, and factoring in locational differences, it is fairly safe to project narrow-blade types within the study area as dating to between about 5000 and 3500 years ago. Vernon projectile points, an indigenous narrow-blade type, have been dated at the Jeffrey–Harris Rockshelter to 5880 ± 1200 (SI-364) and 5120 ± 160 (SI-363) years ago (Johnson 1968). This site is within the Virginia Piedmont just west of the study area.

Evidence suggests that broad-blade projectile point types within the study area should date to between approximately 4200 and 3000 years ago. Stephen Potter (1982) and Gregory Waselkov (1982) have dated Holmes projectile points on the Coastal Plain to between about 4100 and 3500 years ago. Potter's assays from the Plum Nelly site date to 4105 ± 85 (SI-4228) and 3905 ± 95 (SI-4229) years ago. Waselkov's date from the White Oak Point site is 3500 ± 75 (DIC-1771) years ago. A date of 4070 ± 80 (Beta-22156) has been reported on Savannah River points, the so-called narrow variant, from the Slade site in Virginia (Egloff and McAvoy 1990:74). Two additional radiocarbon assays are available from Virginia sites, and both are from late in this period. A date of 3260 ± 90 (UGa-3346) years ago has been reported from site 44-HE-313, and another date of 2840 ± 155 (UGa-3347) years ago was obtained at site 44-GO-40. Again, stratigraphic evidence also suggests that broad-blade types appeared slightly later than narrow-blade types. More radiocarbon assays, however, would certainly help clarify the situation.

Assemblages

Variation within chipped-stone assemblages in the narrow- versus broad-blade traditions, at least as now understood, appears negligible. Both assemblages were primarily biface-focused, and, as such, they exhibit continuity with the previous Middle Archaic pattern. So-called projectile points within each tradition appear to have been used for a variety of functions. In fact, the debate over the functions of narrow- and broad-blade formal bifacial implements often dominates the literature. This controversy originated with the publication of Turnbaugh's (1975) ideas on the broad-blade tradition across eastern North America, and it intensified with the almost immediate rejoinder by Thomas Cook (1976).

McLearen (1991a:93–94) does a good job of reviewing more recent thoughts on this matter. There is no clear local consensus at this point. The debate centers most directly on the function of broad-blade bifaces. Some see them as having functioned as knives (e.g., Custer 1989:151–153). Callahan (1974:48–49), based on experimental analysis, believes they could have functioned as both projectiles and generalized cutting tools. Billy Oliver (1985:202–204), relying on experimental studies of delivery systems, argues that broad, heavy projectiles were designed to increase the distance and accuracy of atlatl-propelled spear shafts. In that perspective they served primarily as hunting implements.

If one views these broad-blade implements as knives, the logical extension becomes that they may have been counterparts to narrow-blade projectiles. This deflates what many see as two archaeological entities into a single Late Archaic manifestation. Depending on point of view, it is possible to make an argument for both positions. At this point in time, however, based on a number of factors (see Mouer 1991), many prefer to view *both* narrow- and broad-blade bifacial implements as potentially multifunctional tools, and to see them as two separate and distinct entities. I follow this line of reasoning.

Whatever the case, the remainder of the Late Archaic chipped-stone assemblage is dominated by various generalized bifaces. These are often accompanied by somewhat expedient flake scrapers, drills, perforators, and utilized flakes. Some such implements, for example drills and end-scrapers, were manufactured from broken or exhausted projectile points. Rough-stone cobble tools are also often found in Late Archaic assemblages. The narrow-blade assemblage (Bare Island/Lackawaxen) excavated at the Higgins site in the upper reaches of the region may be fairly typical of that manifestation (Ebright 1992:341–358). Likewise, the assemblage dominated by broad-blade projectiles at the Plum Nelly site about 14 km from the mouth of the Potomac River in Virginia may be fairly typical for that entity (Potter 1982:303). The recovery of a significant number of bone artifacts along with stone implements at that location is especially noteworthy.

Lithic material preference is variable by location. Narrow-blade assemblages were manufactured from a wide variety of materials. In addition to locally available quartz and quartzite, materials from just outside the immediate region, such as rhyolite, appear in these assemblages. This material seems to have been transported through what Stewart (1989:52) has characterized as broad-based, down-the-line exchange networks. Much the same can be said for broad-blade assemblages, although a preference for locally available quartzite is often evident. In all, lithic procurement practices for both entities appear to have been embedded within group settlement areas. Additional nonlocal materials, if present, arrived via exchange with immediate neighbors.

In addition to chipped-stone tools, the Late Archaic assemblage includes a number of ground-stone tool types. Apparently, at least, the accelerated production of ground-stone tools seems more associated with groups using broad blades. Adzes, celts, gouges, and axes all increase in variety and frequency. The Late Archaic appears to mark the beginning of sustained production of the ground-stone, grooved axe (McLearen 1991a:99). For the most part instead of being flaked and then ground, axes were fashioned through pecking and grinding, but were seldom polished. Many comment that the increase in numbers of woodworking tools might be an indication of the presence of a substantial dugout canoe industry. Other ground-stone tools types, such as manos, metates, mortars, atlatl weights, and the like, appear on all Late Archaic sites.

Certainly, the most noteworthy addition to the Late Archaic assemblage is the steatite, or soapstone, bowl. Steatite outcrops along the fall lines of the major tributaries of the Chesapeake Bay. Starting as early as circa 4000 years ago, prehistoric inhabitants of the study area began to carve containers in various sizes and shapes out of this soft rock (see Figure 5.5). The most common vessel form is the shallow, round to oblong, thick-walled bowl. Vessel openings are unrestricted and bowls often have opposing lug handles. Size can vary greatly, and some enormous containers have been recovered. There is also occasional variation evident in the basic form cited above.

These steatite containers appear to have been manufactured at the quarry locations and then transported throughout the region. Manufacturing implements,

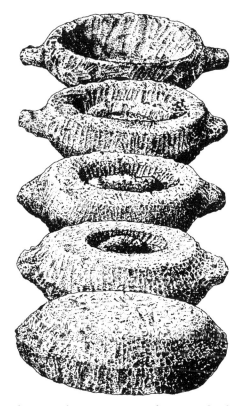

Figure 5.5.   Illustration of the manufacturing sequence of soapstone bowls associated with the Late Archaic in the Chesapeake region (from Holmes 1897).

including chisels and picks, are recovered at the quarries. Bowl preforms were often formed directly on a vein of steatite and then detached for final shaping. Some convenient loose steatite nodules were fashioned directly into containers. Whatever the manufacturing trajectory, the containers appear to have been transported away from the quarries as finished objects. Trace elements analysis (Luckenbach, Allen, and Holland 1975) indicates that steatite from Virginia quarries at least was often transported hundreds of kilometers from its original source.

Steatite containers or fragments appear on a significant number of Late Archaic sites on both shores of the Chesapeake Bay. Waselkov (1982:258) has reported a radiocarbon date of 3500 ± 75 (DIC-1771) on transported steatite along the lower Potomac River. The Harland Mill steatite quarry in Maryland has been dated to 3330 ± 160 (M-2255). Stratigraphic position at other sites suggests an even earlier date for the appearance of these unique artifacts in the region. Although steatite does appear in components assignable to the narrow-blade tradition, it seems to be recovered most frequently and in the largest quantities on broad-blade tradition sites.

One final note about steatite needs to be made. Fragments of steatite with so-called drilled repair holes are recovered in significant numbers on regional sites. All steatite objects recovered on the Eastern Shore, for example, are fragments and a number have repair holes (Custer 1989:236). Some argue that these were net sinkers. Most often these fragments are seen as sherds, the remains of one-time bowls, and many appear to have been thermally altered. Sassaman (1993) has recently suggested that these perforated steatite slabs may actually have been cooking stones used in container boiling. In the same sense, he suggests that many steatite containers were not used directly over fire, but were internally heated.

Site Structure

Late Archaic sites in the region are often dichotomized into large versus small manifestations. The former are often seen as artifacts of increasing sedentism or collective group activity. The latter are interpreted as related temporary camps, usually for the purpose of resource extraction. Such uncritical dichotomies may sometimes be misleading. Some of the large sites, for example, are probably more apparent than real. A significant number of the so-called large, macroband sites are no doubt palimpsests reflecting reoccupations over substantial periods of time. Periodic revisitation, often even by peoples of different traditions, coupled with a lack of vertical separation between occupational episodes represents a real obstacle to any reliable understanding of site structure in the study area during the Late Archaic. It also makes it difficult to present a clear picture of typical site structure for either the narrow- or broad-blade regional components. The only option is to turn to what appear to be reasonably pure, single-component sites representing each grouping. Such sites are not numerous.

In spatial extent, small extraction sites yielding narrow blades are roughly comparable in size to their broad-blade counterparts. At the other end of the spectrum, larger narrow-blade sites often do not match the spatial magnitude of the largest broad-blade sites. As mentioned before, however, size may be deceptive in both instances, and what appear to be truly substantial narrow-blade sites are known from the region. Whatever the case, there appear to be other differences that may represent unique signatures between the two entities in the study area.

Narrow-blade sites, at least as now understood, apparently contain a more limited range of features. Sites assignable to the Clyde Farm and Barker's Landing complexes (Custer 1989) on the Eastern Shore of the estuary may be exceptions, but most narrow-blade sites contain little more than concentrations or scatters of fire-cracked rock. Presumably some of these features were hearths and others represent container dumps. The Rowe site, on the inner Coastal Plain of the Western Shore in Maryland, illustrates the spatial distribution of activity areas within a substantial narrow-blade site. McNett (1974:23–26) isolated a number of discrete activity areas within this site dominated by Vernon projectile points. Specific portions of this site were reserved for tool production, butchering, habitation, and hide processing based on the distribution and functional analysis of recovered implements.

On broad-blade sites the range of features encountered is much more extensive. Concentrations of fire-cracked rock representing various activities are common. In addition, definite formal hearths appear as do very substantial platform hearths. These platform hearths, containing multiple layers of fire-cracked rock placed on the living floor, are sometimes up to 10 m in diameter. Given the location near water of sites with these large features, some sort of fish-processing function is suggested. Mouer (1989:20) comments that many sites with these features are in locations along rivers where fish weir construction was quite likely.

The first definite accumulations of shell appear on broad-blade sites along the lower Potomac River (Potter 1982; Waselkov 1982). Small, globular pits were dug on these sites, often in the middens, for the purpose of steaming open molluscs. Apparent burial pits, containing cremated remains, have been reported at a few locations (Painter 1988). Definite evidence for structures remains lacking on regional Late Arachic sites, although such features are sometimes inferred based on circum-stantial evidence.

Settlement Strategies

Some of the most informative research on regional Late Archaic settlement patterns has been published by Dan Mouer (1990, 1991) of Virginia Commonwealth University. Much of his research was undertaken along the James River in the southern Chesapeake region where Mouer has been working for a number of years. In his study of the Late Archaic, a strong link is made between what he feels to be rather distinct adaptive strategies and the resulting settlement patterns of the narrow- versus broad-blade using groups. Note that Mouer prefers different labels, Late Archaic versus Transitional, for what is herein referred to as the narrow- and broad-blade groupings. In what follows I translate his labels into the terminology of this study.

In essence, Mouer (1991:4–10) views the narrow-blade complex in the study area as reflecting a specialized adaptation to a more sylvan environment found beyond the fall line. This specialization was a factor of the rather homogeneous resource structure of that ecosystem. Here narrow-blade sites were almost equally divided between riverine and upland locations. Sites were situated to exploit nut harvests, deer, and turkey populations. On the Coastal Plain these people, while admittedly rather poorly understood by archaeologists, were perhaps more gener-alized given the patchy, zoned, and seasonal resources encountered in that location. All of this, in either context, results in a generally small band organization, an impermanent or shifting settlement system, infrequent aggregation phases, and low levels of regional interaction. Large sites are not as frequent, and smaller sites in specific locations within the Piedmont or broadcast across the landscape in the Coastal Plain became the norm.

In Mouer's (1991:10–24) opinion the broad-blade complex represented a distinct contrast to this situation. This, he argues, was a response to new conditions in the region. Specifically, this group focused on estuarine resources such as anadromous fish and shellfish as well as the resources of enlarged wetland areas. This shifted the broad-blade adaptation to the linear river valleys of the region's tributaries. In the Piedmont, for example, 96% of the known broad-blade sites were located along watercourses. The effective exploitation of such linear environments required more interaction between groups, with information moving over greater distances and between more people. It should be noted that Mouer (1991:23) implies that goods and information were more mobile than groups or individuals in what he refers to as a "chain" interaction system.

This dictates a different settlement strategy. Site size increased as did total number of sites. No evidence is seen for year-round sedentism, but rather an annual cycle of fusion and fission. The result is a variety of settlements ranging from multiband base camps, to smaller but still substantial band camps, to small microband foray sites. Macroband base camps in the Piedmont and on the Coastal Plain sometimes cover up to 2 ha, while smaller multiband camps typically cover about 450 m². As stated before, most of these sites are located directly on water.

For the most part, many archaeologists would see the above model of settlement strategies as broadly applicable to the Chesapeake region. Nonetheless, in the northern reaches of the Chesapeake region, Custer (1989) argues for a very different settlement strategy during this era. His assumptions about the two archaeological entities are quite different, however, as are his conclusions. And some variation can be seen at more local levels. L. C. Steponaitis (1986:285), for example, sees Late Archaic settlement of the Patuxent River area, both narrow- and broad-blace, as fairly uniform across the Coastal Plain. In all cases, perhaps it is best to keep in mind Gardner's (1986:6) admonition that there may be no such thing as a standard Late Archaic response to the Middle Atlantic landscape.

Subsistence Strategies

Late Archaic subsistence strategies were intimately linked to general patterns of adaptation. Here again most presuppose a real difference between narrow- and broad-blade adaptations. The former is equated with a more specialized sylvan adaptation beyond the fall line with perhaps a slightly more generalized response to the less focused resources of the Coastal Plain (Mouer 1991). The latter broad-blade subsistence focus is linked to the emerging estuarine and riverine resources of the study area.

Evidence that indicates more precisely what resources were being exploited by both groups is now becoming available. Subsistence evidence for narrow-blade groups, while available, is admittedly not substantial. In the early 1970s McNett (1974:15–19) established that sites assignable to this entity in the Potomac Valley often yielded remains of various seeds and nuts. Unfortunately, details on exact species exploited have never been provided. Mouer (1991:4) suggests, based on site locations, that products of the forest mast as well as deer and turkey were major items of consumer choice. Ebright's (1992) analysis of narrow-blade components at the Higgins site on the inner Coastal Plain in the upper reaches of the region points to the exploitation of blueberries (*Vaccinium* sp.), cherries (*Prunus* sp.), and wild legumes (*Leguminosae*) at that location. This supposed pattern of plant exploitation is based on pollen analysis of feature contents. Turkey feather fibers were also recovered.

In terms of the broad-blade groups, Waselkov's (1982) analysis of faunal remains at the White Oak Point site in the lower Potomac River Valley indicates an impressive array of subsistence items. A major subsistence focus at this site was certainly oyster, along with deer. Faunal remains recovered at this site, in addition to the two species listed above, include gulf periwinkle (*Littorina irrorata*), soft-shell clam (*Mya arenaria*), ribbed mussel (*Geukensia demissa*), stout tagellus (*Tagellus plebeius*), and various other species of unidentified fish, snake, and mammal. Floral remains recovered were restricted to acorn. Based on faunal indicators of seasonality, including oyster shell growth ring analysis and tooth eruption studies of deer remains, Waselkov (1982:206) demonstrates that the site was occupied during the spring season.

Potter's (1982) analysis of the Late Archaic component at the nearby Plum Nelly site provides a nice counterpart to these data cited above. Plum Nelly apparently served as a fall–winter base camp (Potter 1982:329). Here, four faunal species, including deer, beaver (*Castor canadensis*), raccoon (*Procyon lotor*), and opossum (*Didelphis marsupialis*), were major contributors to the diet. These species were supplemented by the gathering of oyster, soft-shell clam, ribbed mussel, and stout tagellus. Other faunal species recovered included eastern box turtle (*Terrapene carolina*), passenger pigeon (*Ectopistes migratorius*), gray fox (*Urocyon cinereoargenteus*), dog (*Canis familiaris*), gray squirrel (*Sciurus carolinensis*), fox squirrel (*S. niger*), and cottontail (*Sylvilagus floridanus*). Floral remains recovered in association with the above species consisted primarily of hickory nuts.

Broad-blade sites at or above the fall lines of the Chesapeake Bay's tributaries appear to have been focused around the exploitation of anadromous fish runs (see Mouer 1991:20). In addition, McLearen (1991a:112) reports the recovery of seed remains from within features on the Elk Garden site in Virginia. Specific species identified include wild mustard (*Brassica* sp.) and knotweed or smartweed (*Polygonum* sp.). Here again, many archaeologists suspect a primary focus on riverine resources at interior locations. Deer hunting, especially around interior wetland areas, was probably another focus of the broad-blade groups across the study area.

ARCHAIC PATTERNS AND INTERPRETATIONS

The Archaic period in the Chesapeake region encompassed approximately 7000 years of prehistory. By the standards of local prehistory this is a vast amount of time, and it is axiomatic to state that the Archaic period thus represents an important key toward any understanding of regional prehistory. Two points need to be made in regard to this statement. First, with the archaeological record being what it is, there are and probably always will be gaps in our knowledge of the Archaic period. Still, local prehistorians have to their credit now managed to unearth quite a bit of data on this era. If nothing else, I hope that the previous section of this chapter, which synthesizes many of these data, has demonstrated this fact. Second, I believe that at least some of archaeology's continued search for an adequate understanding of the Archaic period is not a result of what we do or do not know about this archaeological record, but instead is a reflection of the ways in which the scholarly community analytically approaches that very record. This last section of the chapter addresses this matter.

To do this, I ultimately want to produce a general description and interpretation of two broad lifeways that I feel to be characteristic of the local archaeological record of the Archaic period. This represents an attempt to attach meaning to these ways of life. By now, I think regional prehistorians for the most part all agree that there was a significant redirection of human prehistory taking place during the last 1200 or so years of the Late Archaic within the Chesapeake region. Few today would argue that this was not a very important time in local prehistory. That particular redirection is herein labeled the *intensification* effort. Before this, at the very beginning of the Archaic period, an earlier redirection of lifeways is evident that I will argue ultimately continues, with minor modification, up until the intensification era of the Late Archaic. The establishment and continuance of this lifeway, which I descriptively refer to as Archaic hunting and foraging, essentially links the Early Archaic with the Middle Archaic and some of the Late Archaic. I hope to suggest some new ideas about the factors responsible for these phenomena.

To do that, this section is organized as follows. This introduction has identified two significant redirections of lifeways during the Archaic period. One represents a transformation of ways of life away from those of the earlier Paleoindian period. Once established this lifeway continues with some modification until the beginning of the latter portions of the Late Archaic. The second redirection, the intensification effort, commences with subsequent portions of the Late Archaic. These two patterns are viewed, in this context, as areas of concern deserving particular attention. But first I want to present a more specific reconstruction of the ecology of the Chesapeake region during the Archaic period. This concentrates primarily on the spatial structure of the Archaic landscape, and it sets the context that may have been stimulating some of this change. Existing interpretations for both redirections during the Archaic are traditionally linked to this record of ecological change. Last, I focus on the two specific lifeways. I offer a broad description of each, and discuss both in relation to issues of ecological and social change. Ultimately, I argue that adaptation to the changing environment should be an area of our concern in seeking to explain some elements of the Archaic period, but it is increasingly evident that the changing environment is not the only force that needs our attention. In those instances perhaps human agency is also a key explanatory variable.

Ecological Context

If the Archaic period was a time of significant redirection in human lifeways, it was also an era that coincided with equally significant ecological change. This ecological change was triggered by the effects of the end of the Pleistocene with the ensuing retreat of the last glacial intrusion from areas immediately north of the Chesapeake region. Impacts on the study area were twofold. First, as water once trapped in the glacial ice pack returned to the ocean, rising sea levels began to flood the ancestral Susquehanna River thus initiating the formation of the Chesapeake Bay. Second, climatic amelioration across all of eastern North America delivered changes to the flora and fauna of the region. I want to explore the nature of these changes and their impact on the Chesapeake landscape during the Archaic period.

General characteristics of the local ecology from the early Holocene on were outlined in Chapter 3. In quick summary, marine transgression, after first claiming the continental shelf, arrived at the mouth of the present estuary circa 10,000 years ago. It then began a sequence of the flooding and dismemberment of the region's late Pleistocene drainage system formerly dominated by the ancestral Susquehanna River. This transformation was not completed until about 3000 years ago.

Regional floral communities began to respond to change beginning at about 10,000 to 9800 years ago. The dominant late Pleistocene coniferous vegetation was displaced. Its initial replacement appears to have been locally variable and somewhat transitional. After 8200 years ago, oak became the dominant species across the region. Hickory was the primary codominant, although this could vary depending on location. A number of investigators add that they see little in the pollen profiles to indicate any real vegetational change after 5000 years ago.

Corresponding dramatic shifts in terrestrial and aquatic fauna proceeded in concert with the vegetational transformation of the region and the marine transgression. Between 10,000 and 9500 years ago, a unified temperate faunal community replaced the earlier disharmonious animal populations of the late Pleistocene. Estuarine species apparently were not able to establish themselves until much later, about 5000 years ago. It was at this point that the axis of the ancestral Susquehanna River had been completely transgressed, and while sea level rise did continue, it was at a significantly slower rate.

Together these events greatly altered the Holocene ecology of the Chesapeake region. I want to discuss the specific structural properties of this evolving landscape over the 7000 years of the Archaic period. This remarkable period of time is a story of the replacement of an established coniferous floral community by deciduous forests. In the process of this transformation the unique late Pleistocene fauna gave way to a new, strictly temperate fauna. At the same time, aquatic regimes were shifting from riverine to estuarine as the marine transgression radically altered the region's freshwater rivers. What is important to remember, however, is that none of these changes were instantaneous, nor were they felt uniformly across the study area. The paragraphs that follow discuss these changes as both a temporal and spatial process.

Climate across the region was changing by the beginning of the Archaic period. Complete climatic amelioration to modern conditions, from the extremes of the Late Pleistocene during Paleoindian times, was more or less accomplished by circa 5000 years ago. Effective temperature (ET), a statistical summary cited previously that places an ecosystem on a scale of floral and faunal productivity as well as relative seasonality, had risen from approximately $13°$ C during the Paleoindian period to $16°$ C by 5000 years ago. Most investigators (e.g., Carbone 1976) feel this change was the result of shifts in atmospheric circulation during the Holocene. Weather systems originating in southern latitudes increased in duration at the expense of formerly dominant Arctic air masses with corresponding increases in yearly mean temperature and annual amounts of solar radiation reaching the region. Precipitation likewise declined. Of course, while fairly modern conditions were reached by circa 5000 years ago, significant cycles of either warmer–dryer *or* cooler–moister conditions would continue throughout the Holocene.

These changes greatly affected the flora of the Chesapeake region. In general, the boreal forest associations of the late Pleistocene gave way to seasonal temperate, deciduous associations during the Holocene. Such changes were first felt in the southern reaches of the study area. There, an initial and transitional beech–hemlock–birch forest had established itself on the inner Coastal Plain even slightly before 10,000 years ago. Formerly dominant coniferous elements began to decline as oak increased in importance, and by circa 8200 years ago an oak–hickory association dominated on the lower Western Shore. One sees a similar pattern to the north, although it occurred sightly later and involved different species. At the Indian Creek site, again on the inner Coastal Plain but above the middle latitudes of the region, birch initially increased at the expense of both pine and spruce. Oak likewise began to increase. After about 7600 years ago, a deciduous forest consisting of oak and a handful of other species was well established. Oak, it is interesting to note, did not become the clear dominant at that location until circa 5000 years ago.

These data suggest the following in terms of the spatial distribution of arboreal species across the entire Chesapeake region. Between circa 10,000 and 5000 years ago a locationally variable, but clearly temperate, deciduous forest established itself across the region. After 5000 years ago oak and hickory became clear codominants over much of the study area. This was especially true in higher well-drained areas of the Eastern Shore and on the Western Shore above the James River. In the same locations, but where moisture was more abundant, oak along with gum and several other species probably formed a slightly different association. Such an association would have been present along watercourses and near wetland areas along both the nascent estuary and at interior locations. On the Western Shore below the James River, various species of pine that adapted to generally warmer conditions probably represented significant additions to the oak–hickory association. In the same sense, in the extreme northern latitudes of the region, hemlock may have been present in significant quantities with oak, given a generally cooler climate.

However one views the nature of these forests, it is important to keep several facts in mind. Understanding human adaptation during the Archaic, or for that matter during any other period of prehistory, has little to do with knowing the exact percentages of every arboreal species in a forest at any particular point in time. It is instead important to understand that a temperate deciduous forest with a well-developed understory had been established and stabilized around 5000 years ago. The new resources it offered, including new mast products, edible greens, rootstocks, tubers, berries, and starchy seeds, were varied and generally abundant. Carrying capacity was greatly amplified. More important, unlike earlier forests, its resources were zoned in particular locations and appeared at generally predictable intervals. This floral component of the temperate ecosystem would require a different adaptive strategy for effective exploitation.

Great changes in regional hydrology occurred during the Archaic period. In fact, the major hydrologic feature of the late Pleistocene, the ancestral Susquehanna River, was completely transformed from a river into the largest estuary in the United States during this period. Three forces brought about this transformation. First, it is now evident that local subsidence in the earth's crust played a substantial role in the submergence of the ancestral Susquehanna River (Colman, Halka, and Hobbs 1991:14). Aqueous loading and isostatic recoil from glacial withdrawal to the north probably played roles in this process. Second, the ancestral Susquehanna River had had thousands of years during the late Pleistocene to meander across the soft sediments of the Coastal Plain. A natural low-lying basin awaited sea level rise during the Holocene thus mitigating any resistance the river itself could muster. Last, sea levels began to rise significantly with glacial retreat. Sea levels in the study area rose some 56 m during the course of the Archaic period.

The trajectory of the formation of the Chesapeake Bay during the Archaic period was as follows. By the beginning of the period, the ocean had reclaimed the continental shelf and was poised at the mouth of the present estuary. Subsequent transgression of what remained of the lower ancestral Susquehanna River directly within the study area was then fairly rapid. Over a 4000-year period, between 10,000 and 6000 years ago, sea levels rose approximately 50 m thus completely overrunning the river. This effectively transformed the ancestral Susquehanna into a restricted river estuary with seawater now mixing with fresh water along its entire length. Flanking tributaries were themselves turned into subestuaries of this larger body from their fall lines to their confluence with the estuary. Over the next 3000 years, until the end of the Archaic period, sea levels continued to rise another 6 m thereby expanding the estuary into a large coastal bay. The dismemberment of the old Pleistocene drainage system was now effectively complete even though sea levels would continue to rise over the next 3000 years, and indeed continue to rise even today.

In addition to creating the Chesapeake Bay, marine transgression during the Archaic period had collateral effects across the region. One of the most important such effects in terms of resource production was the creation of estuarine as well as interior wetlands. The former, of course, were created as transitional areas between the estuary and dry land. The latter were established inland as subterranean water tables were forced up and perched on impermeable sediments or pooled in poorly drained areas.

Estuarine or tidal wetlands are tremendously productive habitats offering both food and protection for a wide variety of creatures. Formation of these wetlands was an evolutionary process throughout the Archaic period. Incipient tidal wetlands formed along the margins of the ancestral Susquehanna River as it was transgressed, then became inundated themselves as the estuary expanded, and reformed again at the new margins. Radiocarbon dates on submerged and buried estuarine wetlands at the mouth of the bay indicate that such wetland areas were established and expanding by at least circa 9300 years ago. By 3000 years ago, at the end of the Archaic period, tidal wetlands in the region are estimated to have covered some 300,000 ha.

Interior freshwater wetlands likewise were both created or expanded across the inner and outer Coastal Plain of the region. These interior wetlands, like their tidal counterparts, are unusually productive habitats dotting both the Eastern and Western shores of the estuary. Many such interior wetlands were undoubtedly in existence even by the late Pleistocene, and they appear often to have been subsequently expanded during the Holocene. The Great Dismal Swamp, for example, illustrates this process. That wetland, originally covering some 5000 km^2, is primarily the result of ponded water delivered by rising sea levels (Whitehead 1972:313). Other smaller interior wetlands no doubt owe their origins to this same process.

These changes to the landscape of the Chesapeake region had a dramatic effect on animal populations. Over the course of the Holocene an exclusively temperate fauna was established. The fauna of the temperate biome is well known. Standard dominants include white-tail deer, wapiti, turkey, and bear. Many other types of small mammals, birds, reptiles, and amphibians round out the list of species. While this new fauna lacked the diversity in total numbers of species characteristic of the late Pleistocene, those species that did remain could greatly expand their individual populations. This was a matter of less intense competition for available ecological niches as well as the presence of a significantly higher biotic carrying capacity.

The increase in the white-tail deer population is a good example of this process. While that species was certainly present during the late Pleistocene, its numbers could greatly expand during the Holocene. With the establishment of deciduous forests, the amount of browse was greatly expanded, and developing interior wetland areas provided increased favorable habitat. During the Holocene, migratory species likewise benefited from habitat expansion. Flocks of transient waterfowl that wintered in the region, for example, were attracted in greater numbers to the region's evolving tidal wetland areas. At some point in the Holocene the Chesapeake Bay became a major winter waterfowl habitat for flocks traveling the Atlantic Flyway.

Aquatic fauna of the evolving estuary offered many other species for potential human exploitation. The development of seasonal anadromous fish runs up the bay and its tributaries must be an artifact of the Holocene. These new migrants joined a host of other permanent resident swimmer populations. Atlantic blue crab populations were free to expand in numbers. All of these aquatic species represent an enormous potential biomass for human exploitation.

Various nonswimming aquatic species taking up residence in the evolving estuary would eventually become some of the more important items of consumer choice during the Holocene. Within the study area this is especially true of the oyster, and to a lesser degree true of various other shellfish species. Intensive and systematic shellfish gathering, however, apparently did not become commonplace in the region until late in the Archaic period circa 4000 years ago (see Waselkov 1982). Current logic holds that shellfish were not available in significant quantities until that time. Two potential reasons can be offered. First, the Chesapeake Bay required almost all of the Archaic period to evolve into an estuary even close to its current configuration. It remained, in fact, a more restricted river estuary until circa 6000 years ago. Shellfish require generally shallow-water habitats, and humans can only effectively harvest them in those habitats. Such habitats only became available after the river estuary was further transgressed after 6000 years ago, thus creating a large coastal bay with expansive shallow-water areas. Second, even with the creation of suitable habitat, it may have taken a great many years for shellfish to establish themselves in the large reef communities that make human exploitation economically viable.

As a final note, many of my observations on regional ecology offered in this section compare favorably with alternative ecological reconstructions traditionally repeated for the study area, but some do not. On the positive side, this is particularly true about my ideas on the nature and timing of changes in regional faunal populations, and generally true about the changing flora of the region. My statements on rates of estuary formation may differ slightly from other statements given that they are based on new research just now becoming available.

At the same time, however, there are key differences in the present reconstruction versus the most vocally repeated alternative model. For instance, processual archaeologists have over the past two decades argued for a whole suite of climatic episodes triggering numerous corresponding changes in flora through the portion of the Holocene included within the Archaic period (e.g., see Custer 1989:43). As is typical of that explanatory protocol, this series of discontinuities is then used to interpret various changes in human lifeways. One much discussed discontinuity is the so-called xerothermic, a pronounced warm and dry period commencing circa 4500 to 5000 years ago. It is often argued that this phenomenon was the trigger for significant changes occurring near the end of the Archaic—what I have labeled as a time of cultural intensification.

In the discussion of ecological context above, I have remained intentionally skeptical concerning the significance (and maybe even the existence) of this xerothermic interval. First, many of these previous ecological reconstructions used to project a xerothermic are based on pollen data collected well to the west of the Chesapeake region or from selected areas of eastern North America even further afield of the study area. These studies, and more importantly the interpretations behind them, are now close to two decades old. The interpretation I have offered is instead based on a pollen record collected from multiple sites directly within the Chesapeake region. While this local pollen record does occasionally point to *both* dry and wet cycles in the past 5000 years (e.g., see Brush 1986; Delcourt and Delcourt 1985), it does not suggest the presence of a sustained xerothermic interval at that time or after. A regional record of soil erosion and aeolian redeposition is most frequently cited as additional evidence for the xerothermic. Here again, challenges have emerged (e.g., see Stevens 1991) to the interpretation of these geomorphic data. Alternate mechanisms, both natural and humanly imposed, are suggested, and serious questions are ultimately raised about this other evidence for the local xerothermic. Based on these new ideas and the reservations stated earlier in this paragraph, I have come to question the very presence, much less the impact, of the so-called xerothermic on Chesapeake prehistory.

Archaic Lifeways

I now want to return to the two distinct lifeways previously identified as characteristic of the Archaic period in the Chesapeake region. One such way of life dominated all of the Early and Middle Archaic and even some of the Late Archaic, lasting from circa 10,000 to 3500 years ago. I herein label this the Archaic hunter and forager era. The other, what I called the intensification effort, is a phenomenon of the last 1200 or so years of the Late Archaic, spanning circa 4200 to 3000 years ago. While this latter lifeway is obviously in a wider sense an offspring of the former, the gap between the two remains exponential. And this brings us to a host of questions that have long concerned local archaeologists in their efforts to understand the Archaic period. How is the Archaic different from the earlier Paleoindian period? Exactly how much of the change evident throughout the Archaic can be traced to the dramatic changes in the ecology of the Chesapeake region during the Holocene? What changes were instead the result of human agency?

To begin to address these questions, the remainder of this chapter will be organized along the following lines. I want to discuss the two eras identified for the Archaic period each as a separate and distinct entity. Each discussion will elaborate on the ways in which prehistorians traditionally interpret these portions of the archaeological record, basic characteristics, and on the larger issue of how both ways of life came about. A brief conclusion will place the changes of the Archaic period within the context of Chesapeake prehistory.

Archaic Hunters and Foragers: 10,000 to 3500 Years Ago

To conceptualize time we conceive of the archaeological record as a linear phenomenon that at various points fossilizes a series of distinct cultural transformations. The beginning of the Archaic is usually seen as one such event. Nonetheless, the ways in which we think about and write prehistory cannot always necessarily represent the absolute reality of the past. Lifeways did change in the past, but the breaks were often not as crisp and neat as our organizational strategies make them out to be. My point is that while the Archaic period does appear to represent something different and arguably unique after 10,000 years ago, there are still similarities between some elements of the beginning of this era and the preceding Paleoindian period. It is appropriate to say a few words about both these similarities and differences before launching into a description of collective Archaic hunter and forager lifeways.

The reality of the contrast between the Paleoindian and Archaic periods is in some instances a matter of both degree and perspective. The traditional idea that all Paleoindians were primarily hunters of Pleistocene megafauna once clearly served to separate the Paleoindian period from the Archaic. I have, however, unequivocally rejected that notion, as have others, given the lack of hard evidence to date from eastern North America to support such a belief. This effectively blurs the long-standing separation between the two archaeological taxa. And in this sense both Paleoindians and the people of the Archaic in the Chesapeake region are now viewed as hunters and foragers of some of the same species. By extension it may also be realistic to believe that other elements of their lifeways were somewhat similar.

In the existing literature on regional prehistory others have made additional efforts to more specifically link ways of life characteristic of the local Paleoindian period and the portion of the Early Archaic typified by notched projectile points. They follow Gardner's (1975) thoughts developed some two decades ago in the Shenandoah Valley of Virginia, west of the study area. Here a similar lifeway is suggested based on a common settlement pattern and tool assemblage, albeit each tool kit accompanied by very different diagnostic projectile points. In my opinion this particular effort at linkage can be debated directly within the Chesapeake region. Settlement patterns linked to the local Paleoindian and notched sites of the Early Archaic often appear different. Furthermore, although some assemblages containing diagnostic notched projectile points within the region do appear similar to earlier Paleoindian tool kits, assemblages recovered at other components indicate a clear departure. At the very least there is more variation during the beginning of the Early Archaic than had been suspected.

I would argue that in more instances than not the beginning of the Archaic does represent a significant departure from the earlier Paleoindian period. Ecological context, for instance, represented a major point of contrast. Paleoindians occupied a boreal, riverine landscape while the earliest Archaic groups lived within a nascent temperate, estuarine ecosystem. In most cases settlement systems were different. The more temperate, seasonal ecosystem of the Early Archaic allowed repeated visits to areas richer in more predictable resources. Paleoindians, aside from reoccupying some base camps, appear to have encountered resources on a much less predictable basis. Sites thus were often less frequently reoccupied. Site signature likewise varied. The first formal hearths appeared on regional Early Archaic sites and are presumed to be evidence of more extended occupation of settlement locations. Last, projectile points and tools kits began to change at the beginning of the Archaic. A host of new hafting techniques are evident with projectiles, and weapons launch-and-delivery systems may have been changing. Tool-manufacturing processes were certainly being altered during the Early Archaic. All in all it appears safe to state that a new way of life had appeared on the horizon circa 10,000 years ago.

From a technological standpoint, during the Archaic hunter and forager era one encounters unprecedented stylistic variation in what are commonly referred to as projectiles. A host of notched, bifurcate, and stemmed projectiles litter the archaeological record. I suspect that little of this change in form has to do with matters of stylistic variation as an allegory for the definition of group identity. If correct, functional variation becomes the preferred interpretation for all the various projectiles, a case of form following function. Consumer choice and availability of new resources at different times may have often dictated new forms. It is also important to remember that these bifacial implements were increasingly dominating the tool kit and that they were clearly being used for many different purposes. Lastly, the variation in the bases of all these implements probably has something to do with long-term experimentation in hafting technique and ultimately with delivery systems. With atlatl weights appearing in the archaeological record, there is little doubt that more sophisticated launch-and-delivery systems, perhaps requiring increased consideration of aerodynamics or more delicate balance of the dart itself, were then in existence. A lighter projectile, shifting the shaft's center of gravity further back, could dramatically increase weapons range. More open forests may have dictated longer flights from hunter to prey, thus requiring such improvements.

The remainder of the chipped-stone tool kit was clearly in transition during this era. Nonprojectile formalized tools, particularly unifacial types, quickly became rarer as more expedient tools became the norm. Manufacturing techniques had changed. There was a clear movement away from a more sequential, formal core-flake/blade manufacturing process where particular by-products were turned into a limited number of standardized tool forms. During this era bifacial blanks became the norm. These were used as is or fashioned into more formal projectiles. Broken projectiles were sometimes recast as other tool types. Aside from this, amorphous cores, often reduced by the bipolar technique, produced flakes that were used expediently or were quickly turned into less formal, but functionally useful, implements. Lithic raw material usage also changed. Some nonlocal material, rhyolite for example, continued to move into the region, but locally available materials were increasingly utilized. This may be a result of the frequent reuse of sites given the more predictable resource base. Sources of local materials were well known, as were the contingencies to be expected in any task.

A most significant addition to the technological repertoire during this era was the sustained production of ground-stone tools. Axes that were flaked and then ground appeared first. Soon after, pecked and/or ground axes, atlatl weights, pestles, abraders, manos, and metates were being manufactured. This appears to be a clear example of new tools being developed and manufactured to meet the contingencies of a different ecosystem. Woodworking and plant processing became more than occasional activities during this time.

In reviewing the available literature on regional settlement systems of this era it is not unusual to encounter phrases indicating something along the line of "sites are typically positioned to be near productive resource areas." This is a safe, yet ultimately hollow statement. It is difficult to imagine any prehistoric settlement system that would ignore productive areas. Clearly archaeologists must do better than this.

It is evident from a review of the spatial patterning of sites attributable to the Archaic hunter and forager era that a number of more precise observations can be offered. Most apparent is the fact that the inner Coastal Plain as well as the Piedmont were more heavily occupied than the outer Coastal Plain. Two reasons for this can be offered. For one, estuarine resources appear not to have been available in quantities worthy of sustained exploitation until late in this era. For another, sites that once existed along water in that area may have fallen victim to continuing marine transgression. While the latter statement is probably true to a certain extent, I favor the former interpretation based on currently available evidence. It appears that the interior, with its wetland areas, upland forests, more diverse habitats near stream junctures, and riparian floodplain plant communities, offered more predictable resources during this era.

There is some evidence showing that settlement areas did become less expansive over time. Some argue that increasing population numbers were a force behind this phenomenon. I will remain somewhat unconvinced until evidence is assembled or a scenario whereby this would occur is debated. It is difficult to imagine that population pressure would be a significant force in the region until at least the end of this era. Settlement areas could have just as easily been reduced because of the region's rising biotic carrying capacity that was decreasing the amount of land needed to support any one group.

There is evidence to indicate that individual sites during this time were generally limited in spatial extent. As was stated previously, many smaller sites distributed across the landscape would be an effective strategy for keeping people in contact with one another in order to mitigate risks through resource or information sharing. While it is possible to point to a number of sites from this time that do appear to be quite substantial, it remains difficult to unequivocally demonstrate that these were truly large sites occupied by a significant number of people for substantial periods of time. The few buried sites of this era that have been excavated consist of many small occupations superimposed over each other. As combined surface manifestations they would look rather large, but they actually could represent a series of smaller, short-term occupations. It is therefore possible that what appear to be large sites are really palimpsests of many smaller reoccupations over many years.

Focusing within the boundaries of these sites reveals a new site structure with little precedent in the regional archaeological record. Formal site features are reported for the first time on immediately post-10,000-year-old sites and become more common by the end of this era. Some of these features, because of the charcoal and charred food remains they contain, appear to have been formal hearths. Given what is known about Paleoindian sites both in the study area and elsewhere, such features were not constructed during that earlier period. At the very least these features suggest more extended occupation of sites beginning in the earliest portions of the Archaic.

Clusters of fire-cracked rock, which could be viewed as evidence of the adoption of new cooking techniques, have also been recovered at the earliest sites and continue throughout the era. Many of the smaller concentrations of fire-cracked rock are interpreted as container dumps resulting from stone boiling, and the larger features were probably used in baking or steaming. Both small and large features of this type are again unprecedented in the local archaeological record. It is, however, important to note that no subterranean storage features have been recorded on Archaic hunter and forager era sites. Finally, evidence of a cremated human interment was recently reported on an early site. This represents a first glimpse into mortuary practices during this era. All in all, it is hard not to see the appearance and sustained construction of the features mentioned above as anything other than evidence of a distinct change in lifeways just after 10,000 years ago.

Direct evidence of the Archaic hunter and forager subsistence economy, while still scant, is beginning to increase in the region. Faunal remains from reliable contexts have not been recovered, aside from some fibers of turkey feather recovered at one early site. One is therefore left to assume that the typical dominant animals of the temperate biome, especially white-tail deer and other mammals, were being exploited by these groups. More tangible evidence from regional sites, however, would be most welcome.

Floral remains, by contrast, are now being recovered from the earliest sites of the era. Substantial amounts of charred hickory nut along with butternut and possibly acorns have been reported from even Early Archaic sites. Some evidence of the utilization of various starchy seeds and tuberous plants is also being presented. It is reasonable to suggest that similar plant species were being exploited throughout this period of time. All in all, Archaic hunter and foragers evidently quickly turned to the sustained harvesting of the most prolific and reasonably nutritious plant resources offered to them by the evolving temperate biome. The intensity of labor required to collect and process these resources was apparently a factor in consumer choice. Hickory nuts, for example, represent a compromise choice over other more beneficial species, such as walnut. This probably was a labor compromise given the difficulty in opening the outer hull of walnuts. Ample numbers of specialized plant-processing implements recovered from regional sites during this era is further evidence of this belief.

What has been presented in the preceding paragraphs largely characterizes what I have called the Archaic hunter and forager lifeway in the study area. I would like to close with some ideas about how this lifeway came about. In the first chapter of this volume I made the distinction between prehistoric societies that, in a manner of speaking, accommodate nature versus those that socially appropriate nature. The former were typically closely bound to both the constraints and opportunities of the natural environment. In my opinion, such a description largely rings true in the case of the Archaic hunter and forager era under discussion, much like the previous Paleoindian period at a certain level. Extant prehistoric cultures in the Chesapeake region between 10,000 and 3500 years ago practiced a way of life that was intimately attuned to the changes taking place in the ecology of the region during circa the first 6500 years of the Holocene. The archaeological record that results from this era is therefore interpreted as largely a record of adaptation to those changes.

By now I hope that I have demonstrated that the landscape of the Chesapeake region was radically altered during the Archaic hunter and forager era. Some of these changes occurred rather quickly, for example, the replacement of boreal by temperate forests, which was followed by a long period of relative stability. Other such changes, for instance the creation of the estuary, required significantly longer periods of time and were only completed near the end of the era. These two major events, in turn, had differing effects on a series of other elements of the total ecosystem. My argument is that all these changes were met by human populations through the maintenance of a hunter and forager lifeway that was flexible enough to meet new circumstances. The origins of this lifeway are probably to be found in similar situations that had developed earlier deeper within the Southeastern hearth.

For the Chesapeake region, some of the most archaeologically visible local changes were initiated early in the era. Technology was modified with an increased emphasis on bifacial tool forms at the expense of other standardized tool forms. A host of new ground-stone tools were produced to meet the contingencies of this new environment. The chipped-stone assemblage effectively became more expedient, while the new ground-stone tool kit appears to have been more highly curated. This persisted throughout the era.

Settlement organization was modified. The new temperate biome presented a more diverse and plentiful range of resources within predictable locations. The seasonality of that ecosystem offered those resources at specific, regular intervals. Seasonal scheduling became an important element of regional lifeways. The human adaptational response appears to have been one of mapping onto a distinct series of resources through strategic settlement shifts (Binford 1980). The wide diversity of closely packed resources on the inner Coastal Plain and Piedmont zones seems to have been most attractive.

To exploit these resources regional hunter and foragers occupied a series of small to medium-sized sites scattered primarily through these zones. Reoccupation of sites was often frequent given annual resource predictability. Subsistence remains recovered on sites of the era indicate resource selection strategies. It is interesting to note that a subterranean storage capacity is not a feature of this era. This is not to say that storage in portable containers was not practiced, but it does imply that storage was not large scale. With a fairly long growing season it was likely possible to depend on animal exploitation as a solution to the problem of needed resources during crucial overwintering periods when many other resources were unavailable (follows

Binford 1980:15). In this sense animals that have evolutionarily solved the over-wintering problem provided the needed subsistence resources for humans during periods when natural production was otherwise low. A critical dependence on these species may suggest a patrilocal social organization. Finally, the fact that other recognizable features are now reported on sites throughout this era indicates that movement between sites was not as frequent as it had been.

Occupation of a series of sites by smaller groups has some distinct advantages. Parker (1990) has suggested that group size was minimal, and that settlement systems during this era focused around the occupation of smaller-sized sites. This effectively scatters people across the landscape thus increasing the chance that different groups will remain in contact with one another. Communication between groups is thereby stimulated for the purposes of risk avoidance, information exchange, and general group interaction. The nonlocal lithic materials that appear in the region during this era, for example, rhyolite, are perhaps an artifact of this settlement system. Most such exchange is interpreted as low-level, down-the-line exchange. This type of exchange would have been promoted by the type of settlement system described above and its tendency toward more balanced reciprocity.

All in all, I see little reason to further belabor the fact that much of what we prehistorians see in the archaeological record of the Archaic hunter and forager era are the results of a changing adaptation to a newly developing landscape. Changes that occurred after this initial adaptation were the result of the continued evolution of some aspects of the ecosystem, and its eventual stabilization. I am obviously not the first to make that argument, and I think that Chesapeake prehistorians by and large have done a commendable job over the past two decades to bring this process to light. Those achievements can largely be attributed to the positive effects of processual archaeology in the study area. With that said, it is now time to turn to the end of the Archaic and an altogether different matter.

The Intensification Effort: 4200 to 3000 Years Ago

What I have labeled the intensification effort opened a new era in Chesapeake prehistory near the end of the Late Archaic. If the earlier era of the Archaic period represented more of an accommodation of nature, the latter began what might be referred to as the social appropriation of nature. In contrast to the Archaic hunter and forager lifeway just discussed, production during this era was being *intensified* instead of just being *maintained*. Control over the domestic economy was beginning to pass from all of the group to some of the group. In the process, kin ties would eventually be replaced by political ties. The redirection represents the threshold between what Bender (1985b:21) has labeled cold versus hot society.

This era of intensification represented a significant redirection in regional life-ways, yet at the same time I want to be careful of overstatement. Compared to the chiefdoms that would eventually appear within the study area during the subsequent Woodland period, the change under discussion is still comparatively embryonic.

Nonetheless, this is a very important period of time in relation to what had come before, and thus deserves special attention.

The genesis of this intensification effort appears linked to the people who left behind the broad-blade projectiles of the Late Archaic discussed earlier in this chapter. It is generally acknowledged that the earliest such implements first appeared just before 4500 years ago well south of the Chesapeake area, within what is today Georgia and the Carolinas. This brings us to a rather thorny issue in eastern North American prehistory. Two decades ago Turnbaugh (1975) published a paper that argued for a migration of broad-blade using groups out of that more austral area of origin and up the Atlantic coast into the Northeast. The broad-blade implement itself was viewed as perhaps a specialized harpoon used for fishing. These people had presumably successfully adapted to the rich coastal resources of their homeland and then adaptively radiated northward up the coast as other similar areas were established. The anadromous fish runs that were beginning to occur in these areas at this time were viewed as the prime resource attraction.

Turnbaugh's ideas proved both attractive and, of course, controversial. Perhaps the most frequently cited rejoinder to the original set of ideas was Cook's (1976) paper attacking one of the central assumptions of the original article. Cook (1976:351) claimed to be able to demonstrate that broad-blade projectiles in fact appeared as early in the Northeast as they had in the Southeast. If true, this would obviously be damaging to any suggestion of a south-to-north migration. It was enough to cause more than a few archaeologists to dismiss the migration argument.

On closer examination, however, Cook's data appear rather suspicious, if not downright incorrect. Based on a careful reading of the original reports from which they were drawn, the radiocarbon assays he cites to make his case are especially questionable. For example, he cites a radiocarbon date of somewhat more than 4300 years ago on broad-blade projectiles at the Neville site in New Hampshire. According to my reading of that report (Dincauze 1976:113), the Neville site contained only a very small and undated component yielding broad-blades within stratum 3. The radiocarbon date cited by Cook (1976:351) must be the 4390 ± 180 (GX-1749) assay on stratum 4a where the predominant projectiles are assignable to the small point or narrow point tradition (Dincauze 1976:112). Other relevant dates cited by Cook to support his argument are likewise curious, although difficult to check due to lack of adequate reference. In short, I find it rather problematic to reject all of Turnbaugh's ideas based on the data cited by Cook in his reply.

Given this, I strongly suspect that the original stimulus for the intensification effort was imported into the Chesapeake region. This need not have been, as some presuppose, the result of a large, sustained flood of pilgrims into the study area from the south. To my mind the intensification effort was a lifeway whose foundation rested as much on new ideas as it was an adaptational system taking advantage of recently stabilized, ecologically productive coastal areas. This lifeway, in this perspective, is both *historical* and *ecological*. The movement of a unique way of life in prehistory required some movement of people or, at the very least, an exchange of ideas between people. All things considered, the former appears more likely in this case. While I have no way to know how many people might have been involved, evidence does suggest that immigrants into the region planted the seeds of this new lifeway.

Few probably will relish a reconsideration of this issue. So many exchanges have taken place in regional journals and conferences between the migrationists and antimigrationists that an unspoken truce appears to have emerged. Most now are side-stepping the question of origins. Looking at the problem from a wider perspective, however, forces reevaluation. Not many archaeologists question that there were remarkable similarities in broad-blade using groups up and down the Atlantic coast. This does not mean that variation within that entity did not develop over time. It certainly had emerged by the end of the Late Archaic. Still, once a similarity in lifeway is assumed on this scale, two explanations suggest themselves. One is some sort of connection between the widely separated groups, that is, a common heritage. The other is that these groups spanning the entire coast of eastern North America somehow responded with a common adaptation to ecological circumstances, in the process all developing remarkably similar thick, broad-blade implements as well as other similar items of material culture. I simply find this latter position difficult to comprehend. With this background on the question of origins it is now important to describe the archaeological correlates of this new lifeway.

At least three types of distinct broad-blade implements appear most common within the Chesapeake region during this era. These include the Savannah River, Susquehanna, and Perkiomen types. The presence of the three different types is interpreted as a case of inevitable divergence over space once this new lifeway was established both within and outside the region. It is important to note that I assume any of these formal implements could be used for multiple purposes, both as projectiles and knives. These implements were accompanied by other generalized bifaces as well as rather expedient flake scrapers, drills, perforators, and utilized flakes. In addition, various specialized chisels and picks have been recovered at steatite quarries assignable to this era. In many ways the chipped-stone assemblage remained rather conservative, and, aside from the different formal implements, it appears similar to earlier Archaic tool kits in terms of a similar gross technological efficiency. The quarry tools might be the exception to this rule.

I do, however, want to say something about the procurement of lithic raw material for the increasing quantities of chipped-stone tools being produced during this era. Most of the nonlocal lithic material arriving in the study area during this time, principally rhyolite and some argillite, appears to have been traded via what a number of prehistorians refer to as broad-based exchange networks. According to Stewart (1992) these networks were characterized by hand-to-hand, down-the-line exchange through a broad web of common relations. This is a good example of the increasingly interconnected social relations developing in the era.

Nevertheless, many of the broad-blade implements found in the region were manufactured from locally available lithic materials. Although choice could vary depending in location, quartzite in many areas often appears to have been the material of preference. In this regard it is important to make special note of the unprecedented quarry and quarry-related initial reduction activity that occurred within the study area. The famous Piney Branch quarries studied by Holmes at the end of the last century are probably artifacts of this process (Munford 1982:110–111). William Rust (1983) has recently excavated another series of quarry sites in the Piedmont, dating to about 3800 years ago, that duplicate this increased quartzite quarry activity. Caches of unfinished bifaces are found scattered throughout the study area. All of this appears to represent the production of stone tools on a remarkable scale.

Ground-stone tool production was also apparently expanding. Grooved axes of at least two types along with adzes, celts, gouges, mortars, pestles, and manos and metates appear in significant numbers. Potter (1982:328) reports a partially ground slate drill point from a site along the Potomac River. A number of archaeologists have commented that the increased production of woodworking tools may be an indication of dugout canoe construction. The apparent mobility of people during this era would tend to support this assumption, although no such water vessels have actually been recovered. Numerous additional cobble tools have also been unearthed.

The matter of the accompanying bone tool assemblage is becoming clearer during this time. Potter (1982) recovered bone and antler awls, tine flakers, and pins from the middle Chesapeake region. Both awls and pins could be evidence of developed basket and/or net production. While not a matter of technology, tubular beads were also found at the same site. The fact that these bone and antler artifacts were recovered at all, given the generally poor preservation characteristics of the study area, might indicate increased production of such items.

Steatite bowls represent a major new item in the technological repertoire of this era. The uses to which these stone bowls were put are inconclusive at this point. While most are quite heavy, few have sufficient internal volume to serve as practical storage vessels. Mouer (1991) comments that many of the stone bowls he has observed within the region show signs of burning, suggesting use as directly-heated cooking vessels. Sassaman (1993) has just published a detailed analysis of steatite vessels across the Southeast that includes both experimental studies and a review of relevant ethnographic literature. He concludes that these containers were used as cooking vessels, but typically were indirectly heated through the introduction of hot stones. The wide orifice would make it easy to insert the heated stones into the container. This design feature was passed to some of the earliest ceramics in the region and may indicate a similar mode of heating with them. In addition, Sassaman suggests that many of the perforated steatite slabs that are recovered were in fact specialized boiling stones. Ethnographic examples and thermal properties are cited to support this inference. Such an indirect cooking technique is not revolutionary. It was certainly possible even before this era with coated baskets, lined pits, wooden containers, and so on. It may, however, have been enhanced and made more efficient with steatite bowls and heated steatite slabs. Steatite is known even today for excellent thermal retention. The cooking of many food resources could be accelerated, and the presence of a container with an infinitely longer use-life would lessen repair and replacement efforts.

All of the objects of technology discussed thus far are relatively portable objects manufactured of inorganic raw materials. I now want to shift to a discussion of two items that were perhaps not so much objects as they were what might be referred to as appliances or constructions. Certainly neither were portable. Like all objects under examination, however, these constructions played a technological role in the process of subsistence intensification during this era. These constructions include fish weirs or traps and unusually large hearths. Unlike the other objects these admittedly do not appear on every site, and, in the case of fish weirs, I can only point to circumstantial evidence linking them to broad-blade using groups. The very presence of large hearths on a substantial number of sites and the suggestion of the use of fish weirs make both worthy of some further discussion.

Archaeologists have long suspected that anadromous fish runs were important foci of broad-blade subsistence systems. With the estuary beginning to stabilize during this era there is reason to believe that this was true in the study area. Large-scale, effective exploitation of such fish runs requires substantial cooperation and special technology. As John Cavallo (1982) has demonstrated, for maximum return, fish need to be caught in large numbers and then processed quickly. Labor needs are substantial. Payoff, however, is potentially enormous. To catch sufficient quantities of fish most archaeologists agree that fish weirs or traps would have been necessary. There is no doubt that fish weirs at least were built in the estuary's tributaries. Some are still in existence (see Holland 1983; Strandberg and Tomlinson 1968). Neverthe-less, no attempt has yet been made to date such surviving features, and the known weirs are just as likely to be assignable to the subsequent Woodland and Historic periods.

Still, there is a real chance that some of the surviving fish weirs, along with others no longer extant, do date to the intensification era. Such technological features have been linked to this period of time elsewhere in eastern North America. Furthermore, Mouer (1991:20) notes that some broad-blade sites on the James River are in excellent situations for weir or trap fishing. Custer (1989:204) suggests that now-destroyed wooden stakes reported in the Delaware River may have originally been part of a fish weir or trap. These were located near the Naaman's Creek site, which yielded implements from this era. While circumstantial, all these data are at least tantalizing.

It should also be noted that notched cobbles, typically interpreted as net sinkers, are recovered on sites of this era. Tools often used in net making were mentioned previously. While net fishing would have been somewhat less efficient than trap or weir fishing, nets certainly are more portable. Net fishing may also have been more practical in the wider, embayed portions of the lower tributaries in the region given structural limits to the size of a stone or wooden trap or weir.

The case for intensified fishing activity is further solidified by the large hearth features that often appear on sites yielding broad-blade components along major tributaries. Some of these features are actually platform hearths. Such features appear at any number of sites throughout the entire region. Many local prehistorians suggest that these hearths were specialized baking, smoking, or drying features directly associated with the final processing of anadromous fish catches. The logic behind this suggestion is that fish must be cured almost immediately, and the mechanism for accomplishing this should match the scale of the capture technique. At the Scott #4 site in the lower reaches of the study area circular platform hearths up to 10 m in diameter have been reported (McLearen 1991a:112).

During the intensification era settlement focus appears to have shifted and expanded. Many sites appear directly along major waterways in all physiographic provinces of the region, outer Coastal Plain to the Piedmont zone. Some of the most important research in this regard has been published by Mouer (1991) based on his large-scale surveys of portions of the southern Chesapeake region. Mouer (1991:8) reports that out of 85 reported broad-blade components across the southern study area, 87% were located at water's edge while only 13% were removed from that location. He suggests this indicates an emerging, linear settlement of the tributary valleys versus the more diffuse strategy of the previous era. There is good evidence that individual site size varied within this settlement organization. Again, Mouer (1991:23) reports the presence of some relatively large sites in all physiographic zones. These appear to represent what might have been multiple-group gathering sites. At the other end of the spectrum, rather small sites are reported that consist of just lithic debris scattered around a single hearth. Even more common, however, are intermediate-size sites, that cover up to 460 m². These sites, possibly representing the settlement of an individual group, are larger than most sites of the previous era, but smaller than the largest sites mentioned above. This scheme of both settlement organization and site type works well with the distributional pattern and range of site sizes from this era that I have observed in the Potomac River Valley.

The situation described above appears to represent a settlement organization oriented to the increased exploitation of many traditionally available as well as newly available resources. I further suspect that regional settlement systems were shifting more toward what Binford (1980) has characterized as a collector or logistically organized strategy. In such settlement organizations the number of site types increases as people made an effort to overcome incongruent distributions of resources that would otherwise restrict mobility or consumer options. Settlement mobility does become restricted through the occupation of a series of larger, more permanent sites, but procurement parties are then dispatched to distant locations to obtain other seasonally available resources. People still remain relatively mobile, and this fits Mouer's (1991:24) belief that year-round sedentism was not yet possible, while at the same time they became more sedentary than in earlier times. It should be noted that a well-developed storage capacity, one of the elements of Binford's (1980) collector settlement system, cannot be linked to the intensification era in this region. Still, Binford does allow that his forager versus collector dichotomy represents only the extremes of a spectrum modifiable depending on location.

At least two distinct types of hearths appear on broad-blade sites. One type is the more traditional round to oval small hearth defined by hearthstones and various amounts of fire-cracked rock. The other is a larger hearth, often a platform hearth, as reported in the previous section. It should also be noted that scatters and definable concentrations of fire-cracked rock as well as what appears to be stockpiled rock, presumably to be eventually employed in the cooking or heating process, often appear on these sites.

Excavated pit features that probably originally functioned as baking, roasting, and/or steaming appliances are reported on sites assignable to this era. Often they contain traces of charcoal, fire-cracked rock, and the occasional artifact. As an example of this type of feature, Potter (1982:328) reported traces of small globular pits at a site along the lower Potomac River. In the context of this site the pits were probably used to steam open molluscs.

As noted above, broad-blade using groups were turning to newly available estuarine resources. Shellfish represent one such resource, and the first good evidence of more substantial exploitation of these species in the form of small middens appears in the region during this era. While that exploitation did not approach the scale and intensity seen in the subsequent Woodland period, Waselkov's (1982) excavations at the White Oak Point site along the lower Potomac River provide a good example of the new subsistence interest. At that site he recovered evidence of three deposits of shell dating to this era. Shellfish, of a number of different species including oyster, were roasted directly on the ground, and the discarded shells formed the bulk of several small layers and shell heaps (Waselkov 1982:132). The largest such feature he was able to measure assignable to this period of time was 4.3 m in its greatest linear dimension and contained 1.21 m^3 of shell (Waselkov 1982:223). Similar features, of course, can only be expected at sites in appropriate zones of the study area.

Painter (1988) has recently reported the excavation of a basin-shaped pit containing ash, calcined bone, and a number of shattered Perkiomen projectiles (broad-blade variant) along with other artifacts on the western edge of the Dismal Swamp. Based on the possibility that the feature contains a human cremation, it may represent a first look into mortuary practices of the intensification era. One much earlier human cremation has been reported for the study area, and the mortuary feature described above is duplicated on similar sites well to the north of the Chesapeake region. A few additional somewhat similar features containing burned human bone have been reported by regional archaeologists (see McLearen 1991a:105), but there is no real consensus yet on the validity of all these reports in the study area. The mortuary practice described above may be intrusive. On the other hand, more remains may be found. If the latter is true then these features might be interpreted as evidence of increased sedentism. Elaborated mortuary practices are also often the artifacts of expanding sociopolitical activity.

Finally, I want to close this section by mentioning two features that are often recovered on later prehistoric sites in the region, but have proven elusive on sites from this era. For one, it is perplexing that there is not yet good evidence for the remains of domestic structures. Archaeologists in Delaware (see Custer 1989) have reported evidence of small pit houses as well as what appears to be a tent ring. The earliest such pit house has been radiocarbon dated to circa 5200 years ago, but there are no diagnostic artifacts to connect it to any particular group. Another pit house at the Delaware Park site (Thomas 1981) and the so-called tent ring at the Hawthorne site (Custer 1989) are both from late in the intensification era, but assignment is also difficult. While these data are very interesting, we are still searching for unequivocal remains of domestic structures firmly linked to broad-blade groups in the region.

Subterranean storage cists or pits are another somewhat curious omission from the list of features reported at these sites. With the intensification of subsistence production, one might think that archaeologists would recover evidence of these features on sites of the era. Three explanations come to mind. For one, people might have been able to solve all their subsistence needs without having had to resort to storing of foodstuffs. For another, these features might yet be found. There have been some hints of such features reported on sites assignable to this era. They certainly have been reported on sites just subsequent to the period of time under discussion. Last, Warren DeBoer (1988:14) has recently argued that subterranean storage, among other things, might actually have been a means to resist new or potentially oppressive sociopolitical orders. Here stores are concealed for personal consumption or barter. Perhaps social life had not yet reached this state during the intensification era in the Chesapeake region.

Information on subsistence practices of the intensification era include both direct and indirect evidence from the Chesapeake region's archaeological sites. As is typical of the study area, the former is unfortunately less prolific than the latter. Nevertheless, this situation is beginning to change with the increased use of more careful recovery techniques by regional archaeologists.

Archaeologists assume that broad-blade using groups were exploiting a substantial number of resources being offered by the temperate forests of the surrounding region and its estuary that was then beginning to stabilize. The best evidence on the range of such resources comes from the excavations undertaken by Potter (1982) at the Plum Nelly site and Waselkov (1982) at the White Oak Point site. Both of these sites, as mentioned before, are located on the Virginia shore of the lower Potomac River about in the middle of the region.

At Plum Nelly, Potter (1982:328) recovered evidence of exploitation of 11 different species of terrestrial fauna. Deer, beaver, raccoon, and opossum contributed the largest percentage of meat to the diet, while the plant contribution consisted primarily of hickory nuts. Potter (1982:329) suggests the site served as a fall–winter base camp between 4190 and 3810 years ago. White Oak Point, in contrast, was occupied during the spring as a small, temporary camp primarily for the purpose of gathering and roasting shellfish (Waselkov 1982:206). It was revisited a number of times circa 3500 years ago. In addition to shellfish, deer provided most of the meat yield to the occupants of this site, and deer appear to have been individually stalked based on the nature of the remains recovered. Acorn remains are interpreted as supplements to the diet. Both sites also serve as evidence of increased exploitation of estuarine resources. The shell heaps and layers at the White Oak Point site dating to this era have already been discussed. At Plum Nelly shell was either discarded in small pits, originally used to steam open the molluscs, or it was tossed into small heaps that dot the Late Archaic land surface (Potter 1982:328). The shellfish remains discovered at each site indicate that this early shift toward estuarine resources focused on a wide variety of shellfish species. A more exclusive focus on oyster, as would become more typical in later times, had not yet emerged.

An increasing focus on anadromous fish runs has long been discussed as a major element of subsistence practices during this era. Actual faunal remains of this activity, however, do remain elusive. Any number of reasons for this state of affairs can be advanced. The preservation environment for such small remains is minimal given the acidity of regional soils. Without accompanying shell to neutralize such acidity faunal remains are quickly broken down. Large-scale and immediate processing of fish at capture facilities may also play a role in removing these remains from the archaeological record. Nevertheless, there is good indirect evidence for this subsistence focus. I have already discussed the suggested presence of fish weirs and traps for the region, and net sinkers are found in quantities. And the large hearths possibly used to process catches are additional evidence to suggest a focus on anadromous fish.

Last, it is important to entertain the possibility that broad-blade using groups were increasingly exploiting the plant resources of the region. Smith (1989) has drawn our attention to this phenomenon during this time period in the Southeast. Within the Chesapeake study area, many plant-processing implements can be attributed to broad-blade using groups. In addition, a number of investigators (e.g., Rust 1983; Stevens 1991) suggest that during this era people were actively burning areas to promote pioneer species of certain plants. This is essentially a case of human modification of the landscape to promote increased numbers of exploitable plants. Fires may also have been set, effectively lowering primary biomass, in order to promote growth in deer populations and facilitate hunting. Brush's (1986:155) research indicating increased sedimentation in tributaries between 3790 and 2850 years ago is often cited as evidence of this practice. Firing of the landscape removes existing vegetation and thereby increases runoff which, in turn, results in higher sedimentation rates for the study area. Rust (1983:36) cited increased evidence of certain recolonizing species in the pollen record to suggest substantial forest fires.

In sum, there is evidence of shifting subsistence practices during this era. Some of this evidence consists of actual food remains that can be linked to these groups, while other hints are more indirect. While I feel confident that subsistence patterns were shifting and that archaeologists are on the right track in beginning to think about this shift in new ways, we must redouble our efforts to recover unequivocal direct evidence for that shift. It should be possible, even with current methodologies, to substantiate the various elements that form these changing subsistence practices.

The intensification era in the Chesapeake region represented a distinct redirection of lifeways. There does not seem to be much disagreement over that belief.

Definite changes in technology, settlement organization, and subsistence practices can be demonstrated. One would suspect that there were corresponding changes in social organization, and some archaeologists have suggested what direction these changes might have taken. While there is certainly agreement on my part that change was taking place, I am not so sure that we have the appropriate models of social organization to adequately categorize these changes.

Anthropology tends to subdivide the known spectrum of human social relations that once characterized the premodern world into a series of distinct levels or types. Most often this includes the venerable band–tribe–chiefdom–state sequence of types. Prehistorians frequently look to their data as exemplifying one or the other of these characteristic social organizations. Nevertheless, we do need to remind ourselves that while there are definable types or stops along this spectrum, it is still a continuum. And in the past there certainly were as many instances of groups *becoming* these various levels of social organization as there were societies that can be appropriately defined in terms of them. There were probably also totally unique social organizations that did not remain long enough for ethnographers to examine.

Toward that end, I do not see the changes of this era, exemplified by the regional archaeological record, as falling into a single, neat category of our present social typology. I see the intensification era as having consisted of populations that had moved away from the traditional band levels of social organization. Some evidence suggests that these groups may have imported into the Chesapeake region something somewhat similar to a segmentary, tribal organization, albeit one at an amorphous, embryonic stage of development. Fully developed tribal societies contain a pyramid of social groups. Families are joined into larger entities that combine to form even larger local and regional tribal units. As a number of anthropologists (see Sahlins 1968, 1972; Service 1962) have pointed out, coherence or unity is not maintained in tribal society from above by political institutions or sovereign authority. The strength of the social whole is still kin based, and the weakest entity is, in fact, the larger collective, tribal entity. Yet, at the same time, these were not acephalous bands. They did contain integrative units between the two extremes (small domestic and larger collective entities) that would bond people together for specific purposes. In short, such a segmented entity was more than a band, but not much more. At the same time, it was exponentially less than a chiefdom. For a number of reasons I believe that broad-blade using groups may have been organized into a segmentary social organization of sorts. I want to briefly focus on two of these reasons.

First, there are basic structural elements of this lifeway that support the notion of such a social organization. As an example, settlement organization appears to have been shifting toward a collector or logistical system (follows Binford 1980) during this era. Residential moves seem to have been less frequent, and a number of different types of sites were occupied. Goods were frequently moved over considerable distances to consumers. Segments of these societies must have been simultaneously engaged in a variety of different seasonally overlapping extractive efforts. Such activity requires careful scheduling and coordination. Solidarity becomes an important factor. For instance, the part of the population that moved out on the Coastal Plain to harvest shellfish and other locally available resources—while at the same time another segment of the group remained in the Piedmont to catch and process anadromous fish—must remain confident that they too would enjoy the benefits of both activities. There were also what might be called "freight costs" (Filios 1990) on distant procurement of resources of any sort that could only be absorbed by the group as a whole. In short, everyone in a group must have been able to enjoy equity in any activity, even activities with which they were not directly engaged. Segmentary social organizations, with their mechanisms for linking people together beyond small domestic kin units, better serve to coordinate this type of activity.

Second, broad-blade using groups were faced with unique circumstances in moving into the Chesapeake region. They migrated into an area with an already existing resident population. Evidence indicates that the region was and continued to be occupied throughout this intensification era by what I earlier referred to as Archaic hunter and foragers. This resident earlier population did not disappear with the appearance of broad-blade using groups. It has long been suggested that contact and competition between different groups was the most powerful force in creating segmentary societies. This moves us into the realm of the superorganic. A more integrated social organization, beyond basic band-level society, appears necessary to claim already occupied new territory and maintain a stake in the resource base once settlement has occurred. Large technological objects, like fish weirs or traps, are long-term facilities and must be used over a number of years to recapture construction investments. Access to other resources as well as safe passage to them must be maintained. Segmentary social organizations appear better able to provide an environment where this is possible. More will be said about issues of relevance to this situation in the paragraphs that follow.

To begin, I want to make two points that temper my examination of the intensification era directly within the Chesapeake study area. A basic premise is then drawn from these statements. First, as mentioned above, I view the lifeway as an import into the region. It unfortunately remains beyond the scope of this undertaking to offer additional statements concerning an explanation of its earlier origins outside the region. Second, I see this new way of life as having entered a relatively stable local ecological regime. It appears that the resulting new estuarine resources were an already existing attraction and not items that appeared after the fact.

The basic premise of my interpretation is therefore that the intensified lifeway above represented a new and unprecedented social construction within the context of local prehistory. In this perspective, the intensification effort was less an economic phenomenon and more a set of social relations and the ideas that sustained them (follows Thomas 1991:181). Its very essence was a set of internal social mechanisms that began to intensify production, but did so at the expense of more traditional individual autonomy. In the name of larger goals, nature was no longer accommodated. It was now beginning to be socially appropriated.

In this process, much that had characterized the once dominant band-level social organization was breached. Individuals now began the transition from undertaking what might be called *work* to participating in *labor*. Within band-level society individuality remained high through personal as well as group finite production objectives. Here the products of one's work were for direct personal use or were destined for sharing with close kin or associates. Incessant demands by others on the products of this work would eventually be met with resistance. If demands became too great, band-level hunter and foragers had the option of removing themselves from such situations, essentially voting with their feet. A detailed and certainly delightful classic discussion of this way of life can be found in Sahlins (1972).

With the coming of the intensification era all this began to change. Constraints were placed on individual autonomy by new social entities. Work became labor as individuals were more tightly bonded and interdependent within social entities that moved beyond kin groups. This brought about the conditions whereby individuals could begin to lose control over the products of their work. They likewise forfeited the freedom to extract themselves from such circumstances. In short, as soon as individual autonomy became challenged and mobility was constrained, an environment existed where the consequences of a new way of life could begin to assert themselves.

My goal is now to illustrate how this new state of affairs was registered in the regional archaeological record during this era. One way to accomplish this is to point out evidence of increased interdependence and constrained personal autonomy. Here I follow some ideas recently advanced by Elena Filios (1990), although these were modified somewhat for the purposes of this analysis. Another way to see this process is to look for indications of intensified production as expressed through technological innovation and change. Evidence of these two phenomena, one cause and the other effect, can be seen on sites from this era in the Chesapeake Bay region.

Filios (1990:32) points out that constraints on what I have referred to as personal autonomy are an important source of social intensification and increased complexity. The way production was organized ultimately produced new imperatives. Through her research she isolates a number of variables that can lead to such a state of affairs. I will work from an abbreviated list of her original variables and, in the interest of brevity concentrate on a limited number of elements from the era under examination that support her arguments. As Filios (1990:48) remarks, each variable in isolation may not lead to dramatically decreased personal autonomy, but together they constitute an argument for this condition. A number of variables are discussed below.

Production of group livelihood is subject to significant spatial and temporal variation. Resources were unevenly distributed and appeared at different seasons of the year. These variations could be countered in a number of ways. At a basic level choices can be made to move people to goods or, conversely, to move resources to people. This defines Binford's (1980) forager versus collector dichotomy. It has already been noted that groups during the intensification era were moving toward the collector end of the spectrum. Simply put, moving the entire group to resources (foragers) allows more individual access and thus promotes autonomy. By contrast, the practice of collectors moving goods to consumers can begin to erode autonomy. Certain people were dispatched to procure particular resources. Soon, knowledge of the entire resource base fell into the hands of fewer people. Transportation costs also became higher and could only be absorbed by the larger entity. People became more interdependent and circumscribed by the collective operation.

Increased subdivision of the labor process compromises autonomy. Stone tool production practices provide a good example. On the one hand, with band-level social organization it is likely that people individually obtained raw material and fashioned it, through a number of steps, into a completed implement that they then used for a particular task. This is a good example of what was referred to as work. During the intensification era, on the other hand, I have pointed out an apparent case of the subdivision of this process. Specialized quarry and quarry-related reduction sites were identified where the large-scale production of lithic blanks or preforms took place. These objects were often cached. Such a phenomenon tends to modularize tasks (Filios 1990:42), and the production process, now labor, was increasingly removed from the hands of any one individual. Different people appear to have been allocated various specific tasks thus increasing interdependence and lessening the possibility of control over all the products necessary to gain a livelihood. As Filios (1990:42) also mentions, this process can be as true of ritual as it is of tool production.

The choices made concerning the scale of labor scheduling impact personal autonomy. Scheduling of resource procurement and processing tasks becomes a much greater problem as the number of concurrent activities increases. During the intensification era, larger sites were occupied for longer periods of time. This is illustrated by the increasing size and signature of sites from this era within the region. Smaller groups of people were then sent out from these locations to procure other resources far removed from the larger settlement. Scheduling such activity requires strategic decisions about deployment of the labor base. Requisite knowledge of scheduling options may fall into the hands of fewer people. The individual that agreed to collect shellfish while others caught and processed anadromous fish must depend ultimately on receiving a share of the products of both activities. Once this commitment was made, it was much more difficult to abandon one's equity in the whole.

Production tasks with might be termed delayed returns also often compromise individual autonomy. Many hunter and forager groups prefer to work with a more immediate return strategy. Resources are procured and consumed in short periods of time, with mobility remaining fairly high. During the intensification era, however, modification of that strategy is evident. Construction of fish weirs or traps, for example, is a relatively large undertaking involving substantial amounts of time. Time spent to build such an object reduces time that can be allocated to other subsistence activities. While the economic return on a weir or trap is potentially enormous, there is a considerable time delay in recouping original investment. Again, the need to enjoy one's equity in these projects begins to restrict autonomy and mobility.

An increasing need for labor and a dependence on the labor of others binds people together, thus further reducing autonomy and mobility. The builders of a fish weir or trap that have successfully caught large numbers of anadromous fish still need substantial numbers of people to process that catch. Much the same can be said of a landscape that has been burnt to promote plant growth or deer congregation. Seeds cannot be collected or processed in quantity nor large numbers of deer driven and killed without requisite help. A dependency on others for large-scale subsistence activities compromises personal autonomy within the group as a whole.

In regard to the need for larger labor pools, I want to make a point about population growth during the intensification era. A number of archaeologists (e.g., Barber 1991; Klein and Klatka 1991) have made arguments for dramatically increased demographic growth during this era. Most note a dramatic increase in the number of sites, artifact densities, and overall site size during the Late Archaic. Population increase is then typically attributed to human physiological responses to increased sedentism (higher female fecundity, lower mortality rates, and the like). While this may be true, I would like to add that increased population levels can just as easily be seen as a social construction. Once large labor pools are needed for new subsistence activities, it would be to any group's advantage to very deliberately promote population growth. There were at that time subsistence tasks within which both the young and the elderly— segments of the population that must have once been viewed in certain instances as liabilities—could actively participate. In this perspective, population growth is an after-the-fact social phenomenon rather than a physiological response.

The preceding several paragraphs document how individual and household autonomy began to be eroded during the intensification era. Once this erosion occurred, even at this embryonic stage, personal and familial alternatives were limited. These smaller social units became mired in circumstances that were difficult to leave given individual or family investment and interdependence. Once the lifeway had spread across eastern North America, empty territory in which to fission was at a premium and much of that was occupied by peoples with a different way of life. Internal change comes to such intensified social systems, if ever, only reluctantly. These were groups in which there was probably no one without authority; at the same time there was also no one with great authority (Gailey 1987). As Filios (1990:33) comments, people were left to make the best of their situation through small individual acts of resistance, group mediation, and ritual.

In the contemporary literature, increasing attention is being paid to the role intensified social demands on labor plays in technological innovation and change (see Bender 1978, 1985a,b; Sassaman 1993; Thomas 1991). As individual and household autonomy is challenged, the response often is to increase technological capacity and improve efficiency. This process appears abundantly evident during the intensification era in the Chesapeake region in even a cursory examination of the expanding technological repertoire. New items, for example, steatite containers, appear in the archaeological record for the first time. Construction of fish weirs or traps and specialized large processing hearths probably date to this era. A number of archaeologists have commented that the increased construction and use of watercraft was likely a feature of this period of time. Ground-stone tool production was certainly expanded, possibly along with bone tool production. In short, it is not difficult to point to significant evidence of both technological innovation and change. And this phenomenon can be interpreted in light of increasing social demands on labor.

I want to make one additional point about these broad-blade intensification era sites in relation to other sites in the region that yield coterminous narrow-blade projectiles. As discussed earlier, some archaeologists have argued that both implements were in fact part of the same way of life. The former served primarily as a knife and the latter was employed more often as a true projectile. Evidence is frequently cited that both implements often appear on the same living surface (see Custer 1989:149–153). Examples of this occurrence are admittedly out there, and I certainly do agree that both lifeways were extant in the region during the same period of time. Nevertheless, I would argue that this co-occurrence of diagnostic artifacts is more likely a case of expected interaction between very different yet contemporary groups, perhaps even evidence of the development of symbiotic dependence. There is great evidence for this process in both the ethnographic and archaeological literature. One could go so far as to say that it is to be expected in situations where one group is pushed into less productive areas by another entity that arrives to occupy very productive ecological niches.

To end, my interpretation of the intensified era in the Chesapeake region makes use of evidence that is well known to many students of local prehistory. Nevertheless, in relation to the dominant or received view, I have chosen to attach a somewhat different meaning to these very same data. In my view, the intensification era was less an economic phenomenon driven by ecological change and more a new way of life based on changing social imperatives. My ultimate intention is not to diminish existing perspectives; my goal is simply to further challenge such interpretations. It is only through the process of creating a critical tension between alternative views of the past that better understandings are produced.

CONCLUSION

A few may be uneasy with the quantity of print that has been devoted to the Archaic period in this chapter. I ask your indulgence and admit that there is probably not a close correlation between the absolute archaeological interest in this period and the amount of space devoted to it herein. The Woodland period, with its richer material record and its chiefdoms described for us in ethnohistorical accounts, is the most fascinating period of local prehistory to many archaeologists. And certainly the great antiquity of the Paleoindian period creates its own share of interest. In comparison, the Archaic period has in some ways less of almost everything to offer.

Nevertheless, as I have argued, the Archaic period does represent the crucial link between both the beginning and the end of Chesapeake prehistory. One story is not complete and the other cannot begin without an appreciation of the developments that transpired during the Archaic period. For this reason special effort was made to situate the Archaic period of the study area in some wider context and to draw together the culture history of the regional Archaic period from many diverse sources. This allowed a discussion of key changes during this period followed by an interpretation of the meaning of these redirections of lifeways.

Such an undertaking would probably not have been possible even a decade ago. It certainly would have been impoverished by less data and a lack of new ideas about the processes involved. I want to close by acknowledging that this improvement in our understanding of the Archaic period can be attributed to the efforts of a great number of archaeologists. The ideas about adaptation during my Archaic hunter and forager era can be attributed to the efforts of processual archaeologists. New ideas about the intensification era come from more recent postprocessual studies. Present-day interest in the health of the estuary is adding greatly to our understanding of its ecological past. Much of the data on which all these ideas depend come from prehistorians, most often cultural resources managers and amateur archaeologists, who worked more out of the backs of their trucks and automobiles than out of the academy. They, especially, have contributed to an emerging new understanding of the Archaic period in this region. Hopefully this chapter has done justice to all their labors.

Chapter 6

The Woodland Period
Expansion, Chiefdoms, and the End of Prehistory

INTRODUCTION

The archaeological record of the Woodland period in the Chesapeake tidewater region is rich and particularly intriguing. At certain places and during certain times it is spectacular. By the conclusion of the three millennia included in this period, the redirection of lifeways initiated at the end of the Archaic reached its fullest expression in the chiefdoms that mark the end of prehistory. Early European explorers and settlers also interacted with native populations in the sixteenth and seventeenth centuries leaving a dramatic documentary record of that event. In the late nineteenth and early twentieth centuries pioneer ethnographers even caught a fleeting glimpse of the remains of traditional ways of life. All of these elements have created a rich environment for archaeological inquiry.

Within the study area the Woodland period is typically understood as extending from circa 3000 years ago to what has been labeled the end of prehistory, that is, the time of early European contact, exploration, and settlement. The beginning is admittedly arbitrary and the end equally amorphous. For the most part, the threshold of the Woodland period is distinguished by the addition of true terra-cotta ceramic wares to the technological repertoire. The later appearance of agriculture and the development of greater social complexity are seen as significant hallmarks of the period. The very end of prehistory was marked by the establishment of chiefdoms followed by their eventual demise in the shadow of early seventeenth-century European colonization. While present knowledge of this period is neither complete nor uncontested, it is safe to make at least one broad generalization. More then ever before the Woodland period was a time when social interaction played an unprecedented role in the lives of local native peoples. This interaction took place between local Chesapeake groups, with other native groups external to the region, and eventually with totally foreign groups arriving from another very different world.

217

In this chapter I will first present a brief synopsis of period archaeology across broader eastern North America. The chapter then turns to a description of the Woodland period directly within the Chesapeake region. Finally, the discussion focuses on an examination of the various lifeways of the Woodland with an emphasis on the expansion of the intensification process, and the appearance of chiefdoms late in prehistory.

WOODLAND ARCHAEOLOGY: WIDER SPHERES OF INFLUENCES

Prior to the Woodland period, influence on the prehistoric inhabitants of the Chesapeake study area was primarily unidirectional, appearing mainly to have emanated from the Southeast region. That state of affairs would soon change. Throughout the Woodland period, at different times and with various degrees of intensity, much of broader eastern North America appears to have played a part in the events taking place within the Chesapeake region. Developments in both the Southeast and Northeast regions, as well as in the Middle Atlantic region itself, were felt locally. All of this, of course, was a prelude to the final influence on the region via the arrival of Europeans. It is not realistic to offer a review of the archaeology of each of these various regions at anywhere near the level of detail undertaken in the two previous chapters. This section of the chapter will therefore only very briefly describe concurrent developments in those greater spheres of influence to set the stage for the regional archaeology that follows. The pertinent specifics of outside interactions will instead be addressed as necessary directly in the review of the Woodland period within the Chesapeake tidewater area.

Southeast

Two of the more cogent recent reviews of the Woodland period in the Southeast have been published by Smith (1986) and V. Steponaitis (1986). Both tend to view the earliest portions of the Woodland period as a time of gradual change, building on patterns that originally emerged during the Late Archaic. One such earlier innovation, the so-called container revolution, produced the first terra-cotta ceramics known from eastern North America. These plant fiber–tempered wares were manufactured as early as circa 4500 years ago in the Southeast. As Smith (1986:35–43) remarks, by 2500 years ago fiber was replaced as a tempering agent by sand, grit, and limestone, and a host of new vessel forms appeared. Decorative motifs allow archaeologists to define over 100 different ware types. Coastal adaptations like those during the Late Archaic were broad based and focused on a variety of resources, especially oyster along the Atlantic coast and a number of brackish water clam species near the Gulf Coast. Both Smith (1986:38) and V. Steponaitis (1986:379) believe that it is logical to assume that garden plots were also being tended during the early part of the Woodland period. It is interesting to note that exchange networks were moving Adena items from the Midwest into the Southeast during this time.

Smith (1986:43–50) reports archaeological evidence for new forms of socio-political organization between 2000 and 1500 (AD 450) years ago, including the emergence of what are ethnographically known as Big Men (Sahlins 1972). Villages dominated by these incipient leaders tended to cluster along what appear to have been group boundaries across the Southeast or near points of access—either water-ways or trails—to other areas. While there is a general continuity with earlier periods in terms of technology, settlement, and subsistence patterns, there is evidence for the emergence of particular mortuary patterns often thought to have been associated with the rise of stronger leaders. The first low, oval to circular earthen mounds appear during this time. Most are less than 4 m in height and 30 m in diameter. Increased evidence of trade and exchange in the finished products from Hopewellian areas in Illinois and Ohio that appear in the region further documents the emergence of such leaders.

Smith (1986:50–53) cites evidence of population growth and readjustment between AD 450 and 950 that anticipated the emergence of Mississippian society. Maize had appeared by AD 405 in the Southeast, originating from across the southern Plains. This was a 12- and 14-row variety race of pop or hard flint maize. It appears to have initially played a minor role in subsistence practices, having been merely incorporated into field agricultural systems already centered on the production of starchy seed plants. Smith's (1986:51) point is, however, that the shift from hor-ticultural garden plots to field agriculture during this time may have preadapted the region to the monoculture farming based primarily on maize that commenced shortly thereafter.

Within the Southeast, the emergence of Mississippian groups is dated to be-tween AD 750 and 950. All investigators agree that this was a time of very significant cultural change and innovation. Limestone and shell became the primary pottery-tempering agents and preceded a proliferation of vessel forms. Subsistence was primarily based on maize agriculture. Household storage capacity increased, and there is evidence of communal storage facilities (Smith 1986:54). Planned villages with public spaces, fortifications, and mounds were common. Trade activity dramati-cally increased throughout the region. And new forms of sociopolitical organization, including hereditary ranking and centralized leadership, became the norm. V. Step-onaitis (1986:392) sees the stress of warfare and a desire to mitigate the risks of crop failure, along with trade interests and the need to accumulate surpluses, as stimuli to Mississippian development. While Mississippian groups were in decline by AD 1600, later historic groupings were spawned by this florescence.

Northeast

Summary reviews for the Northeast are rather disappointing and tend to be either exclusively oriented toward the Midland or to the more coastal northeastern subregions. Many investigators (e.g., Tuck 1978) see the Early Woodland in the Midlands as an extension of what is known as the Lake Forest Archaic. The rather spectacular mortuary practices of Lake Forest groups are viewed as foreshadowing the clearly spectacular mortuary practices of the subsequent Adena groups during the Early Woodland. Most mound-related Adena material is dated to after circa 2500 years ago, even though the larger entity has demonstrable earlier roots. To the east, Funk (1983:334) defines a Middlesex phase as having been directly or indirectly related to Adena. The earliest portion of the Meadowood phase, overlapping in both time and space with Middlesex, may be linked directly with the Lake Forest Archaic. In any case, ceramics are certainly associated with Early Woodland groups in the Midlands and appeared further to the east by circa 2800 years ago. There is some evidence for incipient horticulture being associated with Midland Adena groups, and *Chenopodium* may have played a role in that subsistence base (Tuck 1978:40).

The Middle Woodland in the Northeast is synonymous with the Hopewell florescence in the Midlands beginning circa 2100 years ago. Two centers of Hopewellian development, one in southern Ohio and the other in the Illinois Valley and adjacent areas, are usually mentioned. In both locations Hopewell is defined by its rich material culture including imposing earthworks and mounds, and the Hopewellian interaction sphere was appropriately immense. Archaeologists have long speculated on the Hopewellian subsistence base. While cultivation of certain indigenous species has been demonstrated, Smith (1989:1569) has argued that maize was not a part of the Hopewellian diet. To the east, Funk (1983) discusses a host of phases that define the Middle Woodland. Most of these smaller phases are grouped within what is known as the Point Peninsula tradition. Some of these may have had some links to more western groups, but many appear to have been typical indigenous hunters and foragers.

What archaeologists refer to as Hopewell begins to decline after AD 300 and is replaced by a variety of different archaeological manifestations. In time, Mississippian-related groups would begin to dominate the Midlands area. Certainly the greatest expression of this Mississippian domination is the Cahokia site outside of St. Louis, Missouri. There is no doubt that maize had by then become the primary cultigen. Further east, in the original Adena–Hopewell heartland, Fort Ancient groups appear clustered along the Ohio River and its tributaries. These sites, dating to between AD 900 and 1600, were also definitely supported by maize agriculture. Smith (1989:1570) suggests that a new eight-row variety of maize, which was adapted to the shorter growing seasons of more northern latitudes, was associated with Fort Ancient. Within eastern Ohio, northern West Virginia, and western Pennsylvania, Monongahela groups predominated at about the same general time period. In all of these later manifestations, however, it is difficult to suggest a relationship to subsequent historic tribes.

Still further east, Funk (1983:306) starts the Late Woodland at AD 1000. Much of the research focus during this subperiod is consumed by the in situ development of the Iroquois tradition out of an earlier Owasco base. The Owasco foundation is itself dated between AD 1000 and 1300, and it anticipates patterns eventually expressed in historic Iroquoian tribal society. There is little debate that these developments were fueled by maize agriculture supplemented by hunting and foraging. The maize component of this subsistence base was the before-mentioned new eight-row variety that appears related to historic period flint varieties. During the Late Woodland, ancestral groups to the historic Algonquian tribes of the coastal region must have been undergoing concurrent development. The details of this development, however, are sketchy at best, and those manifestations, at least to Funk (1983:359), look archaeologically very similar to their Owasco counterparts.

Middle Atlantic

The Middle Atlantic region, as it is broadly defined, runs from southern New York State down the Atlantic coast to about the Virginia–North Carolina border. Less consensus probably exists on interior boundaries. While no region-wide review of the Woodland period exists for the Middle Atlantic, a number of more temporally or geographically restricted reviews (e.g., Jirikowic 1995; Kinsey 1972; Kraft 1986) have been published. The information in these and other reports can be combined to present a brief summary of the Woodland period across the Middle Atlantic region. It should be noted that the various subperiods of the Woodland in the Middle Atlantic are not based as much on the ascendancy of dominant groups—as archaeologists have been able to define in other areas—as they are on changes in various items of material culture, primarily ceramic types.

As with other regions, the Early Woodland begins circa 3000 years ago and builds on trends initiated in the Late Archaic. The earliest ceramics, generally Marcey Creek wares tempered with crushed steatite and reminiscent in form of earlier carved steatite bowls, first appeared in the southern reaches of the Middle Atlantic. This ware type is followed by a host of what are often referred to as early experimental ceramic types. Most of these subsequent early pottery wares were coil constructed in more typical vessel forms. A number of other early ceramic wares, including Exterior Corded/Interior Smooth and Vinette I, also appear in the northern reaches of the region. Generally it appears that after pottery made its appearance, the tradition of ceramic production spread rather quickly across the Middle Atlantic. At the same time, groups became more sedentary and focused on the intensified procurement of various subsistence items, although year-round sedentism is not universal (Jirikowic 1995). Storage infrastructure does appear on some sites. Various investigators have noted that Early Woodland groups were not trading regional materials at previous levels, but the more focused exchange of selected items from the Midlands, mainly Adena artifacts, is evident on regional sites.

The Middle Woodland subperiod in the Middle Atlantic is usually started around 2300 years ago. Early in the subperiod a variety of different ceramic types are recovered. Net-marking regularly appears on ceramics in addition to both cord- and fabric-marked surface treatments. In time, Mockley ware, a shell-tempered ware with a host of decorative attributes, virtually dominates the Middle Atlantic region. There is some indication that groups appear to have been focusing more on the settlement of the Coastal Plain. There is evidence of intensified food production, especially of shellfish in coastal areas and possibly of plant foods across the region. Most importantly, there is indication of increasing interaction between groups throughout the region. Ceramics with decorative motifs common to the Abbott Farm site in New Jersey, for example, are found on sites in Virginia (Stewart 1992:10). Dramatic evidence of increased levels of sociocultural integration begins to appear in isolated areas. Adena artifacts are recovered at what appear to be mortuary centers within the region, and Gardner (1982) notes the appearance of stone burial mounds in the western interior areas of Virginia, Maryland, and West Virginia.

Developments beginning around 1000 years ago start the Late Woodland subperiod. Two trends after this date are typically mentioned in the archaeological literature (e.g., Jirikowic 1995). For one, a completely sedentary way of life became the norm for most of the Middle Atlantic. For another, there is definite evidence of agricultural subsistence production. In terms of the latter, evidence appears first at more interior locations, but there is no doubt that the standard triad of introduced cultigens (maize, beans, and squash) were present across much of the region by circa AD 1000. Absolute commitment to this subsistence system does, however, vary with location. It is important to note that experience with plant cultivation no doubt had a much deeper past in the Middle Atlantic, although unlike other subregions of eastern North American, it is impossible to be more specific about the nature and trajectory of this history at the present time.

While these economic and settlement changes were occurring, a host of new ceramic types appear across the region. Chipped-stone tool manufacturing becomes more expedient, and the production of triangular projectile points all but predominates in the region. The latter implement is interpreted as conclusive evidence of the adoption of the bow and arrow as the primary weapons delivery system. At the same time, most Late Woodland sites yield evidence of a well-developed storage technology. In fact, many investigators point to indicators of even greater economic codependence among people of this time.

By the end of prehistory, relatively large-scale communities were common in the Middle Atlantic region. Many of these groups represent the historic tribes that were documented by early European explorers and settlers. Herbert Kraft (1986) has traced the prehistoric origins of Delaware-speaking groups in the northern Middle Atlantic. The historic Susquehannock tribe, an Iroquoian-speaking group, had its roots in the more northern Owasco tradition and then migrated south to settle along the Susquehanna River above the Chesapeake Bay at about AD 1500 (Kent 1984). Archaeological correlates of the Piscataway (see Cissna 1986) and Powhatan groups, located further south, can also be identified.

Europeans

The fourth major sphere of influence originated across the ocean in Europe. Aside from some very early Norse forays into the far northern reaches of eastern North America, circa AD 1000, significant European impact on the wider region would not be felt until the early sixteenth century. Nevertheless, the effects of European contact would ultimately be enormous, and it is important to appreciate these developments in some wider context. The few paragraphs below closely follow Eric Wolf's (1982) thoughts on the events leading up to the European penetration of eastern North America.

As a prelude, Europe in AD 800 consisted of a host of petty principalities all scrambling for rights to the pieces of the shattered Roman Empire. If there was any center of power in the Old World at that time it was to be found in the Muslim world to the east. By AD 1400, however, this situation had changed. A smaller number of effective European polities, based on local hegemony, war, commerce, and expansion, were about to launch major overseas adventures. Portuguese, Spanish, Dutch, English, French, and Italian powers were all set to sponsor voyages of discovery and eventually to plant settlement on lands far removed from the Old World.

Iberian fleets first dominated the Atlantic, precluding expansion of most other European states into North America until the end of the sixteenth century (Wolf 1982:158). In the interim, the Spanish were able to explore and, to a certain degree, missionize some of the Southeast. Archaeologists are only now beginning to trace Hernando de Soto's route of exploration and terror throughout the Southeast between AD 1539 and 1543. More importantly, scholars have now begun to see his foray and other similarly early adventures as vectors for the infectious diseases that decimated indigenous populations through pandemics that swept across eastern North America even before later sustained European settlement (e.g., see Ramenofsky 1987; M. T. Smith 1987). By the mid-seventeenth century, Spaniards in *La Florida* were successful in establishing a chain of mission settlements throughout the region. The northern frontier of this effort even included the establishment of a short-lived Jesuit mission settlement within the Chesapeake region in AD 1570.

Nevertheless, this Spanish grip on eastern North America slowly loosened. Jacques Cartier wintered on the banks of the St. Lawrence River in AD 1535, thus establishing contact between the French and local North American Indian groups. The French were soon able to penetrate the Northeast and Great Lakes region in search of pelts to market through the international fur trade network. Early in the 1600s the Dutch, after temporarily seizing Portuguese holdings in Brazil and the Caribbean, established settlements from Delaware to New York. So-called New Amsterdam would remain under their control until AD 1644. After an ill-fated earlier attempt at colonization along the North Carolina coast, the English succeeded in planting colonies in Virginia, Maryland, and New England. That colonial power would eventually lay claim to all of eastern North America.

THE WOODLAND PERIOD IN THE CHESAPEAKE REGION

Study of the Woodland period in the Chesapeake region is a pursuit with considerable tenure. In an historic sense, the latter portions of the Woodland period were directly observed and recorded since at least the sixteenth century. This textual record is attributable to the labors of an assortment of European explorers, traders, proselytizers, and settlers. From the standpoint of archaeology itself, it is probably impossible to document the first real local interest in Woodland period archaeology. From at least the seventeenth century on, various parties have collected artifacts from this period. As early as 1794 the Reverend John Jones Spooner left a resonably detailed description of an archaeological site on the Coastal Plain of Virginia (see Turner 1992:99). By the late nineteenth and early twentieth centuries numerous professional and amateur archaeologists became intrigued with the shell middens that dot the shorelines of the region. New evidence of often spectacular mortuary practices, primarily the large ossuary burials of the Late Woodland, also generated its share of curiosity. By the mid-twentieth century, sustained archaeological investigation of the local Woodland period began in earnest.

The task now at hand is to produce an overview of the Woodland period in the Chesapeake region. For the purposes of this analysis, the Woodland period is subdivided into more limited chronological intervals. Early, Middle, and Late qualifiers are attached. Consensus usually dates the Early Woodland subperiod between circa 3000 and 2300 years ago. The Middle Woodland subperiod is bracketed between circa 2300 and 1050 (AD 900) years ago. The Late Woodland subperiod is begun after circa AD 900. Approach these as nominal chronological boundaries.

In addition to discussing each of these three formal subperiods, I want to separately address two important events in regional prehistory. First, the appearance of Adena-related material in the Chesapeake region between circa 2500 and 1900 years ago will be discussed separately. This Adena material is unique, and it chronologically overlaps both the late Early Woodland and early Middle Woodland subperiods. For another, while this volume does focus on the prehistory of the Chesapeake region, it is difficult to ignore early European observations of the native world. That matter will be addressed as a epilogue in the Late Woodland subsection.

Early Woodland

The Early Woodland subperiod in the Chesapeake region is marked by the appearance of the first pottery traditions. In many ways Early Woodland technology builds on trends initiated in the Late Archaic, although specific additional divergence can be noted. Given the increasing amount of data available on the Woodland period as a whole, I divert slightly from conventions employed in corresponding sections of the previous two chapters. In this section I describe the subperiods in terms of fewer and generally broader categories. For the Early Woodland the discussion that follows focuses on technology, settlement practices, and subsistence economy.

Technology

Regional prehistorians isolate a distinct series of ceramic wares assignable to the Early Woodland. These early wares are differentiated based on technique of manufacture, tempering agent, surface treatment, appliques, and final shape or form. The context of discovery is also considered. In general, the earliest ceramics are referred to as experimental wares (follows Wise 1975). Subsequent to these early wares, more traditional ceramic types appear and dominate throughout the Early Woodland, sometimes overlapping into the Middle Woodland. Table 6.1 lists wares within the two groupings. It also references some of the literature on the definition of these types. Table 6.2 offers a sample of available uncorrected radiocarbon assays on these wares.

Early experimental wares are generally trough- or bowl-shaped vessels with flat bottoms modeled from slabs of clay. Vessel orifices are unrestricted, and these vessels often have lug handles applied at each end. Surface marking varies from plain to some cord-marked surfaces or mat/net-marked bottoms. A few types within this category were coil constructed resulting in the more classic conoidal or rounded-base forms. In appearance, local prehistorians often remark that many of these experimental wares are reminiscent in form of the earlier carved steatite bowls. Indeed, some of these wares, for example Marcey Creek and Selden Island ceramics, are tempered with crushed steatite. Mouer (1991a:47) cites the recovery of one of these vessels that actually looks to have been carved from a lump of clay.

Most of the early experimental wares appear spatially restricted to the Piedmont zone and sometimes the outer Coastal Plain. None are typically recovered in great quantities. In the case of the Coastal Plain, however, many are tempered with agents available only in locations west of the fall zone. Examples of this phenomenon include Bushnell, Croaker Landing, and Dames Quarter wares. Marcey Creek ware was the first such experimental type noted for the region and appears more widely distributed than most of the other early types. The distribution of the Currituck series of wares, possibly a very early ceramic, extends from Albemarle Sound in North Carolina to the lower Chesapeake region. Bushnell ware and Croaker Landing ware

Table 6.1. Early Woodland Ceramics

Ware or series	Temper	Reference
Marcey Creek	Steatite	Manson 1948
Selden Island	Steatite	Slattery 1946
Bushnell	Muscovite schist or hornblende	Waselkov 1982
Croaker Landing	Subangular clay particles	Egloff et al. 1988
Dames Quarter	Hornblende or gneiss	Wise 1975
Currituck	Shell to sand	Painter 1978, 1988
Ware Plain	Sand or quartz	McCann 1950
Accokeek	Sand or quartz	Stephenson and Ferguson 1963
Wolf Neck	Quartz	Griffith 1982
Coulbourn	Clay nodules or fragments	Griffith 1982
Nassawango	Rock and clay	Custer 1989
Wilgus	Shell and clay	Custer 1989
Elk Island	Sand or quartz	Mouer 1991

Table 6.2. Radiocarbon Assays
on Early Woodland Ceramics[a]

RCYBP[b]	Lab number	Site
Marcey Creek		
3170 ± 120	Y-2589	Miller Field, NJ
2900 ± 95	I-5091	Monocacy, MD
Selden Island		
2955 ± 90	UGa-5376	Clyde Farm, DE[c]
Dames Quarter		
2955 ± 90	UGa-5376	Clyde Farm, DE[d]
Bushnell		
3110 ± 70	SI-4377	White Oak Point, VA
3060 ± 75	SI-4375	White Oak Point, VA
3020 ± 70	SI-4376	White Oak Point, VA
Currituck		
2760 ± 260	UGa-2189	Currituck, NC
2610 ± 60	UGa-1424	Currituck, NC
2610 ± 85	UGa-1785	Currituck, NC
Elk Island		
2845 ± 150	UGa-3347	Stoneman West, VA
Accokeek		
3070 ± 75	SI-2793	Cole #1, MD
2960 ± 120	Beta-34389	522 Bridge, VA
2930 ± 100	Beta-34388	522 Bridge, VA
2800 ± 90	Beta-34386	522 Bridge, VA
2740 ± 150	Beta-34390	522 Bridge, VA
2360 ± 95	Beta-11799	LD 15, VA
1870 ± 125: AD 80	M-1605	Martins Pond, MD
Wolfe Neck		
2455 ± 60	UGa-1223	Wolfe Neck, DE
2450 ± 85	I-6891	Dill Farm, DE
2330 ± 85	I-6886	Dill Farm, DE
2240 ± 60	UGa-1763	Wilgus, DE[e]
Coulbourn		
2325 ± 60	UGa-1224	Wolfe Neck, DE

[a]Radiocarbon assays obtained from Boyce and Frye, 1986; Custer, 1989;
Mouer, 1991; McLearen, 1991a,b; Painter, 1978; Rust, 1983; Waselkov,
1982; and Wright, 1973.
[b]RCYBP, radiocarbon years before present.
[c]In association with Dames Quarter ceramics.
[d]In association with Selden Island ceramics.
[e]In association with Coulbourn ceramics.

have only been recovered on the outer Coastal Plain of the Western Shore. Dames Quarter and Ware Plain types are found on the Eastern Shore. Selden Island was first excavated along the Potomac River near the fall line and appears in moderate quantities throughout the region. Most of these earliest ceramic wares date to circa 3200 to 2900 years ago.

Some of this early experimental pottery, for example Marcey Creek, Selden Island, Bushnell, and Croaker Landing, may be unique Chesapeake innovations. Alternatively, Keith Egloff (1991:247), a respected regional ceramicist, has recently argued that all these types were ultimately inspired by earlier ceramics in the Southeast. The Currituck series clearly indicates more southern influences. Dames Quarter and Ware Plain, by contrast, appear to have more northern origins.

Very shortly after 2900 years ago, the production of ceramics quite literally blossomed across the study area. Variation was slightly reduced as native potters shifted to coil production techniques and began to produce the more typical bag- and globular-shaped vessels with conoidal or rounded bases. Cord and net marking became the most common surface treatments, although some fabric impression has been noted. Vessel capacity of these new wares increased exponentially, although many of these containers remained extremely friable. Any number of investigators have remarked that these later second-generation wares indicate a complete and rather quick acceptance of a ceramic-making tradition and set the stage for most subsequent Woodland pottery. If earlier vessels were indirectly heated through the introduction of hot rock, these new forms suggest that direct heating was becoming more common.

Accokeek ware, tempered with coarse to medium-fine sand or crushed quartz, appears across much of the Western Shore and south of the Choptank River on the Eastern Shore. Both cord- and net-marked varieties are recovered. Wolf Neck ware, tempered with crushed quartz and having the same surface treatments, is especially prevalent on the upper Eastern Shore. Three cognate types, Coulbourn, Nassawango, and Wilgus wares, appear in that same area, and are tempered with clay and various other admixtures. Recently, Mouer (1991a:39) has argued for an Elk Island series as a local variant of Accokeek wares in the southern study area along the James River, especially beyond the fall line. He sees that series as distinct from Accokeek ware because of some vessel forms with flat bases and lug handles. These second-generation ceramic wares of the Early Woodland date between circa 2900 and 2300 years ago, although some types overlap into the subsequent Middle Woodland subperiod. Many second-generation wares seem to have originated to the west beyond the fall line. Wolfe Neck ware may be related to other more northern pottery traditions (Custer, 1989:171), with cognate types possibly being later in situ developments.

Shifting to the chipped-stone component of the Early Woodland, no simple one-to-one correlation can be demonstrated between individual ceramic ware types and corresponding projectile point types. Given the nature of changes taking place in ceramic styles, it would probably be unusual if such a direct correlation were to exist.

Some of the early experimental wares are associated with what are known as small variant Savannah River projectiles or with later derivatives such as the Fishtail types. Calvert projectile points, however, were clearly associated with early wares at the White Oak Point site (Waselkov 1982:277). Most of the second-generation ceramic types are recovered in association with either Calvert or Rossville projectile points. Mouer (1991a:39) notes that small foliate and lanceolate projectile points are also recovered in association with Elk Island ware. A few archaeologists insist that "Piscataway" projectile points, considered by others to be a Late Archaic type never recovered with pottery, are in fact recovered with early ceramics. Other prehistorians strongly believe that these so-called Piscataway projectiles are actually the somewhat similar, but chronologically later and larger, type known as Rossville. I fall into this last camp, although I acknowledge that the evidence does need to be thoroughly reviewed by all. Last, classic Adena projectile points have been recovered in association with the clay-tempered wares on the Eastern Shore (Custer 1989:173). More will be said about this phenomenon later. Table 6.3 lists a sample of available radiocarbon assays on projectile point types, and Figure 6.1 illustrates various projectile point types.

Beyond projectile points, Early Woodland chipped-stone assemblages generally mirror those of the Late Archaic intensification era. Small bifaces are recovered along with rather expedient drills, perforators, and scraping implements as well as numerous utilized flakes. McLearen (1991a:117) mentions the presence on Early Wood-

Table 6.3. Radiocarbon Assays on Early Woodland Projectile Points[a]

RCYBP[b]	Lab number	Site
Calvert		
3110 ± 70	SI-4377	White Oak Point, VA
3060 ± 75	SI-4375	White Oak Point, VA
3020 ± 70	SI-4376	White Oak Point, VA
1870 ± 125: AD 80	M-1605	Martins Pond, MD
1590 ± 75: AD 360	UGa-3498	Delaware Park, DE[c]
1310 ± 155: AD 640	UGa-3439	Delaware Park, DE[c]
Rossville		
2680 ± 575	UGa-3466	Delaware Park, DE
2430 ± 80	Y-2590	Miller Field, NJ
1960 ± 80	UGa-3500	Delaware Park, DE
1590 ± 75: AD 360	UGa-3498	Delaware Park, DE[d]
1345 ± 400: AD 605	UGa-3437	Delaware Park, DE
1310 ± 155: AD 640	UGa-3439	Delaware Park, DE[d]

[a]Radiocarbon assays obtained from Boyce and Frye, 1986; Custer, 1989; Waselkov, 1982; and Wright, 1973.
[b]RCYBP, radiocarbon years before present.
[c]In association with Rossville.
[d]In association with Calvert.

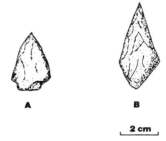

Figure 6.1. Illustration of typical Early Woodland projectile point types recovered in the Chesapeake region: A, Calvert; B, Rossville.

land sites of bipolar flake tools that may have functioned as scrapers, gravers, and generalized cutting implements. Generalized rough-stone implements such as grubbing tools, hammerstones, anvil stones, and net sinkers are reported along with mortars, pestles, manos, and metates. The grooved, stone axes of the Late Archaic continue in the Early Woodland as do ground-stone celts and adzes. A significant number of ground-slate pendants and gorgets are likewise recovered. As for lithic material choice, there appears to have been a preference for local materials. Quartz is widely used along with almost any other locally available material. Trade networks, for lithic material at least, do not appear to be as extensive as they were in earlier times.

Bone tools have likewise been recovered from Early Woodland sites. Waselkov (1982:226) reports recovery of a polished deer antler tine along with a mammal bone splinter awl and deer metapodial splinter awl from the White Oak Point site. Painter's (1988:25) Early Woodland Currituck components include projectile points manufactured from bone, antler, turkey spurs, stingray barbs, and shark's teeth. As McLearen (1991a:126) notes, other objects made from both bone and shell are reported on these sites in the lower Chesapeake and from areas further to the south.

Settlement Practices

The matter of Early Woodland settlement practices will be addressed from the perspective of community patterning within sites and in terms of the distribution of sites across the landscape. A number of investigators point to evidence of increased sedentism during the Early Woodland. Mouer (1991a:26) argues that sedentary life had fully emerged in the Piedmont zone during this period of time. Whatever the degree of sedentism, such changes began to alter settlement practices during the Early Woodland.

Within sites, definite evidence of subsurface storage features begins to appear on sites in the Piedmont zone (Manson 1948; Mouer 1991a; Slattery 1946; Thomas 1981).

Such features also eventually appear at sites on the outer Coastal Plain (McNett 1974; Stephenson and Ferguson 1963). The appearance of these small subterranean cists indicates increased storage of foodstuffs, and many later served as refuse receptacles. Mouer (1991a:39–40) points out that thick midden deposits along with dense and extensive occupational debris begin to appear on sites along the James River. A pit containing a probable human cremation is reported on the Stoneman West site. Formal hearths are also common on Early Woodland sites along with substantial deposits of fire-cracked rock. The White Oak Point site on the outer Coastal Plain of the Potomac River yielded substantial shell midden deposits (Waselkov 1982:225–227). Together these features and observations reflect strong evidence of increasing duration of site use and the intensification of on-site activities.

Remains of domestic structures are difficult to delineate for the Early Woodland, indeed for the entire Woodland period in the Chesapeake region. Mouer (1991a:40) suggests the presence of such structures based on patterning in other features at the Scott #2 site along the James River. Custer (1989:197–198) points to evidence of a pit house at the Clyde Farm site in the Delaware portion of the Eastern Shore. A nearby platform hearth was assayed to 2955 ± 90 (UGa-5376) years ago, and it is associated with Selden Island and Dames Quarter ceramics. Other similar pit structures have been identified in Delaware and were discussed in the previous chapter. Some of these features clearly date to the Late Archaic, but the Clyde Farm structure does appear to be Early Woodland. Such continuity in house form between the Late Archaic and the Early Woodland in that area of the region should probably not be viewed as unusual given similarities between the two subperiods.

McLearen's (1991b) excavations at the 522 Bridge site, well west of the study area on the North Fork of the Shenandoah River near Front Royal, Virginia, no doubt provide the clearest evidence of Early Woodland domestic structures. At that site he recovered unprecedented data on subperiod structures and associated features. Evidence of eight to nine structures was unearthed along with a striking repetition in the placement of associated features, including storage features as well as hearths, in and around these structures (McLearen, 1991b:124–126). Accokeek ceramics were in a majority at this site, and the presence of this ware may make it safe to assume that similar structures once existed at other Early Woodland sites directly within the study area. Figure 6.5, presented in a subsequent section of this chapter, illustrates two of the house patterns from the 522 Bridge site.

Early Woodland settlement systems have recently been receiving increased attention. As mentioned above, evidence indicates that local groups were becoming much more sedentary, effectively occupying certain larger sites for longer periods of time. At the same time, populations at these major large sites were being serviced by numbers of smaller associated resource extraction sites. Such a strategy fits in Binford's (1980) collector strategy and mirrors changes initiated during the Late Archaic in this region. This general theme of larger, more permanent sites supported by smaller special-purpose sites reverberates throughout the literature on the Early Woodland in the Chesapeake study area.

For coastal areas, Gardner (1982:56) sees subperiod settlement systems as having been centered around major base camps linked to more transient, limited purpose interior sites. At more interior locations further west, he sees a similar fusion–fission settlement model focused around freshwater versus estuarine locations. Mouer (1991a:65–70) has recently proposed a similar settlement model based on his research in the James River area. Here individual Early Woodland groups occupied large sites on either the outer Coastal Plain or at interior locations beyond the fall line. The inner Coastal Plain, between these two zones, then served as a buffer zone and was shared by both groups. Outer Coastal Plain groups tended to use it during the fall and early winter seasons, while interior groups visited the zone during late winter and early spring. Visits by either group were dictated by periods of resource scarcity in home areas. Shared buffer zones may also have fostered some group interaction. Custer (1989:189) has presented a similar settlement system for groups on the Eastern Shore of the estuary. This system focuses on the occupation of what he calls macroband base camps supported by numerous microband base camps and associated procurement sites.

Subsistence Economy

Evidence of Early Woodland subsistence practices is beginning to become available. Ronald Thomas (1981:V25) sees fish processing, nut gathering, and other related activities as major foci at the Delaware Park site. Carbonized hickory nut shells were recovered at the Selden Island site along the Potomac River (Slattery 1946:265), and remains of these and other nut-bearing species have been reported at a number of other Early Woodland sites. All of these sites are within the Piedmont zone. On the outer Coastal Plain, Waselkov (1982:312) reports recovery of remains of hickory nut, various species of shellfish, crabs, fish, and deer at the White Oak Point site. Increased exploitation of oyster to the exclusion of other shellfish species appears to have started during the Early Woodland. A number of other investigators report the recovery of similar subsistence remains at other sites on the Coastal Plain.

In addition, although current evidence is not abundant, it appears as if Early Woodland groups were focusing on the intensive exploitation of seed plants. Custer (1989:231) makes this observation for sites on the Eastern Shore. Mouer (1991b:261–262) presents evidence of a small variety of seed remains recovered at Early Woodland sites west of the fall line on the James River, where charred seeds of mustard plant (*Brassica* sp.) and chenopod (*Chenopodium* sp.) are reported. These data might be interpreted as direct evidence of plant promotion in the study area during the Early Woodland.

Adena Influences

Adena is a well-known, albeit incompletely understood, Early Woodland tradition of the American Midlands initiated circa 2500 years ago, but having demonstrable roots even before that date. It is widely recognized for its unique material culture and mortuary program. The distinctiveness of these elements is perhaps only matched by the mystery of Adena everyday life in that heartland. One can therefore imagine the astonishment of local prehistorians a number of decades ago when Adena-related artifacts in association with distinctive mortuary centers were first reported for the Chesapeake tidewater region. These newfound Adena artifacts and associated sites initially represented an enigma of the highest order.

A number of sites related to this western manifestation have been excavated on the Coastal Plain of the Chesapeake Bay. On the Western Shore, the West River Adena site has been reported by T. Latimer Ford (1976). For the Eastern Shore, the Sandy Hill site (Ford 1976) along the Choptank River and the Nassawango Creek site (Wise 1973) on a tributary of the Pocomoke River contain Adena manifestations. Several related Adena sites in nearby Delaware include Killens Pond (Cubbage 1941) and the Frederica site (Jones 1965), both on the Murderkill River, and the Saint Jones site (Thomas 1976) on the Saint Jones River. It is important to note that Adena artifacts also appear in nonmortuary contexts in Maryland, Delaware, and Virginia, although they are not as numerous in the latter state (MacCord 1985).

Local prehistorians' confusion centered on how to view the relationships between regional mortuary sites yielding Adena artifacts and the western Adena sites. Early on, Ritchie and Dragoo (1959:45) maintained that Chesapeake Adena sites were the result of the actual transfer of groups from the Midland home area to the east. The stimulus for this supposed migration was attributed to Hopewell encroachment into the central and upper Ohio Valley. Griffin (1961), while not denying a relationship, quickly challenged the notion of an actual migration of Adena people into the Chesapeake region.

Fortunately, Thomas (1969, 1970) undertook a comprehensive review of available evidence. Based on observation of significant differences in assemblage composition and mortuary practices between the homeland and the Chesapeake region, Thomas (1969:14) suggested that a direct west to east migration did not seem plausible. He instead argued for the existence of extensive trading networks to deliver Adena artifacts into the region. Stewart (1992:21) has outlined the conditions that might stimulate such trade, and this is where the matter stands at the moment.

I would like to review the nature of the major sites containing Adena artifacts in the Chesapeake region. The West River site (Ford 1976) on the Western Shore near Annapolis, Maryland, included a large "ceremonial pit" containing five smaller cremation pits and three fire pits. Postmolds were located around this feature, and Thurman (1987:136) contends that a charnel house once stood on the site. In addition, a reburial pit was also reported. The associated artifact assemblage consists of 34 blades of distinctive nonlocal cherts, tubular pipes, gorgets, pyramids, a paint cup, grooved hematite, copper beads, fossils, and what is described as a "medicine bag" of unknown material (Ford 1976:66–74). All of these artifacts are distinctly Adena, and red ocher was present in significant quantities. Figure 6.2 is a photograph of a sample of artifacts from this site. Table 6.4 lists available radiocarbon assays from this site and

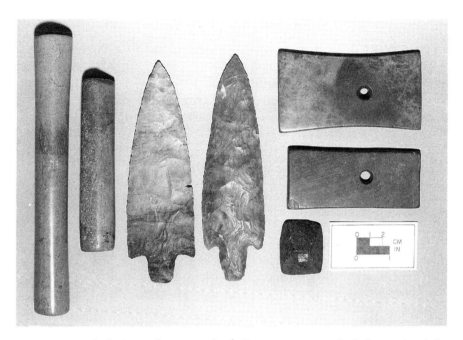

Figure 6.2. Sample of Adena artifacts recovered at the West River site in Maryland. Photograph includes blocked-end tubes, bifaces, gorgets, and a pyramid. Courtesy of the Archaeological Society of Maryland, Inc., and the Maryland Historical Trust.

Table 6.4. Radiocarbon Assays on Adena-Related Sites[a]

RCYBP[b]	Lab number	Site
2735 ± 75	SI-2191	Nassawango Creek, MD
2445 ± 100	SI-2188	Nassawango Creek, MD
2330 ± 80	Y-933	Saint Jones, DE
2310 ± 200	M-416a	West River, MD
2300 ± 200	M-927	West River, MD
2190 ± 70	SI-2189	Nassawango Creek, MD
2190 ± 100	SI-2190	Nassawango Creek, MD
2110 ± 200	M-420b	West River, MD
2030 ± 200	M-418	West River, MD
1960 ± 200	M-419b	West River, MD
1850 ± 200: AD 100	M-417a	West River, MD
1700 ± 250: AD 250	M-419c	West River, MD
1615 ± 45: AD 335	Pitt-429	Frederica, DE

[a]Radiocarbon assays obtained from Boyce and Frye, 1986; Custer *et al.*, 1990; and Thomas, 1970.
[b]RCYBP, radiocarbon years before present.

other Chesapeake Adena-related sites. Eliminating extreme dates, most of these manifestations date to between circa 2500 and 1900 years ago.

Wise (1973) reports Adena material at the Nassawango Creek site on the Eastern Shore along a tributary of the Pocomoke River. Among the 17 features reported at this multicomponent site, Wise uncovered four burial features and five fire hearths. The fill of these burial features consisted of pockets of burnt or ashy soil containing cremated bones and copper beads. Two contained the poorly preserved in-flesh interments of two juveniles accompanied by strings of copper beads. The fire hearths contained charcoal and thoroughly burnt bone. A pendant, paint cup, fabric, and red ocher are also reported.

Ford (1976) has made attempts to reconstruct the Sandy Hill site on the south side of the Choptank River near Cambridge, Maryland. Much of his report was based on interviews with parties who collected materials at various times during the site's unfortunate destruction during the 1930s and 1940s. Artifacts recovered included blades and knives of nonlocal cherts in typical Adena styles, tubular pipes, an effigy pipe, gorgets, gorget blanks, pendants, bar stones, bird stones, paint cups, pestles, atlatl weights, copper beads, fossils, hammerstones, and red ocher (Ford 1976:77–86). Although details are sketchy, Ford felt that two different burial episodes were represented, with both cremated and uncremated human interments present. Thomas (1969:3), apparently privy to information not available to Ford, indicates that graves were aligned in at least five rows and all had a north–south orientation. He further believes that many of the interments, though not all, were extended burials with large concentrations of red ocher.

The Frederica site, located on the south bank of the Murderkill River near Frederica, Delaware, was originally reported by Jones (1965). Artifacts recovered consist of bifacial blades, gorgets, pendants, tubular pipes, copper beads, copper awls, copper and stone paint cups, copper gorgets, and copper breast plates, as well as fossils and shell disc beads (Thomas 1969:16–17). Red ocher was also present. Human interments, as disarticulated bundle burials and cremations, were concentrated in an area approximately 30 m in diameter.

Another Adena-related site, the Killens Pond site, has been reported less than 8 km upstream from the Frederica site (Cubbage 1941). This site apparently contained at least two separate concentrations of graves (Thomas 1969:5). The nature of one concentration is unknown, but the other appeared to contain articulated extended burials with grave goods. Artifacts recovered at the site include a number of bifaces manufactured from nonlocal lithic materials, some apparently having been cached, along with gorgets and tubular pipes.

The Saint Jones site, located on the east bank of the Saint Jones River near Dover, Delaware, has been reported by Thomas (1969, 1970, 1976). Associated Adena-related artifacts include bifacial blades of nonlocal lithic materials, gorgets, tubular pipes, copper beads, copper gorgets, stone paint cups, faceted hematite, and mica. The site contained a large number of human burials, perhaps 50 in all. These interments consisted of dry bone cremations and unburned, disarticulated bone as well as cremated and uncremated bone of adult males, females, and subadults (Thomas 1976:96).

In his comparative analysis of the above sites, Thomas (1969) makes some interesting observations. For one, he was left with the impression that either more than one cultural manifestation was involved in the creation of these sites or, at least, there were significant temporal separations. For another, he notes obvious differences in artifact treatment at the various sites. Over 40% of the artifacts at the West River site appear to have been intentionally "ritually killed" (i.e., broken), while at other sites the percentages are much lower (Thomas 1969:14). Last, funerary practices certainly vary from site to site, and they also often vary within sites. For example, at the Saint Jones site Thomas (1976:107) reconstructs a complex sequence that started with initial preparation of a fresh corpse, temporary in-ground interment, later secondary preparation, and then final interment. The Nassawango Creek data (Wise 1973) offer possible indication of differential treatment of juveniles. Only cremations appear at the West River site (Ford 1976).

The obvious question in relation to all these sites centers on what local groups obtained these artifacts and then created and used these unique mortuary centers? Custer (1989:256–257) suggests that groups manufacturing clay-tempered wares on the Eastern Shore were responsible for these sites. Citing similar Adena artifacts recovered at the Wilgus site in Delaware, he links them to groups manufacturing Coulbourn ceramics. Wise's (1984) recovery of Coulbourn and Nassawango ceramics at the K-713 site adjacent to the Killens Pond Adena site strengthens this association. Custer (1989:268) goes further and suggests that these groups had reached the prehistoric equivalent of ethnographically known Big Man types of social organization. For the Western Shore, groups manufacturing Accokeek wares or possibly later Mockley or Popes Creek wares—both subsequent Middle Woodland ceramics—are typically linked to this phenomenon (Thurman 1985, 1987).

Middle Woodland

The Middle Woodland subperiod is dated to between circa 2300 and 1050 years ago, or AD 900. During this subperiod the Chesapeake region witnessed a period of what might be referred to as technological homogenization. Ceramic and projectile point variability becomes limited to fewer types across the study area. At the same time, a number of redirections are evident with regard to other elements of regional lifeways. I discuss the archaeology of the Middle Woodland below in terms of the categories employed with the earlier subperiod.

Technology

The predominant ceramic wares of the Middle Woodland across almost all of the Chesapeake region include the Popes Creek and Mockley types. The former dates to between circa 2500 years ago and circa AD 250. Popes Creek is a thick-walled ware, tempered with coarse to medium-grained sand, and usually with net-impressed exterior surface treatment. Interiors are often scored or combed. Mockley ware appears later and is typically dated to between circa AD 200 and 900. This ware is tempered with coarsely crushed, unburnt oyster shell, or occasionally with fresh-water shell. Exterior surface treatments include cord marking, net impressions, and plain surfaces. Stephen Potter (1993:71) cites evidence that cord marking becomes less frequent over time as net marking increases. It should be noted that Mockley ware may be a Chesapeake innovation that spread rapidly into the northern Middle Atlantic and Northeast regions. Custer (1989:276) suggests a technological contin-uum in local wares marked by the use of increasing amounts of shell tempering from late Early Woodland to Middle Woodland times.

Within this area of Popes Creek–Mockley ceramic hegemony, other more re-stricted types do appear occasionally at various specific locations throughout the region. Within what is known as the Southside area of the Coastal Plain, below the James River in Virginia, a number of different ceramic types occur that are more in the southern tradition. Some of these ceramics belong to the Stony Creek and Hercules ware series (Blanton 1992:74–75). Stony Creek ware, a sand-tempered type, is earlier. Hercules ware, tempered with crushed granite and gneiss, appears to be later. On the inner Coastal Plain above the James River one preexisting and one new ceramic type, Prince George ware and Varina ware, respectively, are apparently local innovations that crosscut the main ceramic tradition (see McLearen 1992:41–45). Prince George ware is distinctive for its pebble temper and typically dates between 2500 years ago and AD 250. Varina ware is tempered with coarse sand and crushed rock and it should date to after circa AD 230.

Somewhat further north, Nomini ware, tempered with rounded quartz particles, has been recovered by Waselkov (1982:291–293) on the lower Potomac River and dated to circa AD 850. Smallwood ware, similar to Popes Creek but with thinner vessel walls and the addition of shell to the temper, appears on sites above the Potomac River. It is thought to have a similar age to the early Middle Woodland Popes Creek type. In the northern areas of the Eastern Shore, some of the Early Woodland wares continue up into this subperiod. After AD 500, a new ceramic known as Hell Island ware appears, tempered with finely crushed quartz and mica (Custer 1989:289). All of the various wares mentioned above were manufactured in the typical bag-shaped forms with rounded or conoidal bases. Table 6.5 lists these various types with pertinent references, and Table 6.6 lists a sample of available uncorrected radiocarbon assays.

Projectile point assignment becomes somewhat less difficult during the Middle Woodland, although variations on the scenario outlined below do exist. The chipped-stone projectile points recovered with the earliest ceramic wares of the Middle Woodland are perhaps the most problematic. In a paper that is a bit of a classic, Handsman and McNett (1974:6) suggested a linkage between the Calvert projectile point and Popes Creek. Since that time this ware has also been linked to Rossville (Steponaitis 1980:15; Waselkov 1982:230) and a variety of unnamed stemmed forms.

Table 6.5. Middle Woodland Ceramics

Ware or series	Temper	Reference
Popes Creek	Sand	Holmes 1903
		Handsman and McNett 1974
Mockley	Shell	Stephenson and Ferguson 1963
Stony Creek	Sand	Evans 1955
Hercules	Granite and gneiss	Egloff and Potter 1982
Prince George	Pebbles and sand	Evans 1955
Varina	Sand and rock	McLearen 1992
Hell Island	Quartz and mica	Wright 1962
		Griffith 1982
Nomini	Quartz	Waselkov 1982
Smallwood	Quartz with shell	Wright 1973

The search for an association between Mockley ware, the later Middle Woodland ceramic type, and projectile points is less difficult. Prehistorians typically recover Mockley in association with Selby Bay (Handsman and McNett 1974; Potter 1993; Wright 1973) or the closely related Fox Creek projectile points (Custer 1989:276). The latter type name is preferred in the northern Chesapeake, and the projectile points may indeed be slightly different. During the late Middle Woodland, Nomini ware is associated with a projectile point of the same name on the lower Potomac River (Waselkov 1982:234–237). Jack's Reef Pentagonal projectile points are associated with Hell Island ceramics (Custer 1989:291). Figure 6.3 illustrates various projectile point types, and Table 6.7 lists a sample of available uncorrected radiocarbon assays for projectile points. Refer back to Figure 6.1 and Table 6.3 for Calvert and Rossville details.

In regard to lithic material choice, an interesting change corresponds with the shift to Selby Bay–Fox Creek projectile points. Before this time there appears to have been a greater reliance on local materials such as quartz. The exception might be groups occupying the northern Eastern Shore. As Selby Bay–Fox Creek projectile points appear later in the Middle Woodland, however, definite efforts were made to obtain nonlocal lithic material. Rhyolite, the dominate exotic material of choice, originated up the Potomac River in western Maryland and in south-central Pennsylvania. Argillite from Pennsylvania was also imported to the Eastern Shore in particular.

As an example of this general phenomenon, at the late Middle Woodland Boathouse Pond component below the Potomac River in Virginia, fully 94% of the Selby Bay–Fox Creek projectile points were made of rhyolite (Potter 1993:71). And such high percentages of rhyolite projectile points during this time are not that unusual in the region. This material apparently arrived in the form of blanks or preforms flowing from western sources toward the east and then throughout the

Table 6.6. Radiocarbon Assays
on Middle Woodland Ceramics[a]

RCYBP[b]	Lab number	Site
Popes Creek		
2460 ± 100	SI-450	Piscataway, MD
2440 ± 95	I-5247	Loyola Retreat, MD
2270 ± 95	SI-2900	Abells Wharf, MD
2235 ± 100	AA-3867	Chapel Point, MD
1760 ± 100: AD 190	Beta-16217	Aignor #3, VA[c]
1700 ± 60: AD 250	Beta-16212	Aignor #3, VA[c]
Mockley		
1940 ± 60: AD 10	Beta-61317	Taft, VA
1930 ± 70: AD 20	Beta-25913	HT 36/37, VA
1910 ± 80: AD 40	Beta-25914	HT 36/37, VA
1775 ± 65: AD 175	SI-3669	Rose Haven, MD
1750 ± 90: AD 200	SI-449	Piscataway, MD
1750 ± 90: AD 200	I-5817	Carey Farm, DE
1740 ± 260: AD 210	AA-321	KE 17, MD
1720 ± 60: AD 230	Beta-12834	Addington, VA
1710 ± 70: AD 240	UGa-1762	Wilgus, DE
1690 ± 60: AD 260	Beta-12119	Great Neck, VA
1650 ± 70: AD 300	Beta-25915	HT 36/37, VA
1650 ± 70: AD 300	Beta-12832	Addington, VA
1650 ± 110: AD 300	I-6060	Hughes–Willis, DE
1625 ± 160: AD 325	UGa-1273b	Wolfe Neck, DE
1620 ± 65: AD 330	UGa-1273a	Wolfe Neck, VA
1565 ± 90: AD 385	SI-2899	Abells Wharf, MD
1550 ± 80: AD 400	Beta-54249	Maycocks Point, VA
1540 ± 60: AD 410	Beta-12121	Great Neck, VA
1490 ± 90: AD 460	Beta-12120	Great Neck, VA
1490 ± 120: AD 460	GX-2266	James River, VA
1370 ± 120: AD 580	M-1608	Luce Creek, MD
1250 ± 90: AD 700	SI-3670	Rose Haven, MD
1175 ± 75: AD 775	SI-4942	Slaughter Creek, DE
1135 ± 95: AD 815	I-5246	Loyola Retreat, MD
1100 ± 60: AD 850	Beta-5199	Bartlett, VA
1050 ± 140: AD 900	Beta-27174	Patuxent Point, MD
Hell Island		
1345 ± 400: AD 605	UGa-3437	Delaware Park, DE
1310 ± 155: AD 640	UGa-3439	Delaware Park, DE
1305 ± 55: AD 645	UGa-1441	Cedar Creek, DE
1210 ± 90: AD 740	I-6338	Island Field, DE
Prince George		
1700 ± 60: AD 250	Beta-16212	HE 596, VA
1675 ± 85: AD 275	UGa-4817	HE 470, VA
1615 ± 85: AD 335	UGa-4683	HE 470, VA
Varina		
1700 ± 85: AD 250	UGa-1817	Reynolds–Alvis, VA
1720 ± 100: AD 230	Beta-16206	Aignor #9, VA

Table 6.6. (*Continued*)

RCYBP[b]	Lab number	Site
Stony Creek		
910 ± 50: AD 1040	Beta-54245	Partridge Creek, VA
870 ± 70: AD 1080	Beta-54247	Partridge Creek, VA
820 ± 70: AD 1130	Beta-54246	Partridge Creek, VA

[a]Radiocarbon assays obtained from Boyce and Frye, 1986; Curry and Kavanagh, 1991; Custer, 1989; Gleach, 1985; McLearen, 1992; McNett, 1974; Norton and Baird, 1994; Archives of the Virginia Department of Historic Resources; and Archives of the Virginia Commonwealth University Archaeological Research Center.
[b]RCYBP, radiocarbon years before present.
[c]Large vessel fragments of Popes Creek ware in association with small numbers of sherds of various other types.

Chesapeake region (Stewart 1992:21). Some of this distribution reflects broad-base exchange networks, but direct procurement from the source was also taking place.

Accompanying stone tool assemblages for the Middle Woodland closely mirror those previously described for the Early Woodland. One may refer to the technology section on that subperiod for a listing of lithic tool types. Bone tools are better known

Table 6.7. Radiocarbon Assays
on Middle Woodland Projectile Points[a]

RCYBP[b]	Lab number	Site
Selby Bay–Fox Creek		
2020 ± 130	Beta-27175	Patuxent Point, MD
1775 ± 65: AD 175	SI-3669	Rose Haven, MD
1750 ± 90: AD 200	SI-449	Piscataway, MD
1370 ± 120: AD 580	M-1608	Luce Creek, MD
1370 ± 140: AD 580	Beta-13226	Countryside, VA
1250 ± 60: AD 700	Beta-27070	Thomas Point, MD
1250 ± 90: AD 700	SI-3670	Rose Haven, MD
1210 ± 70: AD 740	Beta-6701	Countryside, VA
1135 ± 95: AD 815	I-5246	Loyola Retreat, MD
Jack's Reef		
1305 ± 55: AD 645	UGa-1441	Taylor Cedar Creek, DE
1210 ± 90: AD 740	I-6338	Island Field, DE[c]
Nomini		
1090 ± 60: AD 860	DIC-1763	White Oak Point, VA
1070 ± 60: AD 880	DIC-1769	White Oak Point, VA

[a]Radiocarbon assays obtained from Boyce and Frye, 1986; Custer, 1989; Rust, 1983; Waselkov, 1982; and Wright, 1973.
[b]RCYBP, radiocarbon years before present.
[c]Additional series of radiocarbon assays for Island Field recently published by Custer et al. 1990 also likely dates these implements, but establishment of exact association is difficult based on present publication.

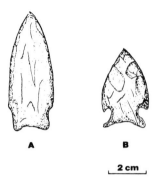

Figure 6.3. Illustration of typical Middle Woodland projectile point types recovered in the Chesapeake region; A, Selby Bay–Fox Creek; B, Jack's Reef corner-notched.

for the Middle Woodland. For example, Potter (1993:74), excavating in a late Middle Woodland context, reports bone awls, an antler awl, an antler projectile point, a fragment of bone needle, and a fragment of a spatula-shaped bone awl that may have been used in basket making. At the White Oak Point site in a Middle Woodland context, Waselkov (1982:231) recovered a mammal long bone shaft that is scored and appears to represent a blank for bead production. Numerous antler projectile points are reported for the Middle Woodland. In general, much of this bone and antler material is being recovered from shell deposits littering subperiod sites that greatly reduce soil acidity, thus improving preservation.

Settlement Practices

I once again want to examine community patterning both within sites and across the distribution of sites. As with the Early Woodland, sites typical of this subperiod can range in size from rather extensive to quite small depending on original function. Potter (1993:68–76) presents data on the range of later Middle Woodland site sizes through his survey of an area of the Northern Neck of Virginia. For general comparison, the largest single site from this time (Boathouse Pond) covers a little over 5 ha, while a nearby intermediate site (Plum Nelly) is spread over slightly less than 1 ha, and the smallest sites average around 1000 m^2. Middle Woodland sites across the region contain within their boundaries the same range of features as seen on Early Woodland sites, including dense midden debris along with subterranean storage cists, storage cists recycled as trash receptacles, hearths, roasting pits, and concentrations of fire-cracked rock.

Special note needs to be made of the shell middens that appear within or near Middle Woodland sites on the Coastal Plain. While it is an extreme example, the Popes Creek site along the Potomac River illustrates the potential amount of oyster harvesting undertaken during this time. This shell heap north of Popes Creek originally covered some 6 ha with up to an 8-m-thick layer of shell. To the south of the creek another corresponding midden covered about 8 ha and was 4 m deep in places. Shell middens, although not as large, appear on many Middle Woodland sites located near the estuary or its embayed tributaries.

Evidence of Middle Woodland domestic structures is somewhat scarce. Potter (1993:71) reports excavation of postmolds at the Boathouse Pond site that might be the remains of some type of pole-supported structure. Unfortunately, the entire structure could not be completely exposed. Gardner et al. (1989) have recently reported a possible Middle Woodland house pattern from a site (18 CV 272) along a small tributary of the Patuxent River in the middle reaches of the region. At that site a 9- by 4-m pattern of postmolds appeared to outline a domestic structure. A large pit with a puddled clay floor, measuring 2.5 m deep and 3 m in diameter, was situated at one end of the structure. Four additional postmolds around this pit appear to suggest some sort of associated protective cover. More than 200 sherds of Mockley ware and rhyolite Selby Bay projectile points were recovered in association with the structure, which appears to have represented part of a small hamlet occupied during the fall–winter season.

Good information is available on Middle Woodland settlement patterns within the context of the broader landscape. In the earlier portions of the Middle Woodland, according to Handsman and McNett (1974:10), groups making Popes Creek ware in the Potomac Valley seem to have focused on the inner Coastal Plain in ecotonal settings. These two authors suggest that the Popes Creek site was a major settlement during the fall and winter with satellite procurement sites for specialized hunting and foraging activities. During the spring some of these occupants traveled upriver to constricted areas near the fall line to exploit anadromous fish runs. In the summer a similar move was made to other nearby areas to collect freshwater shellfish and to hunt. Populations would then congregate again at the major settlement in the fall.

More recently, Potter (1993:100) has described the later Middle Woodland settlement pattern for a portion of the Northern Neck area of Virginia. For this purpose he develops a typology of site sizes applicable to his study area (Potter 1993:Table 3). Between AD 200 and 550 a dichotomy between small and intermediate-size shell midden sites and small interior sites seems to have existed. During seasonal fusion episodes, possibly during the fall and winter, groups would congregate at intermediate locations such as the Plum Nelly site. At other seasons, what were probably family-size groups would occupy the small shell midden and interior sites. Change in the local settlement system, however, was eventually evident. Sometime after AD 550, very large midden sites were occupied on necklands adjacent to coves or embayments of tributaries. The already mentioned Boathouse Pond site, an example of this phenomenon, seems to have been a village where the entire local band gathered at seasonally optimal times, and perhaps some members occupied this site most of the year. When not resident at this very large site, most of the population appears to have fissioned out into small and intermediate-size sites in coastal and interior locations. There were no doubt other sites outside this area linked to this settlement pattern.

In addition, Custer (1989) has presented settlement models for the Middle Woodland period in the northern reaches of the Chesapeake Bay region. His model for much of the Middle Woodland period is similar to those systems discussed above (see Custer 1989:189). Late in the Middle Woodland period, however, he notes the development of a unique settlement system attributable to the groups that left behind Hell Island ceramics sometime after AD 500. During this time, what he terms mortuary-exchange centers appear as additions to the previous basic settlement pattern. The most well known of these sites is the incredible Island Field site on the lower Murderkill River in Delaware, but other sites include the Hell Island site itself, as well as the Oxford and Riverton sites on Maryland's Eastern Shore. Custer (1989:294) adds that these sites, while located in unproductive ecological zones, were perfectly situated within what he sees as trade corridors. He further suggests that this phenomenon is reminiscent of earlier Adena manifestations, and it is probably evidence of the reemergence of more complex forms of sociocultural integration.

As a final note relating to territorial definition, a number of investigators (e.g., McLearen 1992:45; Stewart 1992:16) point out that a clear boundary had developed at the fall line between groups on the Coastal Plain and those further west in the Piedmont. This boundary would continue to exist throughout the remainder of the Woodland period. Additionally, it must be noted that materials were still circulating between the Chesapeake and other regions. Rhyolite procurement and trade and what appear to be exchange centers on the upper Eastern Shore have already been discussed. A number of sites in Virginia have also yielded sherds of a distinctive pottery that is very similar to a ware typically recovered at the well-known Abbott Farm site near Trenton, New Jersey. Stewart (1992:11) feels that this elaborate Abbott zoned-decorated pottery originally served in a more symbolic realm, and it might have been offered as gifts to visitors from the Chesapeake region. Whatever the explanation, it is new evidence of increased interaction between the various regions of eastern North America.

Subsistence Economy

Good data are available to document Middle Woodland subsistence practices in the Chesapeake region. Remains representing typical temperate forest, estuarine, and, where appropriate, freshwater faunal species are available from a variety of sites. The large-scale exploitation of oysters from the estuary and its embayed tributaries is a well-documented fact for the Middle Woodland. A host of other shellfish, both estuarine and freshwater species, were exploited to a lesser degree. Remains of crab, fish (anadromous and resident), and various reptiles are well represented at regional sites. Deer and wapiti remains as well as the bones of numerous other smaller mammals are recovered along with those of various avifauna species, especially migratory waterfowl and turkey. In short, most available species were being exploited. Large herd animals, such as deer, and turkey flocks appear to have been favorite resources. In terms of the former, at least at the White Oak Point site in Virginia, there appears to be no evidence of a shift from stalking to more intensive mass capture via deer drives (Waselkov 1982:202). Age ranges of deer remains recovered at that location indicate that stalking was still the dominant hunting technique. This might not, however, be the case at more interior locations.

Evidence of the exploitation of the flora of the region is available from many sites. Products of the forest mast, especially hickory nut, walnut, and acorn, are especially prevalent on local sites. One can assume that intensive harvesting and storage of these resources were taking place. Many other seed types are also recovered (see Potter 1993:73) in Middle Woodland contexts. Some 17 different species of floral remains dating to this subperiod were recovered at the Delaware Park site (Thomas 1981:ix). Great numbers of amaranth and chenopod seeds were recovered from the middens at the Wilgus site (Custer 1989:257). These data appear indicative of at least more intensive promotion and harvesting of certain plant species. The issue of when actual plant cultivation began cannot be addressed at this time, but the seeds from likely plant candidates are available to begin to look into this matter. Some have suggested that the late Middle Woodland subperiod is a likely candidate for the beginning of such practices.

A recent reanalysis of the Island Field site in Delaware (Custer et al. 1990) indicates that the small population interred in the site's cemetery were hunters and foragers, but that their lifeway involved a more sedentary existence than is typical for most such peoples. At the same time, a carbohydrate-rich diet is indicated by the higher frequency of dental caries in the population. Custer et al. (1990:199) feel that the intensive exploitation of amaranth, chenopod, and possibly wild rice (*Zizania* sp.) could have been providing the high amounts of carbohydrates in that diet and that this was clearly a population midway between hunting and foraging and agriculture. The major portion of the site dates to circa AD 410 to 1180.

Late Woodland

The Late Woodland subperiod begins after circa AD 900 and ends with the arrival of Europeans in the sixteenth through seventeenth centuries. That ensuing brief period of interaction, followed by eventual European domination, is a matter unto itself, and I will address it in a short epilogue following this section. In that epilogue I describe the native world on the eve of European arrival, and I take a moment to examine European textual accounts of the native inhabitants of the Chesapeake. This comment is offered solely from the perspective of the light that these texts might shed on late prehistory. First, however, I want to describe the Late Woodland archaeological record in terms of its precontact development.

Technology

At the dawn of the Late Woodland subperiod the distribution of a new ceramic ware, locally including four distinct types within what is known as the Townsend series, approximates the earlier distribution of Mockley ware across the study area. In a general sense, some archaeologists see Townsend ware as a derivative of Mockley. In a reanalysis of this pottery, Daniel Griffith (1980:34) points to an area of origin to the northeast, probably in the Delaware Valley, followed by expansion across central New Jersey to the Eastern Shore and then over to the Western Shore of this region. Rappahannock Fabric Impressed and Rappahannock Incised appear to be the earliest types within the Townsend series, and investigators note the distributions of these two types across the Eastern Shore and upper Western Shore (Griffith 1980) as well as on the lower Virginia Western Shore (Turner 1992) by the early Late Woodland. Table 6.8 provides a listing of the various subperiod ceramics, and Table 6.9 offers a sample of available uncorrected radiocarbon dates.

By the end of the Late Woodland, well below the Potomac River in Virginia, Townsend ware is concentrated in the core area of the subsequent Powhatan chiefdom and further east along the York River and portions of the lower Rappahannock River (Turner 1992:103). At the same time, Gaston, Cashie, and Roanoke wares appear on or below the James River. Gaston and Roanoke wares, in particular, are now being recovered on late prehistoric and Contact period sites assignable to the Powhatan chiefdom along the James River (Mouer et al. 1992:105–106; McLearen and Mouer 1994:63).

On the Northern Neck of Virginia just below the Potomac River, Potter (1993:77) reports that one of the Townsend types, Rappahannock Fabric Impressed, first appeared circa AD 900 and lasted into the early seventeenth century. Another

Table 6.8. Late Woodland Ceramics

Ware or series	Temper	Reference
Townsend	Shell	Blaker 1963
		Griffith 1980
Potomac Creek	Quartz/sand	Stephenson and Ferguson 1963
Moyaone	Sand	Stephenson and Ferguson 1963
Sullivan	Shell	Wright 1973
		L.C. Steponaitis 1986
Currioman	Shell/quartz	Waselkov 1982
Yeocomico	Shell	Waselkov 1982
		Potter 1982
Gaston	Quartz	Mouer et al. 1992
Cashie	Quartz	Egloff and Potter 1982
Roanoke	Shell	Mouer et al. 1992
Minguannan	Grit/sand/quartz	Custer 1989
Killens	Shell/grit	Wise 1984

Townsend type, Rappahannock Incised, also is common there in the early Late Woodland along with a local type, Currioman Fabric Impressed (Waselkov 1982: 293–294). Potter (1993:81–83) reports that after AD 1300 simple broad-line incised motifs become more common on Rappahannock Incised pottery, and Townsend Corded, another type in the Townsend series, appears along with Sullivan and Potomac Creek wares. The latter two pottery wares are more typical on the opposite shore of the Potomac River and northward. During the protohistoric era after AD 1500, Yeocomico and Moyaone wares appear on the Northern Neck (Potter 1993:87).

Above the Potomac River on Maryland's Western Shore, Townsend series ceramics, especially Rappahannock Fabric Impressed and Rappahannock Incised, are found in Late Woodland contexts. Another more local pottery, Sullivan ware, appears north of the Patuxent River (Wright 1973:22–23) after circa AD 565. Potomac Creek ware would become the most prolific pottery in this area after circa AD 1300. It was first described by Holmes (1903:155–156), and since that time other prehistorians have refined our understanding of this ware. McNett (1974:273), for example, has offered an internal development sequence for this ware. A number of archaeologists (e.g., Clark 1980; MacCord 1984; Potter 1993) view the development of this pottery as a result of groups known as the Montgomery Complex being forced eastward out of the Piedmont and onto the inner Coastal Plain. Paul Cissna (1986:31), citing Piscataway oral traditions and linguistic data, argues for consideration of an alternative hypothesis. He suggests tracing the original makers of Potomac Creek ware to an antecedent Eastern Shore homeland. Whatever the case, Potomac Creek ware was being made by Piscataway groups in the upper Western Shore area at the time of contact. Moyaone ware, most fully defined by Stephenson and Ferguson (1963), represents another local ware after circa AD 1300.

For the Eastern Shore, Griffith (1977, 1980) has documented various types of Townsend ware at sites across the peninsula. More recently, Custer (1989:305–308) has recognized other distinct forms of Late Woodland pottery. He defines another unique series, labeled Minguannan, that has design motifs similar to the Townsend series and may be a derivative of earlier Hell Island ceramics in Delaware. A third local Late Woodland ceramic, Killens ware, has recently been defined by Wise (1984). Killens ware is likewise similar to both Townsend and Minguannan wares.

Before concluding this discussion of regional Late Woodland ceramics, it is important to note that many of these local pottery types have both a core area and an area of greater distribution. Interaction between various regional groups was not uncommon and was probably more extensive than we now realize. Potomac Creek ware, for example, clusters around the Potomac River area on the Western Shore, but this pottery also appears on the Eastern Shore, at least as far south as the James River, and well past the fall line in the western interior, albeit in much less dense concentrations.

The chipped-stone projectile points that accompany these ceramics almost all appear to be triangular in form. Investigators assume that these triangular projectile points were delivered to their targets with bow and arrow. According to Blitz (1988),

Table 6.9. Radiocarbon Assays
on Late Woodland Ceramics[a]

RCYBP[b]	Lab number	Site
Townsend		
1070 ± 70: AD 880	Beta-27073	Thomas Point, MD
980 ± 80: AD 970	Beta-27069	Thomas Point, MD
975 ± 60: AD 975	SI-4946	Slaughter Creek, DE
950 ± 60: AD 1000	SI-2686	Lankford No. 2, MD
945 ± 70: AD 1005	SI-4374	White Oak Point, VA
935 ± 55: AD 1015	UGa-1760	Prickly Pear Island, DE
920 ± 110: AD 1030	Beta-11638	Duck Run, MD
905 ± 60: AD 1045	SI-2684	Lankford No. 1, MD
880 ± 50: AD 1070	Beta-27074	Thomas Point, MD
865 ± 75: AD 1085	UGa-923	Mispillion, DE
850 ± 55: AD 1100	UGa-1440	Bay Vista, DE
825 ± 65: AD 1125	SI-4230	Blue Fish Beach, VA
810 ± 60: AD 1140	UGa-5403	DO 15, MD
810 ± 80: AD 1140	Beta-11639	Duck Run, MD
725 ± 75: AD 1225	SI-4232	Blue Fish Beach, VA
715 ± 60: AD 1235	SI-2188	Lankford No. 2, MD
710 ± 90: AD 1240	SI-3671	Wessel, MD
705 ± 125: AD 1245	UGa-1547	Governor's Land, VA
690 ± 50: AD 1260	UGa-1461	Governor's Land, VA
680 ± 50: AD 1270	SI-4944	Slaughter Creek, DE
665 ± 75: AD 1285	UGa-925	Warrington, DE
660 ± 70: AD 1290	SI-6731	Locust Neck, MD
640 ± 50: AD 1310	DIC-1764	White Oak Point, VA[c]
610 ± 55: AD 1340	DIC-1768	White Oak Point, VA[d]
605 ± 60: AD 1345	SI-4943	Slaughter Creek, DE
580 ± 60: AD 1370	UGa-924	Poplar Thicket, DE
565 ± 55: AD 1385	SI-3665	Waveland Farm, MD
490 ± 45: AD 1460	DIC-1766	White Oak Point, VA[e]
420 ± 100: AD 1530	SI-6404	Locust Neck, MD
360 ± 120: AD 1590	SI-137	Deshazo, VA
Potomac Creek		
790 ± 50: AD 1160	Beta-46955	Taft, VA
750 ± 55: AD 1200	UGa-1761	Robbins Farm, DE
590 ± 60: AD 1360	Beta-49255	Hartwell, VA
620 ± 50: AD 1330	Beta-46954	Taft, VA
430 ± 90: AD 1520	Beta-34804	Little Marsh Creek, VA
390 ± 130: AD 1560	Beta-46956	Taft, VA
375 ± 90: AD 1575	Data-13560	18 CH 281, MD
Moyaone		
640 ± 50: AD 1310	DIC-1764	White Oak Point, VA[e]
490 ± 45: AD 1460	DIC-1766	White Oak Point, VA[e]
Currioman		
610 ± 55: AD 1340	DIC-1768	White Oak Point, VA[e]

Table 6.9. (*Continued*)

RCYBP[b]	Lab number	Site
Gaston		
215 ± 200: AD 1735	M-527	Gaston, NC
Yeocomico		
440 ± 75: AD 1510	DIC-1765	White Oak Point, VA
410 ± 55: AD 1540	DIC-1770	White Oak Point, VA
375 ± 65: AD 1575	UGa-4571	Cumberland, MD
345 ± 70: AD 1605	SI-4231	Blue Fish Beach, VA
320 ± 55: AD 1630	DIC-1767	White Oak Point, VA
305 ± 70: AD 1645	SI-4372	Blue Fish Beach, VA
260 ± 55: AD 1690	DIC-1762	White Oak Point, VA
Sullivan		
910 ± 60: AD 1040	SI-3666	Waveland Farm, MD
640 ± 70: AD 1310	Beta-15936	Solomons, MD
620 ± 50: AD 1330	Beta-13050	Solomons, MD
565 ± 55: AD 1385	SI-3665	Waveland Farm, MD[e]
530 ± 70: AD 1420	Beta-13051	Solomons, MD
Roanoke		
620 ± 00: AD 1330	Beta-12117	Great Neck, VA[e]
435 ± 70: AD 1515	UGa-3294	Great Neck, VA
440 ± 50: AD 1510	Beta-38915	Great Neck, VA[e]

[a]Radiocarbon assays obtained from Boyce and Frye, 1986; Curry and Kavanagh, 1991; Custer, 1989; Gleach, 1985; Hodges, 1993a; Norton and Baird, 1994; Potter, 1993; Waselkov, 1982; Wright, 1973; and Archives of the Virginia Department of Historic Resources.
[b]RCYBP, radiocarbon years before present.
[c]In association with Moyaone.
[d]In association with Currioman.
[e]In association with Townsend.

that delivery system first appeared in Arctic areas of North America some 5000 years ago and it then diffused throughout much of the rest of the continent. It may have appeared in eastern North America as early as AD 600 to 700, possibly reaching the Chesapeake region circa AD 900. One notices many different qualifiers being attached to regional triangular forms. The literature is littered with mention of Levanna, Yadkin, Roanoke, Clarke, Madison, Potomac, and Hamilton type designations as well as other purely descriptive labels. Figure 6.4 illustrates both large and small varieties and Table 6.10 offers uncorrected radiocarbon assays on both types. Choice of lithic material tends toward locally available sources, and the finished products were fashioned from both small expedient cores and flakes. In addition, it should be noted that both bone and antler projectile points appear on regional sites. Finally, metallic triangular projectile points also appear after contact.

The rest of the assemblage during the Late Woodland is large and varied. Stephenson and Ferguson (1963), for example, report the discovery of scrapers, per-

2 cm

Figure 6.4. Illustration of typical Late Woodland projectile point types recovered in the Chesapeake region.

forators, choppers, hoes, and net weights along with ground-stone axes, mauls, celts, adzes, mortars, pestles, grinding slabs, manos, metates, pendants, bannerstones, boatstones, and abraders at the Accokeek Creek site along the Potomac River. Shell artifacts from the Late Woodland at least include various scraping implements, pendants, and bead forms. Antler was fashioned into numerous decorative and tool forms. The bone assemblage includes awls, bodkins, beamers, pins, needles, fish hooks, and beads. This latter item of adornment, made from shell and bone, would be quickly replaced by glass trade beads as soon as they became available. In addition to

Table 6.10. Radiocarbon Assays on Late Woodland Triangular Projectile Points[a,b]

RCYBP[c]	Lab number	Site
1090 ± 60: AD 860	DIC-1763	White Oak Point, VA
945 ± 70: AD 1005	SI-4374	White Oak Point, VA
875 ± 60: AD 1075	UGa-2983	Countryside, VA
810 ± 110: AD 1140	Beta-8319	Countryside, VA
780 ± 75: AD 1170	UGa-2819	Countryside, VA
730 ± 80: AD 1220	Beta-14817	Countryside, VA
660 ± 50: AD 1290	Beta-41367	Hughes, MD
580 ± 60: AD 1370	Beta-49133	Hughes, MD
580 ± 60: AD 1370	UGa-924	Poplar Thicket, DE
510 ± 50: AD 1440	Beta-41368	Hughes, MD
440 ± 75: AD 1510	DIC-1765	White Oak Point, VA
420 ± 60: AD 1530	Beta-49132	Hughes, MD
410 ± 55: AD 1540	DIC-1770	White Oak Point, VA
320 ± 55: AD 1630	DIC-1767	White Oak Point, VA
260 ± 55: AD 1690	DIC-1762	White Oak Point, VA

[a]Radiocarbon assays obtained from Custer, 1989; Dent and Jirikowic, 1990; Rust, 1983; and Waselkov, 1982.
[b]Triangular projectile points are almost always found in association with the Late Woodland ceramics cited on Table 6.9.
[c]RCYBP, radiocarbon years before present.

ceramic vessels, clay tobacco pipes, as well as some stone forms, are common on Late Woodland sites. Native copper beads and pendants, though rare, are known from prehistoric Late Woodland sites.

Settlement Practices

During the Late Woodland it is evident that most groups were becoming increasingly sedentary. This high and eventually complete degree of sedentism is reflected in the archaeological record in any number of ways. Occupational debris of all sorts becomes substantial on subperiod sites. Shell middens were laid down on many sites near the estuary or on embayed tributaries. Refuse middens are common on larger sites. Often relatively substantial amounts of earth were moved to create ditches and trenches for various purposes. All the items of site infrastructure mentioned on earlier Woodland period sites appear in the Late Woodland. Subterranean storage cists still appear, but there is also evidence that groups were shifting to aboveground storage in domestic structures, special warehouses, and granaries.

Ample evidence of Late Woodland domestic structures on regional sites is now becoming available. Much of the following description of these structures draws on the recent review by Turner (1992:110–112). During the 1930s a partially exposed longhouse structure was evident at the Patawomeke site along the Potomac River (see Stewart 1992). Domestic structures have more recently been exposed on a number of additional Virginia sites. A well-preserved longhouse with apparent internal partitioning is reported at the Great Neck site (see Egghart 1986; Hodges 1993a). Two other possible structures exist on this same site. Numerous house patterns are also reported along the James River in Prince George County at the Jordans Point, Flowerdew Hundred, and Hatch sites. The 20 or so small oval house patterns at Jordans Point range from approximately 5.5 to 9 m in length and 4 to 5 m in width. Three house patterns at Flowerdew are 6.5 to 6.75 m long and 4.5 to 5 m wide. The Hatch structure measures 5 by 3 m according to Gregory (1980). More recently a number of spectacular structures have also been excavated at the Governor's Land site. In addition, Turner (1992:112) notes recent discoveries of house patterns at two other sites. One site is on a tributary of the Appomattox River, and the others are further south along the Nottoway River. The house patterns on the former site, a small interior camp, are smaller oval structures, possibly indicating that house form was adjusted to circumstances (see Egghart 1989). Most of these structures date to very late in prehistory or to the early Contact era.

Further north on the Western Shore at the Juhle site off the Potomac River a number of post holes outlining the rounded western end of an apparent structure about 6 m in width have been uncovered (Smith and Meltzer 1982). The entrance to this structure is defined by an L-shaped external alcove and an associated gap in the wall post pattern. The probable structure, never fully excavated, is radiocarbon dated at 435 ± 155: AD 1515 (SI-4819), and it is interpreted as a mortuary house because of its proximity and orientation to a nearby ossuary. Its rounded end and width dimension are at least similar to some of the structures in Virginia. A number of semi-subterranean pit houses have also been excavated in Delaware, and some are associ-ated with Late Woodland Townsend ceramics (Artusy and Griffith 1975).

Some of the above domestic structures appear to be parts of nucleated villages, and others were undoubtedly situated within small hamlets or larger more dispersed villages. Figure 6.5 illustrates a sample of outlines of Chesapeake domestic structures from various subperiods, and Figure 6.6 is a photograph of a reconstructed long-house. The reconstruction by Callahan (1985, 1986) is a two-thirds replication of the Great Neck, Virginia, structure. Callahan earlier undertook a more massive project in experimental archaeology, complete with numerous domestic structures, on the Pamunkey Indian Reservation in Virginia (Callahan 1976, 1981).

In addition, a number of Late Woodland sites in the region were fortified with substantial stockades. Some of these stockades appear to have encircled small parts of larger dispersed villages, perhaps chiefly residences or sacred areas, and others may have enclosed much of the settlement. In the former instance, the palisades may have served as symbolic enclosures rather than actual fortifications (Jirikowic 1995). Archaeologists also suspect that double palisades were simultaneously present on some sites. Exact determinations are difficult, however, because palisade rebuilding often took place within the life of any one site. Potter (1993:173–174) reconstructs five to seven episodes of palisade construction at the Accokeek Creek site and perhaps three to five at Potomac Creek site. Both sites are along the Potomac River. It is certainly evident that palisades on Chesapeake sites predate European contact and that warfare among native groups was endemic throughout the later portions of the Late Woodland. At least three palisade lines were recently exposed at the precontact Hughes site in the Potomac Piedmont.

In terms of Late Woodland site distributions, Potter's (1993) survey of a portion of the Northern Neck of Virginia reports some of the best currently available data on Late Woodland settlement systems. He was also able to isolate important changes within the subperiod. I use it here as an example of potentially similar settlement systems across the region. At the time of contact the area of Potter's survey was occupied by the Chicacoan group. Potter (1993:79–81) could locate no large sites in the locality dating to between AD 900 and AD 1300. Both banks of the nearby Coan River were settled by a population dispersed among intermediate-size sites serviced by a series of smaller sites. The intermediate-size sites are interpreted as semiperma-nent villages or hamlets. After AD 1300, large sites appear only on the east bank of the Coan River (Potter 1993:85). Intermediate-size sites decrease in number, with those remaining perhaps representing small outlying house clusters or favored extraction locations, while most of the rest of the population appears to have coalesced into one large, dispersed or nonnucleated village. This same general pattern holds true for the protohistoric and historic eras, although the total number of components increases due to larger populations.

A number of other investigators mention a similar pattern of larger permanent sites late in the Woodland period serviced by outlying smaller extraction sites. Many of these larger sites also appear to have had associated outlying hamlets. The post–AD

1300 Late Woodland component of Potter's (1993:85) Boathouse Pond site, which covers 4.5 ha, illustrates the size of these larger sites. In comparison, the more highly nucleated Accokeek Creek site further up the Potomac River on the Maryland shore covers about 1.6 ha. This site, though apparently very densely occupied, was fortified, and this fact may account for its smaller size. Both Turner (1976) and Potter (1993) believe that proximity to suitable soils for agriculture may have been a major factor in large village location.

It is apparent that the Late Woodland settlement systems of any one group were restricted by other nearby groups. Coastal Plain groups were constricted by one another or by potentially hostile groups to the west and/or north. As noted earlier, the fall line of the major rivers appears to have represented a cultural boundary from at least the end of the Middle Woodland through the Late Woodland. Generally unoccupied buffer zones between the Powhatan on the inner Coastal Plain and the Monacan, a Siouian-speaking group west of the fall line (Hantman 1990), appear to have been maintained by the end of the Late Woodland. The Piscataway chiefdom on the Western Shore above the Potomac River likewise appears to have observed a buffer zone between its core settlements and the Susquehannock as well as other groups to the north. These buffer zones may have served as game preserves of sorts (see Waselkov 1978), or they could simply be the result of the tendency of chiefdoms to nucleate populations for the purposes of control.

Subsistence Economy

Like before, there is little doubt that people in the Late Woodland were exploiting many of the abundant faunal, aquatic, and floral resources offered by the surrounding temperate biome and its associated estuaries and rivers. A variety of faunal remains have been recovered at a growing number of Late Woodland sites, and those recovered at the Accokeek Creek site, for example, may be fairly typical for the region (Stephenson and Ferguson 1963:58). At that site, deer represented about 80% of the identifiable remains. Elk, bear, turkey, squirrel, duck, bobcat, raccoon, rabbit, skunk, and wolf remains were also recovered. Remains of terrestrial species of turtle are also abundant on Late Woodland sites. In addition, migratory waterfowl and passenger pigeon (*Ectopistes migratorius*) appear in Late Woodland contexts.

Aquatic resources were, of course, also heavily exploited. Oyster remained a favored resource along with other species of shellfish, especially in freshwater settings. Waselkov (1982:207) notes even more intensive harvesting of oyster beginning in the early Late Woodland. Crab and aquatic species of turtle, appear in significant numbers on many sites. Fish, especially anadromous species, were also heavily exploited. Immense amounts of sturgeon (*Acipenser sturio*), gar (*Lepisosteus* sp.), and other unidentified fish species were recovered at the Accokeek Creek site (Stephenson and Ferguson 1963:58). At the White Oak Point site in Virginia, Waselkov (1982:181–182) has identified a variety of other fish species.

Floral resources were also exploited in significant quantities. Almost every

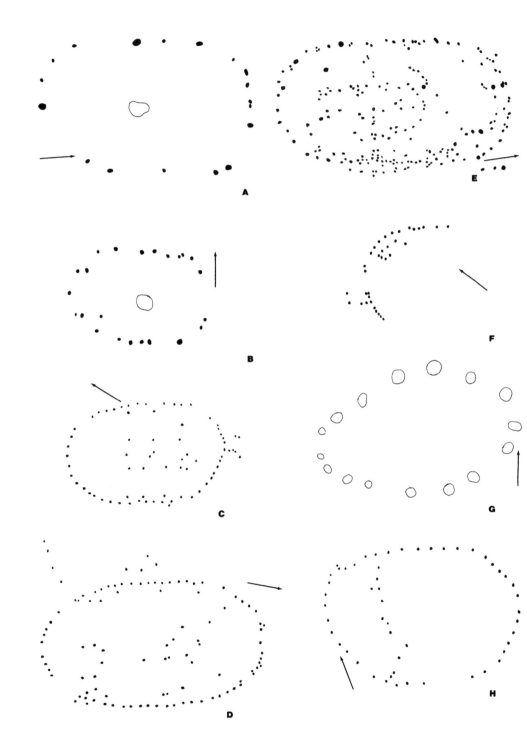

A

B

C

D

E

F

G

H

Figure 6.6. Reconstructed Late Woodland longhouse near St. Marys City, Maryland, by Errett Callahan. Reconstruction is based on a house pattern excavated at the Great Neck site in the lower Chesapeake region.

←───

Figure 6.5. Postmold patterns of domestic structures of various subperiods from Chesapeake archaeological sites (arrows accompanying each figure indicate north): A and B, Early Woodland structures with central hearths from 522 Bridge site (44 WR 329). Approximate dimensions 8.5 × 5.2 m and 5.5 × 3.6 m, respectively. Courtesy of Virginia Commonwealth University (McLearen 1991); C and D, Typical domestic structure and larger structure, possibly occupied by *werowance*, from Governor's Land site (44 JC 308). Occupancy interpretation suggested by location within site, size, and construction details. Both structures date to very early seventeenth century. Approximate dimensions 6.8 × 4.3 m and 8.6 × 4.6, respectively. Note evidence of partitioning within larger structure. Original drawings by Mary Ellen N. Hodges and Diane E. Masters, courtesy of Governor's Land Associates; E, Late Woodland structure from Great Neck site (44 VB 7). Approximate dimensions 9.3 × 4.8 m (Egghart 1986); F, Partial exposure of structure with L-shaped alcove from Juhle site (18 CH 89). Proximity to nearby ossuary suggests structure served as a mortuary facility; G, Small Late Woodland structure from Bull Hill Run site (44 PG 316). Approximate dimensions 4.9 × 3 m (Egghart 1989). Courtesy of Virginia Commonwealth University; H, Domestic structure from 44 PG 303, part of the Jordan's Point excavations. Structure occupied by protohistoric Weyanoke. Approximate dimensions 6.5 × 4.6 m (McLearen and Mouer 1993). Courtesy of Virginia Commonwealth University.

variety of nut available in the region is recovered on Late Woodland sites, along with many starchy and oily seeds and tuberous plants. Exploitation of amaranth and chenopod may have been especially intensive. Lists of other exploited floral resources from Late Woodland sites within the region are somewhat meager in part because many of these sites were excavated before flotation and other fine-scale recovery techniques became standard procedure. Excavations at the Reedy Creek site (Coleman 1982) in the very southern reaches of the study area, however, recovered a wide variety of floral resources, but exploitation of native flora during the Late Woodland no doubt went far beyond even these species.

Archaeological evidence of the shift to agriculture is available, but not abundant, in the Chesapeake region (see Turner 1992:106–108). The earliest agricultural communities using tropical cultigens appear to have been located west of the fall line. Sites in the Potomac Piedmont, for example, have yielded the earliest evidence of maize (see Table 6.11). This maize, at least at the one site where it has been typed, appears to have been an eight-row, flint variety. Potter (1993:144–145) and Dennis Curry and Maureen Kavanagh (1991) cite numerous radiocarbon assays on cultigens from the Piedmont region. The earliest dated material is in the circa AD 825 to 1000 range and it continues up to circa AD 1500.

Direct archaeological evidence of tropical cultigens from the Coastal Plain itself is not abundant. Squash (*Cucurbita* sp.) and beans (*Leguminosae*) have been recovered and dated at the Reynolds–Alvis site along the Chickahominy River in Virginia by archaeologists with Virginia Commonwealth University. Maize has been dated at the Stearns site in Maryland by Jefferson–Patterson Park and Museum archaeologists. Remains of maize from flotation samples appear at the White Oak Point site in Virginia (Waselkov 1982:312). Maize was also recovered in flotation samples at the Great Neck site (Turner 1992:107) in Virginia along with minor amounts of squash (*Cucurbita pepo*) and bottle gourd (*Lagenaria siceraria*). The Ritter site, on the Eastern Shore, is the sole site in that area that has yielded corn remains (Custer 1989:327).

Local prehistorians differ on their assessment of the impact of agriculture on the Coastal Plain of the Chesapeake region. Some feel that it was not a major component of the subsistence system until a demand was created by early European colonists (e.g., Custer 1989), while others feel that it may have represented around 50% to 75% of the subsistence base (e.g., Turner 1992:107). Along the Potomac River, Potter (1993:143) argues that plant husbandry based on tropical cultigens gradually diffused from the Piedmont to the Coastal Plain sometime circa AD 900, and that the activity was intensified after AD 1300.

Mortuary Practices

Regional mortuary programs across the Chesapeake region during the Late Woodland left a series of unique features—ossuaries—within the archaeological record. The often substantial ossuaries that appear across the Coastal Plain have been a focus of research for some time (e.g., Graham 1935; Mercer 1897; Reynolds 1883).

Human biological analyses of a number of these features have been undertaken by physical anthropologists, including T. Dale Stewart (1940a,b,c) and Douglas Ubelaker (1974) of the Smithsonian Institution and Joan Chase (1988, 1990) of American University.

As Turner (1992:117) points out, however, mortuary practices in the region are diverse and nonossuary interments did exist. Both extended and flexed burials are reported on a number of Chesapeake sites, often in conjunction with nearby ossuaries. A number of features containing minor amounts of human bone have also been reported, suggesting movement of remains after initial interment. Cremated remains are somewhat rare. Moving toward the truly bizarre end of the spectrum of mortuary practices, over 100 dog burials were excavated at the Hatch site in Virginia. Two such dog burials were recovered in association with human arms severed at the elbow. Grave goods, if present with Late Woodland interments, usually include utilitarian items and bone as well as shell beads. Large amounts of grave goods and more spectacular inclusions (e.g., see Figures 6.7 and 6.8) generally do not appear until the Contact era.

The most common Late Woodland mortuary practice on the Chesapeake nevertheless appears to be ossuary burial. Most remains in these ossuaries are secondary interments, and they must have been originally curated in some fashion before final placement in the ossuary. About 25 small ossuaries, most containing 10 to 20 individuals, have been recorded on Virginia sites along the James and York river drainages and on the Eastern Shore. A number of similar smaller ossuaries, although one might have contained up to 100 individuals, have also been excavated along the Nanticoke and Choptank Rivers on the Maryland portion of the Eastern Shore (see Ubelaker 1974). Many of these smaller ossuaries appear to be early, circa AD 1300. Ossuaries in the vicinity of the Potomac River on the Western Shore tend to be considerably larger, sometimes containing the remains of hundreds of individuals. Ubelaker's (1974) analysis of Ossuary II at the Juhle site off a tributary of the Potomac River is the most detailed for the region. Three ossuaries have been reported at this site (see Figure 6.9). The latest such feature was radiocarbon dated to 435 ± 155: AD 1515 (SI-4819) and is presumably associated with a nearby structure, itself possibly a mortuary house. A nearby village may also have been associated with these ossuaries.

Ossuary II contained the remains of 188 individuals. Following Ubelaker (1974:28–31), three of the individuals were interred completely articulated and appear to represent people who had died shortly before the ossuary was created. A few possible cremations are present. The majority of the remaining interments are represented by partially articulated bones, sometimes deposited in bundles. Indications are that complete skeletons often did not make it to the ossuary. Some bones may have been lost to scavengers or the elements during initial interment, or they were missed by those involved in the collection of remains. Certain bones may have served as proxies for the deceased.

Whatever the case, Ubelaker (1974:40) sees the ossuary as containing a relatively complete representation of the local population. Based on laboratory analysis, the

Table 6.11. Radiocarbon Assays on Tropical Cultigens[a]

Site and Date in RCYBP[b]	Cultigen
Coastal Plain	
Reynolds-Alvis, VA	Squash and beans
1030 ± 75: AD 920 (UGa-4684)	
Stearns, MD	Maize
491 ± 125: AD 1459 (UGa-5581)	
White Oak Point, VA	Maize
640 ± 50: AD 1310 (DIC-1764)	
490 ± 45: AD 1460 (DIC-1766)	
Great Neck, VA	Maize, squash, and bottle gourd
620 ± 80: AD 1330 (Beta-12117)	
435 ± 70: AD 1515 (UGa-3294)	
440 ± 50: AD 1510 (Beta-38915)	
Above Fall Line	
Winslow, MD[c]	
635 ± 80: AD 1315 (SI-37)	Maize
665 ± 100: AD 1285 (SI-47)	8-row flint
1125 ± 150: AD 825 (MI-189)	
Shephard, MD[d]	
320 ± 240: AD 1630 (SI-257)	Maize
890 ± 280: AD 1060 (SI-258)	
320 ± 280: AD 1630 (SI-259)	
750 ± 60: AD 1200 (SI-553)	
750 ± 50: AD 1200 (SI-554)	
Hughes, MD[e]	
660 ± 50: AD 1290 (Beta-41367)	Maize
580 ± 60: AD 1370 (Beta-49133)	
510 ± 50: AD 1440 (Beta-41368)	
420 ± 60: AD 1530 (Beta-49132)	
Moore Village, MD[f]	
200 ± 50: AD 1750 (Beta-6782)	Maize
530 ± 50: AD 1420 (Beta-6783)	
450 ± 50: AD 1500 (Beta-6784)	
550 ± 70: AD 1400 (DIC-2639)	
Rosenstock, MD[g]	
935 ± 60: AD 1015 (SI-4582)	Maize and beans
910 ± 90: AD 1040 (Beta-51754)	
860 ± 80: AD 1090 (Beta-51756)	
850 ± 120: AD 1100 (Beta-51755)	
740 ± 80: AD 1210 (Beta-55786)	
720 ± 70: AD 1230 (Beta 55048)	
700 ± 90: AD 1250 (Beta 55047)	
615 ± 60: AD 1335 (SI-4579)	
530 ± 60: AD 1420 (SI-4578)	
520 ± 80: AD 1430 (Beta-55044)	
500 ± 30: AD 1450 (SI-4581)	
475 ± 60: AD 1475 (SI-4580)	
380 ± 70: AD 1570 (Beta-55045)	

Table 6.11. (*Continued*)

Site and Date in RCYBP[b]	Cultigen
Cresaptown, MD	
1095 ± 60: AD 855 (SI-7026)	Maize and beans
Paw Paw, MD	
940 ± 65: AD 1010 (SI-6447)	Maize
Onion Field, VA	
440 ± 50: AD 1510 (Beta-56594)	Maize
	8-row flint
Point of Fork, VA	
920 ± 75: AD 1030 (UGa-3793)	Maize
Reedy Creek, VA	
800 ± 65: AD 1150 (UGa-1258)	Maize and beans

[a]Radiocarbon assays obtained from Boyce and Frye, 1986; Curry and Kavanagh, 1991; Dent and Jirikowic, 1990; Potter, 1993; Turner, 1992; Archives of the Maryland Historical Trust; Archives of the Virginia Department of Historic Resources; and Archives of the Virginia Commonwealth University Archaeological Research Center.
[b]RCYBP, radiocarbon years before present.
[c]Probable occupation circa AD 1285–1315.
[d]Probable occupation circa AD 1200.
[e]Probable occupation circa AD 1400.
[f]Probable occupation circa AD 1420.
[g]Maize is directly dated at AD 1090 and beans at AD 1210.

Figure 6.7.   Shell maskette with "weeping eye" design motif from burial on Potomac Neck along the Potomac River in Virginia. Dimensions: 12.7 × 14 cm. Smithsonian Institution.

Figure 6.8. Shell maskette with stylized human face from burial on Potomac Neck along the Potomac River in Virginia. Smithsonian Institution.

highest frequency of death occurred through the first five years of life. This was then followed by a dramatic decline in mortality through childhood into early adolescence. Maximum adult death frequency was between 30 and 35 years of age, followed by a steady decline after age 35. The oldest individual represented was between 65 and 69.9 years old. This ossuary appears to represent a three-year accumulation of the dead. In addition to the human interments, a concentration of large shell beads cut from *Busycon carcia* was found in the middle of the ossuary, and smaller beads, pottery sherds, and projectile points were scattered throughout the remaining fill. Most of the pottery was Potomac Creek ware, and the ossuary appears to date to just prior to contact.

A substantial number of other ossuaries have been excavated, although not carefully analyzed, at other sites along the Potomac River. The nearby Accokeek Creek site included numerous individual interments and three ossuaries within its stockade lines. An additional ossuary was located about 300 m southeast of the main

Figure 6.9. Ossuary excavated by Douglas Ubelaker at the Julile site along the Potomac River in Nanjemoy, Maryland. Courtesy of Douglas Ubelaker, Smithsonian Institution.

village. Interments in each ossuary varied from an estimated 618 individuals in the largest to 155 individuals in the smallest (Stephenson and Ferguson 1963:71–74). Two ossuaries were uncovered along the Anacostia River, a tributary of the Potomac, just outside of Washington, D.C., with between 63 and 70 individuals in each pit (Ubelaker 1974:14). Last, the Patawomeke site further south along the Potomac River yielded five ossuaries. The largest contained an estimated 287 individuals and the smallest 41 individuals (Ubelaker 1974:14). One of these ossuaries also contained artifacts of European manufacture and is thought to date to the early Contact period.

Epilogue: Prelude to the End

The nationality of the captain and crew of the first European ship to sail between the southern capes and enter the Chesapeake Bay is lost in history. The fact that these two capes at the mouth of the estuary are known by their Anglicized names, Cape Henry and Cape Charles, colors much of what we know about earliest Chesapeake history. England became the dominant colonial power in this region, and much of history is written in its favor. This short section describes the earliest phase of the

European conquest of the study area and it presents a brief sketch of the native world in the early seventeenth century.

European Arrival

Most historians suspect that the first European ship to enter the Chesapeake Bay carried either the Spanish or possibly the French flag. During the sixteenth century the Spanish were actively exploring North America from their colonies to the south, and the French had gained a foothold far to the north. From the perspective of the Chesapeake, French privateers, after preying on Spanish shipping in the Caribbean, often reprovisioned and traded with native populations further up the Atlantic coast before turning eastward to Europe (Jennings 1982:217). One or more of these French ships, or possibly a ship associated with other early French exploration parties, may have entered the Chesapeake.

The Chesapeake Bay was cartographically known near the end of the first quarter of the sixteenth century. It appears on official Spanish *Padron General* charts as the *Bahia de Santa Maria*. The Spanish explorer Pedro de Quexos, who sailed in 1521 and again in 1525, is probably the source of these cartographic details. Documents also indicate that the Spanish took a local native from the Chesapeake region captive on one of their reconnaissance voyages circa 1560 (Lewis and Loomie 1953:15). This native, baptized Don Luis and educated in Spain and Cuba, was later returned with a small group of Jesuits under the sponsorship of La Florida Governor Pedro Menendez de Aviles in 1570. They established a very short-lived mission somewhere on either the James or York River (see Lewis and Loomie 1953). Whatever the location, almost all the missionaries were shortly thereafter slain by the local native population, apparently in cooperation with the repatriated Don Luis. A supply ship could not find the mission in 1571, and a punitive raid was launched in 1572 to rescue the one surviving Spaniard, a young boy, and to revenge the loss through the killing of a number of the local population.

The next known period of active exploration was undertaken by the English in concert with the Roanoke voyages between 1584 and 1590. One of the two ships in the earliest 1584 reconnoitering expedition possibly entered the Chesapeake Bay (Hulton 1984:4). Certainly, during the larger 1585 expedition it appears that the Englishmen Thomas Hariot, John White, and others entered at least the mouth of the Chesapeake Bay searching for a secure harbor and knowledge of local inhabitants. The would-be colonists, however, had to return to England due to inadequate supplies. In 1587, another effort was made to establish a permanent English settlement in the New World with specific orders to settle within the Chesapeake Bay. That effort unfortunately once again made shore at Roanoke Island in present-day North Carolina. While its leaders returned to England to lobby for supply and support, those left behind entered history as the famous lost colony (Hulton 1984:12–16). This entire effort became an important lesson in mistakes, and it ultimately focused attention on the Chesapeake region as a more hospitable environment for the next attempt at establishing an English beachhead. In the meantime, it is almost certain that the English explored the Chesapeake Bay at least once again between 1603 and 1605 (Quinn 1977:438).

In December of 1606 three vessels sailed out of the Thames River bound for the Chesapeake Bay. By the spring of 1607 they entered the Chesapeake Bay and made land slightly west of Cape Henry. Shortly thereafter they sailed up the James River and selected a site some 80 km inland from the river's confluence with the Chesapeake Bay. While this site, eventually known as Jamestown, was a questionable choice for many reasons (see Earle 1979), it did become the permanent base of operations for English expansion into the region.

From this base Captain John Smith set out to explore the Chesapeake Bay in 1608, stopping first on the Eastern Shore and then crossing the estuary and sailing up the Potomac River. On a second exploration that year he sailed the length of the Chesapeake Bay and into its northern headwaters. Trade was initiated with various native groups, and a new era had begun. The written accounts of this period by Smith (Barbour 1986) and others record the ensuing intercourse between natives and Europeans. Smith's 1612 map of the region (see Figure 2.9) and his published descriptions of experiences with various groups represent the most important early documentary record of native life in the study area.

Less than three decades thereafter, in 1631, William Claiborne set up a trading settlement on Kent Island off the Eastern Shore in the more northern reaches of the Chesapeake Bay. Soon, a second formal colony, under charter to Lord Baltimore, was planted along the Potomac River. This Maryland colony, especially given the turn for the worse in Anglo–native interactions to the south in Virginia, opened a new chapter in relations. A settlement was established at St. Mary's City, and a string of Jesuit missions eventually stretched from southern Maryland up to near present-day Washington, D.C. (see Beitzell 1960). This sequence of events in Maryland, and the trading efforts operating in concert with it in the northern Chesapeake, left behind another group of documents that chronicle native life around the Chesapeake Bay.

Native Worlds at Contact

On his map of the Chesapeake Bay region, Captain John Smith recorded the locations of 166 different native settlements. Most of the residents of these villages and hamlets spoke dialects of the Algonquian language, and many of the individual settlements mapped by Smith were elements of larger social and political groupings. In fact, Smith employed a symbol on his map to differentiate locations with *Kings Howfes* ($n = 60$) versus *Ordinary Howfes* ($n = 106$). These groups, as identified through surviving early European textual accounts and some archaeological excavation, have been the subject of a number of recent books (e.g., Potter 1993; Rountree 1989, 1990, 1993) and articles (e.g., Feest 1978a,b; Hodges 1993; Turner and Opperman 1993). I want briefly to describe the native world that early European explorers and settlers encountered in their conquest of the region. Some of what was recorded, which I will turn to in the next section of this chapter, has a bearing on the earlier prehistory of the region.

At the time of contact, evidence indicates that the northern and western boundaries of the study area were ringed with non-Algonquian-speaking groups. These external groups, although often hostile, represented important trading partners to regional groups. The Iroquoian-speaking Susquehannocks were located along the lower Susquehanna River to the north of the Chesapeake Bay, but claimed territory on both sides of the northern estuary. The Monacan and Mannahoac were situated beyond the fall line on the Western Shore below the Potomac River. Both of these related groups were apparently Siouan speakers (Hantman 1990). The situation west of the fall line above the Potomac River is less clear. That area may not have been occupied by any single group (Dent and Jirikowic 1990). The Potomac River Valley appears to have been a major corridor in and out of the region, and there is evidence that various groups resided there at different times. It must also be noted that groups far removed from the study area were making forays into the region. Bernard Hoffman (1964) established that various Iroquoian groups from far to the northwest were regularly visiting the Chesapeake.

The Powhatan represents the major group within the study area (see Figure 6.10). Given the corpus of early texts that document Powhatan and English interaction, this group has been the focus of numerous studies. While there is some disagreement, the territory of what one writer labels Powhatania was nominally bounded by the Rappahannock River to the north, and it extended somewhat beyond the James River to the south. The heart of the group was located on the inner Coastal Plain, with the whole forming a crescent of sorts. The Chickahominy, apparently somewhat independent of the Powhatan, represented an island near the center of this area. At various times other groups, further north and south as well as on the lower Eastern Shore, were confederated with the Powhatan and formed what Rountree (1989:14) refers to as Powhatan's ethnic fringe.

The paramount chief of this group throughout a significant portion of the early Contact era was known to the English as Powhatan. He was succeeded, before his death in 1618, by one of his brothers, *Opechancanough*. At the time of contact the Powhatan territory was divided into numerous territorial units or districts led by local chiefs known as *werowances*. One of the more interesting and unique aspects of the Powhatan and of some other study area groups was the fact that they had effectively transformed themselves into what anthropologists would refer to as a chiefdom. The recognition of this transformation is one of the hallmarks of contemporary archaeological and ethnohistorical research in the study area. The Powhatan represent the most extensive and well-developed example of such a chiefdom in the study area. Binford (1964:101) was the first to recognize this fact, and since that time a number of others have advanced ideas to explain this phenomenon (e.g. Barker 1992; Feest 1978b; Haynes 1984; Potter 1993; Rountree 1989; Siebert 1975; Thurman 1985; Turner 1976). Numerous passages in early textual accounts support this interpretation.

Moving up the Western Shore, various groups on the Northern Neck between

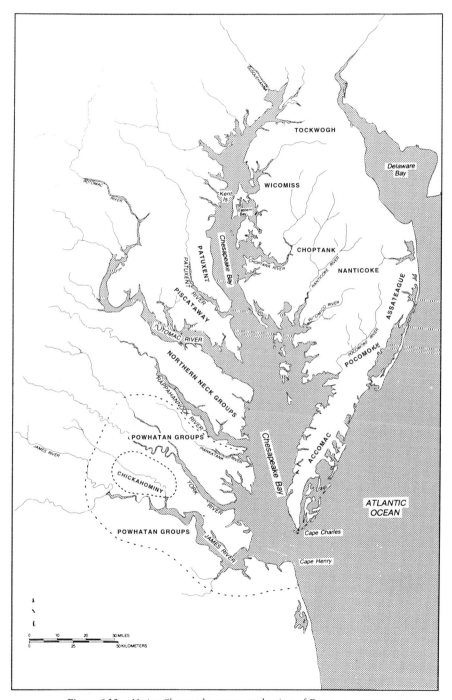

Figure 6.10. Native Chesapeake groups at the time of European contact.

the Rappahannock River and the south bank of the Potomac River were either a part of Powhatan's ethnic fringe or remained independent. In the latter case, Potter (1993:18–19) makes the case that the Patawomekes and the Tauxenents were probably not aligned with the Powhatan. Even if independent, however, it is safe to say that all these groups remained mindful of the activities of their powerful neighbors to the south. Recent population estimates for all Algonquian speakers on the Virginia Coastal Plain at contact are often around 15,000 persons (Turner 1992:114), but one set of estimates argues for up to 21,000 people (Feest 1978b: 256).

Above the Potomac River, the Piscataway (or Conoy) represents another well-documented chiefdom at the time of contact. Most of the textual accounts of this group are precipitates of the Maryland colony and its Jesuit missionaries that settled in the midst of this chiefdom in 1634. Both Paul Cissna (1986) and Potter (1993) have produced important recent analyses of the Piscataway. Dominion over this group was by the *tayac*, who served as paramount chief over six or seven smaller constituent groups, each again led by *werowances*, or subchiefs. Most population estimates range from 5000 to 7000 people, although Cissna (1986:53) favors a lower count of about 3600 people. Apparently groups on the nearby Patuxent River were largely autonomous of the Piscataway.

A substantial number of native groups on the Eastern Shore of the Chesapeake Bay have been documented to a certain degree during the period of initial contact. Less textual information, however, is generally available on these groups given the delay in European settlement of that area. Larger native political groupings apparently did not exist on the Eastern Shore. Nonetheless, a number of scholars (Davidson 1982; Feest 1978a; Weslager 1983) have recently reviewed available information. Following Feest (1978a:240), investigators typically identify at least seven significant groupings in the early seventeenth century. Most of the lower Eastern Shore was inhabited by the Accomacs, with the Pocomokes situated north of that group. The Accomacs, at least, were aligned with the Powhatan on the opposite shore. The Atlantic side of the peninsula was apparently controlled by the Assateagues. Nanticoke and Choptank groups occupied the drainage systems of the two rivers that still bear their names in the middle reaches of the Eastern Shore. The little-known Wicomiss and Tockwogh were situated, respectively, on the Chester and Sassafras rivers of the upper peninsula. In general, all these groups were small, with the Nanticoke representing the largest population concentration of around 665 people (Feest 1978a:242).

WOODLAND LIFEWAYS IN THE CHESAPEAKE: EXPANSION AND REDIRECTION

The approximately 3000 years of the Woodland period are fossilized within a rich and diverse regional archaeological record. From this record local prehistorians have managed to construct a substantial culture history of the period, document a significant redirection in lifeways near the end of prehistory, and produce some very interesting interpretations for various patterns isolated within the record. My goal in this last major section of the chapter is to review existing interpretations as well as to introduce some new ideas on various developments.

As in previous chapters, the section that follows will rest on the descriptions of the archaeological record of the Woodland period just presented. It also draws on arguments advanced about the intensification effort in the previous chapter. I contend that the redirection in regional lifeways begun during the Late Archaic continues, albeit with significant modification, throughout much of the Woodland period in the Chesapeake region. In addition, it is evident that one additional transformation of native lifeways did take place circa AD 1500. This redirection relates to the rise of chiefdoms in parts of the study area. In the paragraphs below I want to focus on producing a general description and interpretation of the expansion of the intensification process followed by a similar treatment of the subsequent rise of chiefdoms. Adena related material within the region will be examined as a short-lived phenomenon of the former pattern. In all cases, my goal is to begin to sort out the meaning behind these two dominant ways of life during the Woodland period. Before beginning this I will offer a brief statement on the regional ecology.

Ecological Context

At the beginning of the Woodland period the temperate biome that continues to exist today was well established in the Chesapeake region. In its pristine state this was an ecosystem of incredible richness. While on several occasions the first Europeans colonists did almost succeed in starving themselves in the midst of these natural riches, they more often than not were impressed enough to leave accounts that touch on the abundance of the land. For example, pen was put to paper when 148 "fowles" (probably geese or duck given the season) were dispatched with three "shots" on one of Captain John Smith's exploratory and diplomatic forays in 1608 (Barbour 1986:245). This was a natural environment plentiful on a scale that no European visitor had ever experienced. I want to briefly outline the nature of this ecosystem during the Woodland period. It is my contention, however, that while this was and continues to be a dynamic ecosystem, perturbations during this period had little real or lasting effect on native lifeways.

Any number of researchers (Brush 1986; Kraft and Brush 1981; Stenger 1982) remark that they see little in available pollen profiles to indicate any significant regional vegetational change over the past 5000 years. They do add (e.g., Brush 1986:150) that relative abundances of various species fluctuated somewhat in response to minor climatic variation, most notably a sporadic series of wet and dry cycles. Based on pollen data and historical plant collections, well-defined oak–hickory, oak–gum, and oak–pine associations were present throughout the study area. On higher, well-drained areas of the outer and inner Coastal Plain an oak–hickory association is noted. Chestnut may have been a major addition to this association in the northern reaches of the region. In lower, less well drained areas on both the Eastern and Western shores an oak–gum association prevailed. The oak–

pine association was restricted to certain locations on the Eastern Shore and on the Western Shore below the James River. Again, even with both wet and dry cycles on occasion altering local flora, I see little evidence to suggest significant ecological impact on Woodland groups within the Chesapeake region.

Much the same can be said in regards to the prevailing temperate terrestrial fauna of the study area. By the Woodland period the typical animal species of the temperate biome were well established and prolific. Faunal assemblages recovered to date on regional archaeological sites indicate exploitation of temperate species such as deer, wapiti, wild turkey, and bear as well as other available small mammals, reptiles, and amphibians. Aboriginal clearing of land, through intentionally set forest fires to lower primary biomass and eventually for the propagation of certain plant species, served to further enhance habitat for certain species.

The estuary, itself, did continue to expand during the Woodland period. Over that 3000-year span of time, local sea level rose significantly. This effectively completed the transformation of a more restricted river estuary into the large coastal estuary of today. Sea level continues to rise, averaging at the present about 1.5 to 3 mm per year (Colman et al. 1991:20). Aqueous loading and isostatic adjustment are likewise still affecting the configuration of the estuary along with both shoreline erosion and internal sedimentation. It is reasonable to suggest that collateral impacts via this marine transgression on interior wetland areas continued to take place during the Woodland period.

Within the estuary and flanking subestuaries along the lower reaches of its tributaries, it appears that numbers of associated aquatic species could have increased during the last 3000 years of prehistory. Nonswimming bottom dwellers, such as oyster, no doubt expanded into easily exploitable, newly created shallow-water locations. As estuarine wetlands continued to expand and subsurface vegetation stabilized, habitat for various other swimming aquatic species increased. These wetlands also increased winter habitat for migratory waterfowl. In all, throughout the Woodland period, a very stable and prolific ecosystem became even richer in terms of the opportunities for human exploitation.

Given the statements offered above, I do not consider the environment to have played a significant role in prehistoric sociocultural change during the Woodland period. The major changes in the archaeological record outlined below are considered the result of prehistoric peoples in the local area reacting to socially induced circumstances rather than to a changing regional ecology. This does not preclude shifts in settlement or subsistence systems in reaction to the changing resource distributions or the availability of certain resources brought on by cycles of wetter or dryer conditions across the region.

Woodland Lifeways

Much of the Woodland period continues the trends initiated during the intensification era of the Late Archaic subperiod. In the section that follows I want to focus on these subsequent adjustments to the intensification process after 3000 years ago. I will not repeat the more detailed discussion of this phenomenon outlined in the previous chapter. Attention instead will only be given to new developments attributable to the last period of regional prehistory.

After circa AD 1500, near the end of the Late Woodland subperiod, another major transformation of lifeways occurred across much of the study area. This era was characterized by the appearance in some parts of the Chesapeake region of politically centralized and socially ranked societies, anthropologically known as chiefdoms. The appearance of these chiefdoms was a unique phenomenon in its own right and certainly had impacts on the smaller and more independent nonchiefly regional groups. In addition, much of the interplay with native groups external to this region and eventually with Europeans arriving to colonize the study area was in the context of these chiefdoms. Special attention will be given to the development of chiefdoms in the Chesapeake region in the last major section of this chapter.

Expansion of the Intensification Process

The intensification era, as I have defined it, started during the Late Archaic circa 4200 years ago and continued, with some significant modification, throughout much of the Woodland period. The resulting lifeway originally represented a new and unprecedented social construction within local prehistory. The very essence of this lifeway was a different set of internal social mechanisms that effectively served to increase productive activities, but did so at the expense of more traditional individual and familial autonomy. In the name of larger goals, the natural environment was increasingly being socially appropriated.

Technological Development during the Woodland Period. The expansion of the container revolution through the manufacture of ceramics, initially the so-called early experimental wares dating to circa 3000 years ago, is a prime example of local technological development during the Early Woodland. Many of the early ceramic wares appear to have been developed in the Piedmont zone. Ceramic technology then spread rather rapidly throughout the study area. Soon thereafter, second-generation pottery types appeared across the region. These later coil-constructed ceramics, with their bag- or globular-shaped vessel forms, rounded or conoidal bases, and increased volumes, seem to represent the adoption of new cooking techniques. Direct heating of contents became more common possibly in response to the need to process food more efficiently, to feed larger populations, or for the processing of different or new resources. Limited storage of food supplies in these larger vessels may also have been more practical than in the early shallow steatite or ceramic bowls.

Subterranean storage cists begin to appear in the region, first on early ceramic-yielding sites. In general, most archaeologists interpret these features as a definite indication of the full adoption of delayed-return subsistence strategies. Resources could be harvested in quantities when available and then stored to increase their usability beyond the shorter season of availability. Recently, DeBoer (1988) has also argued that these constructions were instead more regularly used for the caching of site furniture during periods of site abandonment or for concealment of personal supplies in defiance of group demands on individual production activities. There is no reason why the storage cists could not have been used for all these purposes.

Another interesting item of technological development was the local adoption of the bow and arrow weapons system after circa AD 900. This adoption may have dramatically improved hunting success, increasing effective range and accuracy as well as perhaps making better hunters of more of the population. The bow and arrow almost certainly allowed a wider range of hunting, strategies, and it is important to note that bow and arrow hunting could have further individualized the hunting process. There has been a good deal of recent discussion of what is known as garden hunting, where people tending field crops exploit animals drawn to those locations. The bow and arrow may have made hunting a less gender-specific activity, thereby increasing hunting returns to the group as a whole. The bow and arrow no doubt also played a large role in personal and group defense, as intergroup warfare appears to have been endemic well before European contact.

Changing Subsistence Economy. It appears evident that beginning in the Early Woodland subsistence practices were shifting toward the fuller exploitation of the resources of the still-expanding estuary. By the Middle Woodland this process was mostly complete. Shellfish gathering, especially of oyster, was a major focus of local subsistence systems, which also included the exploitation of many other available faunal and floral resources. The question of when and how intensively local plant species were cultivated cannot be answered for the study area at this time. Certainly chenopod and other prolific plant species appear to have been encouraged in the Chesapeake area and were at times intensively harvested, but actual evidence of early garden horticulture with derivative domesticated species is not available. Perhaps the general ecological richness of the Chesapeake region made this practice unnecessary.

The first definite evidence of the arrival in the region of tropical cultigens—the typical maize, beans, and squash triad—appears in the Piedmont circa AD 900. The practice then spreads down onto the Coastal Plain. Production of these domesticates in both zones seems to have been intensified after circa AD 1300. Even with the adoption of these domesticates, however, subsistence practices seem to have still included the exploitation of many wild floral and faunal resources. There is, in addition, evidence of active efforts to increase certain harvests, for example, fostering browse for deer and maybe some other faunal species. Such efforts would encourage the proliferation of certain faunal species and thereby facilitate larger-scale group hunting tactics, thus increasing meat yields.

Social Experimentation. In my discussion of the beginning of the intensification era during the Late Archaic, I made an argument for the appearance of an embryonic segmentary, tribal organization in the Chesapeake region. It seemed evident that populations of this era had moved away from traditional band-level social organization. My principal reason for suggesting an organization approaching the segmentary, tribal level has to do with the evident need for integrative units above the individual and familial levels. In that section I outlined the archaeological evidence for technological, settlement, and subsistence activities suggesting such larger corporate groups in the Late Archaic. I suspect that this type of social organization continued to exist for most of the Woodland period, until circa AD 1500. After this initial breech of the more domestic mode of production characteristic of earlier band-level society, circumstances existed where individuals could manipulate group activities. Ethnographically known Big Man societies are examples of such manipulation whereby primitive headmen begin to stimulate production beyond the usual aim of domestic livelihood. Since headmanship is achieved rather than ascribed, competition can develop between existing leaders and other would-be leaders. Increased technological development, surplus production, the creation and control of symbolic commodities, and the like soon begin to appear. Competition naturally leads to expansion in the search for new resources, new partners, and new advantages.

I suggest that episodes of this occurrence—that is prehistoric equivalents of so-called Big Men—are evident during the late Early Woodland and Middle Woodland subperiods in the Chesapeake region. The Adena material as well as some of the other more spectacular mortuary sites that appear in or near the study area may be the result of this phenomenon. Custer (1989:295) has done a good job of making this argument for late prehistoric groups in Delaware and across the Eastern Shore of the region. Given that headman positions are achieved and not ascribed, evidence of these groups may appear to wax and wane, as is the case in the Chesapeake archaeological record. Sites with evidence for this phenomenon would also be expected to appear at locations that would facilitate trade and contact with other groups. This is often precisely the case with the materials mentioned above within the Chesapeake region.

Interpretation.   This new way of life, in both the Late Archaic subperiod and through much of the Woodland period, was generated by a set of social mechanisms that served to expand group production activities and increase efficiency. This, at least, is how the results of this phenomenon appear to us today within an archaeological context. Many of the innovations of the Woodland period, in particular the initial development of a local ceramic tradition and the later agriculturally based subsistence practices, emanate from a Piedmont hearth just beyond the fall lines of the Chesapeake Bay's major tributaries. The ultimate source of both innovations probably lay in the Southeast and/or the Midland areas of eastern North America. Once these innovations appeared in the Piedmont, they apparently spread rapidly across the study area. I want to examine the expansion of the intensification process during the Woodland period through the elements of analysis employed in the previous chapter.

Any number of archaeologists have noted that increased social demands on group labor play a vital role in stimulating technological development and change. Such technological development, in fact, appears to be a hallmark of the expansion of a new lifeway in the Chesapeake during the Woodland period. The initial development and spread of a regional ceramic tradition can be seen in this light. This is especially true in terms of the development of the second-generation pottery wares along with the adoption of what seem to be new cooking techniques in higher-volume containers. The adoption of agriculture and the associated construction of subterranean storage cists, which facilitated intensified harvesting and storage of foodstuffs, is another example. Much the same can be said for the adoption of the bow and arrow later in the Woodland period. All these events were technological innovations leading to the possibility of intensified subsistence activities.

In my interpretation of the intensification era at the end of the last chapter, I pointed out a number of instances where archaeological evidence could be cited to indicate increased interdependence between people accompanied by corresponding constraints on individual and familial autonomy. These instances followed ideas advanced by Filios (1990) on how such constraints on autonomy, brought about by new social imperatives, can lead to intensification and increased complexity. Filios's ideas focus on how spatial and temporal variations in resource procurement, costs of moving goods to consumers, the subdivision of the labor process and scale of labor scheduling, delayed-return subsistence systems, and the need for larger labor pools erode personal and familial autonomy. Each of these elements again appears particularly relevant in the interpretation of the local archaeological record for much of the Woodland period. During this time, people appear to have increasingly sacrificed personal and household autonomy in the name of larger group goals. Patterns in the Woodland period apparently follow earlier precedents.

In my opinion, the appearance of the prehistoric equivalent of Big Man types of social organizations in the study area during the Woodland period is further evidence of some sort of an established earlier region-wide tribal, segmentary lineage system. An achieved status such as headmanship is generally not known to arise from band-level society. As any number of anthropologists have stated, the various individual elements of band-level society are systematically interrelated and effectively serve to keep one another in check so that significant development or expansion of any one element is met by resistance from other elements. Band-level society is built around the principle of finite goals. The classic ethnographic example of this phenomenon is the well-known case where the introduction of more efficient steel axes led one group to longer daily naps rather than to increased productivity.

Archaeological evidence of occasional social organizations at least similar to ethnographically known Big Man systems appears in the Chesapeake region sporadically throughout the Woodland period. Procurement of exotic items is one hallmark of the entrepreneurial activities of such actual or would-be primitive leaders. The direct procurement of rhyolite from outside the region and its distribution throughout the study area during the late Middle Woodland may be an example of this process. The Adena artifacts that appear in the Chesapeake region near the end of the

Early Woodland and the beginning of the Middle Woodland subperiod appear to be even more graphic evidence of the phenomenon. I have also always been impressed by the degree to which many Adena mortuary sites seem to have been isolated from the habitation sites of the groups that must have produced them. At the same time, mortuary treatment at these sites indicates that the interred individuals had achieved some greater status in life respective to other members of society. I would argue that the burials at these sites represent achieved rather than ascribed status. If ascribed status, legitimized through links to certain ancestral lines, had emerged, one would expect that the cemeteries would have been placed directly within habitation areas to display and reinforce these associations (Hodder 1982:196). This certainly becomes the case when ascribed ranking does appear with chiefdoms late in the Woodland period.

In any case, it does seem that an environment existed throughout much of the Woodland period in which some social experimentation was possible. Such was not the case before the beginning of the intensification era in the Chesapeake region. As stated before, control over the domestic economy was now beginning to pass from all of the group to some of the group, and in the process traditional kin ties were being challenged by new political ties. The Big Man type of social organization is an early example of that event. This phenomenon would soon reach its ultimate expression in the Chesapeake region with the appearance of chiefdoms.

The Rise of Chiefdoms and the End of Prehistory

Sometime after circa AD 1500, evidence suggests a final transformation of regional lifeways. As mentioned earlier, the first Europeans to arrive in the Chesapeake region described many native peoples living within societies that match what anthropologists refer to as chiefdoms. Such chiefdoms are typically politically centralized and internally ranked. These are also what might be termed redistributive societies with those in power collecting as tribute part of their subjects' production. The most important position was that of paramount chief, but nominal leaders also included various subchiefs, the religious leadership, and minor councilors as well as other people in various positions of authority. The major chiefdoms of the Western Shore at the time of contact included the Powhatan and Piscataway. Eastern Shore chiefdoms, although not as complex or extensive and certainly less well documented, are thought to have existed at certain points in time. No doubt other nonchiefly groups also existed in the local area and often entered into alliances with the more dominant groups in their respective areas.

The first Europeans to settle on the shores of the Chesapeake Bay necessarily interacted with these chiefdoms. Virginia colonists could not ignore, and were at times dependent on, the Powhatan. After a long period of sometime mutual alliance and occasional hostility, the Powhatan felt threatened enough in AD 1622 to strike a coordinated blow at English settlements and they succeeded in killing about one-quarter of the colony's population. After that time, the Virginia colony constantly raided Powhatan villages, undercut chiefly authority (see Potter 1993:220), and opened up alliances with other non-Powhatan groups. The Maryland colony, which landed in AD 1634, subsequently made efforts to maintain better relations with the more northern Piscataway. Ultimately, however, trade and the chronic need for land for tobacco production had much the same effect (see Cissna 1986). Much the same can be said for the Eastern Shore groups. By AD 1646, the Powhatan had reached a state of near collapse, and the Piscataway met a similar fate soon thereafter (see Feest 1978a,b).

In the paragraphs below I focus on the various explanations for the rise of these chiefdoms, especially the Powhatan and the Piscataway, within the Chesapeake region. This section of the chapter is exclusively interpretive, as it would be redundant in this case to repeat the previous discussion of various elements of the archaeological record. These chiefdoms arose out of the same technological, settlement, subsistence, and social base that has just been presented for the rest of the Woodland period. I do, however, want to discuss various elements of this new lifeway that point to the presence of chiefdoms and review existing interpretations of the origins of this final transformation. Last, I add some additional thoughts of my own on this final transformation.

Chiefly Lifeways. For illustrative purposes, I will focus on elements of Powhatan lifeways that led modern scholars to conclude that these people effectively constituted a chiefdom at the time of contact. By definition, anthropologists expect to see evidence of certain features or types of behavior in chiefdoms. The descriptions of these elements in Chesapeake society that I review below were left to us by early European explorers and settlers.

Chiefdoms coordinate activities across large areas and are most often led by paramount chiefs. The paramount chief of the Powhatan was known to the English as Powhatan. His Algonquian birth name was *Wahunsenacawh*. Powhatan political organization and its matrilineal pattern of inheritance is well documented. Captain John Smith wrote:

> The forme of their Common wealth is a monarchicall government, one as Emperour ruleth over many kings or governours. Their chief ruler is called Powhatan. . . . Some countries he hath which had been his ancestors, and came unto him by inheritance. . . . His kindome des-cendeth not to sonnes nor children, but first to his brethen, wherof he hath 3. Opitchapan, Opechancanough, and Catataugh, and after their decease to his sisters. First to the eldest sister then to the rest and after them to the heires male and female of the eldest sister, but never to the heires of the males. (Barbour 1986:173–174)

Powhatan's providence apparently originated with six to nine districts along the James and York rivers, and the remainder (up to 31 districts) were subsequently acquired through force or coercion. Each district was governed by a local chief or *werowance*.

A number of early writers commented on the importance of kin ties within the

Powhatan chiefdom. At least six, and probably more, of the lesser local chiefs were directly related to Powhatan himself. It is evident that the extension of kin ties was viewed as an important mechanism for establishing or strengthening the chiefdom's alliances. The AD 1614 marriage of Pocahontas, a daughter of Powhatan, to Johne Rolfe, an Englishman, is a well-known effort to cement alliances through kinship. No doubt more than a little confounded by English actions, Powhatan tried to offer them a place in the chiefdom. Rolfe, at least in Powhatan's eyes, was now more or less a *werowance*, and Jamestown was to be yet another district in the larger native empire. In another passage (Barbour 1986:217), Powhatan also referred to Captain Newport of the Jamestown colony as a *werowance*. The English, however, failed to appreciate the significance of this fact or chose to ignore it.

Chiefdoms actively define status through actions and material culture. The reproduction of such status can be appreciated in the following description of an audience between Captain John Smith and the paramount chief, Powhatan. Smith wrote:

> Arriving at Werawocomoco, their Emperour proudly lying upon a Bedstead a foote high upon tenne or twelve Mattes, richly hung with manie Chaynes of great Pearles about his necke, and covered with a great Covering of Rahaughcums: At his heade sat a women, at his feete another, on each side sitting upon a Matte upon the ground were raunged his chief men on each side the fire, tenne in ranke, and behinde them as many yong women, each a great Chaine of white Beades over their shoulders, their heades painted in redde, and [he] with such a grave and Majesticall countenance, as drave me into admiration to see such a state in a naked Salvage, hee kindly welcomed me with good wordes, and great Platters of sundrie Victuals, assuring me his friendship. (Barbour 1986:53)

Captain John Smith was obviously taken by Powhatan's presence as well as power, and it must be remembered that Smith was probably not easily impressed given his previous travels and encounters with a host of foreign peoples through many parts of the known world.

In deference to his high status, special treatment was afforded a paramount chief. Captain John Smith described the cleansing ritual:

> When he dineth or suppeth, one of his women before and after meat, bringeth him water in a wooden platter to wash his hands. Another waiteth with a bunch of feathers to wipe them instead of a Towell, and the feathers which he hath wiped are dryed againe. (Barbour 1986:174)

Such ritual cleansing behavior is typical of high rank within chiefdoms in many parts of the world.

Ethnographic documents clearly point to the presence of specific centers within Powhatan society to coordinate economic, sociopolitical, and religious activity. These centers were maintained at specific locations by the paramount chief and at various district capitals of the subchiefs. The major such center of the chiefdom appears to have been located near the confluence of the Pumunkey and Mattaponi rivers as they meet to form the York River on the inner Coastal Plain. While the sociopolitical significance of these villages is obvious, it is appropriate to further examine economic and religious function.

It is apparent that particular villages within the Powhatan domain served as centers for economic redistribution. Turner (1985:201–203) notes a tribute on all goods produced along with active efforts to control the flow of trade items into the area. Labor may also have been subject to tribute. William Strachey, writing in the early seventeenth century, described the nature of the tribute system:

> Every Weroance knowes his owne Meeres and lymitts to fish fowle or hunt in (as before said) but they hold all of their great Weroance Powhatan, vnto whome they paie 8. parts of 10. tribute of all the Commodities which their Country yeildeth, as of wheat, pease, beanes, 8. measures of 10.(and these measured out in little Cades or Basketts which the great king appoints) of the dying roots 8. of tenne; of all sorts of skyns and furrs 8. of tenne, and so he robbes the poore in effect of all they haue even to the deares Skyn wherewith they cover them from Could, in so much as they dare not dress yt and put yt on vntill he haue seene yt and refused yt; for what he Comaundeth they dare not disobey in the least thing. (1953:87)

Note should be made of the standardized containers mentioned by Strachey for the collection of tribute. Standardization of measure for accounting and distribution purposes is typical of tribute or tax collecting societies like chiefdoms.

Items or commodities collected through tribute were stored in special houses, often at isolated locations. Captain John Smith described Powhatan's treasury:

> A mile from Orapekes in a thicket of wood he hath a house in which he keepeth his kind of Treasure, as skinnes, copper, pearle, and beades, which he storeth up against the time of his death and buriall. Here also is his store of red paint for ointment, and bowes and arrowes. This house is 50 or 60 yards in length, frequented only by Priests. At the 4 corners of this house stand 4 Images as Sentinels, one of a dragon, another a Beare, the 3 like a Leopard and the fourth like a giantlike man, all made evillfavordly, according to their best workmanship. (Barbour 1986:173–174)

Other tributary commodities, principally maize, are noted as having been stored in special granaries (Spelman 1910:cxii). While some of these goods and items were undoubtedly reserved as grave furniture, other items were redistributed downward to promote and reward service as well as used to forge alliances, support ritual, for feasting, and so on.

It is evident that religious precincts were associated with major villages, although these were apparently removed from habitation areas. Captain John Smith wrote:

> In every Territory of a werowance is a Temple and a Priest 2 or 3 or more. Their principall Temple or place of superstition is at Uttamussack at Pamaunke, neare unto which is a house or Temple or place of Powhatans. Upon the top of certaine redde sandy hils in the woods, there are 3 great houses filled with images of their

kings and Divels and Tombes of the Predecessors. These houses are neare 60 foote in length built arbor wise after their building. This place they count so holy as that but the Priestes and kings dare come into them; not the Savages dare go up the river in boats to it, but that they solemnly cast some peece of copper, white beads or Pocones into the river, for fear their Oke should be offended and revenged of them. (Barbour 1986:169–170)

These centers were maintained by a full-time religious elite, known as *quiocosoughs*, who were segregated from much of society. From documentary sources it is evident that this priesthood played a significant role in maintaining social order within Powhatan society.

Last, I want to say something about differential mortuary treatment for the Powhatan elite. Captain John Smith described the burial of their "kings" in the following manner:

Their bodies are firsy bowelled, then dryed upon hurdles till they bee verie dry, and so about the most of their jointes and necke they hang bracelets or chaines of copper, pearle, and such like, as they use to weare, their inwards they stuffe with copper beads and covered with a skin, hatchets and such trash. Then lappe them very carefully in white skins and so rowle them in matts for their winding sheets. And in the Tombe which is an arch made of mats, they lay them orderly. What remaineth of this kinde of wealth their kings have, they set at their feet in baskets. These temples and their bodies are kept by their Priests. (Barbour 1986:169)

It appears obvious that the careful maintenance of the prepared corpses in these mortuary houses served to remind people of the roots of the established social order.

Based on these data, and other documentary information too numerous to cite, it is clear that Powhatan society represented a chiefdom of significant proportions. Chiefdoms, by definition, have various features that set them apart from other levels of social organization. Documentary evidence for ranking within Powhatan society, from a paramount chief and subchiefs to a priesthood, is substantial. Ethnohistorical data mention specific ways in which the statuses of such leaders were defined and actively displayed in both life and death. Other passages could be cited to document polygyny by high-ranking members of society, the beginning of craft specialization, and other characteristics often linked to chiefdoms. Finally, various redistributive mechanisms within Powhatan society, including tribute and the flow of goods between the general population, subchiefs at various smaller centers, and the paramount chief, appear substantial. All of these characteristics are evidence of the appearance of a new way of life in the study area near the end of prehistory.

If time and space allowed, this same basic set of conditions could be documented for the Piscataway chiefdom above the Potomac River on the Western Shore of the Chesapeake region. Although supporting data are not as numerous, some Eastern Shore groups, for example the Nanticoke, while not as extensive or well known were undoubtedly very similar. The appearance of these chiefdoms, a somewhat radical alteration of lifeways circa AD 1500, was not without cause. It is now important to review existing ideas on this transformation of local native society and to suggest new directions in the interpretation of these lifeways.

Interpretations.   The origins of chiefdoms in the Chesapeake region have represented a special challenge to prehistorians. Suggestions as to the initial temporal boundary for this redirection vary. Often the date cited varies depending on prime cause. Investigators that argue European contact was at least one major factor in the transformation tend to project a date sometime after AD 1500 (Barker 1992; Feest 1978b; Rountree 1989). Other scholars favoring ecological determinates, internal developments, external pressures, and the like are liable to project an even earlier date, circa AD 1300 to 1400, for the transition (Binford 1964; Turner 1976). One Piscataway informant, a brother of the *tayac* or chief, recalled that by AD 1636 some 13 generations of *tayacs* had ruled (see Cissna 1986). By projection, some suggest that the Piscataway chiefdom had by that date spanned at least 100 years. If accurate, this would put the beginnings of the Piscataway chiefdom just after AD 1500.

Existing explanations for this transformation of lifeways focus on factors both indigenous and external to the study area. I want to mention just a few of the existing ideas regarding the origin of this phenomenon. Binford (1964), after first identifying the Powhatan as a chiefdom, noted the presence of major Powhatan villages within the inner Coastal Plain. He argued that people in that zone had an effective monopoly over critical resources, especially anadromous fish harvests, that they were able to manipulate to their own political advantage. Slightly over a decade later, Turner (1976) revitalized interest in the factors responsible for the origins of chiefdoms through his suggestion that population growth, accompanied by increasing population pressure on key horticulturally productive soils, in time resulted in the development of new means of sociocultural integration. The culmination of this trajectory was the Powhatan chiefdom. Both of these interpretations look at ecological factors as prime movers in the transformation.

Very recently Barker (1992) has argued that Powhatan political development is a direct result of sudden depopulation following direct European contact in the Chesapeake region. As a consequence of this interaction there were not enough producers to supply the elite of the political and social hierarchy. This led to political centralization and subsequent expansion. Such external forces, principally European disruptions, likewise figure heavily in Rountree's (1989) and Feest's (1978b) ideas on the evolution of chiefly authority in the Chesapeake.

More recently, Potter (1993:166–168) has presented a model for the rise of complex societies in the study area that builds on some existing ideas and adds a few new elements to the debate. Circumstances here focus on increased contact between different and sometimes potentially hostile native groups, access to critical resources, and control of trade. As Potter (1993:168) remarks, the complex interplay of all those factors gave a selective advantage to groups with more centralized forms of political organization, ultimately giving rise to chiefdoms on the inner Coastal Plain of the Potomac, York, and James rivers.

Finally, I want to make special mention of ideas advanced by John Haynes (1984,

1990) on the transition to chiefdoms. Haynes adds a new dimension to the problem by not focusing exclusively on external stimuli as the only forces behind this redirection. In his perspective, adaptations to resource stress and the like need not necessarily precipitate increased social hierarchy. He therefore turns to internal, structural explanations for the shift to chiefdoms. According to Haynes (1984:176–202) this initially involved the appearance of conical clans that were then expanded through more extensive ramified descent systems. Chieftainship was then both appropriated and legitimized by the directness of descent from a largely mythical yet powerful founding ancestor. In this perspective the local chiefdoms were created or constructed by certain individuals for specific political purposes. It appears to me that a consideration of such a structural transformation must figure into any adequate understanding the Chesapeake chiefdoms.

Another Perspective. It is now important to turn to what I refer to as a unified interpretation of this final redirection of Chesapeake prehistory. Some explanation of the modifier "unified" is necessary. The existing universe of discourse on the appearance of chiefdoms, reviewed above, has been successful in identifying the various elements that no doubt played a large role in the origins of such groups. Binford's (1964) early research was pathfinding in its identification of these groups as chiefdoms, and Turner (1976) deserves a great deal of credit for his revitalization of interest in this subject. Subsequent research has pushed our knowledge of local chiefdoms further yet. The task at hand therefore need not become an exercise in searching for new ideas to explain the development of chiefdoms. Instead it is more a matter of synthesizing existing ideas into an interpretational package that combines various elements, emphasizing some and perhaps putting less emphasis on others. This is my goal in this section.

In this light, the transformation to chiefdoms at the end of prehistory was clearly foreshadowed by previous developments during the intensification era, especially after circa AD 900. Potter (1993:164), for example, is absolutely correct when he argues that a basic lifeway shared by most of the southern Algonquian societies of the Chesapeake Bay and Carolina Sound areas had solidified by the sixteenth century. All of the subsequent study area chiefdoms, as he insists, were an elaboration of a long-standing way of life. And at the same time, seeds of change were present in that existing way of life. The extant segmentary, tribal lineages offered the possibility of manipulation of the social order. Earlier efforts in that direction can be seen in the occasional emergence of the prehistoric equivalent of Big Men throughout portions of the Early and Middle Woodland subperiods.

With that said, what I want to do below is focus on the external *and* internal forces that precipitated the formation of the Chesapeake chiefdoms after circa AD 1500. While all of these forces are based on various existing ideas, perhaps my specific emphasis on both realms pushes our knowledge of this process forward a bit. I will concentrate on external circumstances first and then turn to the important internal developments leading to the appearance of regional chiefdoms.

A common pattern to the two major chiefdoms in the region was the location of their centers or major villages on the inner Coastal Plain. Binford (1964) was the first to explore the significance of this pattern. With the completion of the estuary this area arguably became the richest ecological zone within the study area. It offered the widest variety of seasonally available resources, some in incredible numbers (see Binford 1964; Turner 1976). The structure of this resource base, especially the availability of large numbers of anadromous fish in the early spring when other resources were in short supply, appears to have been a stimulus in the development of chiefdoms. Control of such resources may have offered some economic advantage over other groups in less naturally endowed zones. Scheduling of resource exploitation likewise may have favored the development of a more managed or directed economy. Finally, groups at this central location, between the Piedmont to the west and the outer Coastal Plain eastward, were in a position to control trade arteries in and out of the broader study area. In short, location appears to have been a factor in the late prehistoric transformation under examination.

Another possible stimulus to the development of chiefdoms appears to have been migrations of new groups onto the Coastal Plain of the Chesapeake Bay region. Custer (1989:308), while acknowledging the difficulty of recognizing migrations in the archaeological record, has suggested plausible evidence of northern groups moving into the study area after circa AD 500 and again at circa AD 900 to 1100. The evidence for this movement is the sudden appearance on the northern Eastern Shore of Hell Island and Minguannan ceramic wares respectively. These wares appear to have originated north of the region. Some want to link the spread of the Algonquian language from its proposed Great Lakes homeland via contiguous northern areas and then down into the Chesapeake through one of more of these possible migrations. In this context I only wish to demonstrate that there is some evidence of new peoples moving into the study area just before and during the Late Woodland subperiod.

Anthropologists have long suspected that the arrival of new peoples with different ways of life can be a powerful stimulus to change. Headmen and chiefs are notorious collaborators with outside groups (Wolf 1982:96). These new groups allow the adventurous the opportunity to escape the confines of their own social systems through unbridled interaction and trade. William Divale (1984:22) argues that shifts to matrilineal descent systems may ultimately be stimulated by imbalances created between newly arrived and in situ populations. Such descent systems were certainly in place during and after the transformation under examination. This migration of new groups into the study area was probably another factor in the development of local chiefdoms.

In this regard, I want to discuss another possible migration of people either into or within, depending on perspective, the study area. Quite a while ago Karl Schmitt suggested that groups in the Potomac Piedmont moved eastward onto the inner Coastal Plain of the study area sometime late in prehistory. These Piedmont groups are most frequently identified as what is archaeologically known as the Montgomery Complex. Many argue that this group of immigrants in their new home became the makers of Potomac Creek ceramics, eventually forming the nucleus for the Piscataway chiefdom (Clark 1980; MacCord 1984; Potter 1993). In regard to this matter, there is little doubt that some sort of migration did occur, and that makers of Potomac Creek ceramics did create the Piscataway chiefdom. While acknowledging that migrations are difficult to demonstrate archaeologically, I still want to hold the door open for consideration of an alternate route for this proposed migration. I refer to the possibility of an Eastern Shore homeland for the makers of Potomac Creek, the direct ancestors of the Piscataway chiefdom (follows Cissna 1986).

Most of the supposed linkage between the Piedmont and the later Coastal Plain sites is based on an admittedly obvious similarity between the two ceramic traditions. Nevertheless, there are ceramic wares on the Eastern Shore that are also similar. At the same time, I am impressed by the earlier tradition of ossuary burial on the Eastern Shore that could be interpreted as anticipating the ossuaries associated with Potomac Creek ceramics. Such ossuaries are not associated with sites in the Potomac Piedmont. I am also skeptical of the actual magnitude of ecological forces that are often suggested to stimulate the movement of the Piedmont groups. Finally, I cannot easily dismiss the recorded statement by the brother of the Piscataway *tayac* (Archives of Maryland, 1883[3]:402–403) that 13 generations of leaders had succeeded their first "King from the Easterne Shoare" in AD 1636. Regional prehistorians are quick to calculate the age of the Piscataway chiefdom based on the mention of 13 *tayacs*, and then just as quickly ignore or explain away the point of origins in the very same recorded statement. Is this critical scholarship?

As a last major external stimulus, many feel that the degree of social circumscription or closure that had transpired in and around the study area was a major factor in the formation of local chiefdoms. By circa AD 1500 the Chesapeake was a region of boundaries brought about by the Balkanization of its various constituent groups. This process was magnified by the presence of other groups just beyond study area boundaries. Evidence of this state of affairs is available in the form of material culture remains and from the corpus of historic documents.

Regional archaeologists have long argued that ceramic types often served as signatures of group identity. Just before the beginning of the Late Woodland subperiod the region was blanketed by one major ceramic type, Mockley ware. After AD 900 a host of new ceramic wares appear across the region and are maintained—perhaps even expanded when one considers variation in decorative motif—up until the end of prehistory. These new ceramics can be interpreted as evidence of increasing group definition. The appearance of a defensive infrastructure at prehistoric sites was unprecedented before the end of the Late Woodland subperiod. Fortification may be viewed as the ultimate graphic evidence of group definition.

Historic documentary sources are likewise littered with reference to group identity. Captain John Smith, in his various reconnaissance and diplomatic forays of the region had little trouble ascertaining and recording the names of a host of groups across and beyond the Chesapeake region (see Barbour 1986). Numerous other Europeans chroniclers recorded many other native recitations of the names and territorial boundaries of groups within the study area. The very fact that these groups conceived of themselves as distinct from their neighbors and could list their alliances and enemies, both far and wide, verifies the increasing significance of group identity. Captain John Smith even recorded a mock battle between a group of Powhatan warriors split into two sides, one being the Powhatan and the other acting as rival Monacans (Barbour 1986:166–167). This is an unequivocal example of the clear definition of self versus outsider. Once a similar definition has solidified across the region, even stronger steps are likely to be taken to assure group maintenance.

In the context of regional prehistory, chiefdoms were no doubt the ultimate precipitate of this process of Balkinization and associated territorial closure. From the perspective of most of the native population the benefits of a chiefdom were counterbalanced by some very definite liabilities. Chiefly society makes even greater demands on both personal and familial autonomy. Continued existence was dependent on a careful balance between the goals of the smaller domestic units with the larger forces that sought to control the group. The former was a unit dedicated to underproduction, and the latter sought unlimited production. Few believe that such social organizations would appear and prosper without sufficient cause. Near the end of prehistory some groups in the Chesapeake region must have been convinced that intensification of social relations was the only course open to maintain personal and group existence. Uneasy relations with one's neighbors and increasing numbers of external native visitors were no doubt powerful stimuli to arrive at such a conclusion.

As a last significant external force stimulating the redirection under examination, I want to discuss the potential impacts of European-introduced diseases on the formation of chiefdoms. Various local investigators (e.g., Barker 1992; Feest 1978b; Rountree 1989) have raised this issue in their discussions of the origins of Chesapeake chiefdoms. Potter (1993:166) has recently questioned the evidence for such epidemics, citing seemingly contradictory mortuary evidence of healthy populations (Chase 1990) and even increasing population numbers (Ubelaker 1974) in the Chesapeake region late in prehistory. And he is absolutely correct at the level of currently available evidence. Like much of the archaeological record, however, it is still important to recognize that we have seen only a very tiny percentage of the once extant population through existing analyses of human burials. And only chronic disease can be expected to register itself adequately in skeletal remains. Many of the introduced diseases were of an acute nature. Given what is now coming to light in the Southeast on even indirectly introduced European diseases, the so-called vectors of death (Ramenofsky 1987), I would be amazed if the Chesapeake region escaped significant depopulation through various pandemics starting just after circa AD 1500.

Ramenofsky (1987:171) recently has suggested death rates of up to 90% of the native population across much of eastern North America. She further documents specific losses in both the lower Mississippi Valley and among the Iroquois, specific groups from south and north of the Chesapeake region. And this staggering projected 90% mortality rate does not even depend on direct European contact. Marvin Smith (1987:55) points out that it is clear from the accounts left of the de Soto *entrada* that disease had well preceded that expedition into the interior Southeast. The list of potential disease vectors included a wide variety of viral, bacterial, and protozoal infections against which native populations had little natural resistance. Even if the estimated impact of such diseases for the Chesapeake were off by 50%, the net effect would still be very substantial. I cannot help but believe, as George Milner (1980:47) has argued, that the effects of these diseases necessitated societal reorganization and coalescence of formerly discrete groups to maintain any semblance of social and economic life. Chiefdoms may have been one answer to this desperate situation in the study area.

Given this, I second the calls of various investigators (Barker 1992; Feest 1978b; Rountree 1989) for the need to rethink the potential impacts of disease on this last redirection of native lifeways. We need to think again about the meaning of Powhatan's statement: "that I, having seene the death of all my people thrice, and not one living of those 3 generations, but my selfe" (Barbour 1986:247). The emphasis on capture and documented rules against infanticide in Powhatan society might also be seen as countermeasures to population decline. Perhaps the final irony in documenting the effects of introduced European diseases on native populations is that the descendants of survivors are now so disenchanted with archaeology that it may take many years before real evidence of this tragedy comes to light.

With these external stimuli in mind, it is now time to shift to internal factors in the origins of local chiefdoms. Following Bender (1978:206–218), it is important to look beyond recurrent external phenomena, in this case ecological conditions, population movements, closure, disease, and the like, toward historical events within the social environment of native groups themselves. I follow arguments originally offered by John Haynes (1984, 1990) in this regard.

Societal transformations, such as the case with the appearance of chiefdoms in the study area, involve the invention of new ways for people to relate to one another in a collective group environment. They involve historical processes that are typically the outgrowth of directed social action. External influences are most often not the primary cause of such transformations, but are themselves molded to fit categories of a larger socially constructed worldview. Paraphrasing Sahlins (1985), culture change is often externally induced but always internally orchestrated. If one is to begin to understand the transformation to chiefdoms, it is important to attempt to see how this new level of sociocultural innovation was created within native society itself.

Group identity certainly existed for much of the Woodland period, but membership and group actions were still subject to some negotiation. With the origins of chiefdoms, group membership was no longer negotiated. For this to happen group existence and order had to be legitimized or made to appear natural. Based on the anthropological literature one of the common human solutions to this problem has been the formation of what are labeled conical clans. These conical clans, predicated on ancestor worship, relate the living to largely mythical, dead ancestors. This process binds people to particular groups and rationalizes the existence of a set social order. Certain people within the conical clan gain power over others based on claims of genealogical nearness to the common ancestor. In the case of the Chesapeake region, the argument is that chiefs appeared after circa AD 1500 and were successful in convincing more and more followers of the legitimacy of their interpretation of this order. Power followed from such a conviction.

It should be noted in this regard that I find the recent arguments of Vernon Knight (1990) refreshing. In his revival of the issue of internal social development, Knight (1990:2) makes a case for the analytical priority of regional ethnohistory over studies relying on ethnologically generated ideal social types. He prefers to see the emergence of social stratification in the Southeast arising out of exogamous clans instead of from conical clans. Knight's (1990:5) rejection of the latter is due to their scarcity in North America except on the Northwest Coast. This rarity may be real and therefore significant, or it may be because the Northwest Coast was the only area where anthropologists were able to study conical clans before the total disruption of native social systems. Whatever the case—exogamous or conical clans—I still believe that Knight would be one of the first to argue that we should not ignore the study of the internal development of hierarchical social organization in whatever form it takes.

In conical clan systems, differences between people are no longer negotiated, rather, to a large extent, they are ascribed. While in reality these differences are sometimes actively manipulated, some way must be found to make the status quo or rank appear natural to a majority of the population. In most cases that have been ethnographically documented, the paramount chief, by cosmic ascription, literally becomes an apotheosized ruler representing the physical manifestation of a collective series of supernatural dead ancestors. This earthly god character of a paramount chief, for example, is documented in the historical documents for Powhatan. Captain John Smith wrote, "Yet when he listeth his will is law and must be obeyed: not only as king but as halfe a God they esteeme him" (Barbour 1986:174). I also suspect that mention of "some countries he hath which had been his ancestors," cited previously (from Barbour 1986:173–174), refers to a linkage to Powhatan's supernatural kin rather than his actual relatives.

This usurpation of ancestral power was almost certainly undertaken in collaboration with the religious leadership whose job it was to maintain the memory of the dead ancestors and to interpret through ritual the resulting social order to the living. It is no coincidence that Powhatan, while still the paramount chief, was only restricted in his power by the retention of some authority by his religious leadership. Early writers, such as William Strachey (1953:104) and Captain John Smith (Barbour 1986:119), point out that priests had a large say in many issues and final say in some. Much the same situation can be expected in the other local chiefdoms.

The priesthood, for their part, directly helped maintain the chiefs' needed close genealogical proximity to the mythical ancestors. All power would have been rationalized in this manner. The mortuary temples of the Chesapeake chiefdoms, with dead leaders literally on display, must have been powerful tools in making believed-in events very apparent. Attachment of actual objects—in this cases preserved corpses—to beliefs leads to a more robust ideology. I think that it is significant that these mortuary structures were located in or near major settlements of the local chiefdoms.

This is in contrast to earlier mortuary precincts yielding Adena-related artifacts. I would argue that this locational difference is a factor of achieved rank in the latter versus the ascribed rank of chiefdoms. In this same sense, Jirikowic (1990) has made the argument that the Potomac River ossuaries are indeed artifacts of political forces within the groups that created them and served as powerful reminders of the existing order.

In summary, the structural transformation or internal reordering of social life, described in the paragraphs above, was one way for ambitious (or perhaps desperate) leaders to unite smaller, more independent groups into a cohesive whole. Haynes (1990:20) argues that the rise of chiefdoms went hand in hand with the appropriation of representations from any number of local conical clans that were understood by all members as emblematic of superior social status. Through these known, ramified descent systems, smaller groups were drawn under the control of a paramount chief. Once a critical mass was reached, additional groups could be brought into the chiefdom through force or the threat of force.

The external forces identified earlier were no doubt influential in creating the environment for this transformation, but it is important to remember that the conditions they delivered could have been met in any number of other ways. The process described above is one ethnogrpahically inspired interpretation of how these events might have resulted in the development of chiefdoms in the Chesapeake region. As mentioned earlier, Knight (1990) has suggested another possible scenario based instead on ethnohistorical information. His ideas likewise deserve considera tion, and are in fact very consistent with postprocessualist admonishments that we need to look for the unprecedented in the archaeological record. My point in this context is simply that any interpretation of the origins of chiefdoms must begin to consider such internal transformations, whatever their nature.

To close this section I want to add a few brief thoughts about potential resistance to this radical redirection and say a few words about the final collapse of the chiefdoms. In terms of the former, these social constructions were based on inequality of both rank and consumption (see Barker 1990). One might therefore expect to see some evidence of resistance to them from within. The traditional answer of dissenters, to fission into new areas, was no longer much of a possibility. For other reasons Potter (1993:171–172) has noted that subterranean storage cists are not as numerous as one might expect on sites from this time, and he suggests that a shift to above-ground storage had almost been completed. He uses this idea to explain why few such features, about 40 cists, were noted in the excavation of the large Accokeek Creek site along the Potomac River. In a different sense, I suggest we could also view these same pits as the prehistoric equivalent of what are today tax shelters. Following DeBoer (1988), the pits might have been used for sequestering items from the more formal village economy. This would no doubt lead to fewer storage cists.

The adoption of the bow and arrow likewise has some interesting implications. Hunting or quite possibly revenge could become a more personal endeavor. The latter certainly could also be undertaken from a distance, perhaps increasing the chance of avoiding detection. The triangular arrow points of the time were all very similar and certainly would not reveal ownership. It is interesting to note that, from its contents, Powhatan's personal treasure house at Orapekes (Barbour 1986:173–174) appeared to have been as much of an armory as it was a storehouse. This could be interpreted to mean that access to such weaponry was not universal and may have been controlled. Is this the first instance of what is now debated as gun control? Finally, larger domestic structures likely begin to appear during the Woodland period. While our current sample is certainly not extensive, such larger structures might serve to mask personal accumulations of supplies. Barker (1990:61) has noted that domestic or familial economies are by nature "grudging" in their production of surplus for chiefs. Large domestic structures can keep more from view. Something as simple as eating inside instead of outside, for example, keeps family consumption and resources from public scrutiny. These may have been some of the ways that resistance was expressed in such societies.

Finally, one cannot help but wonder why these chiefdoms finally did collapse in such a short period of time. While this is probably not a question that the approximately one-quarter of the Virginia colony killed during the Powhatan uprising in AD 1622 would find worthy of consideration, it does appear that the English invaders were quite dependent on their native hosts for a good while and could have been driven out at least early on. There have been various reasons advanced for why local chiefs even allowed Europeans to settle (e.g., Merrell 1979). In my opinion, it is by now well documented that, if given the chance, chiefs were notorious collaborators with outside groups (Wolf 1982). This was usually to their own detriment. Potter (1993:210–220) has done a good job of illustrating how the native leadership used and controlled European trade items. As an addendum to his ideas, the inclusion of large amounts of trade items with certain burials might have been intended to remove this currency from circulation thus increasing the value of the supply still at hand as items became more easily obtained.

Nevertheless, as history demonstrates, chiefdoms are still very fragile societies. With sufficient force it is easy to attack their center of power because it is held by a few people. Chiefs, given the inherent inequalities of the societies they rule, also stand at the apex of a people that may be more than a little willing to take their chances with a new leadership. Last, chiefdoms are surrounded by neighbors that have lived in fear of their expansionist tendencies and are often quite willing to help in their demise. The colonial powers of Europe were quick to learn all this, and aboriginal society seemed doomed in the Chesapeake once a firm foothold was established by the Europeans in the seventeenth century.

CONCLUSION

Through this chapter I have presented an historical review of the foundations of the Woodland period along with a short synopsis of this increment of prehistory

, across broader eastern North America. The chapter then turned to a descriptive synthesis of the Woodland period directly within the Chesapeake region. Last, I offered interpretations of the dominant Woodland period lifeway and of a final additional transformation near the end of the period. Thus prehistory came to an end within the study area.

Before ending this chapter, I want to add a few comments about archaeology's successes in explaining events during this portion of prehistory. The Woodland period has arguably been exposed to the longest period of sustained archaeological inquiry of any of the three periods of Chesapeake prehistory. Its rich record immediately caught the attention of early prehistorians. The very foundations of processual archaeology were given a field trial by Binford on sites in the southern reaches of the study area. More recently other archaeologists with even newer ideas have labored to test them against Woodland period data. All of archaeology has no doubt benefited from the fact that two early English colonial efforts settled on the shores of the Chesapeake and left a rich corpus of historical documents describing the native inhabitants of the region.

What I have tried to do in this chapter is to build on both early and contemporary explanations. While my interpretations are clearly drawn from existing research, I hope that the specific ideas offered in this chapter do add additional insights into Woodland period archaeology. These interpretations admittedly arise through the assignment of different meanings to these same existing data. And this is why I have devoted this chapter to looking both at the archaeological record and at the ways in which archaeologists have perceived this record. I am convinced that consideration of both phenomena, here and in the future, will help us to understand this extraordinary period of Chesapeake prehistory.

Chapter 7

Old Traditions and New Directions

INTRODUCTION

The concluding chapter of books such as this one can be written from a variety of perspectives. In this particular case I do not think it would be useful to abstract the details of the 11,000 or so years of the local archaeological record or to recount in detail my interpretations of that prehistory. Both areas of concern were addressed fully in the pertinent chapters. Instead, it might be more beneficial to reinforce a central and unifying theme of the entire book. I refer to the notion that a contemporary understanding of Chesapeake prehistory requires consideration of both old traditions and new directions. In particular, I would like to reflect on four areas of interest that have dominated the previous chapters. These include the study area in its larger regional context, past and present ideas about the meaning of the archaeological record, the culture history of the Chesapeake, and new or different interpretations of study area prehistoric lifeways. With each aspect I would like to revisit and emphasize the interplay of old traditions and new directions. In addition, I then want to take a moment to look at possible directions for Chesapeake archaeology in the future. That look at the future will be followed by the briefest of conclusions.

EASTERN NORTH AMERICA AND THE CHESAPEAKE REGION

Not long ago, after reflecting for a moment on the prehistory of the Chesapeake region, a senior scholar who had earned his reputation in Midwestern archaeology lamented to me that "it is just too bad that Hopewell never made it your way over the mountains." That opinion, albeit good natured in that context, typifies the view many archaeologists once had of the study area. Aside from some rather fortuitous flashes of interest on the part of the professional archaeological community, the Chesapeake languished as an archaeological backwater of sorts for many years. A good many culture historians simply did not see anything unique about the area. At best it appeared to be the recipient of the effects of phenomena that happened earlier or that were expressed more fully elsewhere. Furthermore, prehistorians were never quite sure if the Chesapeake should be linked with the Southeast or the Northeast archaeological regions.

This state of affairs only began to change in the mid- to late 1960s. With the arrival of processual archaeology, the Chesapeake finally began to assume an identity of its own. Prehistorians slowly acknowledged the long record of ecological change as they began to focus on human adaptation. When one considered the regional record of climatic change accompanied by the development of the largest estuary in the United States, the study area began to look much more unique and interesting. Nevertheless, revolutions in thought often breed excess, and most archaeologists now agree that excess was an unintended consequence of processual archaeology. Some two decades later, a few local prehistorians have begun to wonder if our recent near total fixation with prehistoric adaptation to the changing ecology of the Chesapeake region might indeed have become a bit too parochial.

In the previous chapters of this book I have urged that it is time to return to a more balanced perspective on Chesapeake prehistory. For this reason it seemed important to once again situate the study area in the context of larger surrounding regions such as the Southeast and Northeast. It is time to acknowledge the contributions of these broader areas to the archaeological record of the Chesapeake without diminishing the importance or uniqueness of Chesapeake archaeology. Events within the study area can still be seen as larger dramas playing themselves out within a new context. The Chesapeake, given its location, is at the crossroads between two greater archaeological regions. And while Hopewell never made it over the Appalachian mountains, prehistoric people from the Chesapeake did travel west and borrow more than a few ideas and items from earlier Adena peoples. It is time to rejoin the rest of eastern North American prehistory.

IDEAS ABOUT THE PAST

In every chapter of this book I have gone to some lengths to broadly outline how various ideas about the past have influenced our constructions of Chesapeake prehistory. The second chapter focused specifically on how local prehistorians have perceived the archaeological record throughout the history of our interest in its antiquities. Other chapters looked at the impact of more current thoughts on the nature of the past within the larger discipline of archaeology. I want to add a few thoughts about the benefits of such historic reviews to regional archaeologies like this one.

First, there is a coherence over the last hundred or so years in the way Chesapeake prehistorians have approached the local archaeological record. In some instances they were following broader trends within the whole of archaeology. In two cases—the early debate on a North American paleolithic and in a formulation of a so-called processual archaeology—the Chesapeake was an incubator for important new ideas about the nature of the past and how that past should be interpreted. I hope that the specific history of Chesapeake archaeology also reinforces the notion that what we learn from the past is tinted by biases that inhabit any approach, and that within regional archaeology a diversity of ideas is more beneficial than not. The critical tension of old traditions grating against new directions ultimately moves knowledge forward, especially in areas where change often otherwise comes slowly.

Second, Chesapeake archaeology has benefited from changes over the last 50 or so years within the discipline of archaeology. Culture historians, in this case mainly local amateur archaeologists who worked by necessity in the study area, were remarkably successful in reconstructing the major events of Chesapeake prehistory. Subsequent efforts to look at the region's past in different ways would not have been nearly as successful without the basic temporal and spatial framework for the study area established by the late 1950s. The arrival of processual archaeology and its own interest in human adaptation brought a new way to look at the past, and processual archaeologists made great strides in helping us understand the ecological history of the Chesapeake. As just mentioned, this archaeology also did much to promote the study area as a special entity worthy of study in its own right. Any postprocessual archaeology will only be successful on the base of these earlier developments.

CHESAPEAKE CULTURE HISTORY

Interpretations of the prehistoric past by necessity always approach their subject matter with certain inherent biases. The only constant in all this is often the archaeological record itself. What has been discovered is then cast and recast in relation to the particular questions and interests of the moment. I do not claim that this book represents any exception to that rule. And within reasonable limits I have often consciously chosen to focus specifically on certain aspects of the archaeological record of the Chesapeake region that best support my own interpretations of this past. As a consequence, the richness of the overall record is sometimes diminished in the process. Every perspective on the past picks and chooses data to make its case.

For this very reason, I wanted to also include a comprehensive culture history of the region as a separate section of each chapter on the particular periods of Chesapeake prehistory. No current basic reference on the culture history of the study area existed. Existing data languished in a widespread corpus of both primary and what might be called gray literature. Some was in the form of what could only be referred to as oral history. The culture history drawn from all this attempts to focus on basic questions of chronology, diagnostic artifacts, technological systems, the nature of regional sites, settlement organization, and subsistence practices. I made special attempts to collect available radiocarbon dates on regional sites. While the presentation of all these data sometimes does make for tedious reading, the resulting culture history is not only crucial to my interpretations, but should be of use to all archaeologists regardless of their theoretical interests.

In the end, if I am sure of anything, it is that in the future we should avoid our old tradition of performing this exercise only once every century. As mentioned in the opening chapter, it has been that long since a similar attempt was made to draw together much of what is known about the Chesapeake region. Data collection is now simply moving much too rapidly for such a period of time to pass before the next regional archaeology appears.

CHESAPEAKE LIFEWAYS

Regional prehistory, very recently, has more often than not been completely interpreted as a record of human adaptation to late Pleistocene and subsequent Holocene ecological changes. In some instances I feel this is an accurate portrayal of local prehistory over significant portions of archaeological time. In other cases, however, it appears that the belief that all change is ultimately ecologically driven begins to falter as a way to interpret the local archaeological record. For those instances I make the argument—hopefully without having become too polemic— that we instead need to return to seeing change as having been more a consequence of human agency. This is in keeping with current theoretical trends within archaeology as a whole and also responds to some recent calls by a few other local prehistorians. Such a strategy, in my opinion, does result in a more robust understanding of Chesapeake prehistory.

To effect such an interpretation I dichotomize the whole of regional prehistory as having been composed of groups that, in a manner of speaking, accommodated nature contrasted with others that appropriated nature. The former applies to local prehistory between about 11,000 years ago up until circa 4200 years ago, including the Paleoindian period and much of the subsequent Archaic period. The latter commences after 4200 years ago and continues for all practical purposes to the end of prehistory. It includes some of the Late Archaic subperiod and all of the Woodland period.

Processual archaeology represents a powerful tool in understanding how these earlier groups reached such an accommodation with nature. Change throughout this almost 7000-year period of time often appears to have been stimulated by the late Pleistocene and subsequent Holocene record of climatic amelioration and the associated estuary formation characteristic of this region. As different ecological regimes were established throughout this time period, local prehistoric populations responded with new technologies, settlement practices, and subsistence organizations. Kin-oriented social systems appear remarkably homeostatic in their adjustment to the changing Chesapeake landscape and in their maintenance of traditional lifeways. This is not to say that there is no diversity to be seen in the local archaeological record. As one would suspect, given changing ecological conditions, there do appear to be significant differences between Paleoindian and Archaic period adaptations. My interpretations of these differences build on traditional explanations, but also go in a number of new directions.

I argue beginning circa 4200 years ago that a radical break or discontinuity in regional lifeways began to occur. At that time local societies, directly stimulated by new developments that originated further to the south, began to socially appropriate nature in a redirection of lifeways. This is literally a case of people in the past taking old traditions in new directions. It marks the transition from kin- or familial-based society to one that is based increasingly on civil authority. This redirection can be read through the political imprints that mark the archaeological record of this period beginning 4200 years ago. I argue that we can see this new way of life being worked out in much of the Late Arachic through Middle Woodland subperiods. As one would expect, there is evidence from the archaeological record of some interesting experiments and failures toward this end within that period of time. By the end of the Late Woodland subperiod the changes are fully expressed in the chiefdoms that dotted the Chesapeake landscape—that experiment only to be interrupted by the European conquest of the region.

In all, these interpretations offered for the entire 11,000 or so years of Chesapeake prehistory represent my efforts to take old ideas in new directions. At some points I build on traditional thoughts about the meaning of the local archaeological record, and at other points I argue for new ways of looking at the past. To adequately interpret the last 4200 years of prehistory I adopt some of the tenets of postprocessual archaeology that enfranchise human beings in the past as a larger part of the equation. Still, polemics aside, I see nothing in processual archaeology itself, at least as originally formulated, to preclude consideration of social forces and human agency in our interpretations of the past.

FUTURE DIRECTIONS

Books such as this become points on a greater continuum aimed at understanding the past. As such, they should be approached as parts of a much longer conversation. To make an effort to extend this book into the future it is perhaps appropriate, or at least satisfying, to finish by identifying areas of concern for the archaeology of tomorrow. I do not claim any privileged position to prognosticate the future direction of Chesapeake archaeology. Nevertheless, in writing this book I have noticed a few instances where more data would be helpful or perhaps where Chesapeake prehistorians need to think about going in new or different directions. I would like to make five broad suggestions toward this end.

My first suggestion, because of its very nature, is as much concerned with the way we undertake archaeological research in this region as it is addressed toward what specific increments of prehistory need renewed exploration. As to the latter, it is a statement of the obvious to say that we have much yet to learn about the entire archaeological record of the Chesapeake region. This is true of every archaeological region. Every new bit of data is welcome, and every new site found and tested adds to our knowledge. If forced to be more specific for the study area, I would suggest that there are at least three portions of the archaeological column that deserve particular attention.

For example, some exciting new data are beginning to appear on the Paleoindian period in Virginia, below the James River in the lower Chesapeake region, and on the Eastern Shore of the estuary. These data promise a great deal of insight into local Paleoindian lifeways and, for that matter, on the transition from Paleoindian to Early Archaic times. The Middle Archaic subperiod likewise needs renewed attention. Excavations in the northern Chesapeake region, and data from outside the local area, indicate that our typologies need refinement. Finally, the Late Woodland subperiod is an obvious key toward understanding events near the end of prehistory. Many feel that the small, late prehistoric horticultural villages poised in the Piedmont physiographic province of the region hold keys toward understanding later developments on the Coastal Plain. We also need to know more about native and European interaction throughout the seventeenth century.

Given my statements above, I would like to offer some thoughts on how to effect this data collection. Local cultural resources management has been remarkably successful in mitigating the impacts of development on the archaeological record. Those archaeologists engaged in this activity have also been generally more diligent than many university-based prehistorians in turning the results of their labors into the written word, albeit in the form of technical reports with limited distribution. Indeed, without these CRM reports this book would be greatly impoverished. At the same time, the region is desperately in need of sustained pure research programs to address our various unanswered questions about the nature of the regional archaeological record. The results of this activity also need to be published. I suspect that this comment comes as no surprise to most archaeologists. We all continue to be impressed by how many questions get answered when archaeologists conduct goal-oriented pure research. Such research could just as well be undertaken by CRM, government, or trained amateur archaeologists as by university archaeologists. We all need to look to new funding sources to sponsor this research. It is necessary to appeal to traditional funding agencies that largely abandoned the area with the influx of CRM dollars. In a more controversial sense, some redirection of CRM monies is needed. We created CRM; it is not impossible to recreate it and still achieve legally mandated purposes.

Second, archaeology is rapidly developing new techniques to extract even more information from our data base. Some of these new techniques are spin-offs from other sciences that have been transferred to archaeology. A host of new techniques became standard procedure with the ascendancy of processual archaeology. Flotation rather rapidly came into use on local sites by the mid-1970s along with associated floral remains identification. Few archaeologists today excavate a site without a complete program of faunal remains analysis. In the same sense, an understanding of oyster growth rings and the relationship of these features to season of harvest brought a revolution to regional shell midden studies throughout the late 1970s and early 1980s. New techniques are now available and also need to become standard parts of our research and analysis protocols.

Blood-antigen residue analysis and physical residue analysis are already being put to use on regional sites. More testing is needed, and we need to agree on criteria for acceptance of these data. In the same vein, testing for stable carbon isotope ratios promises a wealth of new information on the appearance and the degree of acceptance of tropical cultigens among local prehistoric groups. Almost no such testing to my knowledge has yet been undertaken in the region even though the natural biome of the Chesapeake region, unlike many other areas of North America, consists largely of so-called C3 plants and animals. The appearance and degree of consumption of corn, a C4 plant, should be easily discernable in the local area. AMS radiocarbon assays are also needed on many Late Woodland sites where often erratic dates, many with large sigmas, confound necessary chronological resolution. For that matter, alternative chronometric dating techniques like archaeomagnetism need to be developed for the region. That method of dating in particular has been used with great success in other areas of North America. And there are undoubtedly many other new techniques that would yield good results in the study area.

Third, there is the matter of how the archaeological record in the study area will be interpreted in the future. I am convinced we need to reopen active debate on the appropriate theoretical foundations for local archaeology. To make my point, I want to cite a recent review of a volume of the Council of Virginia Archaeologists' very commendable attempt to publish syntheses of the various periods of Virginia prehistory. This review appeared in *American Antiquity*. My goal is not to criticize the effort by Virginia archaeologists to publish their data, and clearly some of the points made by this particular reviewer are in my opinion misguided. Still, the reviewer (Seeman 1994:582) is on the mark when he notes that many of the theoretical principles that play such prominent roles in current syntheses in the Midwest or Southeast remain largely absent in the Chesapeake region. I see at least two answers to this observation.

For one, the body of theory derived from processual archaeology is certainly robust enough to continue to make valuable contributions to regional archaeology. I doubt, however, if the currently dominant brand of local processual archaeology has much more to offer the study area. I refer to the "square wave" model of the past where human prehistory becomes a proxy of ecological history. That approach has a certain heuristic value for looking at long-term changes, the so-called structures of the *longue duree*, over broad areas. Nevertheless, what are now needed in the Chesapeake region are more temporally limited processual research strategies based on optimal foraging theory, middle-range research, or evolutionary ecology (see Bettinger 1991). Postprocessual archaeology also has much to offer the region. There are already examples of where it has been successfully used to interpret local prehistory, and more efforts in this direction need to made. The region would benefit greatly from

both theoretical perspectives being incorporated in our interpretations of the archaeological record.

Next, I want to make a brief comment concerning the generally uncritical use of
historic records in Chesapeake archaeology. Early Europeans left a wealth of documents concerning the native societies they encountered in their exploration and
settlement of the Chesapeake region. Archaeologists, myself included, regularly pick
and choose passages from these documents to support our arguments about the
nature of the recent prehistoric past and the subsequent Contact era. These documents are indeed invaluable sources on native lifeways.

In another sense, however, these same documents need to be approached much
more critically. We must remember that these are *texts* written for particular purposes.
None were produced to provide an unbiased record of native life in the Chesapeake
region. Biblical scholars, scholars of Elizabethan English, and linguists have recently
made great strides in developing a methodology for the textual interpretation of
historic documents. Until the corpus of historic documents on the Chesapeake region
begins to be approached in such a critical fashion, we must remain skeptical of its
veracity as the final word in archaeological and ethnohistorical interpretation.

Finally, and very briefly, we all need to remember that prehistoric archaeology in
the Chesapeake region has implications for many peoples well beyond the scholarly
community. This includes every constituency from the general public to the North
American Indian community. I feel we need to make renewed efforts to extend our
research findings to the people who ultimately support our activity. The archaeology
of the Chesapeake study area is interesting and could easily make the transfer to
popular literature as well as to the new realms of multimedia and information
technology. Cyberspace should become a venue for Chesapeake archaeology. In the
same sense, the health of local amateur societies should be a matter of concern to all
scholars. As I hope this book has demonstrated, we owe a tremendous debt to this
community.

CONCLUSION

At the very beginning of this book I set out three very basic goals. One was to
produce a current synthesis of the prehistoric culture history of the Chesapeake
region. Another was to offer an integrated interpretation of the common threads that
bind together the many individual archaeological sites of the study area. These goals
required consideration of a substantial body of data and thought both internal and
external to Chesapeake archaeology itself. In my opinion, to begin to satisfy these
goals, it truly becomes a matter of old traditions being taken in new directions. And if
I have been successful in that realm, my third goal of stimulating further scholarly
questioning and debate on Chesapeake prehistory will follow. If nothing else, let this
book be a beginning in that direction.

References

Archives of Maryland, 1883, *Proceedings of the Council, 1636–1667*. Baltimore: Maryland Historical Society.

Adams, W. Y. and E. W. Adams, 1991, *Archaeological Typology and Practical Reality: A Dialectical Approach to Artifact Classification and Sorting*. Cambridge: Cambridge University Press.

Adovasio, J. M., J. D. Gunn, J. Donahue, J. R. Stuckenrath, J. E. Guilday, and K. Lord, 1978, Meadowcroft rockshelter. In A. L. Bryant, ed., *Early man in America*, pp. 140–180. Alberta: Department of Anthropology, University of Alberta Occasional Paper 1.

American Antiquity, 1943, The first archaeological conference on the woodland pattern. *American Antiquity* 4:393–400.

Anderson, D. G., 1990, The Paleoindian colonization of eastern North America: A view from the southeastern United States. In K. Tankersley and B. Isaac, eds., *Early Paleoindian Economies of Eastern North America*, pp. 163–216, Journal of Economic Anthropology Supplement 5.

Anderson, D. G., 1991, Examining prehistoric settlement distribution in eastern North America. *Archaeology of Eastern North America* 19:1–22.

Anderson, D. G., K. E. Sassaman, and C. Judge, 1992, *Paleoindian and Early Archaic Period Research in the Lower Southeast: A South Carolina Perspective*. Columbia: Council of South Carolina Professional Archaeologists.

Arber, E., 1884, *Captain John Smith, Works, 1608–1631*. The English Scholar's Library 16, Birmingham: Unwin.

Arber, E., 1910, *Travels and Works of Captain John Smith*. New York: Burt Franklin.

Artusy, R. E., and D. R. Griffith, 1975, A brief report on the semi-subterranean dwellings of Delaware. *The Archeolog* 27:1–9.

Barber, M. B., 1991, Evolving subsistence patterns and future directions: The Late Archaic and Early Woodland periods. In T. R. Reinhart and M. E. Hodges, eds., *Late Archaic and Early Woodland Research in Virginia: A Synthesis*, pp. 253–258. Richmond: Council of Virginia Archaeologists.

Barbour, P. L., 1986, *The Complete Works of Captain John Smith, 1–3*. Chapel Hill: University of North Carolina Press.

Barker, A. W., 1992, Powhatan's pursestrings: On the meaning of surplus in a seventeenth-century Algonkian chiefdom. In A. W. Barker and T. R. Pauketat, eds., *Lords of the Southeast: Social Inequality and the Native Elites of Southeastern North America*, pp. 61–80. Washington: Archaeological Papers of the American Anthropological Association.

Bastian, T., 1980, The early pursuit of archaeology in Maryland. *Maryland Historical Magazine* 75: 1–7.

Beitzell, E. W., 1960, *The Jesuit Missions of St. Mary's County, Maryland*. Privately published.

Bender, B., 1978, Gatherer-hunter to farmer: A social perspective. *World Archaeology* 10: 204–222.

Bender, B., 1985a, Emergent tribal formations in the American midcontinent. *American Antiquity* 50: 52–62.

Bender, B., 1985b, Prehistoric developments in the American midcontinent and in Brittany, Northwest

France. In T. D. Price and J. A. Brown, eds., *Prehistoric Hunter-Gatherers: The Emergence of Cultural Complexity*, pp. 21–58. Orlando: Academic Press.

Bennett, C. R., 1989, The Evergreen collection. Maryland *Archaeology* 25:5–10.

Benthall, J. L., 1979, *Daugherty's Cave: A Stratified Site in Russell County, Virginia*. Richmond: Virginia Department of Historic Resources.

Benthall, J. L., and B. C. McCary, 1973, The Williamson Site: A new approach. *Archaeology of Eastern North America* 1:127–132.

Bergsland, K., and H. Vogt, 1962, On the validity of glottochronology. *Current Anthropology* 3:115–153.

Bettinger, R. L., 1991, *Hunter-Gatherers: Archaeological and Evolutionary Theory*. New York: Plenum Press.

Binford, L. R., 1962, Archaeology as anthropology. *American Antiquity* 28:217–225.

Binford, L. R., 1964, *Archaeological and Ethnohistorical Investigation of Cultural Diversity and Progressive Development among Aboriginal Cultures of Coastal Virginia and North Carolina* (Doctoral dissertation, University of Michigan). Ann Arbor: University microfilms.

Binford, L. R., 1980, Willow smoke and dogs' tails: Hunter-gatherer settlement systems and archaeological site formation. *American Antiquity* 45:4–20.

Binford, L. R., 1983, *In Pursuit of the Past*. New York: Thames and Hudson.

Binford, L. R., 1991, *Cultural Diversity among Aboriginal Cultures of Coastal Virginia and North Carolina*. New York: Garland.

Blaker, M. C., 1963, Aboriginal ceramics: The Townsend site near Lewes, Delaware. *The Archeolog* 15: 14–39.

Blanton, D. B., 1992, Middle Woodland settlement systems in Virginia. In T. R. Reinhart and M. E. Hodges, eds., *Middle and Late Woodland Research in Virginia: A Synthesis*, pp. 65–96. Richmond: Council of Virginia Archaeologists.

Blitz, J. H., 1988, Adoption of the bow in prehistoric North America. *North American Archaeologist* 9: 123–147.

Borster, J. B., and M. R. Norton, 1992, Paleoindian projectile point and site survey in Tennessee: 1988–1992. In D. G. Anderson, K. E. Sassaman, and C. Judge, eds., *Paleoindian and Early Archaic Research in the Lower Southeast: A South Carolina perspective*, pp. 263–268. Columbia: Council of South Carolina Professional Archaeologists.

Bottoms, E., 1964, The Dime site. *Chesopiean* 2:145–148.

Bottoms, E., 1966, The Richmond site: A Paleoindian locality in Chesterfield County, Virginia. *Chesopiean* 4:40–50.

Bottoms, E., 1972, The Paleoindian component of the Richmond site, Chesterfield County, Virginia. *Chesopiean* 10:115–135.

Bottoms, E., 1974, The Paleoindian component of the Dime site, City of Nansemond, Virginia. *Chesopiean* 12:88–106.

Bottoms, E., 1985, Additional Paleoindian artifacts from the Dime site. *Chesopiean* 23:28–32.

Boyce, H., and L. Frye, 1986, *Radiocarbon Dating of Archaeological Samples from Maryland*. Baltimore: Maryland Geological Survey Archaeological Studies.

Boyd, V. G., E. A. Moore, and R. J. Dent, 1990, *Phase III Archaeological Investigations of 18 AN 57, Anne Arundel County, Maryland*. Washington, DC: Potomac River Archaeology Survey.

Braidwood, R. J., 1952, From cave to village. *Scientific American* 187:62–66.

Braidwood, R. J., 1960, The agricultural revolution. *Scientific American* 203:130–141.

Braun, E. L., 1950, *Deciduous Forests of Eastern North America*. New York: Free Press.

Brennan, L. A., 1974, The lower Hudson: A decade of shell middens. *Archaeology of Eastern North America* 2:81–93.

Brose, D. S., 1973, The northeastern United States. In J. E. Fitting, ed., *The Development of North American Archaeology*, pp. 84–116. Garden City: Anchor Books.

Brose, D. S., 1978, Comment. *Current Anthropology* 19:729–731.

Brown, L., 1979, *Fluted Projectile Points in Maryland*. Paper distributed by the Council for Maryland Archaeology.

Brown, M. L., J. L. Reveal, C. R. Broome, and G. F. Frick, 1986, *Aspects of the Ecological and Vegetational History of Colonial Maryland*. Unpublished manuscript.

Broyles, B. J., 1966, Preliminary report, the St. Albans site 46 KA 27, Kanawha County, West Virginia. *West Virginia Archaeologist* 19:1–43.

Broyles, B. J., 1971, *Second Preliminary Report: The St. Albans Site, Kanawha County, West Virginia*. Report of Archaeological Investigation No. 3, West Virginia Geological and Economic Survey.

Brush, G. S., 1986, Geology and paleoecology of Chesapeake Bay: A long-term monitoring tool for management. *Journal of the Washington Academy of Sciences* 76:146–160.

Bryan, A. L., 1962, *Paleo-American Culture History—A New Interpretation*. Unpublished thesis, Harvard University.

Bryson, R. A., 1965, Recent climatic episodes in North America. *Proceedings, 21st Southeastern Archaeological Conference, Bulletin 3*, pp. 78–81.

Bushnell, D. L., 1906, The Sloane Collection in the British Museum. *American Anthropologist* 8:671–685.

Bushnell, D. L., 1907, Virginia—From early records. *American Anthropologist* 9:31–44.

Bushnell, D. L., 1934, Stone relics of oldest Americans? *Literary Digest* 117:22.

Bushnell, D. L., 1940, Virginia before Jamestown. *Smithsonian Miscellaneous Collections* 100:125–158.

Byers, D., 1954, Bull Brook—A fluted point site in Ipswich, Massachusetts. *American Antiquity* 19:343–351.

Byers, D., 1955, Additional information on the Bull Brook site, Massachusetts. *American Antiquity* 20:274–276.

Byers, D. S., 1959a, An introduction to five papers on the Archaic stage. *American Antiquity* 24:229–232.

Byers, D. S., 1959b, The eastern Archaic: Some problems and hypotheses. *American Antiquity* 24:233–256.

Caldwell, J. R., 1958, Trend and tradition in the prehistory of the eastern United States. *American Anthropological Association, Memoir 88*.

Callahan, E., 1974, *Experimental Archaeology Papers #3*. Richmond. Virginia Commonwealth University.

Callahan, E., 1976, *The Pamunkey Project Phases I and II* Richmond: Virginia Commonwealth University.

Callahan, E., 1979, The basics of biface knapping in the eastern fluted point tradition. *Archaeology of Eastern North America* 7:1–180.

Callahan, E., 1981, *Pamunkey House Building: An Experimental Study of Late Woodland Constructional Technology in the Powhatan Confederacy* (Doctoral dissertation, Catholic University). Ann Arbor: University microfilms.

Callahan, E., 1985, The St. Mary's longhouse experiment: The first season. *Quarterly Bulletin of the Archaeological Society of Virginia* 40:12–40.

Callahan, E., 1986, A reply to Thurman. *Quarterly Bulletin of the Archaeological Society of Virginia* 41:97–105.

Campbell, L., 1986, Comment on the settlement of the Americas. *Current Anthropology* 27:488.

Carbone, V., 1976, *Environment and Prehistory in the Shenandoah Valley* (Doctoral dissertation, Catholic University). Ann Arbor: University microfilms.

Cavallo, J., 1982, *Fish, fires, and foresight: Middle Woodland Economic Adaptations in the Abbott Farm National Landmark, Trenton, New Jersey*. Paper presented at the annual meeting of the Eastern States Archaeological Federation, Norfolk, Virginia.

Chapman, J., 1975, *The Rose Island Site and the Bifurcate Point Tradition*. Knoxville: University of Tennessee, Department of Anthropology.

Chapman, J., 1977, *Archaic Period Research in the Lower Little Tennessee River Valley*. Knoxville: University of Tennessee, Department of Anthropology.

Chapman, J., 1985, Archaeology and the archaic period in the southern ridge-and-valley province. In R. S. Dickens and H. T. Ward, eds., *Structure and Process in Southeastern Archaeology*, pp. 137–153. University: University of Alabama Press.

Chapman, J., 1985b, Tellico archaeology. *Report of Investigations No. 43*. Knoxville: University of Tennessee, Department of Anthropology.

Chapman, J., and J. M. Adovasio, 1977, Textile and basketry impressions from Icehouse Bottom, Tennessee. *American Antiquity* 42:620–625.

Chase, J. W., 1988, *A Comparison of Signs of Nutritional Stress in Prehistoric Populations of the Potomac*

Piedmont and Coastal Plain (Doctoral dissertation, American University). Ann Arbor: University microfilms.

Chase, J. W., 1990, *Analysis of Skeletal Material from the Thomas Site 18 CA 88.* Report prepared for the Maryland Historical Trust.

Chomko, S., and G. Crawford, 1978, Plant husbandry in prehistoric eastern North America: New evidence for its development. *American Antiquity* 43:405–408.

Cissna, P. B., 1986, *The Piscataway Indians of Southern Maryland: An Ethnohistory from pre European Contact to the Present* (Doctoral dissertation, American University). Ann Arbor: University microfilms.

Clark, W. E., 1980, The origins of Piscataway and related Indian cultures. *Maryland Historical Magazine* 75:8–22.

Clark, W., and W. D. Miller, 1975, U.M.B.C. site: The projectile points. *Miscellaneous Papers No. 10*, pp. 32–89. The Archaeological Society of Maryland.

Clarke, D. L., 1978, *Analytical Archaeology.* London: Methuen.

Clausen, C. J., A. D. Cohen, C. Emiliani, J. A. Hoffman, and J. J. Stipp, 1979, Little Salt Spring, Florida: A unique underwater site. *Science* 203:609–613.

Cleland, C. E., 1976, The focal-diffuse model: An evolutionary perspective on prehistoric cultural adaptations of the eastern United States. *Midcontinental Journal of Archaeology* 1:59–76.

Coe, J. L., 1964, The formative cultures of the Carolina Piedmont. *Transactions of the American Philosophical Society*, 54.

Coleman, G. N., 1982, The Reedy Creek site, 44 HA 22, South Boston, Virginia. *Quarterly Bulletin of the Archaeological Society of Virginia* 37:150–209.

Collingwood, R. G., 1939, *An Autobiography.* Oxford: Oxford University Press.

Colman, S. M., and J. P. Halka, 1989a, *Maps Showing Quaternary Geology of the Northern Maryland Part of the Chesapeake Bay.* Washington, DC: U.S. Geological Survey.

Colman, S. M., and J. P. Halka, 1989b, *Maps Showing Quaternary Geology of the Southern Maryland Part of the Chesapeake Bay.* Washington, DC: U.S. Geological Survey.

Colman, S. M., J. P. Halka, and C. H. Hobbs, 1991, Patterns and rates of sediment accumulation in the Chesapeake Bay during the Holocene rise in sea level. *Contribution Number 1668 of the Virginia Institute of Marine Science.*

Colman, S. M., and C. H. Hobbs, 1987, *Quaternary Geology of the Southern Virginia Part of the Chesapeake Bay.* Washington, DC: U.S. Geological Survey.

Colman, S. M., and C. H. Hobbs, 1988, *Maps Showing Quaternary Geology of the Northern Virginia Part of the Chesapeake Bay.* Washington, DC: U.S. Geological Survey.

Conant, R., 1945, *An Annotated Check List of the Amphibians and Reptiles of the Del-Mar-Va Peninsula.* Wilmington: The Society of Natural History of Delaware.

Cook, T. G., 1976, Broadpoint: Culture, phase, horizon, tradition, or knife. *Journal of Anthropological Research* 32:337–357.

Cooke, M. T., 1929, Birds of the Washington, D.C., region. *Proceedings of the Biological Society of Washington* 42:1–80.

Craig, A. J., 1969, Vegetational history of the Shenandoah Valley, Virginia. *Geological Society of America, Special Paper 123*, pp. 283–296.

Cresthull, P., 1971, Chance 18 SO 5: A major Early Archaic site. *Maryland Archaeology* 7:51–52.

Cresthull, P., 1972, Chance 18 SO 5: A major Early Archaic site, part 2. *Maryland Archaeology* 8:40–53.

Crook, W. W., 1992, The Marine Spring Branch site: A late Paleoindian campsite in Chesterfield County, Virginia. *Quarterly Bulletin of the Archaeological Society of Virginia* 47: 123–128.

Cubbage, W. D., 1941, Killens Mill Pond. *Bulletin of the Archaeological Society of Delaware* 3:23–24.

Curran, M. L., 1984, The Whipple site and Paleoindian tool assemblage variation: A comparison of intrasite structuring. *Archaeology of Eastern North America* 12:5–40.

Curry, D. C., and M. Kavanagh, 1991, The Middle to Late Woodland transition in Maryland. *North America Archaeologist* 12:3–28.

Custer, J. F., 1984, *Delaware Prehistoric Archaeology: An Ecological Approach.* Cranbury: Associated University Presses.

Custer, J. L., 1989, *Prehistoric Cultures of the Delmarva Peninsula: An Archaeological Study*. Newark: University of Delaware Press.

Custer, J. F., K. R. Rosenberg, G. Mellin, and A. Washburn, 1990, A reexamination of the Island Field site 7K-F-17, Kent County, Delaware. *Archaeology of Eastern North America* 18:145–212.

Davidson, T. E., 1982, Historically attested Indian villages of the Lower Delmarva. *Maryland Archaeologist* 18:1–8.

DeBoer, W. R., 1988, Subterranean storage and organization of surplus: the view from eastern North America. *Southeastern Archaeology* 7:1–20.

Delcourt, H. R., and P. A. Delcourt, 1985, Quaternary palynology and vegetational history of the southeastern United States. In V. M. Bryant and R. G. Holloway, eds., *Pollen Records of Late-Quaternary North American Sediments*, pp. 1–37. Austin, Texas: American Association of Stratigraphic Palynologists.

Dent, R. J., 1984, Archaeological research at the Accokeek Creek site. In E. S. Biles, ed., *The Accokeek Creek Complex and the Emerging Maryland Colony*, pp. 7–21. Accokeek, Maryland: Alice Ferguson Foundation.

Dent, R. J., 1985, Amerinds and the environment: Myth, reality, and the upper Delaware Valley. In C. W. McNett, ed., *Shawnee Minisink: A Stratified Paleoindian-Archaic Site in the Upper Delaware Valley of Pennsylvania*, pp. 123–163. New York: Academic Press.

Dent, R. J., 1991, Deep time in the Potomac River Valley—Thoughts on Paleoindian lifeways and revisionist archaeology. *Archaeology of Eastern North America* 19:23–41.

Dent, R. J., 1993, Paleoindian occupation of the Potomac River Valley. *Current Research in the Pleistocene* 10:12–14.

Dent, R. J., and C. A. Jirikowic, 1990, *Preliminary Report of Archaeological Investigations at the Hughes Site*. Washington, DC: Potomac River Archaeology Survey.

Dent, R. J., and B. E. Kauffman, 1985, Aboriginal subsistence and site ecology as interpreted from microfloral and faunal remains. In C. W. McNett, ed., *Shawnee Minisink: A stratified Paleoindian-Archaic Site in the Upper Delaware Valley of Pennsylvania*, pp. 55–79. New York: Academic Press.

Dietrich, R. V., 1970, *Geology and Virginia*. Charlottesville: University Press of Virginia.

Dilks, M. D., and G. M. Reynolds, 1965, Preliminary Survey of Fluted Points in Maryland. *Journal of the Archaeological Society of Maryland* 1:9–10.

Dillon, W. P., and R. N. Oldale, 1978, Late Quaternary sea level curve: Reinterpretation based on glaciotechnic influence. *Geology* 6:56–60.

Dincauze, D. F., 1976, *The Neville Site: 8000 Years at Amoskeag*. Cambridge: Peabody Museum of Archaeology and Ethnology.

Dincauze, D. L., 1981, Paleoenvironmental reconstruction in the Northeast: The art of multidisciplinary science. In D. R. Snow, ed., *Foundations of Northeast Archaeology*, pp. 51–96. New York: Academic Press.

Divale, W. T., 1984, *Matrilocal Residence in pre-Literate Society*. Ann Arbor: UMI Research Press.

Doran, G. H., D. N. Dickel, W. E. Ballinger, O. F. Agee, P. J. Laipis, and W. W. Havswirth, 1986, Anatomical, cellular, and molecular analysis of 8000-year-old human brain tissue from the Windover Archaeological site. *Nature* 323:803–806.

Dragoo, D. W., 1976, Some aspects of eastern North American prehistory: A review 1975. *American Antiquity* 41:3–37.

Driskell, B. N., 1992, Stratified early Holocene remains at Dust Cave, Northwest Alabama. In D. G. Anderson, K. E. Sassaman, and C. Judge, eds., *Paleoindian and Early Archaic Period Research in the Lower Southeast: A South Carolina Perspective*, pp. 273–278. Columbia: Council of South Carolina Professional Archaeologists.

Duke, P., 1991, *Points in Time*. Niwot: University Press of Colorado.

Dunbar, J. S., and B. I. Waller, 1992, Resource orientation of Clovis, Suwannee, and Simpson age Paleoindian sites in Florida. In D. G. Anderson, K. E. Sassaman, and C. Judge, eds., *Paleoindian and Early Archaic Period Research in the Lower Southeast: A South Carolina Perspective*, pp. 279–294. Columbia: Council of South Carolina Professional Archaeologists.

Dunnell, R. C., 1986, Five decades of American archaeology. In D. J. Meltzer, D. D. Fowler, and J. A. Sabloff, eds., *American Archaeology Past and Future*, pp. 23–49. Washington, D.C.: Smithsonian Institution Press.

Earle, C. V., 1979, Environment, disease, and mortality in early Virginia. In T. W. Tate and D. L. Ammerman, eds., *The Chesapeake in the Seventeenth Century*, pp. 96–125. New York: Norton.

Ebright, C. A., 1992, *Early Native American Prehistory on the Maryland Western Shore: Archaeological Investigations at the Higgins site Vols 1–3*. Baltimore: Maryland State Highway Administration and Department of Natural Resources.

Edwards, R. L., and K. O. Emery, 1977, Man on the continental shelf. In W. S. Newman and B. Salwen, eds., *Amerinds and Their Paleoenvironments in Northeastern North America*, pp. 245–256. Annals of the New York Academy of Sciences, 288.

Edwards, R. L., and A. S. Merrill, 1977, A reconstruction of the continental shelf areas of Eastern North America for the times 9500 B.P. and 12,500 B.P. *Archaeology of Eastern North America* 5:1–43.

Eggan, F., 1953, Karl Schmitt, 1915–1952. *American Anthropologist* 55:237–239.

Egghart, C., 1986, *Archaeological Investigations at Great Neck Site 44VB7 on Lot #11 of the Green Hill Subdivision in Virginia Beach, Virginia*. Richmond: CRM report on file Virginia Division of Historic Landmarks.

Egghart, C., 1989, *Phase 3 Archaeological Investigation on the Bull Hill Run Site 44PG316, a Multicomponent Prehistoric Site in Prince George County, Virginia*. Richmond: Virginia Commonwealth Archaeological Research Center.

Egloff, K. T., 1991, Development and impact of ceramics in Virginia. In T. R. Reinhart and M. E. Hodges, eds., *Late Archaic and Early Woodland Research in Virginia: A Synthesis*, pp. 243–252. Richmond: Council of Virginia Archaeologists.

Egloff, K. T., M. E. Hodges, J. F. Custer, K. R. Doms, and L. D. McFaden, 1988, *Archaeological Investigations at Croaker Landing 44JC70 and 44JC71*. Richmond: Division of Historic Landmarks.

Egloff, K. T., and J. M. McAvoy, 1990, Chronology of Virginia's Early and Middle Archaic periods. In T. R. Reinhart and M. E. Hodges, eds., *Early and Middle Archaic Research in Virginia: A Synthesis*, pp. 61–80. Richmond: Council of Virginia Archaeologists.

Egloff, K. T., and S. R. Potter, 1982, Indian ceramics from Coastal Plain Virginia. *Archaeology of Eastern North America* 10:95–117.

Eldredge, N., 1985, *Time Frames: The Rethinking of Darwinian Evolution and the Theory of Punctuated Equilibria*. New York: Simon and Schuster.

Eldredge, N., and S. J. Gould, 1972, Punctuated equilibria: An alternative to phyletic gradualism. In T. J. M. Schopf, ed., *Models in Paleobiology*, pp. 82–115. San Francisco: Freeman, Cooper.

Emory, K. O., R. L. Wigley, A. S. Bartlett, M. Rubin, and E. S. Barghoorn, 1967, Freshwater peat on the continental shelf. *Science* 158:1302–1306.

Escowitz, E. C., G. W. Hill, and R. Bowen, 1988, *Map Showing Bottom Topography of the Mid-Atlantic Continental Margin, Cape Cod to Albemarle Sound*. Washington, DC: U.S. Geological Survey.

Evans, C., 1955, *A Ceramic Study of Virginia*. Smithsonian Institution, Bureau of American Ethnology, Bulletin 160.

Evans, J., 1984, *Late Archaic Projectile Points: What's in a Name*. Paper presented at the Middle Atlantic Archaeological Conference.

Fausz, F. J., 1985, Patterns of Anglo–Indian aggression and accommodation along the mid-Atlantic coast, 1584–1634. In W. W. Fitzhugh, ed., *Cultures in Contact*, pp. 225–270. Washington, DC: Smithsonian Institution Press.

Feest, C. F., 1978a, Nanticoke and neighboring tribes. In B. G. Trigger, ed., *Handbook of North American Indians, Northeast*, pp. 240–252. Washington, DC: Smithsonian Institution Press.

Feest, C. F., 1978b, Virginia Algonquians. In B. G. Trigger, ed., *Handbook of North American Indians, Northeast*, pp. 253–270. Washington, DC: Smithsonian Institution Press.

Feest, C. F., 1983, Powhatan's mantle and skin pouch. In A. MacGregor, ed., *Tradescant's Rarities*, pp. 130–137. Oxford: Clarendon Press.

Ferguson, A. L., 1937, *Moyaone and the Piscataway Indians*. Washington, DC: National Capital Press.

Ferguson, H., 1960, Preface. In A. L. Ferguson and H. G. Ferguson, eds., *The Piscataway Indians of Southern Maryland*, pp. 5–7. Accokeek, Maryland: Alice Ferguson Foundation.

Figgins, J. D., 1927, The antiquity of man in America. *Natural History* 27:229–239.

Filios, E. L., 1990, *Thresholds to Group Mobility among Hunter-Gatherers: An Archaeological Example from Southern New England* (Doctoral dissertation, University of Massachusetts). Ann Arbor: University microfilms.

Fitting, J. E., 1965, A quantitative examination of Virginia fluted points. *American Antiquity* 30:484–491.

Fitting, J. E., 1968, Environmental potential and postglacial readaptation in Eastern North America. *American Antiquity* 33: 441–445.

Fitting, J. E., 1977, Social dimensions of paleoindian adaptation in the Northeast. In W. S. Newman and B. Salwen, eds., *Amerinds and Their Paleoenvironments in Northeastern North America*, pp. 369–374. Annals of the New York Academy of Sciences, 288.

Ford, J. A., and G. R. Willey, 1941, An interpretation of the prehistory of eastern North America. *American Anthropologist* 43:325–363.

Ford, T. L., 1976, Adena sites on Chesapeake Bay. *Archaeology of Eastern North America* 4:63–89.

Foss, J. E., D. S. Fanning, F. P. Miller, and D. P. Wagner, 1978, Loess deposits of the Eastern Shore of Maryland. *Soil and Science Society of America Journal* 42:329–333.

Fowke, G., 1894, Archaeologic investigations in the James and Potomac valleys. *Smithsonian Institution Bureau of American Ethnology Bulletin 23*.

Fowler, M. L., 1959a, Modoc Rockshelter: An Early Archaic site in southern Illinois. *American Antiquity* 24:257–270.

Fowler, M. L., 1959b, *Summary Report of Modoc Rockshelter*. Illinois State Museum Report of Investigations, No. 8.

Fried, M. H., 1967, *The Evolution of Political Society*. New York: Random House.

Funk, R. E., 1976, *Recent Contributions to Hudson Valley Prehistory*. Albany: New York State Museum.

Funk, R. E., 1978, Post-pleistocene adaptations. In B. G. Trigger, ed., *Handbook of North American Indians, Northeast*, pp. 16–27. Washington, DC: Smithsonian Institution Press.

Funk, R. E., 1983, The northeastern United States. In J. D. Jennings, ed., *Ancient North Americans*, pp. 303–372. San Francisco: W.H. Freeman.

Funk, R. E., 1988, The Laurentian concept: A review. *Archaeology of Eastern North America* 16:1–42.

Funk, R. E., D. W. Fisher, and E. M. Reilly, 1970, Caribou and paleoindians in New York state: A presumed association. *American Journal of Science* 268:181–186.

Gailey, C. W., 1987, *Kinship to Kingship*. Austin: University of Texas Press.

Gardner, W. M., 1974, *The Flint Run Complex: Pattern and Process during the Paleoindian to Early Archaic*. Catholic University: Occasional Publication No. 1, Archaeology Laboratory.

Gardner, W. M., 1975, *Paleoindian to Early Archaic: Continuity and Change in Eastern North America during the Late Pleistocene and Early Holocene*. Unpublished manuscript.

Gardner, W. M., 1977, Flint Run Paleoindian Complex and its implications for eastern North American prehistory. In W. S. Newman and B. Salwen, eds., *Amerinds and Their Paleoenvironments in Northeastern North America*, pp. 257–263. Annals of the New York Academy of Sciences, 288.

Gardner, W. M., 1978, *Comparison of Ridge and Valley, Blue Ridge, Piedmont, and Coastal Plain Archaic Period Distribution: An Idealized Transect*. Unpublished manuscript.

Gardner, W. M., 1980, *The Archaic*. Paper presented at the 1980 Middle Atlantic Archaeological Conference, Dover, Delaware.

Gardner, W. M., 1981, Paleoindian Settlement Pattern and Site Distribution in the Middle Atlantic. In R. H. Landman, L. A. Bennett, A. Brooks, and P. P. Chock, eds., *Anthropological Careers*, pp. 51–73. Washington, DC: Anthropological Society of Washington.

Gardner, W. M., 1982, Early and Middle Woodland in the Middle Atlantic: An overview. *American Indian Archaeological Institute, Occasional Paper, No. 3*, pp. 53–86.

Gardner, W. M., 1983, Stop me if you've heard this one before: The Flint Run Paleoindian Complex revisited. *Archaeology of Eastern North America* 11:49–64.

Gardner, W. M., 1986, *Summary Statement Late Archaic to Early Woodland in the Shenandoah Valley and Potomac River*. Paper presented at the annual meeting of the Eastern States Archaeological Federation, Wilmington, Delaware.

Gardner, W. M., 1989, An examination of cultural change in the Late Pleistocene and Early Holocene circa 9200 to 6800 B.C.. In J. M. Wittkofski and T. R. Reinhart, eds., *Paleoindian Research in Virginia: A Synthesis*, pp. 5–51. Richmond: Council of Virginia Archaeologists.

Gardner, W. M., and C. W. McNett, 1970, The Rowe site. *Maryland Archaeology* 6:1–29.

Gardner, W. M., C. Nash, J. Walker, and W. Barse, 1989, *Excavations at 18 CV 272*. Woodstock: Thunderbird Research.

Gardner, W. M., and R. Verrey, 1979, Typology and chronology of fluted points from the Flint Run area. *Pennsylvania Archaeologist* 49:13–46.

Geier, C. R., 1990, The Early and Middle Archaic periods: Material culture and technology. In T. R. Reinhart and M. E. Hodges, eds., *Early and Middle Archaic Research in Virginia: A Synthesis*, pp. 81–98. Richmond: Council of Virginia Archaeologists.

Gleach, F. W., 1985, A compilation of radiocarbon dates with applicability to central Virginia. *Quarterly Bulletin of the Archaeological Society of Virginia* 40:180–200.

Gleach, F. W., 1987, A working projectile point classification for central Virginia. *Quarterly Bulletin of the Archaeological Society of Virginia* 42:80–120.

Goodyear, A. C., 1979, *A Hypothesis for the Use of Cryptocrystalline Raw Materials among Paleoindian Groups of North America*. Research Manuscript Series, University of South Carolina, Institute of Archaeology and Anthropology.

Goodyear, A. C., 1982, The chronological position of the Dalton horizon in the southeastern United States. *American Antiquity* 47:382–395.

Goodyear, A. C., 1989, A hypothesis for the use of crytocrystalline raw materials among Paleoindian groups of North America. In C. J. Ellis and J. C. Lothrop, eds., *Eastern Paleoindian Lithic Resource Use*, pp. 1–9. Boulder, Colorado: Westview Press.

Graham, R. W., 1979, Paleoclimates and late pleistocene faunal provinces in North America. In R. L. Humphrey and D. Stanford, eds., *Pre-Llano Cultures of the Americas: Paradoxes and Possibilities*, pp. 49–69. Washington, DC: Anthropological Society of Washington.

Graham, R. W., C. V. Haynes, D. L. Johnson, and M. Kay, 1981, Kimmiswick: A Clovis–Mastodon association in eastern Missouri. *Science* 156:1115–1117.

Graham, W. J., 1935, *The Indians of Port Tobacco River, Maryland, and Their Burial Places*. Washington, DC: Privately published.

Gramly, R. M., 1982, *The Vail Site: A Paleoindian Encampment in Maine*. Buffalo: Buffalo Museum of Science.

Gramly, R. M., and R. E. Funk, 1990, What is known and what is not known about the human occupation of the northeastern United States until 10,000 B.P. *Archaeology of Eastern North America* 18:5–31.

Gregory, L. B., 1980, The Hatch site: A preliminary report. *Quarterly Bulletin of the Archaeological Society of Virginia* 34:239–248.

Griffin, J. B., 1952, *Archaeology of Eastern United States*. Chicago: University of Chicago Press.

Griffin, J. B., 1961, Review of the eastern dispersal of Adena. *American Antiquity* 26:572–573.

Griffin, J. B., 1967, Eastern North American archaeology: A summary. *Science* 156:175–191.

Griffith, D. R., 1977, *Townsend Ceramics and the Late Woodland of Southern Delaware*. Master's thesis, American University.

Griffith, D. R., 1980, Townsend ceramics and the late woodland of southern Delaware. *Maryland Historical Magazine* 75:23–41.

Griffith, D. R., 1982, Prehistoric ceramics of Delaware: An overview. *Archaeology of Eastern North America* 10:46–68.

Grimes, J. R., W. Eldridge, B. G. Grimes, A. Vaccaro, F. Vaccaro, N. Vaccaro, and A. Orsini, 1984, Bull Brook II. *Archaeology of Eastern North America* 12:159–183.

Guilday, J. E., 1962, The pleistocene local fauna of the natural chimneys, Augustana County, Virginia. *Annals of the Carnegie Museum* 36:87–122.

Guilday, J. E., and H. W. Hamilton, 1973, The late pleistocene small mammals of Eagle Cave, Pendleton County, West Virginia. *Annals of the Carnegie Museum* 44:45–58.

Guilday, J. E., H. W. Hamilton, and A. D. McCrady, 1966, The bone breccia of Bootlegger Sink, York County, Pennsylvania. *Annals of the Carnegie Museum* 38:145–163.

Guilday, J. E., P. S. Martin, and A. D. McCrady, 1964, New Paris No. 4: A Pleistocene cave deposit in Bedford County, Pennsylvania. *Bulletin of the National Speleological Society* 26:121–194.

Guilday, J. E., P. W. Parmalee, and H. W. Hamilton, 1977, The Clark's Cave bone deposit and late Pleistocene paleoecology of the central Appalachian Mountains of Virginia. *Bulletin of the Carnegie Museum of Natural History* 2:1–87.

Handsman, R. G., and C. W. McNett, 1974, *The Middle Woodland in the Middle Atlantic: Chronology, Adaptation, and Contact.* Paper presented at the Middle Atlantic Archaeological Conference, Baltimore, Maryland.

Hantman, J. L., 1990, Between Powhatan and Quirank: Reconstructing Monacan culture and history. *American Anthropologist* 92:676–690.

Harrison, W., R. J. Malloy, G. A. Rusnak, and J. Terasmae, 1965, Possible late Pleistocene uplift Chesapeake Bay entrance. *Journal of Geology* 73:201–229.

Hay, O. P., 1923, *The Pleistocene of North America and Its Vertebrated Animals from the States West of the Mississippi River and from the Canadian Provinces East of Longitude 95 Degrees.* Washington, DC: Carnegie Institution.

Haynes, C. V., 1983, Fluted points in the east and west. *Archaeology of Eastern North America* 11:24–27.

Haynes, C. V., 1987, Clovis origin update. *The Kiva* 52:83–93.

Haynes, J. H., 1984, *The Seasons of Tsenacommacoh and the Rise of Wahunsenacawh: Structure and Ecology in Social Evolution.* Thesis, University of Virginia, Department of Anthropology.

Haynes, J. H., 1990, *Mamanitowick: An Examination of Powhatan Social Organization.* Paper prepared for the Anthropological Society of Washington.

Hinsley, C. M., 1976, *The development of a profession: Anthropology in Washington, D.C., 1846–1903* (Dissertation, University of Wisconsin, Madison) Ann Arbor: University microfilms.

Hinsley, C. M., 1981, *Savages and Scientists: The Smithsonian Institution and the Development of American Anthropology 1846–1910.* Washington, DC: Smithsonian Press.

Hodder, I., 1982, *Symbols in Action.* Cambridge: Cambridge University Press.

Hodder, I., 1991, *Reading the Past.* Cambridge: Cambridge University Press.

Hodges, M. E. N., 1993a, *Middle and Late Woodland Settlement at Great Neck Site 44VB7 in Virginia Beach, Virginia.* Thesis, University of Tennessee, Knoxville.

Hodges, M. E. N., 1993b, The archaeology of Native American life in Virginia in the context of European contact: Review of past research. In T. R. Reinhart and D. Pogue, eds., *The Archaeology of 17th-Century Virginia,* pp. 1–66. Richmond: Council of Virginia Archaeologists.

Hoffman, B. G., 1964, Observations on certain ancient tribes of the northern Appalachian province. *Bureau of American Ethnology, Anthropological Papers, No. 70,* pp. 191–245.

Holland, C. G., 1949a, Contributions to the archaeology of Albemarle County number two—Mehring Site. *Quarterly Bulletin of the Archaeological Society of Virginia* 3:7–13.

Holland, C. G., 1949b, Contributions to the archaeology of Albemarle County number four—Preliminary definition of two foci. *Quarterly Bulletin of the Archaeological Society of Virginia* 4:9–13.

Holland, C. G., 1953, Further data on preceramic sites in Albemarle County, Virginia. *Quarterly Bulletin of the Archaeological Society of Virginia* 8:4–9.

Holland C. G., 1955, An analysis of projectile points and large blades. In C. Evans *A Ceramic Study of Virginia,* pp. 165–195. Smithsonian Institution, Bureau of American Ethnology, Bulletin, 160.

Holland, C. G., 1983, Dams. *Quarterly Bulletin of the Archaeological Society of Virginia* 38:80–107.

Holland, C. G., and J. Moldenhauer, 1994, Blackwater and Pigg Rivers Old Fish Dams. *Quarterly Bulletin of the Archaeological Society of Virginia* 49:65–72.

Holmes, W. H., 1890, A quarry workshop of flaked stone implement makers in the District of Columbia. *American Anthropologist* 3:1–26.

Holmes, W. H., 1897, *Stone Implements of the Potomac–Chesapeake Tidewater Province*. Washington, DC: United States Bureau of American Ethnology, Fifteenth Annual Report, 1893–1894.

Holmes, W. H., 1903, *Aboriginal Pottery of the Eastern United States*. Washington, DC: Twentieth Annual Report of the Bureau of American Ethnology.

Hranicky, W. J., 1991, *Projectile Point Typology and Nomenclature for Maryland, Virginia, West Virginia, and North/South Carolina*. Special Publication Number 26, Archaeological Society of Virginia.

Hranicky, W. J., and F. Painter, 1991, *A Guide to the Identification of Virginia Projectile Points*. Richmond, Archaeological Society of Virginia.

Huffington, W., 1938, *The Delaware Register*. Dover.

Hughes, R. B., 1980, *A Preliminary Cultural and Environmental Overview of the Prehistory of Maryland's Lower Eastern Shore Based on a Survey of Selected Artifact Collections from the Area*. Annapolis: Maryland Historical Trust Manuscript Series 26.

Hulton, P., 1984, *America 1585*. Chapel Hill: University of North Carolina Press.

Hunter, W. H., 1964, *The Story of America's Oldest Museum Building*. Baltimore: Peale Museum Historical Series.

Jennings, F., 1982, Indians and frontiers in seventeenth-century Maryland. In D. B. Quinn, ed., *Early Maryland in a Wider World*, pp. 216–241. Detroit: Wayne State University Press.

Jirikowic, C. A., 1990, The political implications of a cultural practice: A new perspective on ossuary burial in the Potomac Valley. *North American Archaeologist* 11:353–374.

Jirikowic, C. A., 1995, The Hughes village site: A Late Woodland community in the Potomac Piedmont (Doctoral dissertation, American University). Ann Arbor: University microfilms.

Johnson, A. F., 1968, New dates for the Archaic. *Quarterly Bulletin of the Archaeological Society of Virginia* 22:172.

Jones, E. A., 1965, The Frederica site and the Delmarva Adena problem. *Journal of the Archaeological Society of Maryland* 1: 12–25.

Judd, N. M., 1967, *The Bureau of American ethnology*. Norman: University of Oklahoma Press.

Kent, B. C., 1984, *Susquehanna's Indians*. Harrisburg: The Pennsylvania Museum and Historical Commission.

Kinsey, W. F., III, 1959, Recent excavations on Bare Island in Pennsylvania: The Kent Hally site. *Pennsylvania Archaeologist* 29:109–133.

Kinsey, W. F., III, 1972, *Archaeology in the Upper Delaware Valley*. Harrisburg: Pennsylvania Museum and Historical Commission, Anthropological series No. 2.

Kinsey, W. F., III, 1977, Patterning in the Piedmont Archaic: A preliminary view. In W. S. Newman and B. Salwen, eds., *Amerinds and Their Paleoenvironments in Northeastern North America*, pp. 375–391. Annals of the New York Academy of Sciences, 288.

Klein, M. J., and T. Klatka, 1991, Late Archaic and Early Woodland demography and settlement patterns. In T. R. Reinhart and M. E. Hodges, eds., *Late Archaic and Early Woodland Research in Virginia: A Synthesis*, pp. 139–184. Richmond: Council of Virginia Archaeologists.

Knight, V. J., 1990, Social organization and the evolution of hierarchy in Southeastern chiefdoms. *Journal of Anthropological Research* 46:1–23.

Kraft, H. C., 1975, *The Archaeology of the Tocks Island Area*. South Orange: Seton Hall University Museum.

Kraft, H. C., 1986, *The Lenape*. Newark: New Jersey Historical Society.

Kraft, J. C., 1977, Late quaternary paleogeographic changes in coastal environments of Delaware, Middle Atlantic Bight, related to archaeological settings. In W. S. Newman and B. Salwen, eds., *Amerinds and Their Paleoenvironments in Northeastern North America*, pp. 35–69, Annals of the New York Academy of Sciences, 288.

Kraft, J. C., and G. S. Brush, 1981, *A Geological–Paleoenvironmental Analysis of Sediments in St. John's Pond and the Nearshore Zone Near Howard's Wharf at St. Mary's City, Maryland*. Unpublished manuscript.

Kuhn, T. S., 1970, *The Structure of Scientific Revolutions*. Chicago: University of Chicago Press.

LeeDecker, C. H., 1991, *Excavation of the Indian Creek V Site 18 PR 94 Prince Georges County, Maryland*. Washington, DC: Louis Berger and Associates.

Leidy, J., 1889, Notice and description of fossils in caves and crevices of the limestone rocks of Pennsylvania. *Geological Survey of Pennsylvania Annual Report, 1887*, pp. 1–20.

Leone, M. P., 1978, Time in American archaeology. In C. L. Redman, M. J. Berman, E. V. Curtin, W. T. Langhorn, N. V. Versaggi, and J. C. Wanser, eds., *Social Archaeology*, pp. 25–36. New York: Academic Press.

Lepper, B. T., 1983, Fluted point distributional patterns in the eastern United States: A contemporary phenomena. *Midcontinental Journal of Archaeology* 8:269–285.

Lepper, B. T., 1985, The effects of cultivation and collecting on Ohio fluted point finds: A reply to Seeman and Prufer. *Midcontinental Journal of Archaeology* 10:241–250.

Lewis, C. M., and A. J. Loomie, 1953, *The Spanish Jesuit Mission in Virginia, 1570–1572*. Chapel Hill: University of North Carolina Press.

Lewis, T. M. N., and M. K. Lewis, 1961, *Eva: An Archaic Site*. Knoxville: University of Tennessee Press.

Lowery, D., 1989, The Paw Paw Cove Paleoindian site complex, Talbot County, Maryland. *Archaeology of Eastern North America* 17:143–164.

Lowery, D., 1990., Recent excavation at the Paw Paw Cove site: A Maryland Coastal Plain Paleoindian habitation. *Current Research in the Pleistocene* 7:29–30.

Lowery, D., and J. F. Custer, 1990, Crane Point: An Early Archaic site in Maryland. *Journal of Middle Atlantic Archaeology* 6:75–120.

Luchterhand, K., 1970, *Early Archaic Projectile Points and Hunting Patterns in the Lower Illinois Valley*. Illinois State Museum, Report of Investigations 19.

Luckenbach, A. H., R. O. Allen, and C. G. Holland, 1975, Movement of prehistoric soapstone in the James River Basin. *Quarterly Bulletin of the Archaeological Society of Virginia* 29:183–203.

Luckenbach, A. H., W. E. Clark, and R. S. Levy, 1982, Rethinking cultural stability in eastern North American prehistory: Linguistic evidence from Eastern Algonquian. *Journal of Middle Atlantic Archaeology* 3:1–33.

Lundelius, E. L., R. W. Graham, F. Anderson, J. Guilday, J. A. Holman, D. W. Steadman, and S. D. Webb, 1983, Terrestrial vertebrate faunas. In H. E. Wright, ed., *Late Quaternary Environments of the United States*, pp. 311–353. Minneapolis: University of Minnesota Press.

MacCord, H. A., 1990, *The Archaeological Society of Virginia—A Forty-Year History*. Archaeological Society of Virginia, Special Publication Number 21.

MacCord, H. A., 1984, Evidence of a Late Woodland Migration from Piedmont to Tidewater in the Potomac Valley. *Maryland Archaeology* 20:7–18.

MacCord, H. A., 1985, Evidence for Adena influences in Virginia. *Quarterly Bulletin of the Archeological Society of Virginia* 40:41–47.

MacDonald, G. F., 1968, *Debert: A Paleoindian Site in Central Nova Scotia*. Anthropology Papers, No. 16, National Museum of Canada.

MacGregor, A., 1983, *Tradescant's Rarities*. Oxford: Clarendon Press.

Manson, C., 1948, Marcey Creek site: An early manifestation in the Potomac Valley. *American Antiquity* 13:223–227.

Martin, P. S., 1967, Prehistoric overkill. In P. S. Martin and H. E. Wright, eds., *Pleistocene Extinctions: The Search for a Cause*, pp. 75–120. New Haven: Yale University Press.

Martin, P. S., and R. G. Klein, 1984, *Quaternary Extinctions: A Prehistoric Revolution*. Tucson: University of Arizona Press.

Martin, P. S., G. I. Quimby, and D. Collier, 1947, *Indians before Columbus*. Chicago: University of Chicago Press.

Maryland Historical Trust, 1986, *The Maryland Comprehensive Historical Preservation Plan*. Annapolis: Department of Economic and Community Development.

Mason, O. T., 1889, The aborigines of the District of Columbia and the lower Potomac—A symposium. *American Anthropologist* 2:225–268.

Mason, R. J., 1962, The Paleoindian tradition in eastern North America. *Current Anthropology* 3: 227–278.

Mason, R. J., 1981, *Great Lakes Archaeology*. New York: Academic Press.

Mayre, W. B., 1935, Patowmeck above ye inhabitants: A commentary on the subject of an old map. *Maryland Historical Magazine* 30:114–137.

Mayre, W. B., 1936, Former Indian sites in Maryland, as located by early colonial records. *American Antiquity* 2:40–46.

Mayre, W. B., 1937, Patowmeck above ye inhabitants: A commentary on the subject of an old map. *Maryland Historical Magazine* 32:293–300.

Mayre, W. B., 1938a, The Annocostin Indian Fort. *Maryland Historical Magazine* 33:134–148.

Mayre, W. B., 1938b, The Wiccomiss Indians of Maryland. *American Antiquity* 4:146–152.

Mayre, W. B., 1939, The Wiccomiss Indians of Maryland Part II. *American Antiquity* 5:51–55.

Mayre, W. B., 1963, An Indian camp site of the Archaic period: Bryn Mawr school property. *Maryland Historical Magazine* 58:211–232.

McAvoy, J. M., 1965, An early chert assemblage in Chesterfield County, Virginia. *Quarterly Bulletin of the Archaeological Society of Virginia* 20:48–51.

McAvoy, J. M., 1968, A descriptive study of tools and projectile points of two early hunter camp sites on the Atlantic Coastal Plain. *Chesopiean* 6:62–75.

McAvoy, J. M., 1979, The Point-of-Rocks Paleoindian site. *Quarterly Bulletin of the Archaeological Society of Virginia* 34:3–111.

McAvoy, J. M., 1992, *Nottoway River Survey Part-I Clovis Settlement Patterns*. Richmond: Archaeological Society of Virginia and Nottoway River publications.

McCann, C., 1950, The Ware site, Salem County, New Jersey. *American Antiquity* 15:315–331.

McCary, B. C., 1947a, Folsom Point survey. *Quarterly Bulletin of the Archaeological Society of Virginia* 1.

McCary, B. C., 1947b, A survey and study of Folsom-like points found in Virginia. *Quarterly Bulletin of the Archaeological Society of Virginia* 2.

McCary, B. C., 1947c, Report of additional Virginia Folsom points. *Quarterly Bulletin of the Archaeological Society of Virginia* 2.

McCary, B. C., 1951, A workshop site of early man in Dinwiddie County, Virginia. *American Antiquity* 17:9–17.

McCary, B. C., 1983, The Paleoindian in Virginia. *Quarterly Bulletin of the Archaeological Society of Virginia* 38:43–70.

McCary, B. C., J. C. Smith, and C. E. Gilliam, 1949, A Folsom workshop site on the Williamson Farm, Dinwiddie County, Virginia. *Quarterly Bulletin of the Archaeological Society of Virginia* 4:1–8.

McCauley, R. H., 1945, *The Reptiles of Maryland and the District of Columbia*. Privately published.

McDowell, E. E., 1972, *The Archaic Stage of the Potomac River Piedmont: A Techno-ecological Approach to Archaeological Data*. (Doctoral dissertation, American University). Ann Arbor: University microfilms.

McKern, W. C., 1939, The Midwestern Taxonomic Method as an aid to archaeological culture study. *American Antiquity* 4:301–313.

McLearen, D. C., 1991a, Late Archaic and Early Woodland material culture in Virginia. In T. R. Reinhart and M. E. Hodges, eds., *Late Archaic and Early Woodland Research in Virginia: A Synthesis*, pp. 89–138. Richmond: Council of Virginia Archaeologists.

McLearen, D. C., 1991b, *Phase III Archaeological Investigations of the 522 Bridge Site 44WR329 Warren County, Virginia*. Richmond: Virginia Commonwealth Archaeological Research Center.

McLearen, D. C., 1992, Virginia's Middle Woodland period: A regional perspective. In T. R. Reinhart and M. E. Hodges, eds., *Middle and Late Woodland Research in Virginia: A Synthesis*, pp. 39–64. Richmond: Council of Virginia Archaeologists.

McLearen, D. C., and L. D. Mouer, 1994, *Jordan's Journey III*. Richmond: Virginia Commonwealth University Archaeological Research Center.

McNett, C. W., 1974, *The Archaeology of the Potomac River Valley*. Unpublished manuscript.

McNett, C. W., 1985, *Shawnee Minisink: A Stratified Paleoindian–Archaic site in the Upper Delaware Valley of Pennsylvania*. Orlando: Academic Press.

Meltzer, D. J., 1983, The antiquity of man and the development of American archaeology. *Advances in Archaeological Method and Theory* 6:1–51.

Meltzer, D. J., 1984, *Late Pleistocene Human Adaptations in Eastern North America* (Doctoral dissertation, University of Washington). Ann Arbor: University microfilms.

Meltzer, D. J., 1988, Late Pleistocene human adaptations in eastern North America. *Journal of World Prehistory* 2:1–53.

Meltzer, D. J., and R. C. Dunnell, 1992, *The Archaeology of William Henry Holmes*. Washington, D.C.: Smithsonian Press.

Mercer, H. C., 1897, Exploration of an Indian ossuary on the Choptank River, Dorchester County, Maryland: Researches upon the antiquity of man in the Delaware Valley and the eastern U.S. *University of Pennsylvania Publication Series in Philology, Literature, and Archaeology* 6:87–98.

Merrell, J. H., 1979, Cultural continuity among the Piscataway. *William and Mary Quarterly* 36:548–570.

Michels, J. W., and J. S. Dutt, 1968, *Archaeological Investigations of Sheep Rock Shelter, Huntingdon, Pennsylvania*. Occasional Papers in Anthropology, No. 5. The Pennsylvania State University, Department of Anthropology.

Miller, C., 1958, Russell Cave–New light on stone age life. *National Geographic Magazine* 113:427–437.

Milliman, J. D., and K. O. Emery, 1968, Sea levels during the past 35,000 years. *Science* 162:1121–1123.

Milner, G. C., 1980, Epidemic disease in the postcontact Southeast: A reappraisal. *Midcontinental Journal of Archaeology* 5:39–56.

Moeller, R. W., 1980, *6 LF 21: A Paleoindian Site in Western Connecticut*. Occasional Paper, No.2, American Indian Archaeological Institute.

Moeller, R. W., 1982, *Practicing Environmental Archaeology: Methods and Interpretations*. Washington, Connecticut: American Indian Archaeological Institute.

Mooney, J., 1890, The Powhatan Indians. *American Anthropologist* 3:132.

Mooney, J., 1907, The Powhatan Confederacy, past and present. *American Anthropologist* 9:29–52.

Moorehead, W. K., 1938, *A Report of the Susquehanna River Expedition*. Andover. Andover Press.

Mouer, L. D., 1989, Beyond fluted points: Prospects for Paleoindian studies in Virginia for the 1990s. In J. M. Wittkofski and T. R. Reinhart, eds., *Paleoindian Research In Virginia: A Synthesis*, pp 183–187. Richmond: Council of Virginia Archaeologists.

Mouer, L. D., 1990, *The Archaic to Woodland Transition in the Piedmont and Coastal Plain Sections of the James River Valley* (Doctoral dissertation, University of Pittsburgh). Ann Arbor: University microfilms.

Mouer, L. D., 1991, The formative transition in Virginia. In T. R. Reinhart and M. E. Hodges. eds., *Late Archaic and Early Woodland Research in Virginia: A Synthesis*, pp. 1–88. Richmond: Council of Virginia Archaeologists.

Mouer, L. D., D. C. McLearen, R. T. Kiser, C. P. Egghart, B. J. Binns, and D. T. Magoon, 1992, *Jordan's Journey*. Richmond: Virginia Commonwealth Archaeological Research Center.

Munford, B. A., 1982, *The Piney Branch Quarry Site: An Analysis of a Lithic Workshop in Washington, D.C.* Thesis, George Washington University.

Oliver, B. L., 1985, Tradition and typology: Basic elements of the Carolina projectile point sequence. In R. S. Dickens and H. T. Ward, eds., *Structure and Process in Southeastern Archaeology*, pps. 229–242. University: University of Alabama Press.

Owens, J. P., K. Stefansson, and L. A. Sirkin, 1974, Chemical, mineralogic, and palynologic character of the upper Wisconsin–lower Holocene fill in parts of the Hudson, Delaware, and Chesapeake estuaries. *Journal of Sedimentary Petrology* 44: 390–408.

Painter, F., 1978, The beaker makers of Currituck: Carbon 14 dates. *Chesopiean* 16:67.

Painter, F., 1988, Two terminal Archaic cultures of S.E. Virginia and N.E. North Carolina. *Journal of Middle Atlantic Archaeology* 4:25–38.

Parker, A. C., 1920, *The Archaeological History of the State of New York*. Albany: New York State Museum Bulletin.

Parker, S. K., 1990, Early and Middle Archaic settlement patterns and demography. In T. R. Reinhart and M. E. Hodges, eds., *Early and Middle Archaic Research in Virginia: A Synthesis*, pp. 99–118. Richmond: Council of Virginia Archaeologists.

Norton, B., and E. A. Baird, 1994, The Taft site: A Middle and Late Woodland assemblage from the Virginia coastal plain. Unpublished manuscript.

Peabody, C., 1908, The exploration of Bushey cavern near Cavetown, Maryland. *Phillips Academy, Department of Archaeology, Bulletin IV.*

Peck, R. M., 1969, A Paleoindian camp site in Isle-of-Wight County, Virginia. *Chesopean* 7:2–12.

Peck, R. M., 1985, *The Williamson Site, Dinwiddie County Virginia.* Privately published.

Phillips, J. L., and J. A. Brown, 1983, *Archaic Hunters and Gatherers in the American Midwest.* New York: Academic Press.

Porter, F. W., 1981, The foundations of archaeology and anthropology in Maryland: A summary essay. *Man in the Northeast* 21:61–73.

Porter, F. W., 1983, Salvaging the past: The roots of modern archaeology in Maryland, 1900–1940. *Maryland Historical Magazine* 78:143–157.

Potter, S. R., 1982, *An Analysis of Chicacoan Settlement Patterns.* (Doctoral dissertation, University of North Carolina). Ann Arbor: University microfilms.

Potter, S. R., 1993, *Commoners, Tribute, and Chiefs.* Charlottesville: University Press of Virginia.

Pritchard, J. G., 1964, Quail Spring Paleo Occupation Site, Princess Anne County, Virginia. *Chesopean* 2:60–61.

Proudfit, S. V., 1889, Ancient village sites and aboriginal workshops in the District of Columbia. *American Anthropologist* 2:241–246.

Quinn, D. B., 1977, *North America from Earliest Discovery to First Settlements.* New York: Harper and Row.

Ramenofsky, A. F., 1987, *Vectors of Death: The Archaeology of European Contact.* Albuquerque: University of New Mexico Press.

Rappleye, L., and W. M. Gardner, 1979, *Reconnaissance and Impact Area Assessment of the Great Dismal Swamp National Wildlife Refuge, City of Suffolk, Chesapeake and Nansemond Counties, Virginia.* Washington, DC: U.S. Department of the Interior.

Renfrew, A. C., 1982, Explanation revisited. In A. C. Renfrew, M. J. Rowlands, and B. A. Seagraves, eds., *Theory and explanation in archaeology,* pp. 5–23, New York: Academic Press.

Reynolds, E. R., 1883, Ossuary at Accotink. *Smithsonian Miscellaneous Collections* 25:92–94.

Riley, T. J., R. Edging, and J. Rossen, 1990, Cultigens in prehistoric eastern North America: Changing paradigms. *Current Anthropology* 31:525–541.

Ritchie, W. A., 1932a, The Algonkin sequence in New York. *American Anthropologist* 34:406–414.

Ritchie, W.A., 1932b, The Lamoka Lake site. *Researches and Transactions of the New York State Archaeological Association* 7:79–134.

Ritchie, W. A., 1961, *A Typology and Nomenclature for New York Projectile Points.* Albany: New York State Museum and Science Service, Bulletin no. 384.

Ritchie, W. A., and D. W. Dragoo, 1959, The eastern dispersal of Adena. *American Antiquity* 25:43–50.

Ritchie, W. A., and R. E. Funk, 1973, *Aboriginal settlement patterns in the Northeast.* Albany: New York State Museum.

Rogers, R., 1992, *An Investigation of Submerged Prehistoric Site Potential along the Proposed Chesapeake Bay Bridge and Tunnel Parallel Crossing Virginia Beach–Northampton County, Virginia.* Austin: Espey, Huston, and Associates.

Root, D., 1984, *Material Dimensions of Social Inequality in non-Stratified Societies: An Archaeological Perspective.* (Doctoral dissertation, University of Massachusetts). Ann Arbor: University microfilms.

Rountree, H. C., 1989, *The Powhatan Indians of Virginia.* Norman: University of Oklahoma Press.

Rountree, H. C., 1990, *Pocahontas's People.* Norman: University of Oklahoma Press.

Rountree, H. C., 1993, *Powhatan Foreign Relations.* Charlottesville: University Press of Virginia.

Rust, W. F., 1983, *Phase Three Archaeological Investigations of the Countryside Planned Community Loudon County, Virginia.* Leesburg: Coastal and Piedmont Studies Associates.

Sahlins, M., 1968, *Tribesmen.* Englewood Cliffs, New Jersey: Prentice-Hall.

Sahlins, M., 1972, *Stone Age Economics.* Chicago: Aldine.

Sahlins, M., 1985, *Islands of History.* Chicago: University of Chicago Press.

Salmon, M. H., and W. C. Salmon, 1979, Alternative models of scientific explanation. *American Anthropologist* 81:61–74.

Sassaman, K. E., 1993, *Early Pottery in the Southeast: Tradition and Innovation in Cooking Technology.* Tuscaloosa: University of Alabama Press.

Schmitt, K., 1952, Archaeological chronology of the Middle Atlantic States. In J. B. Griffin, ed., *Archaeology of Eastern United States*, pp. 59–70. Chicago: University of Chicago Press.

Schubel, J. R., 1981, *The Living Chesapeake.* Baltimore: Johns Hopkins University Press.

Sears, W. H., 1948, What is the Archaic? *American Antiquity* 2:122–124.

Seeman, M. F., 1994, Review of Middle and Late Woodland research in Virginia: A synthesis. *American Antiquity* 59:582.

Semken, H. A., 1974, Micromammal distribution and migration during the Holocene. *American Quaternary Association Abstracts for Third Biennial Meeting* 25.

Semken, H. A., 1983, Holocene mammalian biogeography and climatic change in the Eastern and Central United States. In H. E. Wright, ed., *Late Quaternary Environments of the United States*, pp. 182–207. Minneapolis: University of Minnesota Press.

Service, E. R., 1962, *Primitive Social Organization.* New York: Random House.

Service, E. R., 1971, *Primitive Social Organization* (Second Edition). New York: Random House.

Sheehan, B., 1980, *Savagism and Civility.* New York: Cambridge University Press.

Siebert, F. T., 1975, Resurrecting Virginia Algonquian from the dead. In J. M. Crawford, ed., *Studies in Southeastern Indian Languages*, pp. 285–453. Athens: University of Georgia Press.

Sirkin, L. A., 1967, Late Pleistocene pollen stratigraphy of Western Long Island and Eastern Staten Island, New York. In E. J. Cushing and H. E. Wright, eds., *Quaternary Paleoecology*, pp. 249–274. New Haven: Yale University Press.

Sirkin, L. A., C. S. Denny, and M. Rubin, 1977, Late pleistocene environment of the central Delmarva Peninsula, Delaware-Maryland. *Geological Society of America Bulletin* 88:139–142.

Slattery, R. G., 1946, A prehistoric Indian site on Selden Island, Montgomery County, Maryland. *Journal of the Washington Academy of Sciences* 36:262–266.

Smith, B. D., 1986, The archaeology of the southeastern United States: from Dalton to de Soto, 10,500–500 B.P. *Advances in World Archaeology* 5:1–92.

Smith, B. D., 1989, Origins of agriculture in eastern North America. *Science* 246:1566–1571.

Smith, B. D., and D. J. Meltzer, 1982, *The Juhle Site: Investigation of Late Prehistoric Mortuary Practices in the Tidewater Potomac.* Grant Proposal, National Geographic Society.

Smith, M. T., 1987, *Archaeology of Aboriginal Culture Change in the Interior Southeast.* Gainesville: University of Florida Press.

Speck, F. G., 1915, The Nanticoke Community of Delaware. Contributions from the Museum of American Indian, Heye Foundation, *Indian Notes and Monographs, 2.*

Speck, F. G., 1925, The Rappahannock Indians of Virginia. Museum of the American Indian, Heye Foundation, *Indian Notes and Monographs, 5.*

Speck, F. G., 1928, Chapters of the ethnology of the Powhatan Tribes of Virginia. Museum of the American Indian, Heye Foundation, *Indian Notes and Monographs, 1.*

Spelman, H., 1910, Relations of Virginia. In E. Arber, ed., *Travels and Works of Captain John Smith*, pp. ci–cxxi. Edinburgh: John Grant.

Spiess, A. E., 1984, Arctic garbage and New England Paleoindians: The single occupation option. *Archaeology of Eastern North America* 12:280–285.

Spiess, A. E., M. L. Curran, and J. L. Grimes, 1985, Caribou (*Rangifer Tarandus* L.) bones from New England Paleoindian sites. *North American Archaeologist* 6:145–159.

Stenger, C. A., 1982, *A Palynological Study of Sediments from the Chesapeake Bay.* Masters thesis, Johns Hopkins University.

Stephenson, R. L., and A. L. Ferguson, 1963, *The Accokeek Creek Site: A Middle Atlantic Seaboard Culture Sequence.* University of Michigan Anthropological Papers, No. 20.

Steponaitis, L. C., 1980, A survey of artifact collections from the Patuxent River Drainage, Maryland. *Maryland Historical Trust Monograph Series, No. 1.*

Steponaitis, L. C., 1986, *Prehistoric Settlement Patterns in the Lower Patuxent River Drainage, Maryland* (Doctoral dissertation, State University of New York at Binghamptom). Ann Arbor: University microfilms.

Steponaitis, V. C., 1986, Prehistoric archaeology in the Southeastern United States, 1970–1985. *Annual Review of Anthropology* 15:363–404.

Stevens, J. S., 1991, A story of plants, fire, and people: The paleoecology and subsistence of the Late Archaic and Early Woodland in Virginia. In T. R. Reinhart and M. E. Hodges, eds., *Late Archaic and Early Woodland Research in Virginia: A Synthesis*, pp. 185–220. Richmond: Council of Virginia Archaeologists.

Stewart, R. M., 1989, Trade and exchange in Middle Atlantic prehistory. *Archaeology of Eastern North America* 17:47–78.

Stewart, R. M., 1992, Observations on the Middle Woodland period of Virginia: A Middle Atlantic perspective. In T. R. Reinhart and M. E. Hodges, eds., *Middle and Late Woodland Research in Virginia: A Synthesis*, pp. 1–38. Richmond: Council of Virginia Archaeologists.

Stewart, T. D., 1940a, *Further Excavations of the Indian Village Site of Patowomeke.* Washington: Explorations and Fieldwork of the Smithsonian Institution in 1939.

Stewart, T. D., 1940b, The finding of an Indian ossuary on the York River in Virginia. *Journal of the Washington Academy of Sciences* 30:356–364.

Stewart, T. D., 1940c, A report on the skeletal remains from the Piscataway Creek Ossuary. *American Antiquity* 6:4–18.

Stewart, T. D., 1990, A story of archaeology in letter form. *Quarterly Bulletin of the Archaeological Society of Virginia* 45:75–83.

Stewart, T. D., 1992, *Archaeological Exploration of Patawomeke: The Indian Town Site 44 ST 2 Ancestral to the One 44 ST 1 Visited in 1608 by Captain John Smith.* Washington: Smithsonian Contributions to Anthropology.

Stewart, T. D., and W. R. Wedel, 1937, The finding of two ossuaries on the site of the Indian village of Nacotchtanke Anacostia. *Journal of the Washington Academy of Sciences* 27:213–219.

Stoltman, J. B., 1978, Temporal models in prehistory: An example from Eastern North America. *Current Anthropology* 19:703–746.

Storck, P. L., and A. E. Spiess, 1994, Paleoindian occupation at the Udora site, Ontario, Canada. *America Antiquity* 59:121–142.

Strachey, W., 1953, *The Historie of Travell into Virginia Britania.* London: The Hakluyt Society.

Strandberg, C. H., and R. Tomlinson, 1968, Photoarchaeological analysis of Potomac River fish traps. *American Antiquity* 34:312–319.

Taylor, W., 1948, A study of archaeology. *American Anthropological Association, Memoir 69.*

Thomas, D. H., 1975, Nonsite sampling in archaeology: Up the creek without a site? In J. W. Mueller, ed., *Sampling in Archaeology*, pp. 61–81, Tucson: University of Arizona Press.

Thomas, D. H., 1989, *Archaeology.* New York: Holt, Rinehart & Winston.

Thomas, J., 1991, *Rethinking the Neolithic.* Cambridge: Cambridge University Press.

Thomas, R. A., 1966. Paleoindian in Delaware. *Delaware Archaeology* 2:1–11.

Thomas, R. A., 1969, *Adena Influence in the Middle Atlantic Coast.* Manuscript on file at Maryland State Archaeologist office, Baltimore.

Thomas, R. A., 1970, Adena influence in the Middle Atlantic Coast. In B. K. Swartz, ed., *Adena: The Seeking of an Identity*, pp. 56–87. Muncie: Ball State University Press.

Thomas, R. A., 1976. A re-evaluation of the St. Jones River Site. *Archaeology of Eastern North America* 4:89–110.

Thomas, R. A., 1981, *Archaeological Investigations at the Delaware Park Site.* Dover: State of Delaware, Department of Transportation.

Thurman, M. D., 1972, *Re-excavation of the Accokeek Creek Site: A Preliminary Report.* Paper presented at the Society of American Archaeology Meeting, Miami, Florida.

Thurman, M. D., 1985, A cultural synthesis of the Middle Atlantic Coastal Plain part I: "Culture area" and regional sequence. *Journal of Middle Atlantic Archaeology* 1:7–32.

Thurman, M. D., 1987, A funny thing happened to archaeological data coming back from Delaware: Some models for Middle Atlantic archaeology. *Journal of Middle Atlantic Archaeology* 3:125–141.

Trigger, B. G., 1978, *Time and traditions: Essays in archaeological interpretation.* Edinburgh: Edinburgh University Press.

Trigger, B. G., 1989, *A history of archaeological thought.* Cambridge: Cambridge University Press.

Tuck, J. A., 1978, Regional cultural development, 300 to 300 B.C. In B. G. Trigger, ed., *Handbook of North American Indians, Northeast,* pp. 28–43. Washington, DC: Smithsonian Institution.

Turnbaugh, W. A., 1975, Toward an explanation of the broadpoint dispersal in Eastern North American prehistory. *Journal of Anthropological Research* 31:51–68.

Turner, E. R., 1976, *An Archaeological and Ethnohistorical Study on the Evolution of Rank Societies in the Virginia Coastal Plain* (Dissertation, Pennsylvania State University). Ann Arbor: University microfilms.

Turner, E. R., 1983, VRCA research at the Conover Paleoindian site in Dinwiddie county, Virginia. *Archaeological Society of Virginia Special Publication, No. 10,* pp. 109–117.

Turner, E. R., 1985, Socio-political organization within the Powhatan Chiefdom and the effects of European contact, A.D. 1607–1646. In W. W. Fitzhugh, ed., *Cultures in Contact,* pp. 193–224. Washington, DC: Smithsonian Institution Press.

Turner, E. R., 1989, Paleoindian settlement patterns and population distributions in Virginia. In J. M. Wittkofski and T. R. Reinhart, eds., *Paleoindian Research in Virginia: A Synthesis,* pp. 71–93. Richmond: Council of Virginia Archaeologists.

Turner, E. R., 1992, The Virginia Coastal Plain during the Late Woodland period. In T. R. Reinhart and M N. Hodges, eds., *Middle and Late Woodland Research in Virginia,* pp. 97–136. Richmond: Council of Virginia Archaeologists.

Turner, E. R., and A. L. Opperman, 1993, Archaeological manifestations of the Virginia company period: A summary of surviving Powhatan and English settlements in tidewater Virginia, circa 1607–1624. In T. R. Reinhart and D. Pogue, eds., *The Archaeology of 17th-Century Virginia,* pp. 67–104. Richmond: Council of Virginia Archaeologists.

Ubelaker, D. H., 1974, Reconstruction of demographic profiles from ossuary skeletal samples: A case study from the Tidewater Potomac. *Smithsonian Contributions to Anthropology, No. 18.*

Virginia Department of Historic Resources, 1992, *Guidelines for Preparing Identification and Evaluation Reports.* Richmond: Department of Historic Resources.

Vokes, H. E., and J. Edwards, 1974, *Geography and Geology of Maryland.* Baltimore: Maryland Geological Survey.

Waselkov, G. A., 1978, Evolution of deer hunting in the Eastern Woodlands. *Mid-continental Journal of Archaeology* 3:15–34.

Waselkov, G. A., 1982, *Shellfish Gathering and Shell Midden Archaeology* (Dissertation, University of North Carolina). Ann Arbor: University microfilms.

Webb, S., J. T. Milanich, R. Alexon, and J. S. Dunbar, 1984, A *Bison antiquus* kill site, Wacissa River, Jefferson County, Florida. *American Antiquity* 49:384–392.

Webb, W. S., 1938, An archaeological survey of the Norris Basin in Eastern Tennessee. *Bureau of American Ethnology Bulletin, No. 118.*

Webb, W. S., 1939, An archaeological survey of Wheeler Basin on the Tennessee River in Northern Alabama. *Smithsonian Institution Bureau of American Ethnology Bulletin, 122.*

Webb, W. S., and D. L. DeJarnette, 1942, An archaeological survey of Pickwick Basin in the adjacent portions of the states of Alabama, Mississippi, and Tennessee. *Bureau of American Ethnology Bulletin, No. 129.*

Webb, W. S. and W. G. Haag, 1940, *Cypress Creek Villages.* University of Kentucky Reports in Archaeology and Anthropology, Vol 4.

Webster, W. D., J. F. Parnell, and W. C. Biggs, 1985, *Mammals of the Carolinas, Virginia, and Maryland.* Chapel Hill: University of North Carolina Press.

Weiss, K. M., and E. Woolford, 1986, Comment on the settlement of the Americas. *Current Anthropology* 27:491–492.

Weslager, C. A., 1944, *Delaware's Buried Past* (first edition). Philadelphia: University of Pennsylvania Press.

Weslager, C. A., 1968, *Delaware's Buried Past* (second edition). New Brunswick: Rutgers University Press.

Weslager, C. A., 1983, *The Nanticoke Indians—Past and Present*. Newark: University of Delaware Press.

Wesler, K. W., 1985, Model and sequence in the Maryland archaic. In R. S. Dickens and H. T. Ward, eds., *Structure and Process in Southeastern Archaeology*, pp. 212–228. University: University of Alabama Press.

Wetmore, A., 1962, Birds. In J. E. Guilday, ed., *In the Pleistocene Local Fauna of Natural Chimneys, Augustana County, Virginia*. Annals of the Carnegie Museum, 36, pp. 87–122.

Whitehead, D. R., 1965, Palynology and pleistocene phytogeography of unglaciated Eastern North America. In H. E. Wright and D. G. Frey, eds., *The Quaternary of the United States*, pp. 417–432. Princeton: Princeton University Press.

Whitehead, D. R., 1972, Developmental and environmental history of the Dismal Swamp. *Ecological Monographs* 42:301–315.

Widmer, R. J., 1988, *The Evolution of the Calusa*. Tuscaloosa: University of Alabama Press.

Wilke, S., and G. Thompson, 1977, *Prehistoric Archaeological Resources in the Maryland Coastal Zone*. Annapolis: Maryland Department of Natural Resources.

Wilke, S., J. Demarest, W. Hoyt, and R. Stuckenrath, 1981, *Holocene Geologic History of the Patuxent Estuary and Its Archaeological Implications*. Maryland Historical Trust Manuscript Series, number 20.

Willey, G. R., 1966, *An Introduction to American Archaeology: Volume One. North and Middle America*. Englewood Cliffs: Prentice Hall.

Willey, G. R., and P. Phillips, 1958, *Method and Theory in American Archaeology*. Chicago: University of Chicago Press.

Willey, G. R., and J. A. Sabloff, 1993, *A History of American Archaeology*. London: Thames and Hudson.

Williamson, M. H., 1979, Powhatan hair. *Man* 14:392–413.

Wilson, T., 1889, The Paleolithic period in the District of Columbia. *American Anthropologist* 2:235–241.

Wilson, T., 1890, Results of an inquiry as to the existence of man in North America during the Paleolithic period. *United States National Museum Annual Report, 1888*, 677–702.

Winterhalder, B., 1983, History and ecology of the Boreal Zone in Ontario. In A. T. Steegman, ed., *Boreal Forest Adaptations: The Northern Algonkians*, pp. 9–54. New York: Plenum Press.

Winters, H. D., 1969, *The Riverton Culture*. The Illinois State Museum and the Illinois Archaeological Survey, Reports of Investigations, No. 13.

Wise, C. L., 1973, *The Nassawango Creek Site: Summary Report*. Report in files of Maryland State Archaeologist, Baltimore.

Wise, C. L., 1975, A proposed Early to Middle Woodland ceramic sequence for the Delmarva Peninsula. *Maryland Archaeology* 11:21–29.

Wise, C. L., 1984, *A Cultural Resources Management Plan for Killens Pond State Park*. Dover: Delaware Division of Parks and Recreation.

Witthoft, J., 1953, Broad Spearpoints and the Transitional Period Cultures. *Pennsylvania Archaeologist 23*: 4–31.

Witthoft, J., 1971, A Paleoindian site in Eastern Pennsylvania. In B. C. Kent, I. F. Smith, and C. McCann, eds., *Foundations of Pennsylvania Prehistory*, pp. 13–64. Harrisburg: Pennsylvania Historical Museum Commission.

Wolf, E. R., 1982, *Europe and the People without History*. Berkeley: University of California Press.

Woodland Conference, 1943, The first archaeological conference on the Woodland pattern. *American Antiquity* 4:392–400.

Wright, H. T., 1962, *The Hell Island Site*. Unpublished manuscript.

Wright, H. T., 1973, *An Archaeological Sequence in the Middle Chesapeake, Maryland*. Maryland Geological Survey, Archaeological Studies, Number 1.

Zeuner, F. E., 1952, *Dating the Past*. London: Methuen.

Index

INTERDISCIPLINARY CONTRIBUTIONS TO ARCHAEOLOGY
Chronological Listing of Volumes

THE ARCHAEOLOGY OF GENDER
Separating the Spheres in Urban America
Diana diZerega Wall

ORIGINS OF ANATOMICALLY MODERN HUMANS
Edited by Matthew H. Nitecki and Doris V. Nitecki

PREHISTORIC EXCHANGE SYSTEMS IN NORTH AMERICA
Edited by Timothy G. Baugh and Jonathon E. Ericson

STYLE, SOCIETY, AND PERSON
Archaeological and Ethnological Perspectives
Edited by Christopher Carr and Jill E. Neitzel

REGIONAL APPROACHES TO MORTUARY ANALYSIS
Edited by Lane Anderson Beck

DIVERSITY AND COMPLEXITY IN PREHISTORIC MARITIME SOCIETIES
A Gulf of Maine Perspective
Bruce J. Bourque

CHESAPEAKE PREHISTORY
Old Traditions, New Directions
Richard J. Dent, Jr.

PREHISTORIC CULTURAL ECOLOGY AND EVOLUTION
Insights from Southern Jordan
Donald O. Henry